# THE SECRET LIFE OF STONES

# Also by Michael Adzema

## From the Return to Grace Series

*Culture War, Class War: Occupy Generations and the Rise and Fall of "Obvious Truths."* Volume 1. (2013)

*Apocalypse Emergency: Love's Wake-Up Call.* Volume 3. (2013)

*Apocalypse NO: Apocalypse or Earth Rebirth and the Emerging Perinatal Unconscious.* Volume 4. (2013)

*Wounded Deer and Centaurs: The Necessary Hero and the Prenatal Matrix of Human Events.* Volume 5. (2016)

*Planetmates: The Great Reveal.* Volume 6. (2014)

*Funny God: The Tao of Funny God and the Mind's True Liberation.* Volume 7. (2015)

*Experience Is Divinity: Matter As Metaphor.* Volume 8. (2013)

*Falls from Grace: The Devolution and Revolution of Consciousness.* Volume 9. (2014)

*Prodigal Human: The Descents of Man.* Volume 10. (2016)

*The Necessary Revolution.* Volume 2. (forthcoming)

*Back to the Garden: The Psychology and Spirituality of Humanicide and the Necessary Future.* Volume 11. (forthcoming)

*Primal Return: Renaissance and Grace.* Volume 12. (forthcoming)

## From The Path of Ecstasy Series

*Womb with a View.* Volume 2. (forthcoming)

*Cells with a View.* Volume 3. (forthcoming)

# THE SECRET LIFE OF STONES

## Matter, Divinity, and the Path of Ecstasy

The Path of Ecstasy, Volume 1

## MICHAEL ADZEMA

Gonzo Sage Media: Eugene, Oregon: sillymickel@gmail.com

ISBN-13: 978-1534607439

*This book is dedicated to the five teachers who changed my life and whose ideas are built into the foundation of all I write. In the order they came to me — Carl Jung, Hermann Hesse, Arthur Janov, Stanislav Grof, and Sathya Sai Baba. As well, this book is dedicated to my No-Form family — my strongest supporters and allies — especially Graham Farrant, Martha D. Ello, and Shirdi Sai Baba.*

*My works are achievements of all of us. I couldn't be more grateful, and I love you all.*

# CONTENTS

# PART TWO: TRANSCENDING WORLDS   67

# PREFACE

*"...that is what this book attempts — the returning to the inanimate world of the status of awareness, aliveness, and intention that Western hubris has stolen from it."*

## Consciousness, Begrudgingly Conceded

You will notice a pattern in our acknowledgment of consciousness as existing in the world outside of ourselves — the nonhuman world: Consciousness outside of humans is a gradual and reluctant acknowledgement throughout Western history. Rooted as it is in medieval Christian notions of dominion over Nature and of humans as being uniquely endowed with souls, science is not the least guilty here. Indeed, its crimes in this regard are epic.

The denial of consciousness in planetmates, which is embedded in science from its Newtonian beginnings, is the basis for our modern ability to thingify all of Nature as resources and items of consumption; thus allowing the torture and abuse of all planetmates to our ends — as food, as ingredients in manufactured items, as brutally treated and bloodily used test subjects, and worse. Pseudo-scientific notions regarding relative levels of consciousness in humans has supported the Nazi holocaust and slavery, as well; just as faux religious notions of the diminished status of females and the nonhuman world of Nature earlier perpetrated The Burning Times and the murder of nine million women at the stake.

Not to be disregarded, flawed scientific understanding of consciousness and feeling awareness attributable to our youngest has resulted in modern high-tech obstetrical birthing procedures, which have brutalized neonates and laid a foundation of horror at the roots of modern personalities. This has had incalculable results, as we see for one thing only, in the random and thoughtless eruptions of violence in modern societies and the abilities of organized violence, by nations and terrorist groups, to perpetrate wars, genocides, and other atrocities. Only reluctantly and gradually are newborns not being brutalized, slapped, wrapped, and isolated — as "modern" practices have heretofore dictated — and humane birthing and infancy methods been implemented. The persistence of the notion that newborns are not conscious, supported as it was in the beginning by science, is hard dying.

For its part, feeling awareness and memory in the prenate — established now beyond any question — fails to put to rest other archaic thinking such as mistaken speculations about a link between myelination and memory. So ideas about an unconscious existence for fetuses, convenient as they are in facilitating our nonchalance about nurturing our babies while still in their womb, simply refuse to die the death they are due. Wherever you look, the refusal to acknowledge consciousness or feeling awareness to an entity or thing allows unrestrained brutality and exploitation there.

Hence, just as the civil rights of minorities, indigenous peoples, women, and children have been only gradually and reluctantly acknowledged over the centuries, so also the awareness and consciousness of the nonhuman world is not the place we start when thinking of it, however much that was the case for our original humans. Remember, for primal humans, the world is alive; consciousness and nobility is awarded planetmates; Nature itself, animate and inanimate, is intentional and aware. This is the way we humans saw the world around us for virtually ninety-five to ninety-nine percent of our history as a species.

With civilization, however, and the burgeoning of an overween-ing ego and a controlling addiction, all of that changed drastically ... and conveniently. For the domestication of plants and animals that began civilization allowed an exploitation of the natural world, which burden earlier humans hardly desired. Until we arrive at pervasive Western views which begin with an assumption of non-life, non-awareness for everything nonhuman, and as we have seen, often for humans other than what "we" are like. From there, awareness is as begrudgingly conceded, requiring mountains of indisputable and hard-to-obtain evidence, as one was attributing awareness to a machine, to an artificial intelligence.

Our assumption, from medieval times, is that the world is non-conscious, while humans are ... well, most of us. The history of science in the last hundred years has amounted to a gradual giving back to Nature of its status as aware and conscious that was initially taken away by Western hubris in regard to Nature. So, we have animal rights, the "secret life of plants," the "secret life of the unborn child," and so on, in a gradual procession of acknowledgment. The understandings of consciousness and aliveness in the inanimate world — the world of matter — which are the most recent and necessary conclusions, arising from the findings of quantum physics and modern consciousness research, are the most difficult to arrive at. We find it nearly impossible to see the world as alive, as our ancestors did, regardless what our sciences now tell us. Yet, that is what this book attempts — the returning to the inanimate world of the status of awareness, aliveness, and intention that Western hubris has stolen from it.

# The Book's Structure

To that end, this book is in several parts, some quite different from the rest. They lay out a pattern of progression from what we commonly think to the majestic flights of insights arrived at with Western blinders removed. In the first four parts, I establish the logical philosophical foundation for the rest of the book, which is Part Five, "Matter Is Message." For this is meant not to be some visionary, poetic book, full of inspiration and spiritual insight, merely. It is also a serious argument for the actual state of Reality. It has a rational basis — rooted in the most expanded circles of our understandings in science — undergirding the wide-ranging soarings of thought following.

So, if you have no interest in what is, or why it is, and you already think life to be poetic; and you do not want or need a rational basis for your stance — for such a stance in life — then you could easily go directly to the second half of the book, "Matter Is Message." It is a long book, and I can understand some might want to do that, if only to cut down on their reading. I need mention this because I want all readers to know of the second part of the book and not to miss it. I consider it the most profound, inspirational, and relevant part for these times and the people living in it.

Still, I have constructed the book to be read front to back. It follows a logical order, creating a rational, thoroughgoing, and comprehensive vision, which the latter parts are that much sweeter by. I think you will miss out a little at least by skipping over the earlier chapters.

Whichever of these ways you read it, or some other way — perhaps you are one to have your dessert first and then get your meat and potatoes later, maybe to have dessert then again — my wish for you is that you receive the blessing of reading it with the same joy, and fun, in which I wrote it. I hope the reverence and gratitude I felt as it came through me is sensed by you as well.

In Part One of this book, "Being Shiva — Destroying and Creating Worlds," I advance an argument based on taking a look at some assumptions we clearly do make and upon which we build all of our knowledge, our science, and our beliefs about what is real. It comes down to *anthropocentrism*, which is a species-centrism more disastrous for our understandings of trueness than any of the other centrisms — ethnocentrism, egocentrism, or any other.

In doing that I unveil the layers of reality construction upon which we construct that anthropocentrism. This is an epistemological undertaking, for in doing this the intent is, by pulling away the false pillars upon which we build our world, to find out what can be known instead: What might actually be true. What might give us surer footing from which to view our worlds.

In Part Two, "Transcending Worlds," I begin to advance the notions that we might genuinely consider, once the false ones have been swept away. These are panoramas of understanding that open up once the curtain of anthropocentrism has been pulled to the side.

We find a flourishing new world revealed. One that borders on wonder.

In Part Three, "Science as Myth," I begin, first of all, to touch upon the ways these newer awarenesses have been thought of in the past. And surprisingly, with some of the deconstruction done in the first two parts, we find that science has made some gross misassumptions and thrown away some bathwater that has a viable life in it. I help to resuscitate those ideas, and I show how they actually integrate with some of the outermost rings of our findings from science at this time.

Part Four begins the advance down the freeway to the new world, the new paradigm, the one where matter is discovered to be alive. In "The Consciousness of Stones," I explain how that position is not just plausible, it is the only rational one left, all things considered. I bring forth some of the reasons — some anthropocentric, some simply habits of thought that are correctible — for why this new cosmic overstanding has not been unveiled before, as well as why significant parts of it, which would have revealed the rest, were historically cast aside.

Part Five, "Matter Is Message" is the heart of the book. It is a comprehensive look at what we can learn having arrived at the position to which the first four parts of the book have brought us. I will say this about it: You will find more reason for optimism and more levity in your being from what will become you here. It gives back what was taken; it returns to you your rightful and honorable place.

I invite you to open your eyes to the aliveness around you. I invite you to join me in a new world.

Let me explain....

# PART ONE

# BEING SHIVA — DESTROYING AND CREATING WORLDS

# 1

# Creating Worlds:

Many Beings, Many Worlds … While Our Science Is Built on an Assumption, Rooted in Religion, That Humans Are "God's Chosen Species"

*"…the probabilities are enormous that there are, in fact, other beings, unperceivable entities, unknown and unimaginable realities, and other and different senses … and, yes, as one new physics proposition puts it, an infinite number of 'worlds.'"*

## Our Knowledge Is Biologically Relative

Looking first to science, the findings of research from neurophysiology and neuropsychology are that neural "firings" from external stimuli, after they shoot through interior areas of the brain that deal with fundamental physiological processes, arrive in the cortical areas of the brain where they are then interpreted. Therefore, in a purely psychophysiological way, the world "out there" is not defined in and of itself.

## Cultures Create Worlds

In fact, ultimately our world is defined in the part of the person that stores cultural information — the cerebral cortex. What this is saying is that cultures create worlds. One's view of the world, arrived at through the process of enculturation in a person's development, is determined by one's culture, by the knowledge and experiences one has had in interaction with one's society. The experience of hearing a particular sound is not known to be that of hearing someone talking to us, until the cortex defines those sounds as words.

## Biology Creates Worlds

However, notice that before any cultural interpretation, those "messages" have had a journey through areas of the brain that define them prior to or outside of culture. Before any stimuli are interpreted as words, for example, a part of us determines that they are sounds.

That is to say that the organism does not *detect* the outside world through its senses, it *determines* the outside world through them. Or at least it *interprets* that outside world in a way that is determined by its biological makeup. Whatever is in Reality is being *scanned,* sorted through: In the process of our perceiving, our senses are picking through an infinity of possibilities of what could be detected to select what will be "sensed," perceived. After that, it is *concocted:* What the senses have chosen out of everything possible is then determined in terms of its relation to the biology of the organism, meaning what species it is. Then it is *interpreted:* An understanding of the experience is arrived at which sees it in the context of the culture one is given by one's society.

A sensation does not discern anything initially, at the moment of sensing. The sensation is interpreted *later.* The organism does not even distinguish between pleasure and pain — to use one crude but useful example — until later. The pattern of neural firings created by any particular set of stimuli is "objectively" neutral until "interpreted" by an organism relative to its physiological makeup, its species.

This, of course, makes perfect sense. There is nothing *inherently* painful in a stimulus that is produced by something whose molecules are moving at such a speed and manner that one would measure its temperature at, say, two hundred degrees Fahrenheit. That degree of heat is not "objectively" painful. It would be painful to us, to humans, however. Yet, one could easily imagine a species for which that particular vibrational rate would be within its tolerance range. The quality of pain ... the very existence of pain, even ... is relative to the perceiving organism, its species. It is determined by the species physiology, and in humans this determination is made for us during the journey of the neural firing through interior areas of the brain, far out of our conscious awareness.

Let us take a more subtle example. There is nothing inherently comforting or even pleasurable in a caress — that is, the pattern of stimuli involving the moving of one particular organism's surface against another's, in a particular way. Those "particulars," along with other aspects, are what go into defining *caress* by means of a complex communication among billions of neural cells and their components inside the brain. One can conceive of some biological organisms who would interpret such touching as a dire threat. Again, the interpretations of external stimuli are relative to the biological makeup of the perceiver and are decided upon outside of conscious awareness. The qualities of pleasure and all other experience, sensations, and feelings are relative to the perceiver, its biological makeup ... generally speaking, its species. Different perceivers, different perceived (experienced) realities.

# Our Knowledge Is Anthropocentric

Our examples emphasize that prior to any cultural interpretation — which comes later, during that neural message's continued journey and now through cortical areas of the brain — a "species" interpretation is made based upon the biological "hardware" of the organism. That is to say that these "vibrational rates" of molecules — using once more the example of temperature — are not in and of themselves even "stimuli" except that certain neurons throughout the body, including "lower" parts of the brain, in a complex intercommunication once again, define them as such: Vibratory rates "out there" are *not* patterns of neural firings. And to suppose that there is, in some magical-mystical sort of way, a kind of authentic, exact replication of the "out there" by our particular sensory apparatus is not only to state more than is conceivably possible to be stated … and to reveal an adherence to a kind of "faith" that is more reminiscent of religion than true science … it is also indisputably anthropocentric. For even our thus limited sensory apparatus informs us of other sentient creatures whose sensory systems are different than our own, indeed, vastly different in some cases.

Even among the species that we perceive as having the major five senses as we do, we observe differences: An eagle sees farther and better; its vision is two to four times more acute than humans — certainly its world does not *look* like ours. A dog hears a much wider range of auditory waves — certainly its world does not *sound* like ours. The sense of smell in canines is particularly telling. What can we make of a species whose ability in that regard is one thousand to ten million times better than us humans. One thousand times better than ours at the *low end*. Using this ability they can even "see" back in time. They can detect for example who passed by a certain area the previous day, what direction they were moving, and other details.

Can we even imagine what that kind of world is like? And, jumping ahead, tell me exactly how we, humans, are superior to that.

Elephants can hear infrasound, as low as one hertz; dolphins as high as one hundred-thousand hertz. Keep in mind that our range is approximately twenty hertz to twenty-thousand hertz.

What of the abilities of echolocation that dolphins and bats have. For that matter, what do we make of the ability of fish and amphibious animals, including sharks, bees, dolphins, and platypuses, to sense electrical fields. This is called *electroreception*. With this sensory ability they are able to sense the electrical impulses of other animals. What is it like living in that world? While I'm sure it is nothing like this, just imagine what our world would be like if we could see the fields of wifi around us.

Do humans have anything like the ability of some planetmates to detect the Earth's magnetic field and use it to navigate for migratory and other purposes? Such animals have *magnetoreception*, which amounts to having compasses built into their cells to point them in the right direction. Amazingly, in addition to migratory animals like sea turtles, this includes fruit flies and even some forms of bacteria.

Some snakes can detect infrared light. Bees can detect ultraviolet light.

As for plants, you thought them dumb? What scientists have discovered is that, amazingly, some have a sensitivity to touch that is finer and more sophisticated as what we have with our fingers; that they communicate with each other, including about a possible threat from a new pest and overcrowding and other matters. They have hormones similar to our own. That not enough, they have vision, all of them. What is the world as experienced by a plant? On what basis do we say that our world is better or closer to apprehending reality than theirs?

Furthermore, what of species whose senses, as nearly as we can determine with our own, are vastly different from ours, such as a mantis shrimp, which have sixteen different types of color receptive cones compared to our mere three. What of species with less in number than ours? What is the "world" of an earthworm like? What, that of an amoeba? Real world, please step forward.

# Our Knowledge Is Biased

Indeed, can we assume, in fairness, that our own senses are capable of perceiving all major aspects of "objective" reality, granting, even, if in limited or distorted fashion? By analogy, it would be ridiculous to suppose that an earthworm or an amoeba ... with apparently few, and more limited, senses ... "knows" of the existence of our species in any ways other than, if anything, a series of obstacles, changes in pressure or temperature, or, well, whatever it is that comprises an earthworm's or amoeba's "worldview."

Correspondingly, can we automatically assume that *our* particular number and set of senses, with their particular ranges, are the endpoint, the pinnacle of what is possible in terms of perceiving "world"? If a sixth, a seventh, an eighth, an *nth* number of "types" of senses were possible, how would we know of that possibility with our five? Would we not be in a situation analogous to that of the earthworm to us? And how would we know what would be perceived with those senses? Why would we bother to, how could we, even, measure the referents in the "out there" corresponding to such hypothetical senses in a way that they would somehow be included in our science?

Furthermore, keeping in mind that earthworm, we can assume, for the sake of argument, that it perceives a *Homo sapiens* as something earthwormo-centrically akin to pressure, an obstacle, or earthwormo-molecular vibrations, in other words, earthworm hot-or-coldness. That is how it might perceive us. Are there any among my readers who believe it would perceive us the way *we* do? I doubt it.

Now, understanding that *our* senses are not omniscient either — they are limited — how would we perceive beings or entities that are outside of or not sufficiently perceived by *our* limited senses? Indeed, how would we even know of the existence of such other sentient beings — not to mention other even more unimaginable realities — who or which could hypothetically be outside of the range and/or number of our *biologically unique* senses?

Would we perceive their existence as human changes in pressure, sound, touch, smell, sight, taste? As atmospheric or environmental "ambiance" changes? As solar activity or astronomical phenomena? As change in mood state, or thought pattern? Or hypothalamic or metabolic or heart or respiratory rate change? As *nuemenon*, "aura," Words of God, Music of the Spheres?... Indeed, as leprechauns, ghosts, or elves? Or perhaps as forcible elements in dreams? Inspirational thought or feeling? Poltergeists, angels, "allies," aliens, psychic phenomena?

# Our Knowledge Is Limited

Then again, would we even perceive this other or these other "species" of beings and/or unimaginable realities at all? Would they be totally out of the domain of detection by anything within our experience — whether sensory, cognitive, affective, intuitive, imaginative, hallucinative?

The point is that we have no, absolutely no, way of knowing what is *really* real, what it "all" *real*-ly *looks* like unless we anthropocentrically assume that we are "God's chosen species," the summit of creation, and magically endowed with a one-in-nine-million — that is to say, one out of the approximate number of other known species, excluding bacteria — uniquely correct number of sensations and perfect accuracy of perception. We have no way of knowing even whether or not we are in the same "space" at the same "time" … the quotation marks because space and time are sensorially determined in our species' unique biological way … as other unperceivable beings, even *sentient* ones — though with what senses, again, we do not know.

# There Are an Infinite Number of Worlds

It should be supremely clear by now, especially among those of us with a transcultural or anthropological familiarity — wherein we are made distinctly aware of the truth-shrouding nature of ethnocentrism — that any serious attempt at discerning truth is not compatible with *any* variety of self-serving or egocentric agenda, regardless how invisible it might be to us or how unconscious it might be held. And *anthropocentrism* — the idea that our species, alone, has the inside track, superior to all creation, on perceiving Reality — is such a self-aggrandizing notion.

Thus, it is just as essential to throw off the overweening species-centric intellectual baggage of our Judeo-Christian tradition … which posits "man" as the ruler over nature and as the summit of created species … as it is essential to strive to drop our ethnocentric blinders. Indeed, making this attempt to view from a neutral, Archimedean, non-anthropocentric "window," it follows logically that the probabilities are enormous that there are, in fact, other beings, unperceivable entities, unknown and unimaginable realities, and other and different senses … and, yes, as one new physics proposition puts it, an infinite number of "worlds."

# 2

# Destroying Worlds:

Our Reality Is Species Determined and the Relativity of Science … Culturally Constituted Realities, Biologically Constituted Realities, and Biological Relativity

*We Cannot Unknow What We Know but We Can't Know What We Can't Know*

*"...to these relativities of space, time, and culture, we must now also include species relativity or biological relativity. That this has not been acknowledged already ... can easily be attributed to ... our anthropocentrism...."*

## Relativity of Science

But what of our science, one might ask, which can reputedly extend the range of our senses? Does it not provide accurate-enough "feedback" or "alternative"-enough perspectives to allow us a glimpse of what *is*, for truth, really real? Let us just look at what modern science tells us about the observations it makes on the world.

According to Gary Zukav (1979), the author of a widely read overview of the new physics, a major underpinning of modern physics is the realization and discovery that science cannot predict anything, as had been taken for granted, with absolute certainty. Relatedly, the new physics informs us that there is simply no way to separate the observed event from the observer. That is to say that the observer is, her- or himself, an inexcludable variable and always affects the results of an experiment. In a very fundamental way, the perceiver influences what is seen in even the most "scientifically" pure observations and experiments: "The new physics ... tells us clearly that it is not possible to observe reality without changing it."[1]

Zukav (1979) takes, as an example, that a condition is set up to perceive an event: If it is designed to find waves in light, it discovers waves. If it is designed to find particles, we get particles — in supposedly the *same* "outside world" ... and regardless of the fact that logically light cannot be both a particle and a wave.[2] That is the classic example, of course. The structure of the experiment, designed by the observer, determines what will be found. At base, intent is all-important; it leans us toward "discovering" what we are inclined to see.

Now, what is this saying if not just what I have stated in Chapter 1? Is this not the same as saying that we determine ultimately, because of our specific biology, what we sense? That we therein *determine* the "world" we experience?

# Culture, Brute Facts, and Culturally Constituted Realities

Nevertheless, to some extent our social scientists have yet to get that memo from the hard sciences. For example, in line with Elizabeth Anscombe's (1958) terminology of *brute facts*, John Searle (1969) claims a distinction between "brute facts" and "institutional facts." Anthropologist Roy D'Andrade (1984) elaborates on this and goes on to explain what is meant by *brute facts:*

11

*Not all social-science variables refer to culturally created things; some variables refer to objects and events that exist prior to, and independent of, their definition: for example, a person's age, the number of calories consumed during a meal, the number of chairs in a room, or the pain someone felt.*[3]

D'Andrade is describing a difference ... no doubt one we all would make ... between objects in the world or seeming absolutes such as numbers and that which varies by culture — *institutional facts*, which are also referred to as *culturally constituted facts*, or realities. Simply put, *culturally constituted realities*, or institutional facts, are facts, things, realities that are created by culture. In the terms we used in the last chapter, culturally constituted realities are created in the cortex and they are interpretations of what has been given to the cortex of information concocted by a species biology, in interior parts of the brain, which were fed by neural firings determined by what our senses has selected out of the infinity of possibility of what can be sensed in any particular moment and environment.

## Culture is Our Template for Understanding

So, you see, culture is the set of understandings and everything related to them that is shared in common by a group. It is the way a particular group sees, creates, and "furnishes" the world. It is the matrix, grid, or framework that is projected onto Reality determining what one perceives and then interprets it. It creates the understandings of our perceptions and experiences, as they are configured within the context created by that culture. It is a group's "window" on the world; it is the template stamped upon Reality; it is the blueprint out of which our perceptions and understandings arise.

Consequently, *culturally constituted realities* are realities or facts that are created by individual cultures and which exist only for them. They are distinct from *brute facts*, which can be said to be realities that exist in all cultures: Brute facts can be said to exist *outside* of cultures, independent of them, regardless that cultures determine the interpretation or meaning of them.

Some basic culturally constituted realities are the different languages; the various religious notions with their supernatural realities and the cultural items and artifacts they impel; specific but commonly held ideas about governance, justice, appropriate behavior, work, play, ritual, leisure, courtesy, fairness, as well as the conventions, institutions, and material culture propelled by them; and much, much more that is considered real and true in a culture but which is not seen or at least is not seen that way in *all* cultures.

Now, D'Andrade is saying that not *all* realities are culturally constituted and that there are realities that are independent of culture, and about which all cultures must make determinations and interpretations or with which they must at least interact. The examples he gives of such realities include things like a person's age, the number of calories in a meal, the number of chairs in a place, and the pain a person feels.

## Total Heritage View of Culture Sees It as the Matrix

D'Andrade is speaking to and critiquing a "total heritage" view of culture, espoused by some anthropologists, which holds that *all* reality is culturally determined ... or constituted ... including such "brute facts." In the total-heritage view — espoused in particular by Marshall Sahlins (1976) — even the things we think to be irreducible or independent of cultural interpretations are indeed created by and patterned by ... "constituted" by ... culture.

To understand the total-heritage take on things, one might use the analogy of the Matrix, as it is portrayed in the movie of the same name. In *The Matrix,* people live their lives in a completely *constructed* world, which includes the physical aspects of it — the buildings, parks, highways, everything else one might think of as real, as physical, as material. Naturally, everything that one thinks and imagines is also bounded within that world, knowing no other, after all. It is virtually identical to Plato's cave, in his "Allegory of the Cave."[4]

As many of you know, the "Allegory of the Cave" is a classic explanation of our normal illusory state of consciousness. As most philosophies hold, there is a greater reality than what we know as humans. I was saying much along those lines in Chapter 1. And many wise folks have added that knowing that Reality would enable us to grok the things that are confusing and inexplicable about life.

Now, Plato, in his allegory, compared humans to beings living in a cave and deeming Reality to be the shadows on a wall created by a fire burning behind the participants. The actual reality could be found only by leaving the cave and going into the sunlight outside. So, this allegory is most definitely a total-heritage view, though it does not specify culture as being the factor creating the reflected or illusory quality of our perceptions and understandings. For its part, the total-heritage view, though it considers culture as all-creative of our world, or "cave," is agnostic about there being any *actual* reality outside the cave.

In the movie, *The Matrix*, the only thing other than this comprehensive and totally constructed world that exists, actually exists, are the people in it. However, they exist also in a state outside of the Matrix, but they do not have a clue that they have an existence separate. Again, this is like Plato's cave allegory.

Thus, the total-heritage view of culture sees it as much like the Matrix or the Cave, with our reality — all of it — being culturally constituted. Or at least that we, as humans, embedded in culture, have no possible way of knowing if there are any brute facts outside of the templates we are given by societies to understand and function in Reality.

By contrast to this total-heritage or "matrix" idea of culture, we have the view that there are "brute facts" also which exist outside of culture which are *interpreted by* culture, not totally concocted by them.

# Biologically Constituted Realities, Species-Specific Facts

For now, though — and however much I agree with D'Andrade that there are realities separate from cultural ones — from what I have been saying in the previous chapter about species creating their "worlds" through the different percepters they have, we can see that these "brute facts" may not be culturally constituted as he asserts, but they certainly are biologically constituted. For the age in years one has, the numbers of anything, and especially pain felt are all realities relative to humans, and some *only* to humans. We might remember what I said earlier about vibrational rates — that is to say, heat —

14

and its relativity to the perceiving organism. In that example I was making the case that the very existence of pain and pleasure is relative to the species in question. Hence, these supposedly brute facts are actually *species-specific facts*. They are "brute" only in relation to our particular species.

## If a Tree Falls in the Forest….

You might acknowledge that relativity to the perceiver is true of pain, but balk about my saying that species-relativity is true as well regarding numbers of things, as in the other examples D'Andrade gives. Let me address that by referring to an analogous situation involving an age-old philosophical question. For it follows from the species-specific angle on reality I am presenting that the new-paradigm answer to that question is clear: If a tree falls in the forest and there is no one there to hear it, does it make a sound? That answer, absolutely not! Sound is as much species-relative as the practice of polygamy is culturally relative. In other words, there are species for which sound does not exist. Everything else we consider existing is also only in relation to humans, so it follows that the numbers of anything is a relative "fact," as well.

What we call "existing" is actually what is existence relative to *one* species, *our* species, *Homo sapiens*. And we are merely one species out of an estimated *one trillion* species, which includes bacteria this time, on Earth. That does not even take into account species on other planets, even ones we would be able to perceive, if we were there or they came here. It does not even touch the infinite possibilities of beingness, or "species" that we would have *no* way of knowing or perceiving or that we *would* perceive but in some way so we would not even know it to be a living thing. Remember that earthworm who might only perceive us as heat or pressure, which I mentioned earlier, and how we are likely in a similar situation relative to some other beings and species.

Similarly, the event that we perceive as *sound-tree-and-forest-interacting* may be "perceived" as quite something else with *different* kinds of and/or *more* "senses" or, one might say, from a different vantage point. Indeed, different concoctions of the event — combinations of its elements — may be carved out of it, being relative to the other-than-human perceiver, creating different elements of the event, different "numbers" of any elements in it, and creating vastly different and totally *unimaginable* interpretations! As I said, our senses scan and pick out of an infinity of possibilities of what can be perceived. What it "notices" ... or "creates"? ... is relative to who we are as a species. Even the determination of that falling tree being an *event* is relative, hence questionable, ultimately. Relatedly, whether or not there is actually even a physical world in which it occurs is suspect and is something we will deal with at length and in due time in this book.

## The Bias Invisible in Science

Regardless, the point of all this is that removing our anthropocentric blinders in this way we must conclude that the world, as experienced, is created of realities that are not only culturally constituted, as anthropologists point out. There are also *biologically constituted realities.* The "brute facts" to which D'Andrade refers are — nothing brute about them — *biologically determined facts.* How anthropocentrically arrogant for us to think that *our* brute facts are brute in some conceivable Ultimate Reality that *all* existing or conceivable living beings or entities share, meaning are able to perceive ... indeed are able to perceive ... *pretty much the way we do!*

Yet this is exactly the arrogance that prevails in all of our sciences. When we imagine other beings in our Universe, as we do in some of our arts, we anthropocentrically assume they would have human features, with only slight variations, with senses similar to ours and perceiving the exact same world, and that they would have evolved in some manner parallel to the way we did on Earth. That is forgivable in our arts and cinema, as in *Star Trek* and *Star Wars,* as they are not claiming to be science.

But what is damning and *is* embedded within and constraining the purview of our sciences is this assumption that the Universe as we have come to know it through our science, with its space, time, stars, Big Bang, galaxies, dimensions, planets, and so on, *is* the Universe in some ultimate way outside of our humanly limited perception.

What? You don't think so? You think the cosmos we measure with our humanly-created technology and perceive with our human, our limited, senses, is pretty much *like* the one that exists outside our perception of it? That our perceived and arrived-at cosmos *is* the Cosmos? No doubt you think it *has* to be. You have never questioned it.

However, remember that experiment with the particle and wave, where what we look for ends up being what we see. Ponder that and its implications.

Now, think again for a minute, and you will realize that when science uncovers discrepancies or anomalies, incongruent with their abiding theories, the most they will acknowledge is that their concepts of the elements of the Cosmos are open to reinterpretation and re-inclusion in some other, some grander scheme which, they assume, at some point will validate them in some way they do not see right now. Nowhere do scientists concede their galaxies, black holes, atoms, matter, space, Big Bang, et al, are realities relative only to humans, for all we know. Or, for that matter, that they might not be existing outside of human perception. When it comes to that tree in the forest, there is never any question about it making a sound for scientists. It just does.

Indeed, these are the assumptions scientists all make; except, that is, for a few remarkable ones like Einstein, whose vast perspective on it all led him to conclude there is a spiritual reality for it all beyond and outside of what science can know. Or Roger Jones, the author of *Physics as Metaphor* (1982) who pulled the blinds to the side on the ultimately empty and insubstantial nature of the concepts assumed in science, specifically its most *substantial* one, physics. Other than the few like these, the great majority of less stellar scientists will acknowledge that Reality is indeterminate — as they are prodded, by the new physics, to admit — yet they will assume validity for their established understandings, in the face of contrary evidence, if not in the current scheme, then in some other and future one. Which they further presume will be built upon their current assumptions, which at most, at that time, will be refined in parts.

So scientists assume the cosmos they peer into, measure, and study is the same one all other species apprehend. This is regardless the vast differences in the way that universe is perceived by the beings we know about or, for that matter, the scope of any particular species' perception of it, which we know at least sometimes is far far more far-ranging, advanced, than ours. Despite these facts to the contrary, nowhere in science is it advanced that their interpretations of the cosmos are relative to humans only. Much more about that, upcoming.

Science's reluctant qualification of indeterminacy is quite a bit different from an acknowledgment of what I am putting forth: Which is that there might be a more valid understanding, or perception, by some conceivable other being or species, in which those elements of the universe we consider to be absolute can be seen to be *non-existent or radically wrong*. And beyond that … the most important part of this … that in comparison to whom, our interpretations of things are not seen merely to be to be biased as a result of our species identity, but that the very existence of these supposedly absolute things of our world are found to be projections, in their entirety and thus completely insubstantial, of our human psyche … to be mere projections of our uniquely human perspective on things … creations purely concocted of the elements of our unique distinction from Nature. That is a distinction, which I will not elaborate upon now, but which has us as supremely flawed in relation to the rest of Nature. This is something I have demonstrated in several of my works, in particular, *Planetmates* (2014b) and *Prodigal Human* (2016a).

Furthermore, consider that physicists talk about the possibility of other dimensions intersecting our world. So these alternate realities share the same time and space … or they share whatever Ultimate Reality we exist in … *with* us. Yet how could physicists even define these invisible worlds as "other dimensions"? Think about it, are dimensions not also relative to our species, with some other species conceivably apprehending the Cosmos in a completely different way? Is it not possible there are species whose perceptions of Reality — equal to or more valid than ours — would in no way involve those dimensions … perceptions where those *dimensions* do not exist, as they are overridden by or subsumed within some other perceptual array vastly different from ours? Or, accepting the reality of those dimensions, how can we say with any certainty at all that the brute facts we have in *our* dimension qualify as *brute facts* in *those* dimensions as well?!

At any rate, I am going to leave to the side, for now, the complicating factor of the infinite number of beings and possibilities of existing and perceiving that would exist in *each* of those different dimensions. I will not even get into the fact that this incredible cosmos with these billions of galaxies — an estimated one hundred billion galaxies with an average of two hundred to four hundred billion stars *per* galaxy and god-only-knows how many planets coinciding with all those stars, or suns — and infinite numbers of dimensions is still only the cosmos that *we* — we lowly, humble, and limited perceptually humans — are able to perceive. So how can it not be true that there even *more* possibilities for ways of perceiving Reality, more possibilities of realities, than even the infinite numbers of them we are able to deduce with our limited senses at this particular time with its limited knowledge as well!!??

And, yes, I realize that some of you readers are jumping ahead and even questioning the reality of entities, beings, perceptions, perceptors, perceivers, percepters, senses, and all else, which I have been leaning on in making my case, and would like to challenge me on that.[5] For you will say that they — any being, beings, or entities — also are deduced from what we know from our limited apprehension of the world. So they, too, might be no more than human projections.

Thinking this way, you might say that my theory is empty or insubstantial for it, also, is deduced from our perception of realities, which I am acknowledging to be unspecial and infinitely variable. You might say that even our perception of different and separate *perceivers* — what I am terming, *perceptors* — is questionable. How do we know any entities or beings exist, outside of our own one — oneself — if all that we perceive is determined by what we expect and project? Are there even *numbers* of things — as when D'Andrade asserted numbers were "brute" — let alone beings?

Are we sure that the way we chop up Reality into parts — separate things, separate beings, and so on — so that we might name them and analyze them separate from our perception of them is anything but a product of our biological programming? Does all possible perceptors see the world in terms of parts? How can we say that is the case? Perhaps, indeed, that separation of ourselves from Reality and dissecting of it is just some neurosis or illness ... some

19

delusion … that is particularly human to do so. Or at least that it is unique to humans.

But going off on that tack *is* jumping ahead. For this book will, indeed, take us there and past that point as well. In fact such considerations are specifically addressed in the chapter titled, "The Radical Rational View of Us And It," Chapter 15. Hang on, and congratulations on your forethought, by the way.

## Biological Relativity

At any rate, getting back to culturally constituted facts and those nasty brute facts, again, I was saying there is nothing "brute" about what humans would call *brute facts*. Rather, they are *biologically determined facts*. They are facts relative to our species. These "facts" or truths are *biologically relative*. They are true, with surety, *only* in relation to our species. They might exist for other species as well, certainly they are shared by many, but a) they are not shared by all, and b) we must conclude they are not even facts the way we know them, for they are necessarily perceived *differently* by *each and every* species. That is to say, if they, indeed, even show up as elements or "facts" in their realities, their perceived realities.

Yes, we have another relativity — *species relativity* — to include with the others we have been coming up with in the sciences.

Einstein let us know that our space and time were relative, not absolute.

Franz Boas and all anthropologists after him helped us to see that our cultural realities were relative, as well. That means that all that we conceive and create as cultural elements can only be understood within the context of the culture they exist within. Which means that anyone outside of that culture — that is, not containing that cultural mental set — will *necessarily* not quite understand them the way those in the culture do: In fact, in a basic and profound way they will *misunderstand* them; they will not "get it" the way cultural members do.[6] Indeed, many cultural elements are *invisible* outside of the culture in which they exist. Cultural elements are *culturally relative*, is the way that is expressed. But more than that, cultures create their own elements, unique to them, and these cultural facts are what

D'Andrade above was referring to when he mentioned *culturally constituted realities*.

Therefore, to these relativities of space, time, and culture, we must now also include *species relativity* or *biological relativity*. That this has not been acknowledged already, for it is so obvious, can easily be attributed to the pervasive and unquestioned species-centrism — our anthropocentrism — characteristic of human, especially Western, culture, to date. Again, this is the hidden "flat earth" assumption I was pointing out in Chapter 1, which is reinforced by our religions, especially the Judeo-Christian ones, which assert humans to be superior in Nature and having dominion over all others in Nature. I call anthropocentrism or human superiority to Nature a *flat earth* assumption because it is equally as obviously true yet ultimately wrong, as well as relative to a perceiver, as is a notion the Earth is flat. Not to mention that seeing Reality outside that assumption of anthropocentrism and acknowledging this species relativity instead would be as momentous and world-changing as was the discovery of the heliocentric nature of our solar system.

Incidentally, this assumption of species superiority — species centrism — is also a central component of the *Unapproved and Hidden* I describe in others of my works.[7]

To understand species relativity, we can use those same understandings, discussed above, in regard to time, space, and culture relativity. We will see that all of those understandings are true, as well, for the realities created or constituted by our specific physical constitution, our biology, separate as it is for each species. This is *biological relativity*, and what it adds to our understanding when seen as analogous to the other relativities is that it tells us:

a) Our realities can only be understood within the context of our species … other species could not understand them … and we cannot really understand the realities of other species … lower *or* higher, if in fact there are such categories for species in Ultimate Reality. In some way, large or small, species will misunderstand each other. In fact, in that species are actually distinct from each other, whereas cultures are not … see Note 6 of this chapter … there is much more to biological relativity than there has ever been to cultural relativity.

b) Many elements of our human reality will be invisible to or not even exist within the realities of other species — they are biologically constituted realities. Some things, maybe many or all things, which exist within the perceived and understood realities of other species will be invisible to us or not even exist within *our* possible world: They are species-specific, biologically constituted realities for *them,* as well.

Bringing this all together, we now see that there are *culturally constituted facts:* That is to say, facts that are cultural creations and either do not exist or are not perceived or understood the same from other cultural perspectives — in other words, by people from other cultures. And there are *biologically constituted realities:* That is, there are those *supposed* "brute facts" that either do not exist or are not perceived or understood the same from other *biological* perspectives — in other words, by species, beings, or entities other than the human one. These last are as *biologically relative* as the first ones are *culturally relative.*

# 3

# Infinite Worlds:

The Spectrum of Realities ... Individually, Bioculturally, and Suprahumanly Constituted Realities, and Ultimate Relativity

*"Authentic and convincing experiences of conscious identification with animals, plants, and even inorganic materials and processes make it easy to understand the beliefs of animistic cultures that see the entire universe as being ensouled." — Stanislav Grof*

*"...such transpersonal experiences dramatically change our understanding of the nature of everyday material reality ... others reveal dimensions of existence that are ordinarily completely hidden to our perception. This ... includes discarnate entities, various deities and demons, mythological realms, suprahuman beings, and the divine creative principle itself." — Stanislav Grof*

*"...space, including size, is relative to the perceiver.... At the ultimate tiniest [atomic, subatomic], consciousness might come around ... and present itself as the hugest consciousness, the Cosmos.... So, literally anything can be."*

*"Ultimately our physics ... is going to demonstrate that essentially there is no such thing as matter. All there is, is mind and motion." — Armand Labbe*

# The Spectrum of Realities

Furthermore, we can see that these realities exist on a continuum with culturally constituted realities on one end and biologically constituted realities on the other, for there are many in-between facts, which would have to be called *bioculturally determined facts* or *bioculturally constituted realities*.

## Bioculturally Constituted Realities

How are *bioculturally constituted realities* defined? Well, they are cultural facts that exist because of the common biology we as a species share, each and every one of us. These are facts that are relative to the pain and pleasure humans experience and the way and degrees in which we experience them.

These are facts relative to the birth and death humans experience and the ways we experience and construe them. These are facts relative to the life cycle and stages of life that are uniquely human and the ways we experience and understand and configure them. Thus, these common biological things and events are *facts* for the species we call *human* — they are biologically constituted realities for humans — for they are shared by all humans. Yet they are perceived, construed, interpreted, configured, manifested, acted out, dealt with, responded to, and created around *differently* by each and every culture, at least slightly differently. These bioculturally constituted realities are cultural constructions built on and around our biological facts (constructions). The constructions, or "facts," about or related to our common biological realities that arise from these different cultures are, therefore, *biocultural* facts or realities. They are *bioculturally determined facts*. I will deal with them in more detail in the next three chapters.

So there are biologically constituted facts, bioculturally constituted facts, and culturally constituted facts all existing on a continuum. That continuum measures the degree to which those facts are "real" … or let us say the degree to which those realities are shared. That continuum tells you the number of "individuals" who share those "facts" … who perceive, hold, and/or engage with those facts, while others do not. *Individuals* is in quotes in keeping with our analysis that our conceptualization of other members of other species — known and unknown — is based on one of our biologically constituted realities. Separate beings, or "individuals," itself is a *species-relative* fact.

Getting back to the spectrum, the more astute of you, I know, have already realized that biologically constituted facts and culturally constituted facts are not even absolute ends of that continuum. That continuum extends out at each of its ends beyond those categories. Do you see that? Do you see how that follows from what I was saying in the beginning about many worlds and infinite numbers of perceivers?

## Individually Constituted Realities

If not, follow this: Do you see that even the term *culture* is not a category with clear boundaries and that it might pertain to a huge group of individuals, whereas subgroups of that would constitute separate cultures, each slightly different from the rest, so they are themselves considered cultures. These subgroups are sometimes called *subcultures*.

But even they have subgroups and subcultures within them. For a culture is a particular set of understandings or ways of seeing that is held in common by a group. And every group, in that sense, can be considered a culture for, indeed, that is how we define a group: It is a number of people that share a common understanding or way of seeing things, and that might simply be in its intent. But also it usually includes its goals, procedures, and more: special language, sometimes called jargon; group constructions — physical and organizational ones as well as temporal ones, i.e., events; as well as ways of behavior, manners of speaking, rules of courtesy, and the like.

So who is still with me? Well, if you followed all that, you would see that such groups can be continually broken down ... can be infinitely broken down, you will soon see ... into even smaller subgroups. Neighborhoods can be broken down into separate family cultures, for example. And where from there?

Well, we see that, yes, it is true, each and every individual can her- or himself be considered a culture, in that there are understandings, procedures, ways of thinking, and all the rest that are *not* held in common with anyone else at all but are unique to each individual. That is often referred to as personality, a person's unique personality, but it goes beyond that to unique facts of each individual that are not even, by *other* individuals, observable! The difference between *individual culture* and *personality* is a matter of emphasis in that *individual culture* pertains to patterns, realities, facts, and ways of looking at or construing the world primarily from the perspective of the individual, whereas *personality* usually applies to those things as observed, to the extent they *are* observed, and referred to by others.

Nevertheless, one might say culture, as it pertains to groups and societies, reduced to its foundation, is simply another way of referring to individual psychologies, or personalities, but doing it cumulatively.

Culture is collective psychology, in a sense. It is the obverse of Jung's *collective unconscious,* for it is what is *known* in a culture, not unknown or unconscious. It could be said that culture is the *collective consciousness,* viewed in its widest possible way and including all possible elements of a culture, of a group.

Following that? Okay, then, we can see that this end of the continuum, which we were calling culturally constituted realities, really goes further out from its supposed end point to *individually constituted realities.* These are realities that are unique to an individual and can only be understood within the context of that individual, and when encountered outside of that individual they are likely to be either misunderstood or not seen at all. For those of you following this, we can see that such personal "cultures," if you will, comprised of individually constructed realities, are different, individual to individual, and that some of those cultural elements are shared widely, while some of those individuals have personal cultures with elements that are so unique and unshared that we have a special term for those individuals. Of course you know this one. For what if I were to put it another way and ask you, simply, what do we call individuals who we can see are "living in their own world."

Yes, you are correct. The term for that is *psychotic*.

No, don't go. We're not done yet.

## Suprahumanly Constituted Realities

Okay, then, let us look at the antipode of that end point, newly seen to be individually constituted realities. On the *other* end of the continuum, the one we were indicating as biologically constituted realities, we can see that it extends beyond where we thought it ended as well. How, you say?

Well, as I said, biologically constituted realities are those realities shared by a species, some of which are shared *only* by that species and some are shared to varying degrees, but not to every other species.

Well, the category, *species*, also, is not absolute. (I see, a couple of you already were thinking this. Good for you!) There are certainly realities that are unique to entire groups of species that have important qualities in common. We see that the categorization of species itself is not absolute. For we can easily draw a line around groups of species and create other entities, which for all we know create their own "constituted" realities.

There are realities constituted by the fact that the perceiver is from the vegetable kingdom — you might call them vegetablely-constituted realities, or from the animal kingdom, planetmatedy-constituted realities, or by virtue of being mammalian (you've got it from here), or out of the fact of belonging to one of the many taxonomies or other biological categories of species, or from the fact that all exist on something that they perceive to be Earth ... and so on. For all I know there are realities that are shared by all "elements" or "members" (whatever they might be) in our solar system, but none other (heliocentrically-constituted realities?), or by "members" (whatever they might be) of our galaxy of the Milky Way, but are not seen at all or are able to be perceived in other galaxies, other dimensions, or other....

... and here we get into realities we are not capable of knowing exist.

You say they are not perceivers, however, so they cannot create their own realities out of their perceptions. Good one, on that. But how do you know that is true? As one example, is there not serious consideration to the idea that the Earth itself is a seeing, feeling, perceiving being? A Gaia? How can you say it is not? Would it not fit into the category of possible beings that we are not capable of seeing with our percepters? Like I said, earthworms might perceive humans as an obstacle or hot and coldness. So might we not be in the same position relative to these *greater* beings (or at least, *different* beings)? So that we as humans are perceiving a planet which is in actuality a form of consciousness (an experiential vantage point, a perceiver), but we mistakenly and "brutely" conceive of it as being lifeless ... an Earth that is mere matter and stuff, not conscious or perceiving?

Remember, also, that the majority of humans that have ever lived, which includes many living now, think of, nay they even have direct experience of, Nature and its aspects as being living and to constitute a living, perceiving being. And they deem that Nature to be even higher, far higher in fact, in its apprehension and consciousness than us.

I want to point out that as odd or fantastical as this sounds, this is exactly the notion coming out of some of the consciousness research of the last fifty years. Stanislav Grof, for one, has found that in his modes of LSD psychotherapy, as well as his non-drug modality, holotropic breathwork, people are able to identify with and experience the consciousnesses not only of other planetmates — that is, other species on Earth — but also are able to merge with and experience the consciousnesses of higher orders of beings: the Earth, individual planets, the galaxy, particular collections of people — such as the women of all time (note here that the entities do not even have to be alive in this time and place for them to be part of a collective consciousness ... the relativity of space and time, remember?); and even collectives of supranormal beings and realities — archetypal consciousness and its reality, for example. And it is possible to experience consciousness of supposedly inanimate, non-living forms

28

(the secret life of stones, you see?) and even identify with consciousnesses on the atomic and subatomic levels … which is something coming up. Hold on.

Putting this rather bluntly, Stanislav Grof concurs,

*Authentic and convincing experiences of conscious identification with animals, plants, and even inorganic materials and processes make it easy to understand the beliefs of animistic cultures that see the entire universe as being ensouled. From their perspective, not only all the animals, but also the trees, the rivers, the mountains, the sun, the moon and the stars appear to be sentient beings.*[1]

# Infinite Worlds

## Infinite Organizations of Experience Equals Infinite Beings

Then there is Teilhard deChardin — someone whom Grof cites as presenting a way of conceptualizing the beings and consciousnesses he has come across in his modalities — who advanced the notion that every integrated whole is in fact a form of beingness and that the degree of consciousness inherent in each is relative to the level of complexity of that integrated whole. For reasons that will become clearer as we proceed, I would say there is indeed reason to assert that levels of complexity relate to levels of awareness.

However as for the "higher level" of consciousness being related to the level of complexity — with more complexity being of a higher consciousness than lower complexity — I would say there is evidence indicating the opposite is true. From the perspective of brain-as-reducing-valve, which I will elaborate on shortly, and the viewpoint brought forth in my books, *Falls from Grace* (2014a) and *Experience Is Divinity* (2013c), the simplest organizations, the least complex entities, are the highest orders of awareness, in that each reduction into form and the elaboration of that form is one step further removed from the consciousness of stone, the consciousness of space, of the Void … ultimately, of Divinity. So physical reality with its myriad and ever increasing complexities and organizations of complications are steps in removal from unity with Divinity.

On the other hand, regarding the Experience, or Divinity, that physical reality is removed from ... and while this is not crucial to the argument being presented here, but as a look ahead ... I would say that levels of higher awareness (rather, experience), not physical or energetic complexity, create perceptible and/or conceivable levels of complexity of Experience. That is, that integration of greater and greater complexities of subjective Experience equate to greater levels of consciousness, but that levels of complexity of Experience are an inverse to levels of complexity of matter. But again, that is jumping ahead. Yes, we'll get to that, as well.

Still, I would join with deChardin in saying that, for all we know, every integrated whole is possibly some form of perceptor, some form of consciousness which is receiving information — "sensory" and otherwise — and combining and integrating it in their unique way.

For example, it is not that strange to believe that each planet is a form of consciousness ... just ask astrologers ... and that they interact with each other in their own ways. For we see that cells, looking down below us to a microcosm smaller than us, have all the qualities of consciousness — they act, interact, behave, learn, make decisions based on judgments, and so on. So how do we know that planets, galaxies, star systems ... the All That Is Itself ... would not appear to have the same qualities of an individual actor or perceiver if we were *above* and able to *look down* on them, just like we do in observing cells and organs? And, in so doing, see what from a higher experiential awareness would be just as much signs of life, consciousness, behavior, intentional interaction, or whatever are the things of perception and beingness at that level that would be similar to the ones we see as indications of life, consciousness, behavior, intentional interactions, and the like at our level ... our admittedly non-ultimate level with its limited and ultimately unknowing perception and experience?

As I have said, Grof has reams of evidence that such an amazing possibility is in fact the case.

## Ultimate Relativity

Putting this all together, all realities are relative, all facts can only be understood in context; and those facts and realities can only truly be understood by groups who collectively construct them. So there are an infinite number of beings, an infinite number of species … consequently an infinite number of worlds.

Nope, nothing brute about our facts … at all!!!!!

The continuum we have constructed has on one end the unique individual with mental and experiential constructions that are not shared with anyone else. So these are called individually constructed realities … related to individual psychology. Yes, yes, I know. Some of you are already breaking down that individual into organs and cells and beginning to see that each of these subgroupings also have their unique constructions — their uniquely held "facts" and realities." Although I will be toying with ideas of that later, such as, do those realities have an infinite regress into the atomic, and beyond. And, indeed, if time and space are both relative, as they are said to be, does this end of the spectrum, at the infinitesimally small, ever even come fully around again and link up with the realities on the other end, with Ultimate Reality? But that is enough on that end for now.

On the other end of the spectrum we have biologically constructed realities and whatever it might be called for the larger "cultures" of beingness and perception beyond them. This includes the galaxies, dimensions, star systems, and such, especially and including the things we do not know exist for there is absolutely no way humans can possibly perceive or know of them, even with our technology, even with any possible technology that humans could come up with in any possible human future.…

As Grof explains them,

*While such transpersonal experiences dramatically change our understanding of the nature of everyday material reality, there are others that reveal dimensions of existence that are ordinarily completely hidden to our perception. This category includes discarnate entities, various deities and demons, mythological realms, suprahuman beings, and the divine creative principle itself.* [2]

So, we have the spectrum of realities and facts: individually constitute realities, culturally constituted realities, bioculturally constituted realities, biologically constituted realities, and near the end of the spectrum, the whatever-constituted realities — let us call them *suprahumanly-constituted realities* — of "entities" that comprise those species or "members," in various levels of organizations extending out further than we could possibly see or imagine. The spectrum describes a progression of increasingly valid or "truer" facts and realities. For they are shared with increasingly larger numbers of members who hold them to be true. This spectrum of validity of realities begins with the individually constituted — putting to the side for now that can be further broken down into groups extending into the subatomic — which has the least number of entities holding them to be true, i.e., only one, an individual. And it extends all the way to the suprahumanly constituted realities, which has the largest group of entities, of members sharing those "facts" and "realities" and holding them to be true.

## Ultimate Reality

And then beyond even that we have what we can postulate to be Ultimate Reality, which might not exist, but the term represents whatever reality is or at least comes closest to having realities that are shared — that are "facts," if you will, that are perceived, shared, "gotten" by ALL individuals — or potentially *can* be gotten considering the makeup of the species involved — and entities in the Universe. Here is where we start to use the word, *God*.

So on the other end of the spectrum from the subatomic is Ultimate Reality ... and does, then, Ultimate Reality and the subatomic end up joining? How would we know? How could we say it would not? Since space, including size, is conceivably as relative to humans as time is to us, why, even that is possible. It boggles the mind.

Also, I should point out that even the subatomic can be further reduced into conscious experiential beings. That might be hard to understand, but keep in mind our most scientific understanding of the Cosmos has it that at the Big Bang, at the creation of the Universe, everything, the entire Universe we see around us, with all its galaxies, was contained within and emanated out from a spot the size of an atom…. If that can happen, well, if nothing else then, space, including size, is relative to the perceiver…. And this gives further credibility to the idea that, at the ultimate tiniest, consciousness might come around again and present itself as the hugest consciousness, the Cosmos. Yes, truly mind-quaking stuff.

So literally anything could be.

# Biologically Constituted Realities, Conclusion

Getting back to culturally constituted realities, so do we then, indeed, create our own reality culturally, of which Marshall Sahlins (1976) writes? Marshall Sahlins is a prominent American anthropologist who stressed the power that culture has to shape the world that people discern and act within and is associated with that total-heritage or Matrix view on reality.

Well, yes, I believe we do live within culturally created worlds, separate from other people in other culturally created worlds.

But I believe we do much more than that. I believe we create it biologically too: I believe that our reality is species-determined prior to that. And while that might sound common-sensical, I contend it is a factor affecting our constructions of reality and determining what we think is real that has been overlooked by all our sciences and by all Western overstandings and for all the time of Western civilization. Yet I profess it has huge significance, affecting the very foundations of human knowledge itself. And the implications of that adjustment to our understandings is what I get into in this book.

## Relativity: Cultural and Biological

Finally, however, what does this say about cultural relativity, of which so much is made in anthropological circles? I agree with Sahlins's position on the total and symbolic nature of culture and with it the resulting extreme cultural relativism which he asserts. As D'Andrade (1987) put it, Sahlins's view is extreme enough that it undermines even science's claim to validity and makes of our science, "mere ethnoscience."[3] But I do not imply by my agreement that I believe reality is *only* culturally determined by any definitional stretch of the term *cultural* that Sahlins, even from his "total heritage" perspective, could have had in mind. I intend to go further.

How so, then, could I claim, at the outset, that I believe both positions can be true? How can reality be so thoroughly "created" — not only culturally but biologically as well — and yet there be universal commonalities on which to base analyses and cross-cultural understanding? Where I disagree with Sahlins and emphatically agree with D'Andrade on the existence of "brute facts" standing outside and separate from cultural constructions is where D'Andrade (1987), in referring to a quote from Sahlins, writes

> *I think I agree if ... [he] ... means that people respond to their interpretations of events, not the raw events themselves. However, if this means that culture can interpret any event any way, and that therefore there is no possibility of establishing universal generalizations, I disagree. I believe that there are strong constraints on how much interpretative latitude can be given to biological and social events. While the letters "D," "O," "G," can be given any interpretation,* pain, death *, and* hunger *have such powerful intrinsic negative properties that they can be interpreted as "good" things only with great effort and for short historical periods with many failed converts.*[4]

With this statement of D'Andrade, I enthusiastically agree also. I believe that there are "intrinsic" (biological) determiners of cultures, which create a basic underlying structure. Indeed, as I was saying above, there are bioculturally constituted realities clustered about those biological "facts" of humans.

However, where I feel I take issue with D'Andrade is that I contend that these "intrinsic" determiners are intrinsic to the species, not to the events themselves, as I was delineating above. These brute "facts" are as much biologically relative as items of culture are culturally relative.

This is as important to point out as it is important in physics to keep in mind that particles and waves only exist in relation to an observer. In this regard, as Armand Labbe (1991) put it, "Ultimately our physics ... is going to demonstrate that essentially there is no such thing as matter. All there is, is mind and motion."

At any rate, I contend that our biological "infrastructure," that is, our bodies and the experiences they make possible — which are species-specific but also common to all humans — results in *biocultural*, *species-specific*, and hence transcultural *patterns* of thought and behavior. Further, these transcultural patterns of thought and behavior create transcultural patterns of social structure, "external culture," sociocultural behavior, and so on.

At this time, in the next chapter, we will look at some of those biocultural realities or "facts." Keeping in mind the immense relativity of them — that is, they are only relative to our species, for one thing — unveils startling understandings and revelations and opens the door a little more to the paradigm I am unveiling for you in *The Secret Life of Stones*.

# 4

# The Perinatal Matrix:

Bioculturally Constituted Realities, Part 1 … Our Biocultural World and We Are What We've Experienced — Our Conception, Gestation, and Birth Create Our Windows to the World

*Going Beyond Jung ... Our Prenatal and Perinatal Experiences Predispose the Nature of Our Mind*

*"...our conception, gestation, and birth... can be seen to form our underlying myths ... but much more than that. They also create the very foundational templates upon which we build our view of reality — physical, social, emotional, spiritual, and philosophical...."*

# Our Prenatal and Perinatal Matrix

Carl Jung is one man in particular who decades ago, in many thoroughly encompassing works, expressed similar concepts regarding biocultural patterns as being species-specific for humans — the hereditary remnants of what are called *instinct* in animals, as he put it.

## Beyond Jung

Without diminishing the historical importance of his contributions, I need to stress that what I am asserting goes much further than Jung's contentions. For I believe we biologically determine our view of reality, as a species,

1) in the biological structures that comprise us and orient us in a world of *space*;

2) in the biochemical processes that constitute our changingness and situate us in a world of *time*;

3) and, most saliently, in the individual biological *history* that is universal for us and unique to us as a species.

So I am saying that our biological *structures, processes*, and *history* — i.e., our past experience — create the worlds of *space, time*, and *memory* within which we move and have our existence.

By this last one, *memory*, however, I mean much more than that our past experience comprises the knowledge base or data bank from which we concoct our life schemes and decisions. I also mean much more than that our past experiences affect us in ways of which we are unaware as well, that is to say unconsciously … that we are affected by repressed or forgotten memories. No, I mean to go much farther and deeper than that. I mean that our conception, gestation, and birth — in general, our earliest experiences as a biological organism — can be seen to form our underlying myths … but much more than that. They also create the very foundational templates upon which we build our view of reality — physical, social, emotional, spiritual, and philosophical.

37

How is this idea — that we have biological parameters of structure, process, and events experienced (one's personal history) — different from what you already know and why is it important or helpful to know it this way? Well, we, with our species arrogance, believe we have a mind, intellect, ability to reason and be logical, *which is separate* from all influences … that is somehow detached or transcendent from Reality and Experience. Sure we admit this faculty is imperfect, but we also believe that we can get it more correct using the methods of science. We believe that its incorrectness lies in faulty logic or faulty data. Both of which are correctible.

But what we have no clue about is that these experiences involving our biological reality, separate from that of other types of beings or species, will *determine* how we interpret our findings and conclusions, even in science. More than that, that like any other paradigm, these earliest of our experiences will direct and constrain us even in terms of where we will look to explore … in order to find out anything. And they will force us to interpret the data we find into constructions of assumptions that will skew and often reverse the interpretation that *should* arise from them. Yes, that should *logically* arrive from them. Elsewhere I have called this our basic *wrong-gettedness* (see *Planetmates*, 2014b).

Indeed, from the paradigm I am unveiling, in which everything we know and feel flows out of what we once felt and experienced, our reason is discovered to be no more than just a product of them, and not separate, and so is inherently faulty. This perspective reveals our vaunted logic and intellect to be riddled through with a species-arrogance, for reasons I detail in those other works, which often *overturns* our being able to see what would be obvious to any other species observing the same thing. So, past experience determines the memory out of which we build our logic and reason. We have no detached reason; we only have a species arrogance that we do, which itself emanates from, is determined by, such early experience.

In any case, keep in mind, in asserting all of this, that I am having less of a problem crossing cultural and other boundaries than cognitive psychologists or cultural anthropologists. They are academics who in particular criticized Freud for journeying down this road before me. They were correct. For Freud's theories were rooted primarily in the cognitive array put up by a particular culture, his, which limited his theories and understandings. Jung went further, though, in finding transcultural symbols, archetypes, which were related to universal human experiences. So Jung sought to go outside of culture as well as outside mere concepts. However when we get to Arthur Janov, whose findings are rooted in raw experience, emanating from the body and from species universal facts, we get into theory which can begin to be universally true.

In that tradition of Janov, but taking it further, is where I operate. What I am asserting is rooted in universal human experience, not just experiences of primal pain, but any and all universal human experience. Hence, I am not like they, cultural anthropologists and cognitive psychologists, who, being academics and intellectuals, get all bogged down in the fact that concepts vary from one entity — person or culture — to another. This is because I am operating not out of shared concepts but common experiences, out of which those concepts arise. I might not know *exactly* what you mean when you say *dukkha*, which I can translate into English as meaning *suffering*. For someone in India, that word might have connotations that I would not get. Then again, someone in the same culture might have a similar problem in not fully understanding exactly what you mean by it.

The point is that I know the experience of suffering, and that is common between us. If additionally I see you after a loved one has died and you are visibly distraught — which is something I know and comprehend because I act similarly at times and I know how that *feels* — and you say to me "Life is dukkha," I believe I might know what you are expressing by that on a deep level that compares with and might perhaps even exceed the understandings of that by someone else in your culture, especially if they have not had such or similar experiences.

You see, I know what the word *denotes* — what it means, not relative to other concepts and in a context of the abstract, which would be connotation; but relative to *experience* — experience which is shared between humans. The word for me is connected to an experiential reality which I have had; it is not just a concept connecting other concepts in my mind. This goes for my experience of an emotion or other biological experience but can be expanded to mean the experience of the physical world that we share. So that when you point to a chicken's egg and say *huevos*, I can understand

39

you because I have, in my experience of the world, also the experience of *egg*. I would understand you better than a hypothetical person in your culture who had never encountered an egg, or at most had only heard of one. Regardless that you would share your language with that person and not with me, I would understand you better. When you say *rojo* and you indicate an item that is the color *red* I also share an understanding with you.

The same kind of understandings about common biological experiences occur across cultures as well. Having experienced birth, child-"rearing," pain, death and loss of loved ones, joy of achievement, pleasure of sexuality, friendship, separation and love, and so on, I have a common ground with another human ... with *any* other human. For we have all, more or less, experienced these things. It is on the basis of experience, held in common by all humans, that I build my theories. Those are the closest things to those *brute facts* which I have been talking about. They are biologically constituted realities mixing with culture to create our bioculturally constituted facts.

# Our Biohistorical Experiences Determine Our World

Elsewhere I have detailed how our universal but species-specific patterns of biological experience at conception, and throughout gestation, and at birth ... and continuing from there but with immensely reduced or nonexistent universality ... conditions and shapes all later experience.[1]

## The Past Affects the Present

First, though, do not forget that you already know, and you have no doubt about it, that experiences you have had in the past contribute to what you know, think, and the way you see things in the present. I am not presenting anything strange by looking further back in time to our earliest experiences in Form and unraveling for you how what you learned in your experience at that time has influenced everything you knew and thought, and the way you saw everything, afterward. You do not remember these experiences, and you think you know and see what you know and see within the context of your memory of what you are consciously aware of.

However, Freud dispelled that delusion a long time ago. He showed us, in ways that are obvious to us now, how what we experienced early in our lives taught us things that influenced us ever afterward, *in spite of the fact* we do not remember them. He showed how we are *unconsciously* influenced by such forgotten experiences.

## Our Earliest Events Predispose the Nature of Our Mind

So, when I take this back even further, showing how even earlier experiences than Freud acknowledged have even greater influence on us, for they occurred earlier and all later "Freudian" events were seen through the "knowledge" or template established already by *them*, I am not doing anything unusual and am operating in such a strong tradition of psychology as well as what we commonly know to be true: Which is that past experience and learning plays greatly into what we will see and how we will interpret the present.

The only reason this has not been explored this way before is that it was thought that such early experiences as I describe — conception, womb, birth, early infancy, the prenatal and perinatal events — could not be remembered or "recorded" by us in a way to influence what comes afterward. That was a mistaken notion, and it is widely known to have been wrong, at this point. For a long time, there was misinformation about myelin sheaths being necessary for memory to occur, by now long debunked. Furthermore, there was an assumption that memory and knowledge needed a substrate of physicality, that is, a brain, in order for events to be "recorded" or remembered. My field of prenatal and perinatal psychology has upended that notion, as well. I say a lot about what we now know in science in this regard in many of my books in which I focus on what we have learned in the field of prenatal and perinatal psychology.[2] But this book is not the one to do that. See my others for that.

For here, though, and based on the knowledge that early experiences even at the cellular level of sperm and ovum are remembered, we have had revealed to us some astonishing discoveries about constituted realities that have their roots that far back. Now, let us look at some of them.

# 5

# Cells with a View:

Bioculturally Constituted Realities, Part 2 ...
Conception Creates Our World ... Dualities,
Dichotomies, Dialectics, Dukkha, Duty,
Disillusionment, Gender, Self-Confidence

*We Can't Know What We Can't Know, but We Cannot
Unknow What We Are*

*You cannot convince a fish it lives in water. You can only
give the fish the experience of being in air; then it will
understand.*

My contentions are that these particular ... that is to say, these early,
these prenatal and perinatal ... experience/memory templates are
especially related, but not limited, to the following:

# Our Experience of Conception Results in Fundamental Constructions of Our Worldview

Let us take conception, for starters. Remember that our existences as a sperm and an ovum coming together to create another individual is a truly unique experience for one's life. We have nothing like it afterwards. Even in marriage, its closest correlate, there is not such a combining as to *actually* have "two become one" as some marriage vows relate.

## Duality as a Fact of Existence Creating Self and Other

At conception, the sperm/egg dichotomy of self led us to ever afterward perceive duality in the Universe, where there is not, in actuality. Our universal human experiences of these events at conception cause us to see the world, our entire life, this way. That is, as dual and separated.

You might ask does duality come from an experience of being a sperm and an ovum at the same time? Meaning, do we experience sperm and egg as dual when it happens, prior to conception, and therefore construe the world as dual and separated? Probably not. However, being as we are barely removed from Divinity at that point — barely removed from No-Form and still fairly soulular — there might be some of that going on. Still, I think we probably do not have a consciousness of the experience of the sperm and of the egg simultaneously before they have joined.

However, beginning at conception we are aware that what we are is comprised of two things coming together. Additionally, we have memory of two different lines of experience … two separate histories … around the same event. We have a memory of having been two separate entities, so that, in a sense, we have two parts to ourselves. And that has us thinking there are two parts to ourselves as adults — that we have a physical, bodily, material self (egg) and a mental, soulular, spiritual self (sperm).

It also means that we will see Reality as being comprised of two parts coming together: There is a physical world and there is a mental world.

The point of knowing this is that we might use this to help us see that our dichotomous view of our Reality is a false conception based on early early experience. That in fact there is only one world, it is just that it is viewed from two different perspectives. And there is not even just a within or without, those two distinctions are incorrect.

There is actually just *direct* and *indirect* perception of Reality. Having assumed dualism as well as having assumed separation, both of which are byproducts of our experience around conception, we assume we are separate from each other. We create the boundaries of self which we call our bodies. And we leave off direct perception of each other, which would amount to *experience-sharing* (ultimately *experience-identity* ... that is, all experience is "owned" by one "being" — God — and that totality of experience constitutes that being's identity.) Direct perception of each other means shared experience with another, and is akin to an empathy that is nearly as profound as an identity with another. It also means telepathy. These realities are our common, basic experiences, yet we repress and deny them, for they do not fit with our "assumption" ... arising from our experiences at the time of conception ... that we are dual ... and separate.

But then why would we even want to let go of that assumption of duality that arises from our experiences prior to conception? This is something no one ever thinks of: Might there be darn good reasons to and/or even a *desire* to not see Reality correctly as it is? Or more correctly than we could if we wanted? Are there reasons for the "stupidity" ... the ignorance, the illusion, the forgetting involved ... of coming into Form?

At this point, we might even be crossing over into the way God would view it. Might we *want* to re-create the experience of duality, perhaps ever after in life, for reasons not having to do with retreating from trauma and pain, making a "mistake," or "sinning" as *Genesis* phrases it, or for some other reason implying a bad choice or an unfortunate understanding or simply ignorance?

Might there be other reasons, Divine or Godly ones perhaps, for having those assumptions of duality — which involve us apprehending Reality in a lesser or more diminished way — that are actually decided by us? That are *intentional*? Consider that, after all, that experience of duality of being a sperm and an ovum made for quite an exciting and profound "story" with an ending that hollywood could not match: the coming together of "worlds"!

I believe there are such reasons and such intentions; and at this point I believe we are bumping up against the very reasons for existence itself as a separate living, breathing being, or becoming human. You see, there are often good reasons to come to lesser, more constrained, apprehensions of Reality. One might be that by assuming a dualism, or a separation into parts, of Reality, there is, what comes with that, more *fun* ... at least at times, in the experiencing of it. Just as we might arbitrarily accept the rules of a board game (or make them up) for exactly that result — for *fun*. And by *fun*, I mean a more interesting, engaging story or experience that is illustrative or illuminating of the nature of Reality (or Divinity) in others of its qualities ... other than simply Truth.

What do I mean by that, you ask? I mean that, for example, if we, as God, wanted to manifest the experience of love, in Reality, might we not create separation into parts — separate human bodies, in our case — in order to bring out and glorify the nature of Reality (God) which includes love.

Might God not want a duality involving ugliness to make known, to make experienced, the nature of God (Reality) as actually being Beauty?

The same for creating pain, to glorify pleasure; and so on.

## Duality as a Fact of Ourselves

Another way our experience of sperm and egg contributes to fundamental constructions of our worldview has to do with the possibility that event of a duality of sperm and egg coming together and comprising us at conception might cause us, ever afterwards, or at least as adults, to conceive of self as dual. In the instance just related above, it was that we were led to assume that Reality is dual, containing us and others ... that there are parts, with boundaries. That our experiences of life are not shared or identical but are like each one of us having different movies playing inside the different "theaters" of our bodies, with the only connection between them coming about through external communication between beings, necessarily flawed or at least not exact.

However, in this idea, the experience of duality at conception might contribute to a sense, not just that there is a duality in existence in that there is us and others, but that one's very self is dual: That is, that we have a conscious and an unconscious self, for example. Or in primal cultures, that there is a "this world" self and a "that world" self, associated with the state after death. Or more simply, that humans have a *body* and a *soul*. Or even more commonly, that we have a *mind* and a *body*, which are separate entities and must *interact*.

Note, in relation to this, that going beyond this delusion or early template, which construes and constricts our view of Reality, is vastly important for understanding the overstanding presented in this book and its companion book, *The Cosmic Overstanding* (forthcoming), as well as in *Experience Is Divinity* (2013c), and in "The Mind's True Liberation" part of *Funny God* (2015).

Yet achieving this overstanding, requiring a defiance of or a transcendence of those earliest templates as it does, has traditionally been nearly impossible for any humans to do, except for mystics and very advanced shamans. And it is extremely difficult for contemporary humans to do, even, or especially scientists. I have discovered it is *damn hard* for people to see this, understand this, and go beyond their preconceptions of mind-body duality, even when they are claiming to do that.

For example, in science these days, we say there is no mind-body duality. We hear that in psychology and the behavioral sciences in particular. Yet, most often what they are asserting amounts to eliminating the mind part of the duality. We eliminate subjectivity — a person's lived experience in every moment — out of existence. We think we have solved the Newtonian-Cartesian dichotomy of body and mind by saying one part of that duality simply does not exist, without changing our understanding a wit! For what this claim of non-duality really means is we focus only on the changes in brain and body and thus say no dichotomy, because, abracadabra! No mind!

Similarly, when we *do* talk about experience or mental events, we see them as arising *out of* a physical basis. We say no duality because we acknowledge only one, the physical, and we paint the other, the mental, as a unique and strange outgrowth of that one reality. We as scientists assume that consciousness is a strange and unique aspect of the physical world which, in some imagined future, will be seen to be just as much "physical" as everything else we study and measure.

But what that does not understand about itself is that it is still creating two categories that are separate and that only *magically*, as it were, interact. Scientists know intuitively that mind is not exactly like body, but in order to eliminate having to deal with mind, they assume what they would like to be the truth. Their model becomes elegant, however wrong.

Whereas what I am saying is quite simple, however hard to grasp: Mind and body are merely two ways of viewing the same thing. Not even two sides of a coin. No. They are *exactly the same thing*, viewed from either inside the individual or outside the individual. I will say later how that has to do with direct and indirect perception, as well as reality as it is versus reality shrouded or hidden from us. For now, let me get away with phrasing it that we know our existence through our direct *experience* of it. That is, our subjectivity tells us of our reality. But we know of others through our *perception* of them, through our senses, or by indirect means … not subjectively, but *objectively*. We have created this subject-object dichotomy as per the above.

And indirect perception, that arising from the "senses," is easy to distinguish from direct perception, one's subjectivity. For indirect perception varies greatly — what we perceive and the interpretation of it changes constantly. However, direct perception is constant. We might not understand ourselves, and we might have different emotional states, but what underlies everything of the contents of consciousness and what we come back to and what they are contained within is a constant apprehension of self. That self is the experience we always come back to, regardless what we do and even if we go into nonordinary or even drugged states. There are all sorts of people and other beings indirectly manifesting to us infinitely varied experiences of themselves (which we perceive as bodies and external events), but there is only one "I".

47

So inner and outer are not separate but are simply general areas of a continuum of our awareness, with what is known being considered inner and what we are hiding or forgetting for the purpose of our game (the unconscious) being perceived nevertheless but as outer, as shrouded and distorted by our unknowing and our forgetfulness. This is how we create a "physical" world, other people, and an "outer." I understand that is practically impossible to grasp the way I am meaning it. However, by the end of the book, you will have quite a bit more ability to envision it, as I peel back the conventions of thought we humans hold that keep us from seeing that.

One of the implications of this is that if we wanted to view another person *directly* we would experience *their* experience and not get second-hand information from the set of defenses that is their body (their current incarnation) as observed from outside of them.

What follows from this as well is that as long as you have separate people, you have duality of at least that sort. And to truly transcend duality one needs to eliminate the duality of separate experiences and see that there is one experience ... just one Experience in all Reality ... similar to the way scientists are wont to say that there is only one physical world, one physical cosmos, with mind being some strange appendage to that which pops up magically in evolution ... and not for all species, mind you.

I wish also to point out that this view fits in with my theory of Falls from Grace,[1] as it is related to the *Tibetan Book of the Dead*, where all stages in the descent into Form involve a constriction of awareness, which continues and advances that constriction at conception experience, again through painful womb experiences, again at birth, then the primal scene, and finally the identity-adolescent phases.

Thus, we view subjectively the truth of existence through the lens of all our experiences — cultural and otherwise. However, the experiences that are painful cause us to retreat from the truth (or reality) of existence. So they act as *reductive lenses*.

And yes, within one's subjectivity one does have *direct access* to the Other, the other person, the other anything in the physical universe ... indeed one can even identify with other beings and things, as happens on entheogens or in modalities of nonordinary experience such as holotropic breathwork and shamanism.

Two more fundamental constructions of our worldview arising from our earliest experiences as cells — our separate ones of being sperm and egg — might be, one, the overstanding we hold of the physical world and the nature of Reality. The second might be the nature of Life.

## Duality of the World Creating Matter–Experience or Explicate–Implicate

The first of these assumptions arising from conception experience might give rise to a separation of the world into one that is material and one non-material, of matter and subjectivity, of physicality as opposed to experience. This is an assumption I will be correcting throughout this work as I try to show how there is only one Reality, one of Experience and Subjectivity, with matter being a mistaken view on it. That is implied in the title: There is a "secret life" of stones, that is to say, matter. And matter as being non-alive or non-experiential or non-conscious is a mistaken view which we as Divinity adopt for the purpose of the Game, as I said earlier. For perspective, we have Sathya Sai Baba's continual refrain that "God is all there is." We also have the assertion from Erwin Schrödinger, the renowned quantum physicist and winner of the Nobel Prize in physics, proclaiming that, "Multiplicity is only apparent, in truth, there is only one mind...."

So a division into matter and Experience is a wrong view, but forgotten to be wrong intentionally, just as one might try to forget that one was playing a game and that rules were not "real" in order to be more immersed in the play of it. Or one might let oneself get caught up in a movie, forgetting it is not real, so as to better enjoy it.

## Duality of Wills in Existence ... Separation of Human and Divine Will

The second of these mistaken assumptions emanating from early duality might be the separation between The Game and Divine Intention, or Divinity Itself. The mistake here is we think we are the tokens in the game and are separate from the player playing it, who fundamentally for each of us is God, is our Divinity. It has us thinking there are two realities, one determined by God and one by oneself. That one has free will separate from what one wills as God, or one's Divinity ... regardless there is no reason one would even wish that. For if one is God, the idea of a will "free" from that is ludicrous. Do not worry, you will understand that better by the end of the book. For perspective on this one, we have Sathya Sai Baba's revelation there is only one doer or Actor in the Universe and that is God. Schrödinger's statement on the one mind in the Universe is relevant here as well.

However, one might wish to, and we probably do, have the mistaken belief that we are separate for the purposes of The Game. In this way, again, we choose to forget ourselves for a while, while still knowing in our Divinity that afterward we will remember once again. So this duality is that between our lives and the Divine Life. I believe we are the only species who forgets its Divine essence as thoroughly as we do and who persists in thinking that we are not Divine, are not movements of the Divine in all our life and its actions. Again, this book will, in the latter parts of it, work to repair that mistaken notion of duality and to reunite that Reality. And this topic in particular is taken up in the third parts of both *Experience Is Divinity* (2013c) and *Funny God* (2015).

# The Experience of Conception Results in Fundamental Patterns of Experience and Attitudes to Life

Attitudes towards life is another outgrowth of our biohistorical experiences early in life, which create our biocultural realities, in due course. It seems fundamental patterns of experience that operate throughout our lives to organize the manner in which our lives unfold are laid down at this time, too.

## The Dialectic of Personal Growth and the Dichotomy of Work and Play

For example, the struggle of sperm as compared with the experience of being the peaceful egg — both having been profoundly experienced — could be the earliest origins of the universally apparent alternating or cyclic character of personal or spiritual growth. Even more commonly, and on a daily basis, the universal pattern of alternating work and play, similar to the dialectic of personal growth, is perhaps created here. Let me explain.

In the most general pattern of personal growth, there is a dialectic of periods of outward activity in interaction with the world and other individuals in which one comes upon new information and learning and inevitably encounters obstacles ... just like a sperm does. This alternates with periods of going within oneself to process, to evaluate, and to integrate what was newly taken in during the venturing without in a way to form a greater whole of oneself ... just like the egg did. The sperm ad-ventures, makes an effort, encounters the new, comes up against obstacles. The egg stays put, is complete within itself, does not journey outward but to the contrary draws inside itself all that venturing, effort, and information in the form of the sperm at conception; and processes it, which is another way of describing actual conception; and evaluates it, which is another way of describing a matching up or aligning of chromosomes; and then integrates it, which is another way of saying a combining together of chromosomes to form a new and greater whole. Coincidence? Or is our personal growth this dialectic as I have described it *because* of our earliest template of "personal growth" at a coming together of sperm and egg at conception.

Put another way, we do it this way ever afterward — we grow this way — and cannot conceive of, let alone do, it any other way, because the first time we had an experience of "personal growth" or work/play occurred this way. Remember, we are no different from a river in which every momentary direction taken *determines*, not just influences, *every* direction that can and will be taken afterward. So the

51

course determinations had at its head are the most influential and are irreversible. The earliest "experiences" of that stream cannot be decided differently, for they are part of what it has become at every moment. Even were the river to have the vanity of thought and reason, as we humans do, it cannot decide that its experience has been different from what it was so that its courseway is elsewhere.

## Primordial Guilt and Disillusionment

Another example of distinct earliest experiences creating templates of experience for the rest of our lives is the fertilized egg's experience upon its success of conception: Its survival–achievement at conception is bought at the cost of hundreds of millions of others dead. This results ever after in a primordial guilt about simply being alive. Related to that is the idea that there is a dog-eat-dog quality to existence, a kill-or-be-killed one. It is thought that achievement is had only at others' expense. The idea of win-win solutions is extremely hard for humans to arrive at because of this early experience.

As well, because such euphoric union, and achievement, is followed by such realization of apocalyptic-like death of others, we have within us a prevalent attitude that accomplishment never brings expected rewards. Disillusionment is felt at a deep level — regardless how we avoid, defend against, or counter it in our thinking — to be an unavoidable facet of human experience.

In fact, such early guilt and disillusionment just might be the first fractal of the diminution of consciousness. For in it, one is already applying the notion of duality in that it is felt that the others, the other sperm, are actually separate from oneself. It thus might be the earliest origin of that sense of fallenness or original sin, which shows up so strongly at birth. Which birth also is characterized by both duality and guilt. For at birth one separates from mother and becomes two, or dual; and one's survival is had in the midst of a mother's pain, often excruciating. A neonate cannot help but feel its survival was bought at the cost of another's suffering — hence, guilt.

## Dukkha, Nonsatisfaction as Inherent in Life

Also, the zygote must continue working, must reproduce itself, must move and implant itself … each time or die. This results in an attitude that in life there is no end to struggle, growth, achievement. This quality of life of inherent nonsatisfaction (Buddhist *dukkha*) is felt as a fundamental fact of physical existence.

Jumping ahead, keep in mind that uncovering these attitudes and perceptions of our lives as being products of our earliest experience allows us to entertain the idea that they are not necessary aspects of experience as we have been driven unconsciously to think. Knowing they are merely outgrowths of experience reveals a doorway to a new way of viewing oneself and one's life where those aspects are not required and to a life in which they might be nonexistent. This is what I am talking about when I am referring to "biological transcendence," a few chapters from now. That I just now brought that up in referring to something Buddhists think is inevitable in life, dukkha, points to how *biological transcendence* is related to what they think of as *liberation*.

Enough teaser, for now, however.

## Endemic Self-Confidence, Cooperation, Interconnectedness

On the positive side, the experience, as blastocyst and fetus, of growing as cells in this precise and perfect way so as to construct ourselves into parts of the body and organs and eventually the body with all its finely tuned qualities and abilities might be the basis of a self-confidence in life. Having experienced such perfection and such ability to be doing it, we have forever afterward a felt sense that we can succeed, if we apply ourselves. It is the basis for a supreme self-confidence or belief in oneself.

I know, for I experienced it, and that was the result. Whereas before I relived that early experience I did not have that complete and total belief in myself, quite the contrary. Indeed, having that experience forty years ago changed my life forever.

Even earlier, there are origins of a similar belief: Which is that we are special and uniquely destined to succeed. For each and every one of us was a sperm who *actually did* succeed in making it to join with the egg. Whereas, three hundred million others did not. That leaves one feeling special, and destined for something.

Consider, it is like being the one who wins the presidency of the United States ... the chances of that happening being similar to that of being the sperm and out of so many others getting to join with the egg. I am not saying everyone experiences this sense of specialness and destiny in later life, for it conflicts with many of the negative things coming out of the painful experiences of our life. But I believe it is there inside us, even if it takes therapy to reveal it after clearing up the negative residue overlying it.

It might also be the basis of the belief in being special and uniquely singled out for attention and concern by a Creator God. For, being helped by the other sperm to succeed, we feel that the Universe, in a sense, aids us in our endeavors and wants our success. And, yes, the other sperm do help. It is not a competition to get to the egg, rather it is a joint effort, with some sperm throwing themselves on "land mines" ... allowing themselves to be eaten up by white blood cells, for example ... in order that the sperm-to-succeed makes it ... which was us! It could be compared to being a runner in a football game and having blockers who cooperate with us in getting into the end zone.

One analogy I read recently of the way it works is the way bicyclists in a race work together to further themselves as a group by taking turns in the various positions.

## Gender Beliefs; Gender Attitudes; Sexual Attitudes and Gender Relationships.

Now, keep in mind that I am saying that these experiences *create* our, essentially delusional, realities. I am saying we are *predisposed* to think this way, not that these underlying patterns are necessarily good or recommended. In fact, except for the positive ones, as mentioned above, they are all hindrances in one's life; they are part of our diminution from Total Awareness coming into Form. Indeed, the point of unraveling these roots of ideas and attitudes is so as to be able to *go beyond them* to an overstanding of reality which is not imbued with and slanted by them. One might also say, which is not "tainted" by them.

With this in mind, let's look at another fundamental attitude of human existence, this one relating to female and male distinctions. In this category we see human realities emanating from the characteristics of sperm and egg. That is, that the egg being larger than the sperm and so carrying the bulk of the material of existence leads to ideas that the feminine is related to the world of matter or Nature. Matter's etymological root is in fact, *mother.* The ovum's diameter is thirty to fifty times that of the head of the sperm and contains many thousands of times the amount of mass. This is because the egg provides all the raw material out of which the zygote will be created, while the sperm provides only the chromosomal package.

Also, egg as containing the material or resources out of which the newly formed cell grow and multiply into new cells leads to the beliefs in virtually all cultures that it is the female who is most responsible for the food source. Contrary to what most people think, that the male is the "bread winner," the fact is that in virtually all cultures that have ever existed, women have provided the basic nourishment or resources for life. They do most of the work, including foraging and preparing food.

Whereas the pattern for male behavior nearly universally in primal cultures is that while the women stay close to hearth and home, the men are more mobile, just like the sperm was more mobile. The men do the hunting for the most part, and only on occasion, and intermittently, at that. Remember sperm's motive of hunting or searching out the egg, as related to that. Such that meat is only considered a treat or a special food and in no way a staple. The odds are not high for acquiring meat; it is more of a "gamble." The same with fishing, which is also predominantly a male pursuit.

And men, strangely as well, tend to spend their time hanging out and often playing games of chance. That playing games of chance and lounging is a virtually universal pastime of men, rivaling the time and effort women spend in providing food, is bizarre. Inexplicable. However, our earliest experiences around conception provide a clue, where otherwise there is absolutely nothing to account for this difference in gender roles and activities.

Astonishingly, is that strange pastime, peculiar to men— games of chance — related to the experience of having odds of one in three hundred million at conception? And having won, keep in mind. What would that result in or feel like? Well, if at one time one beat odds of one to three hundred million and it resulted in a prize of life itself, might not one be drawn to continually toy with the fates and be attracted to odds-related activities, forever mining that magical moment of having won in the most unlikely-to-win lottery of all, one's conception or combining with an egg to create a new life? Someone else can look up whether men are more likely to be gambling addicts. Probably true. But I have to keep moving here. I'll get more into all of this in *Womb with a View* and *Cells with a View*, if you are interested.

While the women, on the other hand, predominantly provide the foundation of material nourishment, the staples. They also, almost universally, cook them. And the women raise the children. These things can be considered aspects of egg experience, that is, egg does not travel to accomplish what it needs to do. Similarly, there is most definitely in human societies a tendency for women to attend more closely to hearth and home.

It is significant, also, that the overwhelming majority of societies that have existed have been *matrilocal* — which means that cultures have deemed that after marriage the couple lives with the family of the woman, more exactly, in the locale from which she comes. *Matrilineal descent* is also far more common in human societies, although not so since patriarchy and civilization. Which change to patrilineal lines of descent is a whole other story, see *Planetmates* (2014b) and *Prodigal Human* (2016a). However the great majority of human societies that have ever been have traced their line of descent through the mother, the woman.

So newly mated couples, in primal societies, go to where the woman lives and they establish lines of descent through the woman. Remember, periconceptionally the egg stays in place and sperm(s) come to *it!* Afterwards, it is the egg's home that is the basis of their new life as a combined self, as "mated," and from that spot, cell multiplication, or we might say, "lines of descent" are drawn.

Finally, egg provides the physical material, from its actual much greater amount of cell material, from which all else will be created; just as women, overwhelmingly in societies, bring in the food and other essentials.

Another imprint from conception has to do with the universal perception of woman as the center of male attention from many sources. Woman is the desired; man is the desirer. Man seeks out woman. The social configuration, as adults, of women and men, especially as related to the time of courting is that of individual women surrounded by many men, just as egg was surrounded by many sperm. Also, it is perhaps not coincidence that whereas a man can pretty much have only one orgasm, without a period of usually considerable buildup, that the male "shoots" or "drops its load" just as the sperm did its package of DNA. While the female is capable of many orgasms, sometimes in rapid succession, and can therefore be matched with more than one male at a time, just as the egg is surrounded by many sperm.

Also it is the general and natural pattern that woman is the decider and chooser in the relationship … the one who picks, out of that cadre of males, the chosen one. In the same way, it is the egg who chooses the sperm that will be allowed in to join DNA with her and create the life form. Contrary to popular belief about conception, which has it that the first sperm to reach the egg is the one who enters and without any say by the woman (the egg) — which is both a patriarchal notion (a male ego inflation) and is a kind of rape — the egg actually *chooses* the sperm; it actually refuses entrance to other earlier sperm who are not the chosen one, and finally, that the egg kind of "welcomes" the sperm in … it "eggs it on."

Then, subsequently, the egg "traps" the sperm who might otherwise push away. Which is a rather provocative notion as part of our templates. But as a man I'm hardly dumb enough to venture down *that* road. *chuckle*

At any rate, these patterns of experience of sperm and egg, with female the welcomer and encourager and male as the striver and achiever relates to universal human beliefs about women as "cheerleaders," supporters. There is no greater metaphor of the sperm and egg than that of the football player (the sperm) crossing the "goal" line (the egg's surface) to deliver the football (the DNA package) into the "end zone" (the zone where the sperm ends its journey as its head explodes, exemplified by spiking the ball) with cheerleaders (the egg) cheering and "egging" him on. This can be compared with the egg welcoming the sperm, egging him on — which, indeed, amazingly, the egg actually appears to do — to cross the cellular barrier and spike that DNA package in the end zone of the egg's interior, wherein lies *its* DNA package (the goal posts).

# 6

# Womb with a View:

Bioculturally Constituted Realities, Part 3 … Our Womb Experience Configures Our "Good" and Our "Bad" — Our Spiritual-Religious Beliefs and Our Evil — Our "Human Nature"

*"...these foundational events shape and inform the myths by which we live, the motives that inspire us, the feelings and emotions that move us, and the attitudes that are our thickly matted screens across our windows to the world, and much else."*

## Prenatal Events of Fetal Malnutrition Configure Our Evil

Relative to bioculturally constituted realities, I would also like to share some specific early experiences that I have elaborated upon in a recent work of mine, *Wounded Deer and Centaurs: The Necessary Hero and the Prenatal Matrix of Human Events* (2016b). I pointed out that we go through specific experiences in the last month of gestation which imprint us for life. These experiences create *the matrix of human events*. Most importantly, they are the foundation of what humans consider to be evil.

These experiences of the last month of gestation include experiences emanating out of the fact that we uniquely, as a species, undergo trauma at that time of *fetal malnutrition* — which means that the blood supply, which brings nutrients and oxygen to us at that time, is restricted because of the weight of the fetus pressing on the arteries feeding the prenate through the placenta. This results in an arrest of development during that month. Lacking resources the fetus stops growing and does not pick up its rate of growth until after birth; whereupon it catches up to what it would have been.

The experiences involved in this fetal malnutrition, which happens for all humans if they have the full term of nine months of gestation, are suffocation — from reduction in oxygen; are prenatal poisoning and disgust — from the buildup of waste matters from the blood not taking them away as efficiently and thus not being removed from our bodies as well either; and are prenatal irritation or burning — from the fact that we exist in a kind of a stew of toxins which affects us as a kind of irritation or burning on the surface of the skin.

Another experience occurring at the same time, though not caused by reduced blood flow, is simple crowdedness in the womb. The prenate is at its greatest size prior to birth. As birth approaches, and especially during that final month with all that restricted blood flow and fetal malnutrition going on, there is a traumatic amount of discomfort. The world as free — which was comparable at times to floating in space or in water and having the freedom of movement of a gymnast — is replaced by the world as constricting and oppressive. Everywhere and anyway one wishes to move is blocked or difficult. Just hearing this might be bringing up a frustrated feeling in you right now. For it stays with us for life, and we build much of what we think and believe upon the bedrock of such feelings.

All of these experiences are unusual in Nature. In fact, fetal malnutrition and crowdedness occur only to humans, among all other planetmates, and they did not happen to our earliest primate ancestors, either. They arise out of the factor of having become bipedal; had our pelvic bones become aligned in a way that made birth more difficult; thus creating trauma at birth; which created bigger brains to deal with the trauma; which resulted in more birth trauma; which led to a compromise where we were born before we were ready — human prematurity; and had a time of excruciating suffering just prior to that birth — fetal malnutrition; for all the reasons previous, including the mother's standing up resulting in a reducing of blood flow to the fetus. You need to look to *Planetmates* and *Prodigal Human* for this one. It also is just too involved for elaboration here.

In any case, in *Wounded Deer and Centaurs*, I pointed out that these experiences of crowdedness and fetal malnutrition during the last month of gestation create a template or psychic stamp upon our minds wherein for the rest of our lives we will be predisposed to various feelings and actions. These include

- wars — for we need to expand boundaries in reaction to the crowdedness

- greed — for we need to grasp and struggle for more than we need because of fetal suffocation and starvation

- bigotry — for we feel outside and alien presences near us that are irritating, caused by prenatal irritation

- paranoia — for we felt that we were being force-fed toxins, caused by prenatal poisoning

- pollution — for we keenly felt our existence in a place that was polluted because of the buildup of waste matter not sufficiently removed, which we re-create in air and other pollutions

- greenhouse effect — for we existed in an environment that was lacking in oxygen and higher in carbon dioxide

- environmental destruction — because of being at such odds with our environment in the womb and due to its seeming contrary or assaultive relation to us as a prenate, we pave over and are at war with Nature

- overpopulation of globe and crowded environs, especially in cities — for we re-create the situation of crowdedness in the womb, just prior to birth

- and so on

So, here, with fetal malnutrition, we have other kinds of bioculturally created realities.

## Our Bioculturally Constituted Realities Create Our Human Nature, the Parameters of the Human Game, in Form

Many more examples of how our prenatal and perinatal experiences predispose our world — going back, actually, to our existence still inside our parents, as sperm in the testicles and ovum in the ovarian sac — could be given. And for a more comprehensive understanding I refer the reader to my books, *Falls from Grace: The Devolution and Revolution of Consciousness* (2014a) and *Wounded Deer and Centaurs: The Necessary Hero and the Prenatal Matrix of Human Events* (2016b). For an even more detailed understanding, keep your eye out for two of my works, which are forthcoming, *Womb with a View* and *Cells with a View*.

However, the point I am making is that those early, universal events predispose the very nature of our mind. They do this both in determining the kinds of thoughts and images we will have as well as in modeling the patterns and the connections, associations, and networks among such elements of consciousness.

The thing of all this that makes them the basis of bioculturally constituted realities and not individually constructed realities is that we *all* experience these events. We therefore *all* have these assumptions, attitudes, and beliefs … each of us and in every culture. And we can see that cultures create constructions … culturally constituted realities, or institutionally constituted realities … around and out of these assumptions and beliefs. We base our culturally constituted realities upon understandings (assumptions) that we have a body and a soul (religion); that there is a Divine entity at work in the Universe aiding us (God); that there is separation between people which means there is misunderstanding, necessarily, which means there are differences that must be mediated; that women and men being different and having different roles requires different cultural apparatuses as part of that … and so on and so forth.

## Our Early Events Shape Our Social, Cultural, and Physical Worlds, Which We Create With Our Minds

Those biohistorical events consequently end up configuring our sociocultural structures, which we conceive and modify with less deeply-rooted thoughts and images emanating from idiosyncratic later events. Likewise, these foundational events shape and inform the myths by which we live, the motives that inspire us, the feelings and emotions that move us, and the attitudes that are our thickly matted screens across our windows to the world, and much else. Indeed, in my conceptualization, these biohistorical experiences delineate the very paradigms within which we live; therefore, there is very little of experiential reality that is not in some way linked, modeled, or bounded by the effects of these events. They are, indeed, as all-inclusive and comprehensive as any matrix, like in *The Matrix*, and they are just as much exclusive of and blocking or hiding any reality outside of them.

# Our Experiences in the Womb Result in Fundamental Concepts–Feelings About the Transpersonal

Our concepts–feelings about the transpersonal — that is to say, the religious or spiritual — have roots in our periconceptional and prenatal experiences.

For example, zygote, blastocyst, embryo, and then fetus grow at an incredible pace with enormous number of biological systems perfectly synchronized. This leads to feelings that there is meaning in all one's actions — if in tune with the Divine, i.e., the natural order or Nature. Also, that there is perfect synchronicity of external and internal events in one's world if so attuned.

Also, fetus nurtured, protected, all needs met — especially through umbilical cord at navel — leads

a) to feelings that a spiritual state is one of perfect harmony, being protected, and the Divine provides for all one's needs;
b) to ideas of navel as being "source" of spiritual energy or the place of connection of soul to body;
c) and, finally, it leads to the flow-in < — > flow-out feelings of optimal relationship of person to society, the Divine, Nature, and Experience.

This and the two chapters previous are a cursory overview of what I mean by bioculturally constituted realities as related to cellular and fetal experience. However, I will be expounding on these early biological events and how they shape our worlds and cultures in the two works following this one in The Path of Ecstasy Series, which will be titled, *Womb with a View* and *Cells with a View*. Look for them. In the meantime, see the Afterword for more about them.

# Other Biocultural Determiners

## Biology

There *are* other things, however, that are crucial in the creation of our species worldview. These include, of course, anatomical, biochemical, and other biological shapers and formers of our reality as we generally perceive it as a species, which have to be seen as even more fundamental — representing more pervasive yet subtler determiners and modelers of all above them. As I was saying above, these are what create the very "hardware" of space and time within which this "software" of experience and memory — culture and unconscious — runs its "programs" and "applications." These would be in the category, then, of species-specific, or biologically constituted realities.

## Transpersonal

Then there are the other universal determiners and/or directors of experience that fall under the rubric of *transpersonal* and are truly outside our biological parameters. But there is a completely different "board" for that "game" than the one on which we are working. Specifically, it amounts to "bumping" the Newtonian-Cartesian paradigm that I am working off of in making this argument about biologically constituted realities and adopting instead a holonomic and panentheistic perspective like that which I discuss further on, especially in Part Four: "The Consciousness of Stones."

# Our Biohistorical Experiences and Biology Determine Our Thoughts, Attitudes, and Actions

At any rate, it follows that within our societies and cultures, themselves modeled inside these strictly circumscribed, experientially based outlines, we are also influenced concerning the very things we write about, investigate, study, and then discuss ... and the manner in which we do so. Thus all knowledge of all cultures, including that of science, are contained within these templates of ways of seeing, thinking, and experiencing. Science may not be "mere ethnoscience," as total-symbolic-heritage proponents claim it is; but it is certainly and irredeemably mere *anthropo-science*, meaning relative only to humans.

There is no way to see outside of these parameters in order to even see that they exist. Except for the unusual and only available ways come of new psychotechnologies, which is how I was able to do it. Again, that also, for later.

In sum, in all these ways — conscious and unconscious and unknowable — we create our human "world."

So, what can we know? And why? Well, that is what we look at next.

# PART TWO

# Transcending Worlds

# 7

# What We Can Know:

Why We Know Not, Mind at Large, Levels of
Reality Construction, Paradigm Relativity, and
Ultimate Interconnectedness

*Understanding Our Limitations, We Approach the
Mystical: Paradigm Relativity and the Limitations of
Science*

*"Reality is merely an illusion, albeit a persistent one."*
*— Albert Einstein*

*"A human being is part of the whole called by us
universe, a part in time and space. We experience
ourselves, our thoughts and feelings as something
separate from the rest. A kind of optical delusion of
consciousness. This delusion is a kind of prison for us,
restricting us to our personal desires and to affection
for a few persons nearest to us. Our task must be to free
ourselves from this prison by widening our circle of
compassion to embrace all living creatures and the
whole of nature in its beauty. The true value of a human*

*being is determined by the measure and the sense in
which they have obtained liberation from the self. We
shall require a substantially new manner of thinking if
humanity is to survive." — Albert Einstein (1945)*

# Why We Know Not

What we have arrived at, following from Part One, is that basically our sciences have shown they cannot determine what is real, let alone measure it, because they are extensions of our senses which are themselves imperfect. So we cannot really know what is really real. Further, we find that just as culture creates our reality for us, that prior to that our biology creates the reality upon which culture can build. This means that we are able to understand what is human reality at least, though not Ultimate Reality, by looking at the only reality that all humans share — our biological one.

Additionally, as I showed in Chapters 4 through 6 on the perinatal matrix and bioculturally constituted realities, and will continue to unveil, this means that the way we come into the world — our conception, womb life, and birth — creates the foundations upon which all our other perceptions are built. These being unique to humans means that humans will be the only species seeing the world exactly the way we do.

Finally, while focusing on our biology as a basis for understanding what is fundamental about humanness, we are able to compare cultures in relation to that biology, though not in any other way. What we will see this means is that while we cannot compare cultures for the most part — this is called *cultural relativity* — we can compare them in terms of certain things all cultures share, which have to do with the fact that all humans have the same kind of body and biological history: An example of that would be the way cultures deal with birth, specifically the pain of it.

## Neither Ordinary Reality or Science Is Necessarily Real

Let me put it this way. Our combined efforts in psychology, physics, biology, and anthropology ... examples of which I have been pointing out ... have led us to an impasse. We have been led to conclude that our view of reality is symbolic. We have learned, above all, not what to know, but that we know not ... that is to say, that we are incapable of truly knowing.

In anthropology we see this in Sahlins's (1976) thinking on culture: Cultures create the very realities within which we live, much like The Matrix or The Cave. However, D'Andrade (1987) makes the important point that in Sahlins's theory the total cultural heritage is a symbolic structure. Thus, Sahlins's theory is "epistemologically sealed." Okay, what does he mean by that?

What is meant by this is that this particular theory of culture sees individuals as existing within a totality that is wholly symbolic. There are no intruding "real world" or "brute" elements. Everything is comprehended through the veil of those symbols, including any competing ideas or elements. There can be no conflicting elements or challenging elements or ways to evaluate a particular structure when it is thought nothing exists outside that structure. "The Matrix," you see, cannot be challenged by something that is not seen to exist. Nor can such Matrix be challenged when anything to the contrary, if it is seen at all, is interpreted in a way so as to make it something other than what it is and becoming something that fits in with and supports that Matrix or, let us say, which contributes to that dominant and universally held "illusion."

So D'Andrade does not like the fact that Sahlins can avoid any and all criticism of his theory by simply saying that any challenges to it are not valid for they are products of that system and have no separate validity from which one could compare or evaluate that system.

Indeed, Sahlins's total-cultural-heritage notion of reality is so hard to understand because, not only do we assume a "real" world, a physical world, of "brute facts," against which any and all constructions would need to be measured as to their validity, but we also assume a separate status for our reason. We believe logic to be separate and able to evaluate things, being outside of the things that they are dealing with. However, if one were to say, as Sahlins's theory implies, that both reason and the physical world of brute facts are constructions of our cultures, then no criticism or challenge can be directed at the culture from either quarter, because the basis for each of them, it is said, *is* the culture … it is not outside of it. There is no Archimedean vantage point. Simply, you cannot truly see something that you are part of, in which you are thoroughly and inextricably enmeshed. You cannot objectively see yourself. What follows also from this total-symbolic-heritage view of culture is that different cultures have different "reason" — different logic and ways of evaluating — and different "worlds." So all these realities are arbitrary, and there is nothing upon which to stand in making any judgments or analysis or comparisons.

It is a lot like many religions, which interpret *everything* within its matrix. Even any contrary facts are construed as being in an underlying way faulty because they do not conform to the totality, or are not congruent with all the other elements. So nothing can be challenged, in either the total-symbolic-heritage view or the religious theologies, for any challenge only supports the assumptions being made. In virtually all religions, obedience and adherence to its beliefs are values, and some sort of "sin" is postulated as part of non-compliance or non-adherence. So any challenges are easily subsumed within an understanding that it is not obedient to present them and hence such criticisms are sinful and thus are dismissed out of hand. The challenge only proves the point that sin exists. For the thinking is, "You see! Here is an example of a sin in this impudent statement!"

In the same way, Sahlins's theory would have it that any challenges are themselves symbolic, that is, not standing upon themselves or having any validity outside the symbolic system of understanding. Criticisms have their roots within the system. Any challenge to the theory is a product of the system that produced it, hence it is not valid.

So no challenges can be made; no contrary reality can intrude. Such reality structures … *paradigms* we can call them … are as watertight as The Matrix as in any of its movies. These systems are "epistemologically sealed" … they cannot be disputed or argued for no reality is acknowledged to exist outside them.

This is also not much different from the way political and national paradigms construe everything within their overarching viewpoints, so any challenges only support their contentions. In a totalitarian state which is assumed to be beneficial and superior to any other way, any challenge to it must be, just like those religious "sins" in the previous example, inherently wrong and dangerous. So, revolutions or even progress can never occur in a system where any revolutionary or contrary sentiment is subsumed under a perception of it as "terrorism." For any shaking of the status quo is necessarily wrong and hardly necessary in a system that cannot be improved upon. So nations, political frameworks, religious theologies and their societal paradigms of control … along with cultures viewed in the total-symbolic-heritage way … are unassailable … *by definition of them!*

My point is that since our total biological heritage is also a "symbolic structure" — in the sense at least that it is a species-relative created reality providing analogous representations, survival-oriented metaphors *only* of That Which Is — we are "epistemologically sealed" as regards That Which Is and specifically in terms of understanding other known or unknown species. Our reality is symbolic and "sealed" — that is to say, cut off from all else, any other reality that might exist — prior to the cultural symbolism which creates further obfuscation between people in different cultures.

# What We Can Know … Mind at Large and Levels of Reality

Let me put this all in context. It might be helpful in understanding this to mention Aldous Huxley's (1956) way of viewing this matter. In his classic work, *The Doors of Perception*, he quotes Dr. C. D. Broad on the importance of considering a view of memory and sense perception, originally proposed by Bergson, in which "the function of the brain and nervous system and sense organs is in the main *eliminative.*"[1]

## What Is Outside All Paradigms … Really Real

By way of explanation, Huxley (1956), still quoting Broad, writes

*Each person is at each moment capable of remembering all that has ever happened to him and of perceiving everything that is happening everywhere in the universe.*

*The function of the brain and nervous system is to protect us from being overwhelmed and confused by this mass of largely useless and irrelevant knowledge, by shutting out most of what we should otherwise perceive or remember at any moment, and leaving only that very small and special selection which is likely to be practically useful.[2]*

## Mind-at-Large Is "Really Real"

Huxley (1956) adds

*According to such a theory, each one of us is potentially Mind at Large.*

*But in so far as we are animals, our business is at all costs to survive. To make biological survival possible, Mind at Large has to be funneled through the reducing valve of the brain and nervous system. What comes out at the other end is a measly trickle of the kind of consciousness which will help us to stay alive on the surface of this particular planet.[3]*

This is saying that we can know virtually anything and everything; however — and notice this for it becomes increasingly relevant as we go on — there is an underlying biological rationale for what the brain will end up having us perceive. I emphasize Huxley's point on the criterion of *usefulness* in determining what is normally regarded as real and true ... and especially this usefulness as being relative to biological survival. For we will see how the same criterion determines the "real-world" information that is the usual purview of our sciences.

## The Levels of Reality Construction

The major point I wish to make now is that we may profitably consider each level of reality construction I have been proposing — from the levels of biologically constituted realities down through the various levels of cultural constructions of reality — as levels in the diminution of reality … from Mind at Large down to what is "biologically useful." This human characteristic of creating the reality to be lived by focusing on the specifics to the exclusion of more wholistic perspectives might, and usually does, have more "biological" usefulness.

The point I would add, by the way, is that any scientific endeavor that would seek to be anything more than merely pragmatic … and instead actually venture after truth … must undo or reverse that diminution. It must indeed be aware of the self-constructed nature of the creations with which it is normally, and inevitably, concerned. More about that in a little.

## Paradigm Relativity

In any case, the upshot of all of this paradigmatic way of viewing realities, with each built upon an even deeper one, and each one following subsumed within the one previous, is that the elements … the "particles" as opposed to "fields … operating within any particular paradigm are closed to each other, "sealed." On the other hand, standing on the basis of a "deeper," or more encompassing, paradigm, translation, discourse, and transfer of information can truly occur.

As an example, looked at from the arena of culture, we come to the conclusion of epistemological relativism — that is, that cultures are sealed from one another; no genuine dialogue is possible across their boundaries. However, looking at these same cultures within the playing field — the paradigm or "field" … the morphogenetic field is another way of conceiving it — of the physical or biological — that is to say, standing upon those semi-brute facts of biologically constituted realities — we see that discourse, transfer, and translation occur once again.

We have an ordinary example of that. This is much the same as saying that it is when we share our feelings and personal experience that we have the greatest chance of sharing across individual *or* cultural boundaries. It is no coincidence that these — feelings and personal experience — are to a greater extent physical and biological than "mental."

Another way of understanding this idea of "looked at from the playing field of" or "standing upon the deeper paradigm" is as so: Whenever there is understanding between two entities — be they people, nations, societies, and, here also, cultures — it happens on the basis of *common ground*. That is to say, this whole idea of "sealedness" assumes actual, separate entities. But this is never ever the case. There is no such thing as a person, society, or culture that does not share *some* ways of thinking, experiencing, or behaving with other entities of like kind. There are no sealed units of social reality any more than there are hard and irreducible particles of physical reality.

All seemingly singular and separate units are products of our analytical mind's tendency to "chop up" whole realities into parts that can be compared and evaluated. When actually all seeming units of anything are merely the raised or more apparent characteristics of underlying fields. In this way, elementary particles in physics have been described as "knots," or raised parts, in underlying fields. Compare this with Bohm's analogy of matter being "frozen light" (more on that, later). This thinking is applied to what we are learning about physical reality; I am contending that it can be applied equally well to understanding social realities.

## Ultimate Interconnectedness

The important point is that these social realities, too, are aspects of fields which are interconnected ... a web of fields that ultimately connects everything in the Universe. There is no such thing, ever, as separation, let alone "sealedness"; no such thing as hard and irreducible "particles," whether physical, cultural, epistemological, or otherwise. Thus, when I say "standing upon" or "looked at from" I mean that standing within the realities, understandings, or cultural items held in common — metaphorically, the "fields" undergirding them — there is possibility to understand items that are nearby, related, but not shared as much ... and out from there, items that are not shared at all.

In the ultimate sense, we can see how this would make even metaphysical or supernatural understandings possible between cultures. For we find that even these things have a common ground

— a common core of experiences for all humans. That is something I will talk a lot more about near the end of this book.

In the more immediate sense, it means that, for example, I can understand another person when they react to pain, which I also am subject to. So cultures are hardly epistemologically sealed because *experiential realities* — which are, remember, related to biologically constituted realities — are shared, overlap, and are common, to varying degrees, even if only minimally. And that from these common understandings, less common understandings are possible, if not completely understood in some mind-meld kind of way.[4]

Even saying it that way, you see the flaw in the thinking about cultural relativism of the extreme sort. It assumes that cultures are bounded and separate entities, not arbitrarily delineated, changing, and fluid categories. It assumes that a culture that is shared is understood the same way by everyone within it. It assumes further that someone from a different culture might not have more in common — more common ground of experience — with someone in that culture than someone who also exists in that culture but who has little to nothing of the same kind of experiences. It is probably not coincidental that such an idea about cultures as being bounded arose at a time when cultures were much more distinct than they are today and where conflict of cultures was so extreme actual genocides were perpetrated, as for example upon a multitude of indigenous cultures.

However, in our postmodern world of complex multiculturalism, where folks of all cultures encounter each other everywhere and interact intimately and considerably on social media, the flaws in that thinking are so readily apparent.

In any case, looking at culture and shared understandings from the point of view of biologically constituted realities (or species) and even bioculturally constituted realities (cultural items arising from our common biohistorical experience as a species), we can see why it seems that biological anthropologists and primatologists are so much less bothered by issues of epistemological relativism than are cultural anthropologists.

But then, standing on these "brute" (in other words, biological) facts, we are confronted with a new relativism — that regarding the worldviews of one species over against another. We see that species are epistemologically sealed from one another and that a trans-species reality is seen to be as impossible as a transcultural one was while standing within the playing field of culture.

Thus, though each culture is epistemologically sealed in relation to Reality, it is not so in relation to other cultures ... at least in a relative sense — that is, relative to our separation from Reality as Such. For all cultures of humans exist within a common biological paradigm that is concerned with all that is related to biological survivability ... though not to Reality as Such. It means that cultural paradigms *can*, after all, be compared in relation to common species-specific factors — biological ones.

# 8

# Beyond "Flat Earth" Materialism:

Why We Seek to Know, Usefulness and Limitations of Science, The New Evidence and the New Researchers, The Transpersonal Paradigm, and The Challenge to Know More

*A New Paradigm Emerging: The New Evidence, Pouring Forth from Our Sciences, Has Made Our Common-Sense Materialistic Assumptions About Our Reality as Obsolete as Our Flat-Earth Ones*

*"...wonder of wonders, finally in our evolution — in this very time of ours — there may be more people who are focusing on those keys to possible biological transcendence than ever before.... All of this despite the fact that within the 'real rules' of the Newtonian-Cartesian paradigm [those anomalies] have absolutely no possibility of existing or being able to happen.... Yet they do. Similarly, within the 'real world' of 'brute facts'*

*related to biological survivability they seemingly find no place.... Yet we stumble over them."*

*A Call to Our Sciences to Embrace the Awakening, Which It, Too, Has Been Resisting*

*"...although our very survival depends on a paradigm change, or shift ... it is being resisted mightily by our communities of scientific researchers. This Scientific Awakening is as much a threat to the corporate hegemony over modern culture as are the social and political Awakenings. There has been as much a battle in science over the last fifty years — a scientific culture war, if you will — as there has been the one in our societies around the world ... and for the same reasons. Paradigm shift threatens the status quo..."*

*"The crises of our time, it becomes increasingly clear, are the necessary impetus for the revolution now under way. And once we understand nature's transformative powers, we see that it is our powerful ally, not a force to be feared or subdued." — Thomas Kuhn*

*"It is, I think, particularly in periods of acknowledged crisis that scientists have turned to philosophical analysis as a device for unlocking the riddles of their field. Scientists have not generally needed or wanted to be philosophers." — Thomas Kuhn*

*"The historian of science may be tempted to claim that when paradigms change, the world itself changes with them. Led by a new paradigm, scientists adopt new instruments and look in new places. Even more important, during revolutions, scientists see new and different things when looking with familiar instruments in places they have looked before. It is rather as if the professional community had been suddenly transported to another planet where familiar objects are seen in a different light and are joined by unfamiliar ones as well." — Thomas Kuhn*

*"'Normal' science, in Kuhn's sense, exists. It is the activity of the non-revolutionary, or more precisely, the not-too-critical professional: of the science student who*

*accepts the ruling dogma of the day ... in my view the 'normal' scientist, as Kuhn describes him, is a person one ought to be sorry for.... He has been taught in a dogmatic spirit: he is a victim of indoctrination.... I can only say that I see a very great danger in it and in the possibility of its becoming normal ... a danger to science and, indeed, to our civilization. And this shows why I regard Kuhn's emphasis on the existence of this kind of science as so important." — Karl Raimund Popper*

*"Well-established theories collapse under the weight of new facts and observations which cannot be explained, and then accumulate to the point where the once useful theory is clearly obsolete."*
*[Using Thomas S. Kuhn's theories to frame his argument about the relationship between science and technology: as new facts continue to accumulate, a new, more accurate paradigm must replace the old one.] — Al Gore*

# Why We Seek to Know

So, what can we know? And why should we know it? I mean, in view of all that has been said so far, one might ask, if one cannot have any truly accurate conception or even "sense" of what is really real, why then bother to know anything?

## Ordinary Reality is Useful

The answer? Well, we bother to know because it is a helpful part of our species-specific worldview to do so. Employing the metaphor I have been using, they are the "rules" of the "game" we have chosen in coming here. And it is nice to know them. More specifically, as humans, we have evolved, as nearly as we can determine, through a process of natural selection based on survival. We are, consequently, the end-product of a biological drive to exist, to live — in all that may biologically, or otherwise, connote. Hence, that which we "know," in our most refined science and in our daily lives, is that which is, or has been, in some way useful to the *biological* existence of our species.

This so-called "real-world" information is important because, then, it relates *to* our very biological aliveness. It has worth, and it has value in that. That which comprises our species-world — as opposed to the "World-In-Itself" — is extremely relevant, indeed, to everything that we think of as living and existing ... for our species.

The point I make, however, is that our senses and our sciences — which are extensions of our senses — are not ultimately in any one-to-one relationship to That Which Is. And that our refined as well as cruder perceptions of reality are bioculturally relative. They are even more biologically relative than they are culturally relative in Marshall Sahlins's allegedly extreme theory.

We see that there are therefore levels of applicability of "knowledge." We might think of these as paradigms. But as surely as there are cultural paradigms, there are biological paradigms. I am saying that every configuration of spirit that we perceive in the physical world as a species, with each a different biology, represents a separate paradigm for interpreting reality.[1]

# Usefulness and Limitations of Science

## Ordinary Science is Useful

In this way we see why investigation of this Newtonian-Cartesian universe that we perceive with our senses and that we have constructed with the aid of our sciences is important. For it can provide additional data that has the possibility of being biologically useful.

Contrary to the conclusion from the total-symbolic-heritage view, science can be seen as more than "mere ethnoscience." That is to say, science is not, as those critics claim, merely one more part of a culture and with no more claim to validity than any view about the same things from another culture.

## Levels of Usefulness, Paradigm Comparisons

It seems to me that science has a greater, though not ultimate, claim to validity to the extent it includes and integrates more experiential "facts" in its reality constructions. With the degree of scientific validity — from good ethnoscience to bad ethnoscience — being equal to the number of experiential facts it includes and integrates.

If we were talking about people instead of cultures, we would be saying that cultures, to the extent that they integrate more, have greater "ego strength." Or as I insist it be called, more *self*. Cultural constructions, including science, that include more facts of existence, rather than freaking out in relation to them … not seeing them, repressing, running away from or ignoring them, or simply not knowing them … have, like persons with more "ego strength" or self, more validity, more "reality." Cultural constructions can therefore be compared, although such comparisons do not render any one of them, including science, Ultimate Truth, only "righter" in relation to the others, that is to say, more correct.

This is no different from saying, incidentally, that someone who "knows" more things, in particular experiences or experiential things, is likely to be "righter" in their pronouncements than someone who knows little, or less. Only we are comparing cultures, cultural matrices, if you will, instead of people.

The same would be true if we were to compare biological entities, with one caveat: Since we are human, we simply cannot know how the amount of reality that we are able to perceive compares with the amount any other planetmates are able to apprehend. And that is a huge difference, for as I pointed out in the last chapter, it is just as likely our brainpower is being used to keep *out* reality as that it is being used to include it. This is the *brain-as-reducing-valve* theory. And in this case, *the further down* the chain of biological complexity and size of brain, the more likely the species is apprehending *more* reality … though not *our* reality, or what we humans would be able to see as reality … than bigger-brained and more complex organisms. But, again, that is jumping ahead.

First, following up this idea that apprehending more is "smarter," what follows is that whoever accepts the "larger," more encompassing, more inclusive perspective is necessarily the one who has more "power" ultimately, in that this one's view allows for more accurate predictive and remedial power. That is why, eventually if not immediately, more inclusive paradigms and their proponents attain dominance. And by *power* I mean what it is that emanates from a perspective being more *useful*. And by "useful," I mean that its effectiveness — i.e., bringing about what is intended — is greater. And that's all I mean by that. Despite all the flaws of science, it still has incorporated more experiential — "true" or empirical — facts into it so as to make it capable of the technological wonders of the modern world — in medicine, in electronics, in space exploration. No other cultural paradigm has had enough potency — has embraced enough of actually true, empirical-experiential realities — to accomplish as much.

This is not to say, by the way, that new paradigms do always include all facts that old paradigms include. Or, another way of saying that, it does not mean that all facts *not* included in a subsequent, more "powerful," paradigm are not real or are not true. As just one example, many Native Americans' views included some "facts" — good, experientially and perceptually based objective facts — that were excluded from the paradigms of the Western conquerors who superseded them.

No, this is just to say that more powerful paradigms are ones containing a greater *number* of perceptually and scientifically based — albeit human specific but therefore "objectively" true — facts. It makes no claims as to the relative value of those facts that are included to those that are excluded.

## Paradigm Clash, The Force Behind Evolution

But to continue, since persons holding more inclusive paradigms are more "powerful," eventually if not immediately, they are more likely to be predominant in that they would be chosen by natural selection. If we would slide back our anthropocentric lenses for a minute and attempt to view all other species as simply other problem-solving beings who, as measured by their success, were employing either better or worse paradigms — that is to say, including more or less experiential "facts" — we might say that this is one way of appreciating the force behind continual evolution for all species.

So science has a claim to validity in relation to our species' biological survivability. But as emphasized earlier it has no claim in relation to anything other than that. Its truth is but a limited one. Its truth is relative to a biological context, a specific one, that of *Homo sapiens.*

## A Challenge to Know More

Indeed, this fact of limitation needs to be emphasized more heartily in science today. Anthropological thinking has created a legacy where we have been made fully aware of the relativity of culture and the limitations of culturally constituted facts — those "institutional facts" referred to earlier. It seems an equal and parallel effort is warranted — from the ranks of ecosophists, consciousness researchers, ecopsychologists, tranpersonalists, and others in the know — to point out the limitations and relativity of our species' biologically constituted facts — those (not so) "brute facts" of Anscombe and D'Andrade.

# The New Evidence and the New Researchers

For unless we do this, unless we keep in mind the limitations of our reality constructions — including our "scientific" ones — we have absolutely no way of understanding certain incorrigible and "biologically useless" facts that intrude upon our "real world" and that are scared into the light of our biological parameters by our scientific rummaging through the bushes. These "useless" side effects of our scientific enterprise may indeed contain the keys to our venturing forth, to at least some small degree, beyond the biological real-world confines of our predecessors. For just as we have seen that standing on a deeper, more encompassing paradigm than the cultural makes transcultural discourse and understanding possible, so also standing on one deeper than the biological may bring trans-biological understanding closer.

Following the reasoning I have been presenting, one can speculate that the prospects for bridging the boundaries between species … of both the known and "unknown" variety … as well as between our physical reality and other possible "non-physical" ones are good if we can find a way to look at that physical/biological — that Newtonian-Cartesian — level from a deeper grounding in spiritual, in transpersonal reality. In fact, the evidence from LSD and entheogenic-psychedelic research, some spiritual literature, and various aspects of "new age" phenomena that are washing up on the shores of a variety of disciplines is exactly to that effect.

Indeed, wonder of wonders, finally in our evolution — in this very time of ours — there are more people who are focusing on those keys to possible biological transcendence than ever before. Additionally, these researchers and seekers are scientifically, empirically, and experientially researching, eliciting, and perceiving many such incorrigible and "useless" phenomena and events. Most importantly of all, they are finding that these events can be intersubjectively validated — can be intertemporally and, indeed, empirically confirmed, demonstrated, and/or significantly correlated, so that they can be proven to have intersubjective and/or replicable validity. All of this despite the fact that within the "real rules" of the Newtonian-Cartesian paradigm they have absolutely no possibility of existing or being able to happen.... Yet they do. Similarly, within the "real world" of "brute facts" related to biological survivability they seemingly find no place…. Yet we stumble over them.

If all of this were not enough, we find that these incorrigible facts provide more than a pathway to a glimpse outside our biological blinders, more than a puncture in our epistemological seal, and more than a transcendence of our biological paradigm. We find that this information from "outside" the table of our biological board game is less biologically useless than was thought from within the borders of that board game. We find, indeed, that our species' assessment through natural selection of that which exists beyond it was less than perfect. We find that we are on the verge of re-evaluating that assessment and — to the extent it is possible and driven (once again) by biological survivability — of expanding our biological-cultural constructions to admit and give meaning to some of them.

# The Transpersonal Paradigm Emerging

Stanislav Grof is one such pioneer in this sort of "useless" research.[2] Though he is by no means alone, I mention him in that he has achieved far more than simply demonstrating the validity of particular incorrigible facts that turn our familiar, comfy, Newtonian-Cartesian paradigm on its ear. Additionally, Grof (1985) puts forth a model, a framework for a new paradigm. Bringing together the physicist Bohm's (1980) model of the universe and the neurosurgeon Pribram's (1971, 1976) model of the brain, he presents a holonomic "perspective" or "theory" based upon the idea of a hologram. The important aspect of this perspective is that it allows the inclusion and understanding of these new experiential facts, yet it does *not* contradict the Newtonian-Cartesian view of the world. The model includes the older paradigm, interpenetrating it thoroughly with something approaching a "field model" (my terms) of the universe.

The combined model explains the phenomena of everyday life, of "normal" science, as well as a huge and increasingly accumulating body of unexplainable data and evidence that is continually erupting out of the "new" natural sciences … in physics, chemistry, biology, astronomy, anthropology, and psychology, especially transpersonal psychology; out of the human potential phenomenon and new, experiential psychotherapeutic and growth techniques, such as primal therapy and holotropic breathwork; out of psychedelic, conscious-ness, entheogenic, and brain … especially brain waves … research; out of a half-century-long now Western fascination with and intense engagement with Eastern world-view, philosophy, and spiritual practice; and out of an equally long and parallel interest in the paranormal and the occult.

The holonomic (combined) model is explanatory and predictive. Yet it does so without having to exclude known, observable, empirically validated facts and evidence — without undeservedly casting upon them the light of nonexistence or, worse still, ignoring them, simply because their validity gives rise to a very human "uncomfortableness." Such data trigger a certain insecurity in that they undermine a familiar, habitual, and thoroughly ego-invested commitment to a view of reality.

The purposes of this chapter do not allow an elaboration of either the new evidence or the new paradigm that I have discussed and for that I refer the reader to references being mentioned. An additional good source is a few of my own works, specifically, *Experience Is Divinity* (2013c) and *Falls from Grace* (2014a), wherein I have detailed elaborate overviews of such a paradigm and indicated some of the evidence and research supporting it.

Beyond these works, a good example is found in *Beyond the Brain: Birth, Death and Transcendence in Psychotherapy* (1985). There, Stanislav Grof presents in the first chapter — which comprises ninety-one pages — an insightful analysis of paradigms and historical process along with an exhaustive sampling of the new evidence from the array of sciences, sociohistorical trends, and cultural processes that I have been mentioning. In addition, Grof (1985) constructs a thorough presentation, delineation, and analysis of the holographic model of a new paradigm. I recommend those pages highly.

On-line at youtube, I recommend a video, titled "Holographic Universe," which is an excellent overview of the model and makes the clear case that science has most definitely overturned the materialistic paradigm which birthed it hundreds of years ago.[3]

All that being said, I wish to point out that the recent and rapid emergence of the field of transpersonal psychology itself is pushed by an inability to continually disregard the evidence of our own senses that does not fit with the mechanical paradigms we were taught.

The point I am making in this chapter is that this new evidence, which is pouring forth on the cutting edges of our modern sciences, has made the Newtonian-Cartesian paradigm as obsolete as the flat-earth one.

# Beyond "Flat Earth" Materialism

All this being true, you might wonder why this new evidence and the expanded paradigm it reveals is not more well known in science, if not even adopted by now. There are sad reasons for that.

## Why We Refuse to Know

For one thing, the mere existence of this new data — these keys to biological transcendence, these formerly inexplicable anomalies of science — trigger a certain insecurity in that they undermine a familiar, habitual, and thoroughly ego-invested commitment to a view of reality.

I have noticed a fear and hostility toward the new paradigm and its evidence, even among self-professedly open-minded and

88

fieldwork-seasoned academicians and Ph.Ds. After observing and delving below this reaction for years, I have consistently detected a pattern of irrationality that associates, somehow, all this new stuff with things like having to go to church as a child, hell-fiery father gods, and Pat Robertson. Though nothing could be further from the truth, they confuse this paradigm with right-wing, Tea Party–type politics and evangelical religions. They think it is connected to the attacks on the theory of evolution, the idea of Intelligent Design, and the drives to install Creationism in our schools.

So these people harbor the mistaken notion that spiritual or *transpersonal* realities have something to do with organized religion, when they are quite different and, indeed, often at odds with each other.[4]

## A Call to Know Instead

However, this new evidence and new paradigm is not at all at odds, let alone at war with — as much of the constructs of fundamentalist theology are — our traditional scientific ways or findings. For, similar to the way in which the Earth *is* flat in the particular environs of one's daily life, and for a considerable distance surrounding, the Newtonian-Cartesian paradigm likewise has its limited usefulness. But if we are to get moving on our species' continuing adventure into discovering the nature of reality, we must acknowledge its limitations.

What bodes ill against this happening is an incredible, Jupiterian weight of egoic, economic, and time investment in the old materialist, the Newtonian-Cartesian, paradigm that pushes most people to insist upon its ultimate validity. Historically, this has been the unfortunate fate of every emergent paradigm facing the entrenched one. Decades and even centuries have often been required while the new worldview has been put "on hold" until entire, invested generations have left the scene … totally regardless of the quality, quantity, or indisputability of the new evidence.[5] What a waste! Especially in that when the new ideas are finally accepted and incorporated the effect is that of inspiring a renaissance of new frontiers of research and theoretical enterprise and thus a surging powerfully forth of the released creative tide.[6]

Let me state emphatically, in the face of such dire historical precedents, that there is no inherent insecurity involved in the new paradigm, or inherent danger, or inherent trigger for anxiety, or necessary economic disadvantage ... assuming one has the capacity to change with new developments and thought. So why do we not, then, get on with the incorporation of this new, heretofore unexplainable, data and with the creation of new paradigm models ... not, of necessity, Grof's or my own ... for making sense of it?

Why not rise and reach forth to new and inclusive thought that embraces the facts of existence? Instead of cleaving to a kind of thinking that requires either a psychic numbing to the avalanche of new evidence or a thick and sturdy guard against information from all but thoroughly sanctioned and sanitized, perfectly safe and riskless, or intractably bureaucratized sources?

I must point out that by now many scientists, of diverse fields, have abandoned the old model long ago and, at this point, consider its inadequacy to be well-nigh common knowledge. Having been over to the new paradigm a while, they feel it to be familiar territory; they find it useful (after all!), stable, workable, and even pleasurable terrain. They await the rest of us in the adventure of splicing or merging our insights about an explanatory framework that *has* room for the evidence of the new techniques and sciences; and thereby blowing away the door jammed, opening it wide to the next new phase of discovery of the nature of reality that is called the scientific enterprise.

Scientific awakening is as crucial for paradigm shift as are the social and political awakenings. Of course, this book is an aspect of that effort.

# 9

# Cultural Transcendence:

What We Could Know, Paradigm Dolls, and The Doors of Perception … Only by Leaving Can a Fish Know It Lives in Water

*Each of Us Is Potentially Mind At Large …*
*When Perception Is Cleansed, All Kinds of Nonordinary*
*Things Happen*

*Why Everything Appears Infinite when the Doors of*
*Perception Are Cleansed: "Mind at Large" and The*
*Awakening*

*"If the doors of perception were cleansed, everything*
*would appear to man as it is … infinite." — William*
*Blake*

# Our Knowledge Is Useful, Not Revelatory

Now, let us ask the same question — Why do we seek to know? — in a slightly different way. I have been saying that we want to know basically because it is biologically helpful to do so. It contributes to our physical survival, whether as an individual or a group. However, I want to ask in this chapter why should we bother to know anything outside of the biologically useful, outside of our biologically constituted parameters for understanding and determining value. Is there any reason to seek to know anything outside of the pragmatic?

Reviewing, where we have arrived in this book is that the cumulative efforts in our modern sciences point to a symbolic nature to our reality. Discoveries in psychology, physics, especially quantum physics, biology, and anthropology have brought a standstill to our beliefs that we can know anything with any certainty, as their forerunners earlier in science were wont to do. Our latest understandings are not about what we know, but about the fact that ultimately we do not know. More even than that, they bring the harsh revelation that regardless our trying, we are unable ever to know.

So, we cannot know ultimately, but as we discussed in the last chapter, it is helpful to know the rules of the game. That is, that within the paradigm we operate, there are potent, beneficial reasons for learning them. These relate to their biological usefulness. The theory I advanced, bringing forth from Huxley and Bergson, was that the Universe is essentially Mind-at-Large, or what I call, throughout this book, Divinity; and that we are part of that. That we are "capable of remembering all that has ever happened" and "of perceiving everything that is happening everywhere in the universe," as Huxley phrased it. But that "in so far as we are animals, our business is at all costs to survive."

There's the game and there's those rules of the game. This is saying that in the Form state we have a particular focus than what is possible for us and it is immensely reduced down from what is potential. Quoting Huxley, to live in this world "Mind at Large has to be funneled through the reducing valve of the brain and nervous system." That the result is only that which is helpful for our survival.

The other analogy being used in science, a more recent one, is to compare the brain to a television receiver. Physicists and consciousness researchers explain that the idea that the brain "produces" consciousness was faulty. That would be like a TV coming up with the shows that play on it. Some scientists are now explaining the way the brain works as being similar to the way your television receives the signal — which would be consciousness or the contents of consciousness in the form of the shows that are possible to you, which in theory would be an infinite number of them. Then the television packages it and interfaces with you to view it. An important aspect of this, however, is that the television also selects the channel, that will be viewed, out of many … and in terms of consciousness, out of a virtual infinity of possibilities. I would add that the brain–television receiver has something to do with the "quality of the reception," as well.

In any case, this is virtually the way I explained it initially in this book, in the first chapter, when I pointed out that what our senses (the actual television hardware) does firstly is *scan* and sort through a vastness of experiential possibilities. In the same way a television takes the signal it receives from the coaxial cable feeding it and selects from it in line with what channel the viewer has selected. Then our brain *concocts* it, I explained. This would be analogous to the way the television takes that program, produced and created elsewhere, and turns it into the electrical messages another part of the TV can read and re-create in its interfacing mechanisms with you … in its TV screen, its speaker. The TV takes the signal of the story or program produced elsewhere and turns it into something on the television screen that is viewable. And finally, I pointed out, the brain *interprets* it, which in the television analogy would be that which determines the resolution, color, shadings, and so on, which make it clear and understandable to the viewer. This last I compared with culture. The second could be compared to our biocultural realities. The first, the scanning and then selecting, could be compared to our biologically constituted realities. And the viewer selecting the channel and show to watch would be the person selecting the life to live in reincarnating.

In any case, this television analogy is a more refined way of explaining brain-as-reducing valve, however it fails to emphasize the aspect the earlier analogy did: Which is that whatever signal the television picks up and re-creates to be humanly experienced is selected out of a vastness of what is there or could be. That is to say, there exists a virtual infinity of scripts and stories containing an infinity of experiences and information, analogous to the infinity of possible "channels." And that the brain is not just "selecting," but it is also "rejecting" ... or eliminating a universe of other possibilities. This is the way the reducing-valve analogy stresses something that is important in this chapter: Which is that there is more out there.

I must say, it gets annoying the way our anthropocentric bias suffuses everything we assert. You might say our bias is part of the television that is selecting down from what is possible again. For the television receiver analogy, while more elegant, is also geared to be more palatable. For it panders to human ego to say that the brain is accomplishing something, producing something, in relaying the message or program. The analogy would have us seeing the brain as taking the signal and "doing" something with it to create a channel or viewable program. It still appears to be a brain "creating" something out of random and incoherent data. Whereas actually it is only selecting and tuning into something far beyond itself; that is to say, what is being produced "elsewhere."

More importantly, the television analogy manages to avoid noticing that the process involves leaving out an infinity of What Is, as well, in doing that. The reducing-valve theory emphasizes there are other possibilities for perception, indeed an infinity of them; whereas the television-receiver analogy is slanted toward having a brain that creates something out of what would otherwise be incomprehensible to a human.

Both, no doubt, are true. We can say equally that our biologically constituted realities create the reality — the rules of the game — out of an infinity of what is or could be, so enabling us to function and to have that "biologically useful" information needed — the selected channel. Whereas they are also restrictive of all other possibilities or potentialities.

Whereas the previous chapter emphasized "why we seek to know" and pointed out there are biological survival considerations involved; this chapter will emphasize "what we could know" and focus on what else is Real and True and what value that information left out might have for us.

The previous chapter stressed that a picture is created on the screen. This chapter will focus on the fact that there is much more, equally or more true and valid, that the picture on the screen is leaving out. It focuses on what that might be that is left out, and it evaluates it.

We have gone from, in Chapter 7, "why we know not" and "what we can know."

To "why we seek to know" despite that, in the last chapter, Chapter 8.

In this Chapter 9, we will look into what follows from that, which is, "what we could know," "how we could know more," and "what would be better to know."

You will see that "Transcending Worlds," Part 2 of this book, will finish, in the next chapter, on what everyone will be thinking at that point. Which is, "how we might come to know."

# How We Could Know More

So, we seek to know because it is useful to our biological survival to know. And that which we "know," in our most refined science and in our daily lives, is that which is, or has been, in some way useful to the biological existence of our species. Our sciences have led us to learn that what we call reality is what we have found to be useful for us as a species, but that it is not necessarily what is True and is certainly not all that is true or real. So we find that the Reality of It All or the All That Is gets reduced down from the immensity, indeed the infinity, of what it is to the mere snippet of it that we have found to be biologically useful. And from there it is further reduced to what is useful to us as individuals at a specific time in a specific place.

However let's now consider the other implication of Huxley-Broad's theory. For Huxley (1956) points out, "When this is reversed by various methods, and the brain is itself inhibited from its task of reducing awareness so that Mind at Large seeps past the no longer watertight valve, all kinds of biologically useless things start to happen."[1]

# "Biologically Useless Things Start to Happen"

So, if we wish to know not merely what is practical but what is actually True or Reality — as I am attempting to do in this book, *The Secret Life of Stones,* and in a forthcoming work, *The Cosmic Overstanding* — we need to go way beyond the smattering of facts thrown up by our ordinary senses and the sciences that are extensions of them. There are levels of that diminution of Reality — from All That Is or Mind at Large down through to what the individual knows to be true. I have been describing them as biologically constituted, bioculturally constituted, culturally constituted, and individually constituted realities.

*So to know what is True, beyond merely what is practical; what is helpful; what is powerful for advancing and dominating in this game, on this planet, during this slice of time....*

*in order to transcend those constituted realities; in order to achieve "biological transcendence"; in order to take a step "out of Form," so to speak; to go outside our static state; to go* ec-static *...*

*we need to reverse those reductions in true understanding.*

Helping in that effort is what this book is about. At least, that is to say, in this book the attempt is made to bring forward for inspection the cognitive changes, the mistakes in thinking, the obvious cognitive blinders; and in doing so to pull them away from one's eyes and ways of thinking....

However, nothing put in words — this book or any other or any lecture or youtube presentation or seminar talk — can bring about the changes that only experiences can. As this book continues to point out, it is only an experiential route that can be fruitful and transformative. But as I also point out, words and concepts — and especially overstandings and paradigms made visible — are maps on that experiential journey. And when those overstandings and maps are known and understood, they can have us going back to our life experience with a better orientation, with better ideas of where to expend one's efforts, with helpful insights about additional things to notice about where one is — all of which can contribute to the quality of or maximize the positive results of one's experiential efforts.

At any rate, to this end, I continue....

# What Would Be Better to Know

We find that in doing this reversal, some startling things are revealed.

## Paradigm Dolls

To begin, from the perspective of each greater awareness, each more limited perspective becomes understandable and the different ones of those perspectives can be compared. You might say that in the China Doll construction of the universe of knowing, or overstandings, each larger doll is more likely to understand all the other dolls it contains, but will likely vastly misconstrue what the larger doll or dolls would be like within which it is contained. Substitute overstandings or paradigms for dolls, now.

Incidentally, the fact that an included paradigm will misunderstand its including, more encompassing ones — the ones in which it is contained — explains why folks operating in the old Newtonian-Cartesian paradigm are totally unable to understand the transpersonal paradigm, as I was complaining in the last chapter.

## Cultural Transcendence

However, you ask how this works for encompassing paradigms comprehending its included ones? Okay, we know, for example, that it is difficult for one individual to truly understand another. Nonetheless, standing within a knowledge of psychology in general, we have a better understanding of another and we can compare one individual's reality with another and come up with meaningful and true conclusions, even comparisons and evaluations. That is, indeed, why we have the science of psychology in the first place.

But at the level of cultures, a similar thing happens. Anthropologists come necessarily to the conclusion that another culture cannot truly be understood by someone standing in a different culture. Just as one individual cannot exactly understand another's reality, it is even more impossible for someone from one culture to be able to truly view the world through the lenses or worldview of those born into another culture.

However, here again, we can have a better understanding of each culture and can even compare cultures somewhat when coming from the perspective of our common human biology. For all cultures have to relate to the nature of our body and its abilities, senses, and capabilities. All cultures make constructions about, around, and from the particular biological frame that humans have, so cultures can be compared at least in relation to those commonalities of humans.

This means more than just that cultures can be compared in relation to biological realities like birth and death. For it is even more important and instructive to compare them to more basic realities of human biology such as pain, pleasure, happiness, liberty, and so on. All humans feel and have concepts about these things. And following along the lines of my argument so far, we can say that some cultures can be considered to be superior, based upon the way those biological items are handled.

How, you ask? Well, since we are operating within a biological paradigm to begin with — one that is necessitated by the fact that we are human, and we find that what knowledge we have is because it is biologically useful — we have to say that implies that life is a value inherent in our paradigm. "Biologically useful," broken down, means that a fact, or piece of knowledge lends itself to greater survivability of a biological organism … it furthers, augments, or enhances the life of it.

Now, having life as a value, we can extrapolate from that, that since life is impeded, reduced, and eventually eliminated by pain, that reduction of pain is a value. This would not always be the case, for a particular pain might eliminate the need for a greater pain, which would be even more life-negating. A prick of a needle, which is injecting a cure or an inoculation, might be a pain that has value if it avoids a greater pain of an illness.

But beyond that, since we are talking about paradigms, and biocultural sets of understanding, this is about knowledge. And greater knowledge has a value, as I was saying above, in that true and actual greater knowledge or encompassing systems facilitate greater power, greater life, and greater longevity. With this in mind, some pains might actually be life-affirming if they lead to enhancing those values involving nurturing of life.

We only get confused by these things because we have managed to concoct, with civilization, religions and theologies in which these human values of reduction of pain, reduction of suffering, increase of life, increase of life span, and so on, are put on their head. Whether we are talking about a pleasurable activity like sexuality or any number of satisfying life experiences, they are irrelevant to many Western theologies, and often they are demonized … they are considered sinful.

How this is accomplished is by postulating another time, after death, in which the pain and suffering we experience now, or the earlier death or reduced life expectancy, will lead to greater pleasure, "life," and so on, later, in an afterlife. In this kind of thinking, the suffering, even the facilitation of death, of this world is much like that inoculation — a pain that will prevent a greater pain later, after death. And when you concoct a pain in the afterlife that is of the greatest magnitude and of the longest duration (eternal) … you know I am talking about hell here … you can justify all kinds of horrible and painful actions in life. And, indeed, this has been done. Witness the Inquisition as just one example.

But the problem is that looked at in the broadest historical expanse of humans and from the widest array of cultural perspectives now and of all time, those "sinful" pleasurable and life-affirming activities are *not* considered negative at all!

So you can only propose such a theology by leaving out the evidence of other cultures and other, prehistoric and pre-civilizational, times. And this is exactly what they do. These theologies eliminate outside knowledge and cling to infantile understandings of Reality in order to maintain their dogma of sinfulness.

However, further weight is given to this notion that modern religions have it all backwards in that we can see, even by an understanding of civilizational history, that these religions and notions of morality only came into play with hierarchy in society, come of civilization, when there were higher ups wanting to control those below them,. We must suspect the supernatural status of wrongfulness attributed to normally life-affirming or life-neutral acts when we achieve the understanding that these "sins" are conveniently, and not coincidentally, in the interest primarily of the elite of society.[2]

Furthermore, such views, keeping out the facts of history, culture, and other people's experiences and cultural understandings, are then in the category of that paradigm or overstanding that is less *powerful* because it includes *less* experiential facts of existence. They necessarily will be superseded; since at some point, even if a long time, truth *will* out. It cannot be kept out of the awareness of the masses, as attempts in the Soviet Union and other such societies have shown. What can be known, once it is known, cannot be forever unknown.

So, a greater understanding of human values shows that, in general, less pain is a value, when comparing cultures; less death is always a value, when comparing cultures; more pleasure is valuable to the extent it fosters greater life and/or longevity ... the same with greater happiness and felicity; greater psychological sanity, as for example in cultures having superior prenatal and birthing procedures, is a value in that it also facilitates greater life, longevity, pleasure, and less pain; and ... this one is very important ... greater wisdom or knowledge or paradigm overstandingness is a value in that it facilitates all the rest — less pain, greater felicity, and enhanced life and increased longevity ... and for all we know, it results in a more accepting, peaceful death and a better all-around "time" to be had in the No-Form State, after death.

## Biological Relativity, Species Relativity

All that being said, we see how non-absolute even these human values and realities are as soon as we look at the realities or consciousness of life forms other than human. Can we truly say that a lizard has a feeling of the pleasure or life-enhancing value involved in liberty? Does it even experience happiness, as we do in the way it enhances and magnifies the life value in our species.? Can we say that an amoeba or bacteria feels the pleasure of freedom or the lack of it? We cannot know. They might have elements in their experience of Reality that are analogous or parallel to that which we experience in ours, but a) they would not be identical to our perception of Reality and b) they might not!

So even these larger — more powerful and more valuable, truer — biocultural paradigms encompassing the smaller biocultural ones ... those larger China dolls ... are themselves superseded by biological paradigms relating to species, which are bigger China dolls still, in which they are "understood" or "contained"; but within which their elements and components might be devalued, skewed, or even be seen to be irrelevant, wrong, or nonsensical. This is to say that within the paradigm encompassing all species just on Earth, not even extending out to all the probable species and beings in existence, human values of life, pleasure, freedom, fulfillment, happiness, and longevity are open to reinterpretation, with greater degrees of reinterpretation applicable the further removed from human experience that paradigm is doing its encompassing. Or, let us say, the bigger the China doll is relative to the human one, the human biological paradigm, the greater likelihood the human values within ours would be interpreted differently.

Now, just so this does not sound purely academic, or worse, merely semantic, let me say this: This analysis, this viewpoint or understanding, has value, as one example, in helping us to understand species on our planet who have a different relation to death than us. This is a big one. For it is on this basis that we proclaim our superiority to Nature.

We see Nature as brute and untamed because we see it as brutal in relation to death and pain. Yet, as I explicate in Chapter 29 on planetmates, titled, "The Other Is Our Hidden Face," their reality — their "values" and approaches to life — can be seen as superior in value to ours within a paradigm where a) death is not an absolute end of anything, merely a resetting of life and b) pain, within particular ranges and amounts in life, is seen as enhancing of all good values and feelings, and c) a primary value is put on the adventure, fun, or experiential quality of living not merely its amount of time or amount of pain. You'll see better what I mean there, in that chapter.

The point is that our evaluations, wrought from within our biological paradigm, are flawed and open to reinterpretation once we go outside our species paradigm. So in no way can we use them as a basis upon which to evaluate and judge another or other species any more than one culture can legitimately evaluate and judge another culture, except based upon the more encompassing biological paradigm of humans.

# Biological Transcendence

It follows that to understand truth beyond our biologically constituted realities … to be able to get an idea of what reality might be like for entities and life in general and not just humans, we would need to stand inside a paradigm of understanding that would apply to all species — both known and unknown. We would need to take a stance on the foundation of a trans-species perspective — that is, what is true for all species, not just humans. We would need to find a common ground of understanding from which to view what is related to that for both species.

This is what science says it is attempting to do, but it actually does not. Because we have found that sciences can only look in areas that we as humans ahead of time have an idea that something might be. In other words, science is an extension of our senses. So to do more, we have to expand our imagination to include what might be the perspectives of other species … other planetmates. This is what we are doing with our attempt to understand planetmate consciousness. Indeed, that is exactly what I lay out in my book, *Planetmates: The Great Reveal* (2014b).

# 10

# Species Transcendence and Occupy Science:

How We Might Come to Know … Knowledge Begins Where Arrogance Ends … Dropping Our Species-Centrism, We Transcend Scientific Truth

*Bridging the Barriers Between Species, Biological Transcendence: This Is the Place Where Even Hard Core "Realists" Learn How Little They Know*

*"Ultimately this means that now that we know that common-sense materialism is simply a biological construct of the species human, we can relearn that it is Consciousness that is our only knowable Reality."*

*"…in tossing away our species blinders, we approach a truth far beyond science, though not overturning science…. In doing this we see that it is the mystics and the consciousness researchers who are likely to have the most accurate angle on Reality."*

*A Call to End Science's Culture War and for a Scientific Awakening. Consciousness ... Experience ... is infinite. It is fantastic as well.*

# Species Transcendence

But, you say, how can we do that? How can we know the way another being or life form, other than human, might view Reality? We cannot.

## True Knowledge Begins Where Arrogance Ends

However, the point is we are more likely to come up with something *truer* than what we already know when we at least try to do that. Knowing something *truer* then has a chance of opening other doors not seen before, as well. Whereas complicity in the strictures of any prevailing paradigm *guarantees* stasis and dead ends. Complicity in easy prejudices, such as anthropocentrism, obstructs new knowledge as strictly as adherence to the dogma of Catholicism put a dead stop on intellectual progress for a millennia in Europe during the Middle Ages.

Trying to do that — to find a stance outside one's species-determined one — means starting with dropping the presumption, the arrogance, that humans have a superior and more real understanding of Reality. When we do that, simply that alone, we already find we have a much expanded understanding of what is really Real. For simply knowing that one's human view is biased allows one to consider possibilities, wrought of anomalies and inconsistencies in the current paradigm, that the prevailing paradigm overlooks, ignores, puts on a shelf, and covers up.

For even what we are able to know about other species shows us some of the ways they see things differently than us. So simply by not assuming we are the pinnacle of creation and acknowledging that, for example, a dog really does have more accurate smelling and hearing ability and an eagle a greater ability to see, and imagining what that would mean for our reality in relation to theirs or keeping that in mind, we come to an appreciation of ourselves as a part of Nature, not a ruler of Nature; just as our understandings of the realities-subjectivities-feelings of other humans has led us to know that we are not rulers of other people; just as our understandings of other cultures have led us to know that one culture is not better, superior to, or more dominant over another.

Let me give a specific example of the greater overstandings made possible by the diminishment of arrogance and Ego in the evaluation of the realities of species other than ours.

## Culture Versus Instinct

Fortunately I do not have to go far to come up with one, as this is the most frequently addressed topic when we are comparing our species with other planetmates. That issue is instinct in planetmates versus culture in humans.

To begin, as I have pointed out in several other works, most species are born and are either immediately or soon enough able to fend for themselves. How they are able to do that is attributed to what we refer to as *instinct*.

We arrive at this determination of a factor of instinct, not empirically, but conveniently. By that I mean that *instinct* is not a thing-in-itself that we have discovered in Nature. No. We see that other planetmates are able to do all kinds of things without being taught, and since we do not have that same thing we cannot understand it. Not able to understand it, we give it a name — *instinct*. Problem solved.

But what is it? Well, we say it is genetic. It is behavior laid down in the genes. And we have this further rather magical idea that somehow the pattern of molecules inside a part of the body, inside planetmates, creates behavior. Much like a machine, we imagine that the inner "works" of beings, on the molecular level as DNA, makes them do things just as the tiny gears and such that makes up a watch causes it to move its arms. No consciousness, no subjectivity involved: Things become actions, somehow; physical items in the material body impel beings to do particular things in particular ways … precisely so and with little to no mental mediation.

Which is like saying that my rock garden … I'll even give you, the *pattern* of my rock garden … conceivably makes me, want to or not, get up at seven am, make coffee, put particular and specific clothes on, and travel in a particular car, to a particular place, to engage all day in particular and precise actions, at a particular job. Why, how fantastic!

Not fantastical enough, this behavior is not just of a crude sort, for example, a bird's ability to create a nest. No, somehow instinct is said to account for the fact that birds are able to, not only fly in formation, but make specific split-second and synchronous movements in full flight among all of them, and to do it always and an infinite numbers of times, all without any blemishes in their choreography, mistake, or the slightest bit of collision with each other. That's quite the watch!

Supposedly, these genes of millions of years development know when and how each individual bird in flight, throughout that span of millions of years, is supposed to move in any particular millisecond that each individual bird is in flight. Imagine our robotics engineers programming the precise actions of their creations for all possible events to be encountered millions of years into the future. So these genes of instinct evolved over millions of years somehow knew in advance, millions of years before now, what a particular flock of birds was going to do at a particular millisecond of time … not to mention, *all* birds in all flocks in every millisecond of time over the course of millions of years.

Yet instinct is supposed to be the down-to-earth, real-world, "scientific" explanation for these incredible movements of birds, insects, and other similar planetmates. Instinct implies a kind of foreknowledge, premonition, or clairvoyance wilder than anything imaginable … and all contained within that infinitesimally small package of DNA. But somehow the idea of telepathy — what I call, more descriptively, *mind-sharing* — is considered unscientific and too fantastical to be believed.

The same with dolphins and fish. We see their precise synchronous movements and we say that is instinctive. We cannot know how they could possibly perfectly choreograph their movements far more precisely than any contestants on *Dancing with the Stars* are able to, even after much training. Actually it is more like the choreography of groups of humans that is arrived at after months of hard work to get it right. Even then, such dancers are hardly able to maintain that perfect choreography among all of them while spontaneously making random new changes in their movements — unplanned — the way flocks, swarms, and schools of various planetmates do.

Yet flocks of birds have infinitely creative and seemingly random changes — perfectly choreographed into their movements — in their flight. Changes which are instigated by.... Well, here you see again, how magical! Instigated by no one in particular, they just occur for all participants simultaneously, not even a leader or a director in sight. Yet, imagine those human dancers making endless new patterns in their routines, unplanned, spontaneous, without direction, and perfectly synchronized in the movement and steps among all the participants.

Well, such is instinct ... and the power of it ... supposedly. Even more disingenuous, we attribute the ability of the dolphins and fish to do that to *instinct*, and then we do not have to try to understand it anymore. We give something a name and consider it job done.

And then we say the idea of *shared mind* — a shared field of energy comprised of knowledge or, as I have been asserting, Experience (subjectivity, consciousness), which is the only thing that exists, being shared among multiple perceivers at the same time — which also might explain these wondrous abilities of planetmates, is fantastical, hence absurd. Yet this idea of consciousness shared is an idea that our consciousness research is leading us toward.

In this light, it is likely that ideas like instinct will have as much importance in the future as the convoluted theories of astrologers who, prior to the heliocentric revolution in thought, attempted to make sense out of the movement of the stars employing all kinds of bizarre notions.

For consciousness research, with its findings in related fields such as quantum physics, transpersonal psychology, prenatal and perinatal psychology, and the new biology will, in time, demonstrate to all of science ... it has been proven to those of us in these fields already ... that it is consciousness, Experience, subjectivity, and feelings that are fundamental to Reality. All of science will eventually learn that Experience, Consciousness, and mental-emotional stuff is shared between beings. Beings were formerly, traditionally, assumed to be absolutely separate from each other, though in fact they were not. Science in general will finally be forced to acknowledge that all beings and all the subjective experience of each and every one of them overlaps with other, similar ones, and potentially with all beings and all subjectivities existing. We actually share identity, in a sense; our perception of separate identities is our human illusion.

In correcting these misassumptions of ordinary science, a new-paradigm science will bring clarity to our understanding of these fantastical behaviors of planetmates and make the idea of instinct to be like the emperor with no clothes — sad and laughable.

## Shared Mind: When the Doors of Perception Are Cleansed, the Nonordinary Happens

At any rate, what I am saying is that many planetmates have a kind of overlapping of mind; they share mind stuff. They participate in a kind of field of mind or understanding … and that gives them the ability to know things they were not taught. In a sense, the species did the learning over the course of its evolution, and it is shared mentally by all members. If that sounds unbelievable, realize that what I just described is exactly the way one new biologist, Rupert Sheldrake, describes his theory of *morphogenetic fields*.[1] More about that later.

Now, we humans have lost that shared mind. We have lost that ability. More correctly, we believe we have lost it; for we retain some ability of shared mind, or telepathy. However, for the most part we ignore it, dismiss it, or at least downplay it. And if and when it comes out in social intercourse, we have cultural conventions which have us all ignoring that it happened, colluding in its cover-up.

And you think there is no way I could explain this huge difference between humans and planetmates in regard to instincts? Not quite. As I elaborate upon in other works, the difference between us and the rest of Nature has to do with secondary altriciality and culture.[2] Let me explain:

a)  In the womb just before birth we experience an hellacious time that splits us off from our connection with Divinity.

This is known as *fetal malnutrition,* and because it is a traumatic time, which we needed to push out of our mind, we suppressed others of our abilities along with it. Among them is that mind sharing with other beings and that felt connection with Divinity. So this is part of why we are not able to mind share after birth, but then,

b) Since our brains are too big to be able to stay in the womb for the twenty-one months it would need for us to be born at the level of development comparable to other species when they are born, we are born prematurely with our brains not fully developed enough … perhaps not developed enough to do that "mind sharing" that other species are able to do?

c) At any rate, then we are born with even more pain, birth trauma. This causes us to lose any last traces of connection with Divinity or the participation of the individual consciousness in that of the group. So, indeed, we are born with a "blank slate." Not because we have nothing, no instinct, no sense of self, no prior understandings or proclivities, or even instructions. But rather because all that we did have, unlike all other species, was wiped off our "slate" … our consciousness … during those prenatal and perinatal times of excruciating pain, which caused us to block all that out. We are born with a *tabula rasa* because we have repressed out of our consciousness … and we have created an unconscious of … all that we are and could be if we had not suppressed, repressed, and forgotten who we are. So that,

d) Onto this blank slate we pour all the necessary learnings we need to survive; we do this through a process of parenting. But unlike the mind sharing of other planetmates, we are only going to get any learnings we do as funneled through an even more narrowed consciousness, one even more split from Divinity or the mind we share in common with the Universe. And that more narrowed consciousness is that of our caregivers, one's parents, usually. Thus,

e) Culture — which is the accumulated, infinitely varied, and unavoidably flawed understandings of how to behave and survive in the world, developed over time, different in every society, and transmitted primarily by admittedly imperfect parents — steps in where mind sharing ... what we disrespectfully call *instinct* ... should be.

Okay, you say. Some parts of that I've heard before, no big deal, you might say.

But I ask you: Have you ever heard that described in any way that did not necessarily raise our species onto a pedestal? Be honest and you will see that here is where everyone, including scientists, begin to beat their chests and pontificate on how humans ... and that would include *them*, ahem, ahem, don't you know ... have free will, or *choice*. Which term, *choice*, by the way, is the politically correct way scientists phrase it so as not to sound, oops, *religious*. Scientists bristle at the presumptions of religion, so they are wary of using terms like *free will*. Yet they hesitate not in asserting a power of choice, using the same lazy illogic running along endlessly overused, deep and chiseled channels of egotism — of the special variety of species-centrism — to give us god-like status above other planetmates with magical capacities for free will and choice which planetmates supposedly do not have.

So instinct, as framed the way it usually is by scientists, is used as another way of touting our superiority over Nature (again!!!) instead of it being explained in a way that would tell what that substitution of culture for instinct actually is: Culture is an artificial substitute for what we have lost in splitting from Divinity, or shared mind, and it is a sufficient-for-survival construct. However, culture is not as refined, or as close to Truth and Reality, or perfect, even, as what other planetmates have that is called *instinct*. Culture, in this way, is collective Ego. For Ego can be defined as the artificial consciousness construct that each individual develops to be able to function, after one has lost one's more expanded consciousness that one had in the womb.

Indeed, in our refusing to frame it in any way that is other than a boast, masquerading as science, we see exactly those kinds of indications of Ego. For Ego, to mention one of its effects only, is the way humans turn all their faults into accomplishments.

## Opening a Non-Anthropocentric Window, A World of Possibilities is Viewed

Now, the point of this example is to show how much more can be brought into our understandings when we, as scientists, lower our collective Ego. And that collective Ego we have reified into culture and, therefore, with that as an excuse, or as a curtain to hide us, we feel we are allowed to boast. This is something we need to push to the side to find truer Truths. This is not different from the fact that a person cannot grow in knowledge until that person lets in information besides that which is self-congratulatory. That is to say, for personal growth to occur, a lowering of one's ego defenses is required.

The conclusions from all this understanding is that our sciences are important in establishing facts and reality, but the ones they come up with are only relative to our species, not necessarily to any other species, and not necessarily do they give us a true idea of What Really Is. Hardly do they help us in comparing ourselves with other species, either.

Conversely, that when one steps outside those species conventions, bucking up species survivability, and opens a non-anthropocentric window, all kinds of possibilities arise, which are seen to be obviously more likely than the ones we had that stroked our collective species "ego."

## Scientific Arrogance Is Laughable

You think this is irrelevant to know? Well, to give just one example, think of all our forays into space and our imaginings of other beings from other than this planet. If you take the perspective that I am encouraging here, you will notice how astoundingly naïve are our expectations and how crude the instruments we use to detect other life forms. For they all are built on an expectation of finding beings that are at least somewhat like ourselves.

You say, no, our scientists are not assuming other beings of high consciousness would look like us. But you should know I mean that in our scientists saying what are the building blocks of life — water, carbon, and so on — they are showing a bias about "life" that it is something like what we know. Notice also that even the idea of a "higher" level of consciousness itself has its roots in this idea that a human consciousness is superior to other kinds we know of. So these assumptions built into our science are laughable in their arrogance.

## In Tossing Away Our Species Blinders, We Approach the Mystical

Meanwhile, in understanding how limited and relative is our human perspective, we are able to imagine other possibilities for life and its variations. We begin to approach the perspectives of mystics. We begin to open to a pantheist revelation. We begin to understand the consciousness of matter ... the life that lies in mountains, streams, and planets. We begin to understand how it is not outside the realm of possibility that even what we consider non-life and inanimate to be somehow conscious or a form of consciousness, even if we resist calling it "life" — which is, we see now, itself, as we normally think of it, part of our limited species interpretation.

Yet, with a flip of the switch in our thinking which would allow a lowering of species-ego, we have cast light upon the cosmic overstanding exposing, for one and all, *the secret life of stones.*

So, in tossing away our species blinders, we approach a truth far beyond science, though not overturning science. What Is ends up not, as fundamentalists might think, opposed to science, rather inclusive of science ... but including so, so much more. And in doing this we see that it is the mystics and the consciousness researchers who are likely to have the most accurate angle on Reality.

## Transcending Our Biologically Constituted Materialism, We Relearn That Consciousness Is Infinite, Yes ... But Fantastic as Well

Ultimately this means that now that we know that common-sense materialism is simply a biological construct of the species human, we can relearn that it is Consciousness that is our only knowable Reality. And while that Consciousness, or as I insist it must be called,

*Experience,* is, as I have been showing, infinite, varied, and beyond our ken, still … and this is the point relative to us in all our biological determinedness, which includes values of life, pleasure, and hence interestedness, fun desiring, and curiosity appreciating … it is fantastic as well.

Hence, the attempt to transcend our species parameters is itself driven by that biological existence and its elements. And though it leaves us in a quandary where we see Reality cannot be ultimately known, for it is Infinite, still, it can be *experienced.* And in being experienced in a way as to attempt to go beyond our arrogance, Ego, and species-constituted and species-constricting Realities, it reveals itself as both wondrous and awe-inspiring. We, as humans, will never be able to apprehend Ultimate Reality, but the attempt itself takes us beyond where we would be if not making the attempt. And it leads us toward realities that are both infinite … and wonderful.

## Anomalies Hold the Key

It is the so called "anomalies" of science that hold the keys to the reality that lies beyond science. Looking at them we see a pattern upon which to stand in bringing together the different viewpoints or paradigms that are not reconcilable otherwise. These different viewpoints are the different scientific ones and the different cultural ones as well as the different biological ones — that is, the perspectives or views of different species … the different planetmate views.[3]

The anomalies that we have found to have the most potential, for aiding us in this venture to a greater paradigm or framework within which to comprehend all these smaller views, are those that have come out of consciousness research. This research comes from scientific as well as spiritual sources. The findings and discoveries are often experientially based, though they are hardly just anecdotal since these reports are replicable and verifiable and they are often and can easily be collected and collated scientifically.

These scientific approaches to what were once in the realm of just the spiritual or religious are going on more now than ever before in the history of the world. Whether from fields of the new physics, the new biology, or the consciousness branches of psychology and anthropology, they are uncovering more new erstwhile inexplicable data of events that have heretofore been beyond the views of our sciences and beyond our common-sense materialism. That is to say, beyond our world of "brute facts," which we have found are not incontestable or brute at all but are only solidly true in relation to the fact that we are of the species of humans.

## Knowledge Once Considered Biologically Useless Has Suddenly Become Necessary for Survival

We have found that these new facts are not as biologically irrelevant as was assumed by us, however. In fact, the survival of our species and indeed of the life on our planet probably depend upon us incorporating this information into a newer and more *comprehensive understanding of reality* — or as I term it, an *overstanding* ... ideally a cosmic overstanding.

As Kuhn (1970) wrote,

> *The crises of our time, it becomes increasingly clear, are the necessary impetus for the revolution now under way. And once we understand nature's transformative powers, we see that it is our powerful ally, not a force to be feared or subdued.*[4]

Fortunately the construction of this new framework is being carried out. And it and its implications are astounding, revelatory, and revolutionary in all respects imaginable. My take on, as well as my additions to, this new revolutionary model is revealed in ever increasing detail throughout this book.

# The Scientific Culture War

It helps to keep in mind that science is a good candidate for instigating a revolution. For the political and social revolutions, which we are seeing erupt around the world from Arab Springs to American Autumns and in global Occupy movements, have been going on more quietly and for a longer time in our sciences. Indeed, it may be said that to some extent this scientific Awakening preceded and precipitated the social one.

That contemporary "normal" scientists are deaf to the clarion call of revolutionary science has everything to do with retreating from the world-shattering revelations of the recent past into the familiar surrounds of "normal" science, with all of its bland uncovering of that which was already assumed. Beyond some scientific laziness and lack of the passion of discovery, that cowardice or at least that refusal to be bold has mostly to do with the enslavement of scientific endeavors in the plantation fields ruled by corporate and consumer-driven interests. Real science, in recent times, takes a back seat to practical and applicable science operating to feed the demands of capitalist and ever-hungry-for-trinkets modern societies.

## This Scientific Awakening, However Necessary, Is Seen as a Threat to Corporate Hegemony

Thus — although our very survival depends on a paradigm change, or shift — it is being resisted mightily by our communities of scientific researchers. This Scientific Awakening is as much a threat to the corporate hegemony over modern culture as are the social and political Awakenings. There has been as much a battle in science over the last fifty years — a scientific culture war, if you will — as there has been the one in our societies around the world ... and for the same reasons.

Paradigm shift threatens the status quo. It is seen to have the potential to upset the traditional and engrained financial structures and the social stratification built upon them. That is, this scientific culture war is also class war in disguise. Though these new paradigms or overstandings are more life-facilitating or enhancing, and thus have a great value, relative at least to our species, they are not so much a boon for *every* human in our species. For older overstandings are invested in with the time and energies and lives of humans, so the humans most invested in them will not see any value in anything new, however better.

But scientists and intellectuals are as much a product of an old paradigm even when they propose to not be. So, often they mis-categorize new developments in their fields within old and outdated dualistic frames. In particular they see the findings of consciousness research and misconstrue it as being within the old science-religion debates and struggles. Hence they look not into it and overlook what otherwise would be obvious.

So they are as unable to see old-paradigm influences on themselves and are as clueless in moving beyond them as are their counterparts in the social, financial, and political arenas, where not just old paradigm right-wing folks are blind to the messages of the Awakening but even many traditional liberals are unable to see past their time-worn ways of categorizing in order to understand the message and import of the new-paradigm social and political movements of Occupy and Arab Spring. They misunderstood the Occupy movement's multi-messages and calls for complete re-visioning as being no message. They misconstrued the new-paradigm uprisings for freedom and justice throughout the world and especially in the Arab world in the tired old terminologies of economics and imperialism. They continue to misinterpret heartfelt aspirations for a global coming together and unity of humanity in old-paradigm New-World-Order terms. They misread new-paradigm seekings for consciousness change and revolution being bogged down in old-paradigm, reactionary, medieval even, illuminati concepts.

## A Call for Scientific Awakening

This is a call for sciences to allow themselves to let go of old ways and embrace new visions. In the past, it has taken centuries, at times, for these paradigm shifts to happen. Societies have had to wait, and entire generations have needed to die off before people could enjoy the freedom of being released from old bindings of thought and could realize the benefits of new revelations. We do not have that kind of time right now.

This new paradigm, gestating within the scientific community for fifty or so years previous to the Sixties, erupted out of that academic container and into the global consciousness, at that time, the Sixties, with the social and cultural revolutions begun then. These revolutionary elements have done battle within scientific communities as well as in the society-at-large; and in the same way as those social and cultural movements, they have been beaten back to the peripheries by the overwhelming power of the entrenched interests.

But entire generations have left the scene by now. New generations — the Millennial and Generation Z (the one following the Millennial) — seeded with the new-paradigm visions rained upon them by elder veterans of the culture war and enjoying fruits of wisdom plucked from an ongoing though less visible counterculture born in those times have arisen. So, the time is ripe.

The change is necessary. We can no longer afford to hesitate. The time for the Scientific Awakening is now. The time for a Cosmic Overstanding is equally imperative.

And to this we now turn. Having established that our scientific and other realities are relative; that anything we know only has value relative to its being biologically useful, specifically that it enhances life; and that the search for a truth more encompassing requires us to go, not just beyond the constraints of culture but also the constraints of biology (to the extent we can), and that first and foremost in that effort to look outside our biological blinders requires relinquishing the ego-centric, culture-centric, and anthropocentric entitlements that are part and parcel of what constrains our ability to transcend; that any attempt for anything greater must include greater amounts of experiential reality, thus it is driven by findings in consciousness research and psychology; and that in doing so we open to realities fantastic, but also wonderful; we can see that it is not only a worthwhile thing to do, not only a life-affirming and enhancing thing to do ... meaning it will make us a better and happier person in some sense ... but this effort, this attempt at biological transcendence or, using a word that means the same thing, ecstasy ... this effort at cosmic overstanding will be ... necessarily ...

fun.

Consider this your invitation to join the party. C'mon along as we continue the path of ecstasy to a cosmic overstanding.

# PART THREE

# Science as Myth

# 11

# The Footprint We Have Discovered Is Our Own:

## When Tradition and Religion Break Down, All Truth Is Liable to Bust Out: The Center of the Onion Is Nothing … The Last Secret to Be Told Is There Is No Secret

*"...belief/religion/ritual keep real feeling from happening. They also keep truth from happening. They keep spontaneity and authenticity from happening."*

## The Implications of Matter As Metaphor

Consistently applying the overstanding described so far, this new-paradigm perspective on matter and consciousness — as is attempted in this book … that is, of matter as an epiphenomenon of consciousness and the primacy-of-the-psychic-world postulate — requires a rethinking of theoretical constructions even in the fields of consciousness and psychology, which one would think at first hand to be amenable to this sort of view. However, our cultural context is such, our Western viewpoint so engrained, that even in these fields there seems a huge temptation to bow to the prevailing winds and a consequently understandable reluctance to go out on a limb against those.

Thus, we have many hybrids — theorists who it appears are trying to please too many people, too many former mentors, or whatever; and who find themselves, consequently, unable to go steadfastly forward, following through consistently on the implications of the transpersonal perspective. For example, from a consistent new-paradigm vantage point, Ken Wilber — the "consciousness" guru of the more intellectual, less experiential wing of the transpersonal movement — appears as inconsistent as pre-Copernican astronomers in devolving his theories.[1]

Therefore, much of these next parts will entail addressing the way the perspective presented in the previous parts of this book affects, expands, changes, and reverses the tenets put forth in transpersonal psychology and philosophy — especially those aspects associated with Ken Wilber.

# The Revolutionary Import, in Science, of the New-Paradigm Perspective

But let us set aside transpersonal thinking for the moment to focus on the larger picture. It may also be argued that in the larger context of normal science, in general, the new-paradigm primacy of consciousness is simply irrelevant.

However, I take strong exception to that. It is not simply innocuous that scientists refuse to acknowledge the implications of their findings. For in fact the implications of them would require a revolution and an overturning, and in many cases, a throwing out as obsolete of much of what scientists have paid highly for and struggled long and hard to learn.

# The Lengths To Which They Go

So it should not be too surprising to observe the lengths to which scientists will go in avoiding the implications of their findings. Their actions and behaviors have all the earmarks of what, in therapeutic circles, is called *denial*.

For example, Roger Jones (1982), a physicist, in his remarkable book titled *Physics As Metaphor*, points out how physicists in their day-to-day activities hardly consider the implications of Twentieth Century findings in their field. He begins by noting that, "Quantum mechanics, then, may just possibly imply an essential role for consciousness in the scheme of things…."[2]

Nevertheless, he adds that

> [T]he real issue is whether or not such ideas figure significantly in scientific research. It is, in fact, the rare scientist who is concerned with such matters. The Copenhagen interpretation may be the prevailing philosophy of quantum mechanics today … but it is hardly a hot topic over lunch at the research lab. Most scientists take a rather pragmatic and condescending view of philosophy, and its niceties have no direct bearing on their day-to-day research, thinking, and discussion…. Fifty years after the Copenhagen interpretation forced consciousness on an unwilling scientific community, there is precious little to be found in the research literature of physics to suggest any bridging of the mind-body gap.
>
> In fact, in the last fifty years, the trend in mainstream physical science has been away from consciousness and holism and toward the mechanistic and divisible world of the nineteenth century. Fritjof Capra argues that despite the much touted promises of an ultimate unification in physics, modern elementary particle and quark theory is basically a throwback to the atomistic, thing-oriented notions of premodern physics and is contrary to the holistic, process-oriented currents in modern thought.[3]

## The Emperor's New Clothes

In fact, Jones (1982) goes so far as to say that in teaching physics and in publicly maintaining its precepts he often felt as if he were living a lie:

> *I found myself thinking hard about why and how to interest children in science, and this in turn awakened several philosophical issues that had troubled me over the years. As a practicing physicist, I had always been vaguely embarrassed by a kind of illusory quality in science and had often felt somehow part of a swindle on the human race. It was not a conspiracy but more like the hoax in The Emperor's New Clothes. I had come to suspect, and now felt compelled to acknowledge, that science and the physical world were products of human imagining — that we were not the cool observers of the world, but its passionate creators.*[4]

## The Footprint We Have Discovered Is Our Own

His implication is that physicists are aware of the subjective and arbitrary nature of the pronouncements and assertions they make about physical reality. It follows that they assert, with such authority and with the certitude of fact, things which they know to be only conjecture, or at the most, conjuring.

Jones (1982) concurs,

> *I ... suggest that scientists (and indeed all who possess creative consciousness) conjure like the poet and the shaman, that their theories are metaphors which ultimately are inseparable from physical reality, and that consciousness is so integral to the cosmos that the creative idea and the thing are one and the same.*

> *What else are we to think when the theory of relativity teaches us that space and time are the same as matter and energy, that geometry is gravity? Is this not an equating, an integration, of mind and matter? Is this not an act of poetic, perhaps of divine, creation? And what of the astronomer's black hole, the perfect metaphor for a bottomless well in space from which not even light may escape? Which is the reality and which the metaphor? And what of quarks, the claimed ultimate constituents of matter, locked permanently within*

*the elementary particles they compose, never able to appear in the literal, physical world? Are they not constructs, figments of the mind, symbols for a collection of unobservable properties?*

*How is the quark more real than figurative? ... Indeed, as Sir Arthur Eddington said in 1920, the footprint we have discovered on the shores of the unknown is our own.[5]*

## Science as Idolatry

Finally, Jones goes so far as to equate with idolatry the elevation of such man-made scientific constructs to objective status. And he suggests that such deceptiveness and failure to be completely candid is linked to some of our major modern crises:

*For the full elaboration of the idea of science and the physical world as a construct of the mind or a collective representation, I owe a great debt to Owen Barfield and his writings, especially his book* Saving the Appearances — A Study in Idolatry. *It was Barfield who helped me most to fathom the deceptiveness of science by seeing that when metaphors become crystallized and abstract, cut off from their roots in consciousness, and forgotten by their creators, they become idols. For an idolator is not so much one who creates idols, but one who worships them.*

*This failure to recognize the central role of consciousness in reality and thus to treat the physical world as an independent, external, and alien object has been a chronic problem throughout the modern era of scientific discovery, since the Renaissance and the Enlightenment, and has reached a critical stage in the twentieth century with its unconscionable, and largely unconscious, ravaging of the environment.[6]*

# Breaking This Down: The Dire Import of Scientific Cowardice

Hence, refusing to acknowledge the central role of consciousness, which their own science has demonstrated to exist, scientists can deny consciousness to all of Nature and rape it.

Think back to how science once told us that babies did not feel pain. Remember how it was common for a doctor to smack a baby on the bum and, with infant screaming filling the room, for all and about to smile and congratulate each other on the abilities of its lungs? Scientists still do not acknowledge there is sentience in planetmates (animals) like there is in humans.

With those kinds of attitudes, all of Nature, including all of life, can be raped and exploited. And thus we have the situation today.

But those are just examples. There are plenty more.

Think of how medical science views us as just like machines — that is to say, without real consciousness — instead of holistically like they should. They fix and replace our parts. That is what comes from this attitude.

By contrast, primal peoples certainly do not and never did view humans and themselves that way in indigenous cultures.

Native Americans had planetmate spirit guides, and if they hunted, they asked forgiveness for taking its life. Whereas we treat sentient beings, planetmates, like they are items being produced in a factory … their parts nicely packaged. And they are raised with no consideration that they are conscious beings and feel pain.

When you objectify Nature the way we do, you get to the point, as we are, where we even begin to objectify ourselves and begin acting like things, like machines … like robots … not like souls or spirits with intrinsic, not to mention Divine, worth.

Does "The Matrix" fit anywhere here, one might ask.

Very much so, The Matrix fits in. This artificial construction … this objectification of the person and Nature *is* The Matrix. It is the artificial reality we consider more important — because we have been taught that — than our own lives, than our own loves, than our own feelings and experiences. And part of this, of course, is that we value ourselves not as emotional-spiritual beings but as economic units with specific numerals of measurement in dollars designating us.

The old-fashioned word for this is *dehumanization* … but of course that is only when we are speaking of this process with humans alone. But we do it with all of Nature. With all life, we do this process of reducing everything to its objective status only. And that way it can be *used*.

So you can no doubt see how this attitude in science goes hand in glove with a capitalistic system of economics which seeks to exploit all of Nature for someone's monetary gain.

And that brings us back to the point of this chapter. Science has gone beyond that understanding of reality but refuses to acknowledge that it has. So truth has been dismissed as irrelevant to profit, with dire consequences for everything and everyone on this planet.

# The Elders' "New Clothes"

This overall pattern of behavior, exhibited in our scientific priesthood, has remarkable parallels to something that happened in recent history … several decades ago … among a particular culture in Papua, New Guinea. As the story goes — according to a well-known anthropologist who was studying there at the time and observed the entire sequence of events — this particular tribe, from time immemorial, had perpetuated a sequence of male rites of passage beginning with adolescents of a certain age. The rites were especially brutal and humiliating, including the infliction of physical pain and deprivation and repetitive oral sex to be performed by the initiates for the pleasure of the elders.[7]

But in the course of them, the initiates were led to believe that great value would come from their endurance of the rites. For they would be given certain aspects of "secret" knowledge. Furthermore, they were informed of the various other stages in the rite that they would need to go through in the course of their life — each of which would be excruciatingly painful; but each of which would be rewarded with a little more of the secret knowledge until, near the end of one's life, one would be instructed into the highest knowledge of all: This was the knowledge that was the possession of only the most elderly males, the most "advanced" in said knowledge, in the culture.

These secrets were never shared with women. The women were never let in on any aspect, at any level, of the ceremonies that the males performed and underwent, nor any of the secrets they were told. Indeed, there was such a taboo against women finding out or males sharing secrets with females that death was used as a penalty for either infraction.

It follows that the whole truth was only known by the elders of the tribe.

Now, this anthropologist observed these ceremonies, studied them, and was let in on certain aspects of them. He could not be told "the whole truth" of course; for that was reserved for the elite, the elders — only those who had successfully completed all the stages of the ordeal, only those who had sufficiently suffered. And this anthropologist studied other aspects of the culture and returned again and again over the course of several decades.

But one time when he returned after a several year absence, he was to find everything changed. The elders no longer ruled with an iron hand, in fact they were despised and openly rebuked, especially by women. And the initiation ceremonies were no longer carried out.

The anthropologist, to his amazement, found out that what had happened is that a group of the elders had announced to one and all, in a large community-wide meeting, that *there were no secrets* they held, that *there never were.* The elders revealed that the entire deception of "the secrets" had been maintained for the purpose of getting younger men to go through the ceremonies — with the inducement of greater and greater rewards — and in order to ensure their power and status in the community. Essentially, these elder men "fessed up" that the only last secret to be told was that there was no last secret; that it was all a sham; that the entire foundation had nothing beneath it — like a house of cards built in the middle of the air; that the center of the onion, after peeling back layer after layer, was in fact nothing.

Now, how do we know the elders were telling the truth this time? We know this because they confessed in a state of great distress and guilt. They expressed again and again their shame at perpetuating the system. In fact, they let it be known that a big inducement they had for coming forth with the truth was the guilt they felt, in the rites, at having to follow through on inflicting suffering and torturing the younger men, all the time knowing the truth and the fact that there was no reason to be doing it. They said they simply could not bear the guilt, or the burden of lying anymore.

When I first heard this story, I could not help but think about its striking parallel to my situation in graduate school, where I happened to be at the time as a first-year doctoral student.

The rest of the story is that what had been happening is that the culture had been increasing its contacts and ties with the outside world; the villagers were becoming aware of other beliefs — a cargo cult in particular.[8]

And there were other signs to them of another world out there beyond that of their tribe.

In this light, it was speculated by anthropologists that this awareness of other realities other than that of one's own culture — the one that one was indoctrinated and tortured into accepting — may have had something to do with their losing faith in their way of doing things. It was suggested by such observers of the phenomenon that this had led to the elders finding themselves having remorse about such things as hurting other people — for they would now know that there are other ways of living and being; that everyone does not believe and live as one's own culture does. Hence that the torture and suffering were not absolutely necessary ... as they had once been convinced, and then continued to convince themselves. It might be said that losing ultimate, or "Divine," justification for their actions caused them to view them in the human context of the here-and-now relation. With their sights no longer in the heavens, they could finally observe the tribesmen before them.

Before continuing, I want to point out the congruence of this pattern with the example I was giving before about the ways that religions are able to espouse life-negating beliefs, and the actions emanating from them, by positing another realm where the good is made bad (like hell) and the bad, good (like heaven). Only in this case in New Guinea the justification of the bad, which made it "good," was that time, not in an afterlife, but at the culmination of the rites when the secret would finally be revealed that there was no secret. Suffering was made okay in the present through it being said to be the only way to a greater good.

As I said, looking cross-culturally is a great assistance to seeing beyond such flawed understandings and to bringing one's understand-ings of things in line with one's natural conscience, rooted in quite ordinary, and profound, empathy. As an example, religions that encourage war, clitorectomy, witch-burning, lynchings, and pogroms, viewed in multicultural context, lose their potency in driving such behavior when their rationalization that such atrocity is rectified, indeed made superlative, in some bizarro afterlife where the bad is made good (wars, witch burnings, clitorectomies) and the good is made bad (sexuality, for example) are seen in contrast to the beliefs of other peoples. Given alternatives, through multicultural understanding, and diluting the power of an unassailed belief system to force compliance of cultural atrocity, one is left to rely on simple conscience and fellow feeling. And this changes everything ... and for the better.

Another parallel to Western culture that I see is to that which happened in the Sixties, at the beginning of the postmodern era. For indeed this was a time when the truisms of Western material culture and capitalist-imperialist worldwide hegemony married with conventional religious orthodoxy would be broken down and left in tatters in its confrontation with a multicultural world and an influx of scientific findings which challenged all orthodoxies. The international event that would precipitate this awareness would be the Vietnam War, of course. Here also it was the exposure to an outside world of many cultural understandings that was the precipitating event. And, it would have a similar result: People knowing that alternative ways were possible would question old ways that involved violence that their consciences cringed at but which previously they carried through on when they thought there was no alternative. What followed that was an extravaganza of national finger-pointing and soul searching and a quest to find deeper foundations for right action and life purpose.

Anyway, getting back to New Guinea, this is a true story. Still, it can be seen as a parable or metaphor for many things currently arising and especially so in the sciences. In addition to what it tells us about knowledge and epistemologies, the last part especially might be telling us a lot about the effects, one might say benefits, to be wrought, in terms of truth, by this century's increasing mixing of cultures and races and by the worldwide emergence of a multiculturalism as a common basis of global belief. We might also relate its message to the inauthentic nature of ritual and of initiation. For they bring about individual actions contrary to one's desires, intents, or conscience, and they substitute those of culture and society, especially the elite sectors of that. Without such brutal insistence by outside forces, these actions would not come forth … they simply would not happen under the aegis of one's empathy, conscience, and fellow feeling. This story also says something about how when belief and ritual are removed, real feelings, authentic feelings are possible.

This might be considered a directly opposite interpretation of the normal explanation of ritual/religion/beliefs and their relation to feeling, by the way. The traditional explanation is that without such ritual/religion/belief people are left at the mercy of their aggressive and incestuous inner natures. Thus, when religion breaks down, all hell breaks loose — and then the situation in modern urban societies is usually pointed to, to bear this out.

However my interpretation is that belief/religion/ritual *keep real feeling from happening*. They also keep truth from happening. They keep spontaneity and authenticity from happening. Therefore, when religion breaks down, all truth is liable to break loose. And this is bound to be a bit disruptive at first — as it is true that any dam that holds a river in check is going to see that river explode across the countryside at first until it finally comes to rest in its normal stable peaceful courseway!

But most of all this story reminds me of what Jones wrote about his fellow physicists — those scientists who through the suffering of years of tortuous graduate study and the equally challenging hoops of research, research grants, and university tenure tracks are led to face the foundations of their beliefs as being as equally insubstantial as those tribal elders knew theirs to be. In this respect, Jones's book, *Physics As Metaphor* (1982), is practically the Western equivalent of such a confession as those tribal elders put before their people. Indeed, his feelings at carrying around the lie, the "deception" or "swindle," are remarkably akin to those of the guilt-ridden tribal elders, so many thousands of miles and so many millions of cultural beliefs distant.

So we can be thankful to Jones for the profound insight he affords us. However, and thankfully, we find that he is not alone in doing so.

# 12

# Restoring Nobility to Nature:

Morphic Resonance, Lamarck, Morphogenetic
Fields, and the Mind of God ... All Is
Subjectivity, Everything We Think and Do
Affects All Reality

*"Science itself has now superseded the mechanistic
world view." — Rupert Sheldrake*

## Dire Consequences of Scientists' Closed-Mindedness

Biologist, natural scientist, and philosopher Rupert Sheldrake (1991a)
also describes this radical dissociation between the day-to-day
approach and workings of the common scientist and their best
understandings of the nature of the phenomena they study. And he
explains why this dissociation might occur:

*Although science is now superseding the mechanistic world view, the mechanistic theory of nature has shaped the modern world, underlies the ideology of technological progress, and is still the official orthodoxy of science.*[1]

And furthermore about this reluctance to change: "It has had many consequences, not the least of which is the environmental crisis."[2]

Robert Lawlor (1991), from his cross-cultural perspective, echoes this perception of scientists and their innate conservatism in the face of their own contrary findings:

*Despite the advances in relativity and quantum theory, scientists still expect to view a world in which things are exactly as they appear to be, discrete and unperturbed by the subjective depths of the mind from which our very perceptions and rational intellect emerge.*[3]

And further on:

*Meanwhile, the old thought patterns and linguistic practices, along with the social, political, military, economic, and medical institutions based on Aristotle, Descartes, and Newton go rolling along. Furthermore, the same scientific priesthood, for a price, continues to supply those institutions with the knowledge and technological equipment by which they sustain their power.*[4]

# The Revolutionary Import

And yet, the implications of these empirically-rooted, experimentally reproducible discoveries about the Reality which we share are profoundly important and influential in that they affect the very foundations upon which the rest of science's other findings, discoveries, and theories are built.

Rupert Sheldrake (1991a) points out that the findings of science have overturned all of science's original premises. First he lists nine "essential features of the mechanistic world view":

1. Nature is inanimate
2. Inert atoms of matter

3. Determinate, predictable
4. Knowable
5. Universe a machine
6. Earth dead
7. No internal purposes
8. No creativity
9. Eternal laws[5]

You will notice how many of these aspects of the mechanistic worldview overlap with what is normally called "materialism." At any rate, Sheldrake (1991a) then states, and goes on to demonstrate, that "every one of those essential claims has been refuted by advances of science. In effect, science itself has now superseded the mechanistic world view."[6]

Despite scientists' reluctance to face the implications of their discoveries and their insistence on clinging to the familiar, it is our duty to shed popular or convenient positions when they are contradicted by the evidence ... or else we should give up our scientific endeavor's claim to be a truthful one. In so doing, Sheldrake's (1991a) conclusion is that

> *The modern changes in science have effectively transcended each of these features. These changes in science have not happened as part of a coordinated research programme designed to overthrow the mechanistic paradigm. They have happened in specialized areas, seemingly unconnected with each other, and often without any consciousness that this was leading to a change in the overall world view of science. What I am going to suggest is that we can now see that this has effectively refuted the mechanistic world view within the very heart of science itself.* [7]

But let us just now take one specific example. Let us consider the example of Darwinian evolution. This theory of evolution and natural selection is so widely accepted that it is hard to find an alternative explanation of these processes even presented, let alone discussed, in the textbooks of natural science. And yet there have been those in the past. The Lamarckian explanation is one of them. Emanationism is another.

# Debunking Neo-Darwinism and the Reemergence of Lamarck

For our purposes now, I wish to simply demonstrate how it is that science's current discoveries can be said to overthrow so much of what is considered established about evolution. Rupert Sheldrake gives us a good example of that in his explaining that, in his opinion, based on the evidence for morphic resonance and morphogenetic fields, genes are actually a small part, perhaps even an inessential part of the process of evolution.[8]

He writes,

> At each of these levels there is an organizing field containing an inherent memory, called a morphic field. And the basis of this memory is a process I call morphic resonance, the influence of like upon like. So each baby giraffe, as it grows, tunes in to the experience of all previous giraffes, through morphic resonance. It taps into a kind of collective pooled memory of the species, and in turn contributes to it. This applies, according to this hypothesis, to all animals and plants and people and also to crystals and molecules and planetary systems. It operates at all levels of nature.[9]

And further on:

> This leads to a new interpretation of heredity and evolution. Heredity depends both on genetic inheritance (chemical genes made up of DNA) and also on morphic resonance from past members of the species. In relation to form and behavior, I think that morphic resonance is much the most important component. I am suggesting, in other words, that genes are grossly overrated.[10]

Furthermore: "morphic resonance permits a more rapid evolution than the standard neo-Darwinian theory, based on random mutation and natural selection...."[11]

Thus, all of our elaborate theorizing about genetic factors in evolution are, by the evidence of morphogenetic fields, put in a questionable category. The implications of Sheldrake's theory are no less than that what scientists normally consider to be the causative factors in both heredity and evolution are in fact either only a small, but not very influential, however measurable, aspect of such factors — like the veritable observable tip of a much more expansive iceberg — or that they are *totally unrelated* to the actual causative factors of such processes. In either case, scientists are understandably threatened by such an assault on the foundations of their beliefs, work, and dearly bought academic indoctrination. To paraphrase a joke, it is a morphogenetic night out, and the scientists are nervous.

Furthermore, Sheldrake's theory gives rise to a conception of evolution — one that scientists have been taught to discredit, one which scientists have learned to smugly position themselves above, to pooh-pooh and snicker at. This alternative theory is the Lamarckian view of evolution.

# Restoring Nobility to Nature

What I am saying is it appears that science along with modern consciousness research has unveiled a new-paradigm vision of evolution which overturns the dog-eat-dog Darwinian one. For Sheldrake's theory points to initiative and effort, even honor, as the engine of evolution. Let me explain.

Briefly stated, the Lamarckian view is that repetitive actions made by individual members of a species, leading to certain changes in themselves, will also cause certain changes in the genes, which will then lead to those changes being observed in the offspring.

Essentially the theory states that to some extent, however small, acquired characteristics of the parents can be passed on to offspring. And that it is the buildup of such minute changes in the generations following that we observe as the process of evolution. This view attempts to explain, for example, how giraffes can come to have long necks by saying that it is the result of innumerable generations of giraffe progenitors straining to reach the leaves of high trees.

Supposedly this idea is discredited because it is not seen how either mental events or their resulting repetitive actions — that is to say, either the desires of the giraffes for the higher leaves or the behavior of reaching and stretching — could actually change or affect the physical composition of genes and the basic units of DNA of which they are composed. DNA and genes are only known by scientists to be changed by mutations in their structure through radiation or other actual physical alterations.

All things considered, then, a Lamarckian theory is discredited because of a physicalist perspective ... can we at least at this point begin to use the word *bias*? ... that says that mental or behavioral events cannot be transferred from one generation to the next unless they somehow do this through physical matter. Remember that this is matter as defined by us and is that which is capable of being externally perceptible to us. It is matter that is defined by limited humans and their scientific "toys." And it is matter which has had excluded from it all traces of the only reality one can ever actually know to be true — one's subjectivity. It is matter that is construed by our biologically constituted realities and our bioculturally constituted ones as well, if we would be totally honest.

So we employ our subjectivity, as scientists, following outdated notions from Descartes, Newton, and Aristotle, to blind us to the existence of subjectivity.

If the irrationality of that is not enough, consider the abominable unconsciousness and insensitivity that comported with those beliefs and contributed to their conceptualization. In regard to Descartes, his ideas emanated from a time so blind to feeling that researchers were able to marvel at the magnificent "machinery" of live planetmates who were nailed to wooden frames and cut open — vivisected — to reveal the workings of heart and other organs, while the cat, to take one example, was still fully conscious. Consider the views of Aristotle arising during a time when pedophilia was common ... not to mention misogyny. Their insensitivities are understandable within the context of their eras, but need they be in ours?

We might assert that we have gone beyond such practices as planetmate torture ... though we have not ... and pedophilia ... again, though we have not. But if scientists want to proclaim the attainment of such humanity within themselves, they are not consistent if they simultaneously embrace the philosophical outcroppings of such practices. For example, it was the vivisection that Descartes observed which led him to his ideas of the Universe as being a machine. We see here how an abominably insensitive consciousness gives rise to theologies of its own design, supporting and justifying itself.

If you do not see how the two — the insensitive consciousness and the reasonings and deductions it makes — are inseparable and how reason cannot stand on its own merit for it brings with it innumerable assumptions of moral and philosophical import, consider how observations on the practice of slavery in pre-Civil War times and seeing African Americans as subservient and ignorant ... as they were made to be ... might, if not challenged, lead to philosophies premised on the assumption of an inherent hierarchy of humans, in accordance with race. In fact, if that sounds far-fetched, consider that such philosophical abominations, during the time of the Third Reich in Germany, arose out of the "scientific" observations of that time and place — as full of unacknowledged bias as they were and similar to what we have today in our science — which led to the atrocities of that era.

That we do not still hold such beliefs about Blacks and Jews today has everything to do with the fact that 1) they, as humans and to the extent they could, were able to resist and fight back against such atrocious renderings of their worth, and 2) other humans — those with sensitivity and empathy — were impelled to seek to right what was felt as such an abominable wrong. The first is hardly possible with planetmates and children. We will be waiting a long time if we require the rising up of planetmates against us and/or their creation of symposia on their feeling consciousness before we include that in our understandings of them. With children, the same. So, the revelation of greater understanding relies on the second — the existence of sensitivity and empathy in the rest of us.

And that is what my reasoning here addresses and attempts. It is only be appealing to our sensitivity and feelings of empathy that we can have a chance to see through the biases that lie at the basis of modern beliefs. But the beliefs have the same raison d'être in all situations: That is, the glorification of individual Ego and species ego — anthropocentrism. Do you see what a fallacy it is to think that the greatest truth is had when one eliminates all feeling and emotion from one's thinking?

The opposite is true. It is our feelings that can lead us beyond ourselves and our individual and collective egos of culture and species. We see how it is that very thing, one's conscience and the feelings it gives rise to, which led to the progression out of the blind torture and inhumanity of the initiation rites in Papua, New Guinea in the previous chapter. Whereas, the myth of detached rationality can be seen, with no counter to it able to rise up, to be unconsciously directed along lines to support itself in only what it already, and self-servingly, believes. And that underlying belief is in fact that separation of subject from object.

So, the underlying belief determines the result that will be found … again. Whereas the only truth that we can truly discover — outside of that which we have predetermined with our beliefs — can be arrived at only along with a fully conscious awareness that one is oneself a subjective being with tendencies led by feelings, emotions, and desires. It is only when in full knowledge that one's thinking tends a particular way, when uninhibited, that one can use reason to counter one's proclivities and look into alternatives to it. Whereas, an unknown prejudice reasserts itself everywhere and proves itself beyond a doubt repeatedly. No new truth can ever be seen.

You see, thus, how detached reason, unchallenged, is no different from blind belief. We only thought differently because we, following our prejudices, believed ourselves to be above our biology of feeling and emotion to begin with — that self-repeating anthropocentrism again. It is only by acknowledging the parameters of our understandings that we can at all hope to peek over the fences constraining our beliefs to see what might be truer … not to mention, simply correct.

We pridefully pronounce how we have learned that scientists cannot study reality without changing it, that humans cannot observe the world they live in without in some sense creating it. Yet we ignore the implications of that. What follows from it are that scientific and other attempts at truthful findings cannot be separated from their historical and social contexts. This is not to say that all of science is "mere ethnoscience." According to my earlier reasoning, there are factors of applicability of knowledge that can be used along which to evaluate the truthfulness, or worth, of competing frames of understanding. Yet it should lead at least to a more humble acknowledgment of the relativity of one's conjectures and a greater willingness to afford some respect to alternate, however seemingly "exotic," interpretations of the same observations.

So beliefs in the status of physicality as the only, or primary, reality arise from people who are Nazi-like in their view of other lives, human and other planetmate ... who have repressed their sensitivity, conscience, sense of fellow feeling, and inherent morality. That we should look to such shriveled up souls for insight is an admission of the strange and corrupted sensitivities of our own selves.

In any case, the physicalists we follow — despite that pedigree of tainted origins — in regard to evolution assert, nevertheless, that the only thing that can be transferred to subsequent generations is what is actually given to the next generation by way of the sperm and egg cells of the parents, and at base, the genetic material contained in them, the DNA. And since that genetic material is not in any way altered by such mental or behavioral events, the reasoning goes, there can be no connection between these events in these different generations.

Let us leave aside for now the exciting new research by Bruce Lipton and others demonstrating the alteration of the DNA within a cell as a result of the experience or learning of that cell. This research demonstrates remarkably — along with completely debunking as well as reversing what we have asserted about consciousness arising out of and depending on a physical basis — that indeed it is physicality (the material universe) that arises out of and depends on an experiential basis. However, the point I wish to make at this particular time is that it is *only* after accepting this physicalist bias, and its resulting negation of an alternative hypothesis, that the neo-Darwinian theory of natural selection becomes viable, indeed, becomes at all necessary. It is only after discrediting the preceding, more organically plausible Lamarckian hypothesis, that the theory of occasional genetic mutations by radiation or other extreme factor leading to higher survivability among slightly different offspring begins to look like anything but a strained explanation.

Granted that some changes between generations of offspring do change in this way. That has been proven beyond a doubt in the laboratories. But it has yet to be demonstrated that these seemingly rare occurrences can account for the immense variation of life or the incredible rate of evolutionary change relative to such a mechanism working alone.

Consequently, cutting edge scientists, in biology and elsewhere, are going against this theory on this last point alone. Lawlor (1991) says of them:

> *There is no evidence that random mutations can produce new species or that complex organs can develop as a result of mutation and selection. The eye, for example, could emerge only as a result of thousands of simultaneous mutations — a mathematical impossibility. Nor has it been explained how organisms could develop new behavior patterns to adjust positively to genetic changes. Mathematicians have protested that only one in 20 million mutations can be expected to be positive. Generating new species through natural selection by means of mutated genes seems about as probable, in the words of astronomer Fred Hoyle, "as a tornado sweeping through a junkyard assembling a Boeing 707."*[12]

Still, there *is* the evidence for morphogenetic fields, which not only overturns the need for the Darwinian mechanism of natural selection, but also highly supports the previously discredited Lamarckian view. And I might add it restores to humans a view of natural process much more complimentary to inner-directed behavior and much more supportive of good efforts made in honorable directions than is the Darwinian theory which, in its appearance of support for the physically strongest, and its seeming rationalization of a "dog eat dog" and "kill or be killed" world, has been used to justify all kinds of brutal uses of force — through war and forceful domination and suppression by powerful individuals and groups in governments and other social bodies.

## Morphic Resonance and Lamarck

Sheldrake's morphic resonance theory supports the Lamarckian view and makes the theory of genetic evolution in general obsolete in this way: Basically, the theory of morphogenetic fields is supported by evidence that indicates that information is passed between individuals according to their degree of similarity. Therefore, if knowledge from one generation changes a particular field which can then be picked up by succeeding generations, it means that the whole idea of genetic mutations, and so on, is completely unnecessary; that the whole idea of genetic mutations and evolution, natural selection, and survival of the fittest is simply an explanation that is based upon the assumption of the primacy of the physical universe or the primacy of our concepts of the physical universe.

However if we consider the primacy of consciousness "fields," then we see that if consciousness is considered to be primary, and consciousness is considered to be fields which are affected simply by consciousness, then the whole idea of finding how a physical, biological organism is changed in order to affect evolution is unnecessary. One does not have to try to find a way that actions and their subsequent learnings might lead to future knowing unless one posits ahead of time that learning can only affect knowledge if it is funneled through an infinitesimally tiny dot of matter — the DNA. Furthermore, if consciousness is changed through learning, and consciousness is the basis on which later generations are changed, then we have a complete revolution, a total revolution, a total new-paradigm revolution in theories of evolution and natural selection.

Thus, Rupert Sheldrake's morphic resonance theory relates to a new-paradigm vision of evolution. The essence of this new-paradigm view — as opposed to the old-paradigm stance which holds that the world is basically matter and that consciousness is an epiphenomenon of matter — is that the world is basically consciousness or subjectivity and that the material universe is an epiphenomenon of consciousness.

# All Is Subjectivity ... Simply Thinking New Thoughts or Acting New Behaviors Affects All That Exists

Affirming this idea of the primacy of Consciousness and the epiphenomenal nature of matter, we have Sathya Sai Baba's statement that all there is, is the "I" or the Atma and that this is the foundation for everything else; everything else is illusion. All that really exists is the "I." This is the predominant view of mystics. And it is the same as saying in Western philosophy that subjectivity is the only true reality.

## Subjectivity Is Primary and Morphogenetic Fields

This is in line with the viewpoint — a common Idealist, Eastern, Gnostic, and Jungian one — that the so-called "objective" reality is indirect perception and is dependent upon subjective reality; and so subjective reality is the only true reality that can be known.

Considering this traditional Idealist view together with Sheldrake's ideas and their Lamarckian consequences, one realizes that the predominant view of evolution — that it is based upon natural selection caused by mutations of chromosomes and genes, and so on — is actually a *rationalization* based upon an *a priori* presumption of the prior existence of the material universe. That is, that since the Lamarckian version — which is that changes are made in the biology of an organism based upon psychological strivings — cannot be demonstrated within a Newtonian-Cartesian world view, a materialistic worldview, then and only then we must postulate a mechanism for accounting for biological changes over generations, as in the theory of natural selection.

## "Billiard Balls" ... "Normal" Natural Selection

This theory of natural selection basically states that random changes occur in the chromosomes — mutations; "billiard balls" from the universe come in, so to speak, and rearrange the molecules of DNA, changing the chromosomes — which then have effects on the psychology and the biology of the organism. According to the theory, this may have positive benefits in terms of natural selection. And if they are positive for the species overall, then the members of that species who get those particular physical characteristics will tend to reproduce more and will therefore reproduce those offspring with those physical characteristics.

But all of this is a justification based upon the idea that there needs to be some kind of physical substrate to explain the changes. Whereas, in fact we see that evolution happens much more frequently than would be possible to be explained by natural selection, as just described. Indeed, it happens much more frequently and much faster.

# Science Demonstrates That Psychological, Subjective Changes Affect the Rest of Reality

A Lamarckian view comes necessarily to mind because of this, and the only thing that keeps one from immediately suspecting the Lamarckian view is the old bugaboo of the prior assumption of a materialistic universe.

However, if we consider that all is subjectivity, that subjectivity is the prior reality, then the Lamarckian view stands supreme. Restated in terms of Rupert Sheldrake's theory, it is that certain things that are learned through striving or effort or by a particular organism change the energetic field for the entire universe in that respect. So that not only offspring of that species, but also contemporaries of that species will be more likely to learn that.

What we are saying is that psychological changes — you might say changes in subjectivity — affect all the rest of reality, all the rest of consciousness ... and this can be demonstrated. It can be demonstrated, for example in experiments dating back seventy years which show that successive generations of rats learn specific tasks more quickly than their parents and that a phony Morse code is more difficult to learn than the real one. More recently, studies have supported the theory. For example, it was determined that people will more easily solve a crossword puzzle after it has appeared in print than before, in both cases without any prior exposure to it. In such a situation, the only change is that a great many minds have undoubtedly been working the puzzle after its publication, and this must have some effect, albeit nonphysical, on the performance of the later group.[8]

In another experiment specifically involving Rupert Sheldrake's theory, a group learned a particular random sample of items, memorizing them. It was discovered that just having that group memorize that series of items brought about the situation that in future learnings other groups were more easily able to learn that series of random groupings than other randomly created series.[8]

So what I am saying is this gives us a view of reality which is both deterministic and yet includes the subjective qualities of insight and choice. This is true in that each and every thing that happens in the Universe has a tendency to happen, a probability to happen, based on particular fields that have to do with the way they have happened in the past or what has been done in the past. But these fields are chosen and built up by free choice. Indeed, they were originally created by free choice.

So it is as if all of our actions or the greater percentage of our actions are determined by these fields or are pushed or pulled by these fields; that we have tendencies to act in particular ways; that every thought we have tends a particular way because of these fields of things happening the way they happened before.

But the full story includes the fact that we have the possibility to change those patterns; that we have the ability to choose to create new patterns which are then more likely to happen.

This possibility, this view of the way things work, also helps explain the observed increasing likelihood or possibility for people to deal with their feelings — specifically, even, to re-experience birth feelings — to have increasing access to other unfamiliar (in Western culture) experiences such as cellular memory, ancestral memory, past-lives memory, and so on, when increasing numbers of other people have had those experiences.

## Everything We Think and Do Affects All of Consciousness

This is a new-paradigm view in that it links all events or says that each and every thing that we do is part of a consciousness that we all partake of, and so each and every thing that we do affects the whole in at least a small way.

In fact it affirms that what we do individually affects the whole in a great way if what we do is truly a creative act. We raise ourselves up, thus, together — that is, as a species, not simply individually. In this way we are One Mind, regardless how much we might assert our separateness.

The new-paradigm essence of it is summed up in that — regardless of whether or not the thing was shared or expressed — simply the thinking of new thoughts or the acting out of new behaviors affect Consciousness in its entirety and all of humanity, in particular.

# The Mind of God

This gives us a totally new vantage point from which to survey the vast heavings of evolution over the course of millions and billions of years. For they appear then as the cumulative results of infinite numbers of tiny actions, choices, and efforts by infinite numbers of infinitely varied beings, species. What we see externally, thus, is the outer form of a shared mind that embraces all of Nature on Earth for all time. The overview of evolution on Earth, in its configurations, with all of its intricacies, gives us the closest thing we can get to a look at "God's Mind," exhibiting God's intent. The same is true when we look to astronomy and we overview the nature of the Cosmos and its change and evolution over time.

However, on Earth we see God's intent in "our neighborhood." That is the most illuminating place to start. Looking at the course and contours of evolution in this light is quite a profound meditation on Divinity, revealing somewhat the nature of Divinity. In it we sense somewhat the nature of ourselves. What pops to mind, for example, is this:

## Divinity Is Playful

We see a Universe fervently desiring and intently involved in an infinite variety of experience of Itself, for one.

This shows Nature as playful, sometimes humorous, and as ever expanding in all directions to explore more variety of possibilities of Existence. It is seen as dramatic, yet peaceful.... It shows a value on beauty for its own sake and on pleasure and bliss as the basis of all normal motivations.

## Divinity Is Loving

It includes the attraction of like to like and the ever occurring merger of one with another. It thus manifests both love and empathy as the profound motivating principles of evolution.

## Divinity's Plan Includes Imperfection

It shows a God intent on being imperfect so as to bring about the story of ever increasing achievement toward perfection, with the goal never attainable, yet the process and the path and the experience of that being the point of it. We perceive an infinite learning experience of the Divine, manifesting physically in the anatomies of organisms.

What it does *not* show are those dog-eat-dog, kill-or-be-killed intents we normally attribute to Nature. For, regardless of the existence of those in particular contexts, in all possible wider contexts that we can see, we observe that destruction as being merely infinite leveling mechanisms clearing the field for infinite numbers of new "games," new dramas of excitement and enjoyment. We see how ridiculous it was to think that existence, sustainability, and progress could be built upon motivations of opposing interests negating each other … for what would be left? We see that, whereas that process of mutual opposition leading to negation is part of the mix, that Reality exists, maintains, and moves forward exclusively on the basis of mutual intent, common ground, shared understanding, collective-interest (not self-interest), and cooperation. For the Eastern-minded, this means that whereas the Shiva factor is an important part of the process, the majority of existence relies on the Vishnu factor.

## Divinity Desires Drama

In any case, this puts human intent, and intent of all beings, in the center of the engine of evolution, in the driver's seat of the advance of time. And the result of those intentions, arising out of the mind of God, is the creation of infinite worlds, with infinite and profound variety, with infinite eyes and vantage points for viewing Itself. And it shows a duality, which makes manifest every single thing in contrast to its opposite. The outgrowth of that duality is seen to be the creation of an heroic motive for positive to overcome negative in an endless cyclical process which glorifies the story as the end of it all. With death not existing, yet time being made manifest, this all reveals a Divine appetite, if you will, for narrative, for the entertainment of Itself through a process of a duality of hiddenness and revelation, alternating, and producing delight.

## Divinity Is Ad-Venturing … and Fun

It shows the Universe engaged in an endless game of peek-a-boo with itself, the mind of God as intending to bring joy and enjoyment into existence within a context of infinite wonder and beauty. It shows the Universe as endlessly venturing out of Itself — ad-venturing — for no other reason than the experience of it and the glorification of the All in the appreciation of itself.

It shows the Mind of God, at its base, desiring fun. You heard me right. Gods just want to have fun.

# 13

# Emanationism Revival:

## A Revolution in the Direction of Growth — Panentheism, Krause, and the Cyclical Nature of Time and Change

*Linear versus Cyclical Development ... Ladders and U-Turns*

## Emanationism and the Cyclical Nature of Time and Change

*Emanationism* is another important non-mechanistic perspective that comes out of the new consciousness research, the new physics, and quantum theory. Like the Lamarckian view of evolution and the subjectivity-as-primary postulate of Reality, it, also, is ridiculed and pooh-poohed by the many self-ordained "rational" persons of science. But like the others, it, too, is given new credibility and life through some of those same "inconvenient" findings of science which overturn common-sense materialism and neo-Darwinism.

Emanationism is a view of our changes over time that suggests that we *devolve* from an original pure state to increasingly diffracted, diffused, and more impure states of being. It asserts that, rather than evolving to higher forms, we descend from a highest form to lower and lower forms as we get farther from an original source. On "Emanationism," *Wikipedia* says,

> Emanationism is an idea in the cosmology or cosmogony of certain religious or philosophical systems. Emanation, from the Latin emanare *meaning "to flow from" or "to pour forth or out of", is the mode by which all things are derived from the First Reality, or Principle. All things are derived from the first reality or perfect God by steps of degradation to lesser degrees of the first reality or God, and at every step the emanating beings are less pure, less perfect, less divine. Emanationism is a transcendent principle from which everything is derived, and is opposed to both Creationism (wherein the universe is created by a sentient God who is separate from creation) and materialism (which posits no underlying subjective and/or ontological nature behind phenomena being immanent).*[1]

The importance of such a distinction in the views of the nature and direction of Reality might not be obvious. But it is supremely relevant to just about everything we think of as advance or development: In spirituality or spiritual growth, it determines whether or not one can pile up spiritual "accomplishments," ladder-style, step-by-step and analogous to the way one acquires credits toward a scholastic degree, or whether one needs to let go and *stop* trying to control one's development and instead place the source of one's plan for eternity *outside* of the Ego. It has much to say about the so-called "advances" of civilization and points to an idea that these accomplishments take a much higher toll than they provide benefits; the net result being that we continually retreat, not advance, with technological and cultural elaboration.

It has something to say about our development in life and whether we lose more than we gain as we get older, alongside the measure of perhaps the most important things of life. It might say something to a physicist pondering the Big Bang and its aftermath as well about where one might look for the more optimal state of the

Universe — something we approach, an Omega Point, or something we left behind, an Origin or Source. For the traditional Western view in each case sees all growth and development as linear and upward; whereas the Emanationist view in each case sees Reality more like the ways indigenous folks and our progenitors saw it: Reality as a cycle, with times of decline followed eventually, and fortuitously, by eternal returns to states of renewed vitality.[1]

If you think about it, the two views have two different inherent attitudes in them, corresponding to two different psychologies. As a psychotherapist, they strike me as embodying opposite stances towards life; for example as we get depending on whether we had nurturing times at our origins — that is, in the womb, at birth, and in infancy — which gives rise to a stance of basic trust toward Reality. Or one did not, which gives rise to basic mistrust.

The one, the linear or evolutional embodies basic mistrust and implies effort as the engine of change. For the world is felt to be resistant and not forthcoming. It is felt to be obtuse, ignorant, selfish even, and at odds with oneself — just as one feels about a stiffening, hardening placenta, a difficult birth, and/or an unloving, non-nurturing mother once born. One better pick oneself up and do it, for life is not easy and it will not be given over easily. "There is no free lunch," as they say.

Whereas the other, the cyclical and emanational, implies Reality to be a bounteous and beneficial Other that gives up blessings easily and is supportive and nurturing. One receives these gifts and does with them what one will, and over time they are depleted, to be replenished again. It is similar to the pattern of being fed, in that one receives all that one needs and uses it up over time, for there is plenty more and it will be given again. It implies a benevolent outside world or Other, who or that is giving, gracious, generous. Whereas the other — the linear, effortful, and evolutional — embodies an attitude that nothing comes from nothing and the only thing one gets is what one earns.

When you look at it, these emanational versus evolutional stances are easily seen to be views that are characteristically matriarchal versus patriarchal and primal versus civilizational, and they contain all the implications of those diverse perspectives, in each case.

You see, perhaps, how these stances toward Reality, embodied in the thrusts of civilizations, can be seen to have roots in our earliest experiences and in culture's varying modes of caring for its newest members at and around birth and infancy.

These are hardly ontological stances unaffected by personality and individual or collective psychology ... or by culture, for that matter.

Still, I understand the Emanationist view sounds strange in our times. For we live in an oh-so-effortful and stressful age of solitary individuality, dog-eat-dog capitalism, and Ayn Randian Western assumptions. It is a period of history where Tea Partiers and patriarchal mouthpieces abound on Fox News and in politics and decry the softness implicit in modern trends. This is an era that espouses hard work and individual effort as the only valid mode of advance and that abhors socialism as weakness and turns its back on the collectivism, cooperation, sharing, and tribalism of primal cultures. However, keep in mind that the idea of Emanationism is central in the concepts of rebirthing, of being "born again" in religions, and of renewal of any sort that is sought in any endeavor, spiritual-psychological or secular.

For it is hugely important when seeking to be reborn to have the view that a return to birth is not a loss of all that one has but that a return is one to a fuller state which contains more of what one is but was lost over the course of time. Even psychotherapy needs to understand this notion that — though they apply it only to neurosis — going back to a time before the trauma that created the neurosis or working through that trauma allows one to regain something that was lost that is superior to what one arrived at, in that a person splits off from a healthy development into an unhealthy one because of the trauma. So these notions are not all *that* different from some of the things we already take for granted.

Keep in mind, also, that Emanationism is in line with right-brain or "organic" thinking, which sees progress as growing outward in all directions at the same time from a Source which is also then the End Point. It describes a Reality that is contained within itself and complete.

Meanwhile a traditional view of progress has development being linear and in line with left-brain thinking which posits everything in cause and effect relation from a dim, unforeseeable beginning to an incomprehensible Omega Point at the opposite end of Infinity … which is a mathematical impossibility, by the way, so even it, though linear, is not logical. So, such a linear idea is flat-earth-like in being true and applicable only in limited regions, while not conceivable in any comprehensive or ultimate view.

So while such an idea as Emanationism might sound strange these days … thus reinforcing my argument for the overweening success of the theory of evolution as being an ever advancing movement leading up to magnificent us, of course … yet it was one that was common among ancient philosophers. It was and is a common "primitive" — a better word is *primal* — depiction of the way things work. It is a cornerstone of ancient Gnostic teachings. A good deal of ancient Greek philosophy is presented this way — for example, the writings of Plotinus and Proclus. It is the perception of Hindu cosmology, even up to this day, with the belief in a system of *yugas* or ages — each one being a decline from the previous one.

Strangest of all, it appears in a physical form … almost as if it had to come out somewhere, even if only "reflected" … in the theory of cosmic origins put forth by the scientific community called the Big Bang theory. People this very day have this conception in mind, also, in thinking there might be some renewal on the horizon after the end of the Mayan calendar or coinciding with some other celestial or macrocosmic shift.

However, generally speaking, in this philosophical conception, the Universe is seen as "running down" over time — that is, in a spiritual or moral sense, not a physical one like the scientists' refracted formulation. Consequently, the current age, which we think of as the height of evolution is, in Hindu cosmology, the *Kali yuga*, the lowest level of decline, of degenerate morals, habit, and custom that is possible before the starting up of the cycle all over again from the "top" … which, keep in mind, is also the beginning or "bottom."

**FALL AND RETURN TO GRACE**

## Karl Christian Friedrich Krause and Panentheism

And this viewpoint is expressed magnificently as recently as the early Nineteenth Century by philosopher Karl Christian Friedrich Krause with such import and power that it led to an entire movement outside of Krause's Germany in the country of Spain during the mid-Nineteenth Century and after his death.

Of Krause, *Encyclopedia Brittanica* reports,

> *Karl Christian Friedrich Krause, (born May 6, 1781, Eisenberg, Rhenish Palatinate [Germany] — died Sept. 27, 1832, Munich, Bavaria), German philosopher who attracted a considerable following, especially in Spain, where his disciples, known as krausistas, greatly influenced the direction of Spanish education in the late 19th and early 20th centuries.*
>
> *Krause's system of philosophy, which he called "panentheism" (essentially an attempt to reconcile pantheism and theism), asserts that God is an essence that contains the entire universe within itself but is not exhausted by it. He put particular emphasis on the development of the individual as an integral part of the life of the whole.*

# Ostracizing Emanationism In Our Intellectually "Open" Society

Yet this viewpoint of Emanationism is decried and suppressed these days. Sure of our beliefs in evolution which, conveniently enough, puts us at the top of the ladder of creation, we relegate the idea of Emanationism and the philosophy of Krause, for example, to the trash heap of history. The *Encyclopedia of Philosophy* has this to say about Emanationism as regards its contrast with the theory of evolution: "In modern times, evolutionism has obliterated the emanationist philosophy."[2]

And sure enough, in my computer search of the seven million titles in the entire University of California library system I found *not one* title at all related to the topic of Emanationism. Similarly, of the forty-six titles listed on Krause, only two were in English and both of those were concerned, not at all with Krause's philosophy. One focused on his other major interest — his political views on world peace. The other title was an analysis of the sociological movement that followed from his ideas in Spain. Therefore there was not one title in English on this philosophy! This viewpoint of Emanationism had suffered the consequences it would itself predict: It had been ostracized and had faded from existence.

We may congratulate ourselves on having an open intellectual climate, a freedom of expression and viewpoint, especially in modern and Western-style societies. However, inquiry like I just described forces us to acknowledge the existence of certain forces in our world — be they psychological, political, economic, sociological, or all of these — that severely circumscribe the range of ideas available for consideration by our supposedly "open" minds in this supposedly "open" society and culture.

But I do not wish to make the entire case for Emanationism right now. That has been the task of one of my other works, *Falls from Grace: The Devolution and Revolution of Consciousness* (2014a). In it I presented exactly that proposition: that in the process of coming into the world, in an individual's life, the individual's consciousness proceeds from a state of high awareness and spiritual expansion to lower and more constricted levels of such awareness.

155

This would be ontogenetic emanationism or what I refer to as *devolution* in the course of one's life.

However in two other of my works, *Planetmates: The Great Reveal* (2014b) and *Prodigal Human: The Descents of Man* (2016a), I lay out the manner of this Emanationism as it has occurred for our species. This phylogenetic or cultural Emanationism or devolution is the idea that in the process of the eons of time we have existed on Earth our species has gone from a state of grand awareness and spiritual fullness to increasingly lesser states of such.

# Further New-Paradigm Implications: Child "Development" as Spiritual Devolution

Whatever the weight of the assault I am making on the scientific bias, it must at least be acknowledged, concerning scientific theories, that theoretical positions that ignore the very foundations upon which they are based — that is, the subjectivity of the observer — are going to be the weaker for that.

Yet, acknowledging even that, one could argue that there is no clear idea of how to go about applying these new perspectives. How could they be used? How could they be relevant? What implications might they have?

It is in answer to these questions that I have offered the analysis in my work, *Falls from Grace: The Devolution and Revolution of Consciousness* (2014a). In it, I detail how these new-paradigm perspectives, specifically Emanationism, can be used in the understanding of child "development" and personal growth or spirituality. I propose just such an Emanationist or devolutional model — one that is rooted in the framework provided by Ken Wilber (1977) in his *spectrum of consciousness* theory. It is also one that gives rise to the conclusions that I believe Wilber should have come to, from his theory, but did not.[3]

These conclusions and implications of devolutional or Emanationist ways of viewing human development and our species' evolution are more than just speculative, however. They are based also on the findings of the new-paradigm experiential psychotherapies — that is, the ones that place primacy upon experience over concept, "territory" over "map," and percept over object.

The implications of this approach of devolution, I show, are for no less than the validity of the current direction of child-caring, the effectiveness of mainstream psychotherapeutic and counseling approaches, and the direction of psychological and spiritual growth. It is my belief that such implications are far from irrelevant or unimportant.

# The Transpersonal Perspective Explained

However at this time, in this work, *The Secret Life of Stones*, I wish to provide a more comprehensive philosophical viewpoint which arises from the modern consciousness research. In the next part, "The Consciousness of Stones," I will lay out what I believe *can* be known about Reality. For it is the basis upon which any true knowledge can exist.

# PART FOUR

# The Consciousness of Stones

# 14

# The Consciousness of Stones:

## Idealism, a Profound Overstanding. Matter Matters, It Just Ain't Material

*"All through the physical world runs that unknown content, which must surely be the stuff of our consciousness." — A. S. Eddington*

## Some Assumptions

The perspective contained in this argument on *The Secret Life of Stones* arises out of a set of assumptions that I should make clear at the outset. In addition, certain words are used with particular meanings which might not be clear to the reader initially. These terms are *devolution, regression, the Divine, Experience* , and *metaphor*; and I will deal with each of them in due course. In this Part Four, "The Consciousness of Stones," I will discuss the definitional, epistemological, ontological, and methodological issues that pertain to this and others of my works.

That is to say, I will take you upon a journey deep into the underpinnings of these ideas in the ground of Knowledge and Reality. We will evaluate on what basis these things I unveil can be known — their *epistemology*. Relatedly, we will assess their standing within Reality — their *ontological* status ... just how *real* are these propositions and their theoretical components. To complete our journey, we will do a fly-over of the *ways* and the *modes of research* by which we can, and have, come to know these things — their *methodology* — and we will consider them as to their validity and applicability, and the degree of their soundness as a basis for learning new things. Got that?

Okay, continuing: My books' working set of assumptions is congruent with those of transpersonal psychology and the perennial philosophy as put forth by Ken Wilber (1977), and it is compatible with the metaphysical view constructed by Carl Jung. The basic assumption within that set is that Reality is

1. something that is directly experienced and

2. is not the interpretation of that experience.

That is, that as soon as one begins to interpret, one is already abstracting from What Really Is, one is removing oneself from that Reality and is beginning the process of increasing abstraction, degression, and *devolution* ... meaning the reverse of evolution, the opposite of growth forward ... from What Is.

Let us look at each of these premises, beginning with the first. In subsequent chapters, we will go deeply into the second postulate. However remember that the entirety of the early parts of this book on the effects of the constituted realities on our understanding of Reality could not be clearer in establishing the second — that Reality is not the interpretation of one's experience. For one's experience is immediately interpreted through layers of distorting understandings, beliefs, and information wrought of previous experience and learning.

# 1. Reality Is Something Directly Experienced

First, however, that Reality is something that is directly experienced is related to the position of Idealism, in philosophy, which is contrasted with the position of Common-Sense Realism or Materialism. Not only does Idealism have a strong historical legacy in philosophy, it has vital contemporary and empirical support from both the mainstream and cutting edges of our sciences.

## Debunking Materialism

To establish Idealism more strongly we might want, first of all, to undercut the prevailing notion of Common-Sense Realism or Materialism.

In Chapter 12, I pointed out that from the field of the new biology, Rupert Sheldrake (1991a) — a natural scientist and philosopher as well as prominent biologist — had listed the nine essential features of this mechanistic world view … mechanistic, which is another way of saying Common-Sense Realism or Materialism. As a reminder, they were that Nature is inanimate; that the world is composed of inert atoms of matter; that Reality is determinate and predictable; that it is knowable as well; that the Universe is a machine; that the Earth is dead, that Reality and the Universe contain no internal purposes; and that there exist eternal, immutable laws[1].

Sheldrake's contention is that "every one of those essential claims has been refuted by advances of science. In effect, science itself has now superseded the mechanistic world view."[2] In his work, he then proceeds to support that claim by dismantling these suppositions, one by one.

Why this is not common knowledge is answered by Sheldrake as well. As noted elsewhere, he points out,

> *Although science is now superseding the mechanistic world view, the mechanistic theory of nature has shaped the modern world, underlies the ideology of technological progress, and is still the official*

*orthodoxy of science.*[3]

Furthermore about this reluctance to change, he writes, "It has had many consequences, not the least of which is the environmental crisis."[4] So, these entrenched views are both incorrect and have the most profound and dire consequences for human survival.

Yet if we wish to assert once again the purpose of science as being a venture after truth, we need to resist these forces of complacency and convenience. Sheldrake (1991a) explains this death blow to the foundations of the materialistic paradigm, as so,

> *The modern changes in science have effectively transcended each of these features. These changes in science have not happened as part of a coordinated research programme designed to overthrow the mechanistic paradigm. They have happened in specialized areas, seemingly unconnected with each other, and often without any consciousness that this was leading to a change in the overall world view of science. What I am going to suggest is that we can now see that this has effectively refuted the mechanistic world view within the very heart of science itself.*[5]

And similarly, as concerns Materialism specifically, Sheldrake writes,

> *Inert atoms have given way to the idea of atoms as structures of activity. Matter is not fundamental in modern physics. Energy and fields are fundamental. Energy is what gives things actuality or activity; it's like the flow of change. Fields are what organize the flow of energy. As David Bohm says, "Matter is frozen light," It's the energy of light, or light-like energy trapped within a small space going round and round upon itself within fields. So matter is energy bound within fields. And as Sir Karl Popper has pointed out, "through modern physics, materialism has transcended itself," because matter is no longer the fundamental explanatory entity, no longer the fundamental feature of things. Fields and energy are the most fundamental things.*[6]

## Affirming Idealism

With Materialism in disrepute, it is logical to consider the alternative of Idealism. Idealism is the position, in philosophy, that states that matter's existence is dependent upon our perception of it, that we cannot know that matter exists outside of our perception of it, and hence that what is most fundamental about Reality is the observer, not the observed ... that the observed always presupposes an observer, prior to that.

This position fits in exactly with the idea of biologically constituted realities as I have described it in Part One. This idea is that "worlds," including "physical worlds," are dependent upon the particular biological paradigm that constitutes the observer. Another way of saying that is that the "structure" of the observer ... most notably, what is commonly called the "species" ... determines the "world" that will be apprehended.

By "structure," of observer, I naturally mean a "psychic" structure — one which we mistakenly label a physical structure such as the anatomy of a species, of course, because of our culturally constituted materialist bias. I am implying some psychic configuration or structure as the essential constituent of the observer. You might look at it as analogous to the matter as frozen light analogy above in the sense that, in what I am saying, I intend to imply structural *fields*, comprised of experiential stuff ... of "energy" stuff, if you will as the actual foundation of the bodies of species, their anatomy, much as light is the true essence of matter. So, by *anatomy*, *species*, and *structure* I do not imply, at base, physical structures or the anatomical structures of species.

I am saying that species are different psychic or experiential constructions, existing as entities, which we term anatomies or biologies, out of the physicalist bias we hold. Whereas I am asserting that those experiential configurations of spirit, which we term *species*, are the basis of our worlds, as opposed to species and biologically constituted realities indicating a physical structure. For I need to be consistent: I am, after all, herein arguing for the more fundamental reality of *psyche* over matter.[7]

If this conceptualization is being difficult to grasp, you may lean on Sheldrake's concept of morphogenetic fields as constituting the basis of species and their anatomies, and you won't be too far afield from where I am at.

At any rate, it follows that an infinite number of worlds are possible, corresponding to an infinite number of structured fields of observers. That is to say that perceivers consist in an infinite number of conceivable "biological paradigms"; we call them *species*.

Furthermore, subjective worlds vary as well within the individual biological structures that comprise each species. For the worlds of species vary with the individual perceivers or members which are by definition of similar, but *not identical*, construction to each other.

At any rate, in our materialistic age, such an "Idealist" position that posits the essence of World as psychical or subjective is looked down upon. Indeed, it has been roundly dismissed as "logically impeccable but incredible."[8]

# Rationalism As Egoistic Self-Abuse

Similarly, we have an argument against Idealism — more specifically the version of it called *panpsychism*, which is, by the way, the position being asserted here — by Wittgenstein (1953) in his *Philosophical Investigations*. His conclusion is that the position of panpsychism is unintelligible. Stating "Could one imagine a stone's having consciousness?" he concludes that if one could it would only amount to "image-mongery."[9] The implication is that since we cannot do something adequately, and adequately according to *him* ... that we cannot understand something completely ... there is something wrong with *it!*

This kind of reasoning qualifies for the "All-Time Boners in Philosophy Award." For the argument — while claiming not to be saying anything about the truth or falsity of a position, nor about its provenness or unprovenness — would want us to evaluate positions, and even possibly dismiss them as viable (that is to say, as possibly true), based upon whether we (as a species) are capable of understanding them with our intelligence.

Whereas, not only does this limit our knowledge endeavor — removing it from any possibility of speaking of truth unless it somehow ... miraculously, I suppose, or through some sort of chosen-by-God kind of privilege ... *happens* to coincide with what is intelligible to us. Not only does it *eliminate* the scientific and philosophical enterprises in their attempts at venturing, ever on, after what might actually be true … or at least "truer" than we had previously held. But it presupposes that what is unimaginable at one time, or to one person, will be unimaginable, or unintelligible, to all others in all other times.

When you think about it, it is an example of much of human, especially Western, thinking which has it that what is Real can only be real if it is embraceable by our intelligence … our *human* intelligence. If one asked, such thinkers would never admit to that bias. However, it is woven through just about all of Western thinking, in spite of the proclamations and the efforts of our best. Look around, and one can hardly find an instance where there is not the assumption that human intelligence is the road supreme to, not only determining what is Real, but also to personal growth, therapeutic healing, and pretty much any human advance in life.

How could intellectuals — and it is, after all, intellectuals who are of necessity the ones writing the books and giving the lectures by which lay folk are led — even if they wanted to, not continually fall into that? I confess that it is only because I have such a background of decades-worth of experiential discovery, of knowledge arrived at based upon profound and varied experiences of ordinary as well as nonordinary states, that I can even attempt it, as I am in my works. And I must continually monitor myself lest I begin rolling down those well-travelled rails, laid with empty concept, which we habitually assume to be more valid than experience.

Such is the extent to which we have come to raise human intelligence on a pedestal in Western culture. Expanding it across the skies of our modern existence as we do, hell, we can no longer see it up there. We assume the heavens just happen to be that way. Though from other cultures, different "star systems" are spied.

Indeed, a cross-cultural analysis reveals our Western hubris. Not all cultures deem rationalism as the only route to truth. Many rely on experiential touchstones in making their way. In that sense, they are more "empirical" in their approach than Westerners. More than that, a cross-species analysis, as is being proposed in this book, reveals the rational approach to be downright arrogant, and laughable, in its presumptiveness.

This example from the philosopher, Wittgenstein, is one instance, in particular, where Rationalism displays its circularity, its egoistic self-abuse ... hence its inherent fallacy. For we know by looking at the historical and anthropological record that what is unimaginable at one time, or to one person, ends up being imaginable to another. Reason is not a thing-in-itself that is the same, that is isolated, that is unassailable and incorruptible and that is impervious outside of any context.

Sure, we want to believe reason is detachable from experiential influences and from the circumstances within which it moves. It gives us a tool to deal with our essentially mysterious and incomprehensible reality. But while reason is helpful when it is a servant, it makes a horrible master. For it is indeed affected, if not downright configured, by the contexts it operates within. Those contexts are all the constituted realities — biological, biocultural, cultural, and individual. Reason, though it seems to, does not transcend time and space, existing as some discarnate reality able to observe and make detached judgements on reality. No. Intellect and thought are part of Reality and are molded by the Reality in which they arise.

For example, do we suppose that an early "animistic" hunter-gatherer could imagine a physical universe as we picture it today — with black holes, a heliocentric solar system, a Big Bang, quarks, and quasars?

Do we say that because this primal person could not imagine these that we must dismiss them as possible truths ... that is to say, as possible good models of our reality? Or must we say that our conceptualizations of these things amount to "image-mongery" and thereby dismiss them on those grounds, as Wittgenstein's reasoning would have us do?

As a matter of fact, while Wittgenstein decries such a position as that stones have consciousness .... I would say that stones *are* consciousness, by the way, in keeping with an Idealist, not physicalist stance ... and that to think so is image-mongery, this book attempts to do exactly what he says is impossible.

As you are seeing, how I do that is by, first, clearing the field of inquiry, in Parts One and Two, of its physicalist bias by pointing out that only by asserting a version of egotism that is called *anthropocentrism* can we not acknowledge that everything we know is determined by us as a species and is therefore biologically relative. Subsequently then, in Part Three and following through here, in Part Four, by bringing in some of the new discoveries in science and their reformulations of Reality, I make the attempt to paint a picture of Reality consistent with them — a rendering that abjures the anthropocentric bias in normal scientific and philosophical thinking; which is inclusive of a biological neutrality, in light of biological relativity; and which then, I deem, allows us an understanding of the secret life of stones that is not "image-mongery."

For is it really all that hard, is it really "image-mongery," to assert that stones, mountains, the Earth, the planets, though they speak not to us (at least in *our* language … we will see in the next part — Part Five, "Matter Is Message" — how they *do* speak to us) have consciousness when we similarly are able to attribute consciousness to all other planetmates, including plants, cells, and bacteria? We have heard of *The Secret Life of Plants* and *The Secret Life of the Unborn Child*.[10] Is it really that much of a stretch to consider the secret life of stones?

The only difference is the one — matter, stones — does not observably move … though they all do over time … and it does not *seem* to have intention of its own … though how would we know? Is consciousness dependent upon something's (someone's?) actions correlating with the time line of our own? Does its intentions have to align with intentions as we know of them? Do they have to be human-like or life-like-as-we-know-it intentions? Furthermore, having debunked the idea of duality and separation, can we not see that if we are able to understand a shared mind as existing between species that we already acknowledge, that the fact of separation or not between stones and the rest of matter is irrelevant to the consciousness of something?

Finally, if all the Universe is at base Consciousness, or Experience, or mind-stuff, as is currently being asserted in quantum physics and in Consciousness research circles, does that not imply that matter and stones are, somehow, aspects of that Consciousness, mind-stuff, Experience?

So, this last point leads beyond it in compelling us to realize that *all* forms of what we call "intelligible" venturing after truth are already a matter of "image-mongery." That is to say that all our attempts equate with imagining models of what is; none of which can be said to actually constitute the thing described inasmuch as the map cannot constitute the territory.

Image-"mongery" as a criticism, thus, is only stating that something that is hard for one person to imagine ... or one person and his colleagues to imagine ... cannot be true.

Hence we are led, again, to a realization of the inevitably anthropocentric nature of such arguments as the philosopher Wittgenstein's attack on *panpsychism* — the idea that consciousness or subjectivity exists in everything, including matter. And we cannot help but notice the equivalent degree of arrogance that corresponds with them. For such arguments reduce themselves to "if we can't imagine something, it doesn't exist!"

Leaving behind such a fatuous and uninspired rationale, let us return to the position of Idealism anew.

# Scientific Arrogance Must Cease

For — even admitting these claims of the unimaginability or incredibility of an Idealistic or panpsychic position — that was then, and this is now. It may have been unimaginable in Wittgenstein's time or incredible from Joad's perspective to consider a non-materialistic view of Reality. However, in an age that has witnessed LSD; a revival of shamanism; the emergence of virtual reality; the concepts of quantum physics, holographic paradigms, morphic resonances, entheogens, cellular consciousness, and holotropic minds; and Consciousness research in almost every branch of the natural and social sciences at this point ... in such a day it might be ripe to reconsider some of what has been prematurely, and I might say arrogantly, set aside.

I say "arrogantly" based upon what I have said elsewhere about the anthropocentric bias of scientists. For with an understanding of biologically constituted realities of species we gain an appreciation of the fundamentally limited and species-relative nature of our views of Reality.

Hopefully, we can set aside, to at least a little degree, some of the anthropocentric egotism which obscures any *truly* reasonable attempt at constructing fruitful reality models. That being so, we need to admit of the possibility ... not of the "intelligible-to-Wittgenstein possibility" but of the *real* possibility ... of the prior fundamental reality of psyche over matter, of the observer over the observed. Hence, of the secret life of stones.

# The Footprints on the Shores of the Unknown Are Our Own

From the preceding it should be clear that I believe that consciousness is the only thing of the Universe or that it is at least the only thing knowable of the Universe. It should be just as evident from my line of reasoning why we would have such difficulty in acknowledging this obvious fact. Still, despite our modern difficulties with this worldview, it is not an uncommon position in philosophy. As the author of a comprehensive overview of the field of philosophy, G.T.W. Patrick (1952), described Idealism,

> Idealism, too, asserts that reality is one, that one being mind or spirit. For the Idealist matter is at best a representation or construct of mind. The world of "matter" is but the appearance of mind to itself. The world which the physical scientist talks about is, as Eddington says, in The Nature of the Physical World *(p. xv), a* "world of shadows." What really is, in the final analysis, is of the nature of mind.[11]

Patrick (1952) elaborates further, quoting Eddington:

> A. S. Eddington, at the end of his chapter "On the Nature of Things" closing his striking book on Space, Time and Gravitation, *comes to the conclusion that something of the nature of consciousness forms the essential content of the world.*

> > The theory of relativity has passed in review the whole subject-matter of physics. It has unified the great laws, which by the precision of their formulation and the exactness of their application have won the proud place in human knowledge which physical science holds today. And yet, in regard to the

nature of things, this knowledge is only an empty shell — a form of symbols. *It is knowledge of structural form, and not knowledge of content. All through the physical world runs that unknown content, which must surely be the stuff of our consciousness.*

*Here is a hint of aspects deep within the world of physics, and yet unattainable by the methods of physics. And, moreover, we have found that where science has progressed the farthest, the mind has but regained from nature that which the mind has put into nature.*

*We have found a strange footprint on the shores of the unknown. We have devised profound theories, one after another, to account for its origin. At last, we have succeeded in reconstructing the creature that made the footprint. And lo! it is our own.*[12]

# 15

# The Radical Rational View of Us and It:

I Am You, and You Are Me, and We Are We, and We Are All Together — How You Are God, How the Universe Is Friendly. A Proof of the Existence of God

*Experience Is Divine:  From Solipsism to Transpersonal Reality ... How One Goes from Solipsism to Mysticism*

## From Solipsism to Transpersonal Reality

We need to lay down a foundation based on strict adherence to what can be known. We need to stand on it. We, only then, can reason what might be Real.

Whereas, the problem with all the metaphysics inherent in contemporary science is that they are all built upon assumptions. Assuming such-and-such is the case — that matter, not mind, is the fundamental unit of Reality, for example — then yadda yadda, this-and-that follows. So all of the philosophy of the day-to-day science and the lay understandings of reality are based on circular reasoning. The reason given for that is that there is no other way to go, for anything else is based on *solipsism* — the idea that only oneself exists.

I believe that there *is* another way of reasoning, which is missed by normal science, compelled by contemporary findings in consciousness and related research, and which is logically impeccable.

Let me explain it.

# I Exist

Everything that we say exists is dependent upon our subjective experience of it. So all we really can know exists for sure is a subjective experience of anything. The assertion of anything else as existing beyond that is pure speculation. So essentially all that we can know to exist is *experience* ... is *that which is*, in any particular moment, for oneself — the perceiver or receptor of *experience*.

This is *solipsism*, pure and simple of course. But it is the best place of all to start. As W. T. Stace (1932) wrote, "The initial position of every mind must be solipsistic." And further, that while continued investigation might eventually lead to "very good reason to believe in the existence of other minds," still, "each of us must begin from within his own consciousness" as a "solitary mind."[1]

What this is saying is that to have any possibility of venturing after Truth we must start from what we know and that is essentially a solipsistic starting point. But that, though it is a starting point, it is not necessarily the conclusion. The problem with arguments against a solipsistic starting point, and the reason given for why one needs to *assume* something in order to go beyond it, is that making that argument also assumes that one is unable to reason, logically so, beyond it. It assumes that one will only arrive at where one has begun.

Whereas I will attempt to show in the following how that is not the case. And that starting from the position, only, of what is obviously true — a solipsistic position — one can logically conclude much more, including the existence of God and supernatural beings and that you, yourself, are God. As well as that life is a cosmic game with participants and spectators, actors and audience, Form and No-Form ... incarnate and discarnate ... beings ... and, possibly, actual and potential states. Ambitious, you say? Well, let us see.

# You Exist

And so it is that we start with solipsism, with our assertion of the existence of oneself; it is the foundation upon which we stand. We begin with the assertion that I experience, therefore I am. And, anyone who would dispute that, well, they are saying that they do not exist. So why even bother with what they have to say? Heheh. Indeed, if we want to respect their position, we are required to ignore them.

Anyway, from this initial starting point of solipsism a compelling deduction is next made — and it *can* be made, on the basis of one's experience alone — that others exist. How so?

One deduces the existence of others out of one's experience that there is something outside of the bounds of that which we call one's self which happens to "impinge" on one's self. Or we can say that we discover "wills" other than one's own "will" ... and this is especially obvious when they are at odds or in conflict with one's own will. We know of us and our intent directly. However we unerringly come up against an undeniable truth: There are other intents, hence probably other subjectivities or selves, like the one we know of as ourselves.

We also deduce the existence of an Other from the fact that there are aspects of one's experience that are completely surprising and unintended and thus "unwilled" by oneself — one discovers creations which are to all appearances and upon all reflection other than one's own. Now, these elements alone would imply simply that experience contains the unintended, the contrary, and the surprising. However, these surprising and unintended occurrences can be seen to have meaningful patterns to them. They are meaningful in the sense that we are able to deduce that these "patterns" are themselves centers of experience, centers of will or creation, in much the same way that oneself is. This is a compelling deduction, based on the evidence of one's experience, but is not a necessary one.

Being not a necessary one, it is still the most likely one. At this point we need acknowledge that even our best attempts at understanding anything beyond the boundaries of self are inevitably going to be conjecture.

Still, having a basis for understanding that is one's experience of self is having the only solid foundation from which one can reason with certitude. One posits comfortably based upon the only reality we know without a doubt — our experience, our existence. I experience therefore I am can never and in no way be disputed.

Whereas *cogito ergo sum* ... "I think, therefore I am" ... while it also proves one's existence, does not prove the existence of anything else. Thinking shows itself up to be faulty, exactly as Reason, as I explained above, does. One can think something, but it might be and often is gobbledygook.

Whereas one cannot dispute the facts of one's experience. One might have an "hallucination" of something, which is a way of saying that something one experienced is not possible to be experienced by anyone else. In that case it is like a thought in its insubstantiality. It does not mean it did not happen, in the same way that we can say thoughts happen, though they also might be insubstantial, that is, based on nothing. That is to say, probably not true. Which is to mean, probably not shareable by anyone outside the bounds of self. That is, that in order to even begin to venture beyond self, to go beyond solipsism, these thoughts must be left behind. They must be dropped, from consideration, in order to go forward.

However, experiences are much more likely to be shared realities than thoughts are. Hence, when one begins with an empirical, an experiential, basis, one is more likely to come up with additional realities that can be shared, that can be logically arrived at, together. The point is that thinking and reason are much more likely, being able to be detached from actual empirical, sensed Reality, to be constructions built in the air or as Schopenhauer phrased them, "ideas of Reflection" or "ideas of ideas." And as he said about them, such abstract notions or mere concepts, not connected to empirical reality are like bank notes "issued by a firm which has nothing but other paper obligations to back it with" and that they "move in the air without support."[2]

These metaphors about metaphors can, and very often are, structures built upon structures, having no substance, no actual content. They are *much* more likely to be solipsistic, meaning applicable or real only to oneself. Whereas deductions arising from empirical realities, experiential realities … and the definition of empirical is that they are shared realities … well, these deductions have, by definition, substance. They are good things to build upon. And the first empirical reality is one's experience of self.

So conjecture having a basis of self is better than having no basis at all — as for example in the *a priori* postulation of the physical world and the consciousnesses we ascribe to being in it. This ascribing of consciousness to the world, note, is done arbitrarily and inconsistently; we grant consciousness to most humans and some other life forms and not to other entities in haphazard ways that vary by culture and time period. Well, that should tell you something about the insubstantiality of our postulation of the reality of the physical world with its varying instances of consciousness sprinkled through it. Yet this *a priori* assumption of a physical world, along with this attribution of consciousness to ourselves and those we like, or who are like us (same thing), is what is normally done in science and in common-sense realism.

# They Exist

So we have it that there are Others based upon our *experiences* that our intents and will are contested or inhibited by something(s) that are *outside* of that which we experience (normally, that is) as ourselves. Also we deduce the existence of Others based upon the fact that our *expectations* are continually revised by *experiences* involving the unexpected and surprising, which have sources outside of ourselves. Yet further support for this deduction is that these seemingly Other-emanating events that are unexpected have all the same qualities of events and experiences as we know ourselves to be concocting and intending out of one's own self. So we conclude there is an Other, and then others, just like us outside of us.

Having the compelling conviction that others (that is other experience containers, or experience screens, or experience perceivers) exist, we are informed (in other words, we are "impinged" upon in meaningful [to us] ways) by these "patterns" (entities) of experiences which are *not* like our own. At least we are "told" and led to believe this through the "communications" that we have with these alleged "others." The quote marks are used here because these are arbitrary, not necessary, categories to what are essentially, fundamentally, patterns of experience within self. Yet, what language is, only and at base, is the assigning of terms, verbal constructions, that is, to what are always and everywhere merely patterns of experience within self.

Thus, the World emerges as meaningful patterns of experience within oneself ... within one's experience, one's experiential world ... which reveal themselves as *separate* from us to varying degrees. And we label the degree of separation in accord with their similarity with us. That is, indeed, the definition of separation, when you think about it. Thus we label as *humans* — that which is very similar to us; as *animals* — what is less so; as other *living* things — less again; *inanimate* things — even less; and so on.

Keep this in mind as we continue: Consciousness is a quality that is attributed varyingly according to how similar something is to what we feel ourselves to be ... nothing more.

To say something is conscious is to assert that it is like us. It does not say whether or not something has intention; has will; has ability to experience; has awareness; or has appreciation of itself as in some way singular, in some way separate, however much part of a whole. These are all the things we attribute to the term *consciousness,* but we cannot, fairly, say they are not part of the physical world or anything else we say is not conscious, based upon what we can know. To say something outside of ourselves does not have all those things we consider to be consciousness ... to say a stone does not have consciousness ... is a presumption. And at base, considering all of our constituted realities and our anthropocentrism, it is a *prejudice.* And an unfair one, at that. It does not really say anything about consciousness as a quality of the world. It only says that something is *similar* to us and is therefore *understandable* to us as being conscious like us.

Here again, in doing this, in asserting the non-consciousness of anything outside of ourselves, we are basing our evaluations of the truth of things, like Wittgenstein did, on what is more or less intelligible to us ... which states nothing at all about what exists outside of us. Asserting the non-consciousness of anything is in no way a statement about Reality. It is merely a statement about one's self ... about the limitations of one's ability to understand. That's right. At base, to assert the non-consciousness of anything is to proclaim oneself as ignorant. *Ignorance* is a result of ignoring, whether consciously or unconscioiusly, something real or true ... which is often obvious to others or from some other perspective. Indeed, in every situation where consciousness is denied in something, there is at least *something* that is being ignored by the observer, by the proclaimer of non-consciousness in something. This book will continue to point to those things being ignored, so we might dispel such ignorance.

# We Are Alike

At any rate, so far, so good. Here, with this concoction of there being Others, we have our normal world — the way we normally think of reality.

Then, amid these "communications" from conjectured Others, we hear descriptions of experience that are much like we would describe our own experience. It is as if what is outside of us is not outside of us at all.

We listen more carefully, we share and reveal ourselves again and again, and these have the result that we have more *experiences* of deep and profound sharing with certain others; and to our amazement we cannot help but continually be confronted with this possibility that we are, in fact, *not* separate from Other, in some way that we cannot imagine. Thus, it is our ability to empathize along with our experiences of deep conversation (communication, sharing) with others — which is why it is by the way that psychotherapists like myself unlike normal physical scientists have no problem with this understanding — which give us the experience of hearing of experiences that seem to be ... impossibly from within the understanding of separateness we once had ... similar, practically identical to our own.

This gives rise to a consideration that our experiences are *not* unique, are not separate, are not isolated, are not alone.

We begin to doubt our existence as separate, as solitary ... as a solitary mind and experience of itself. We begin to wonder about the connection between us and Other, about the status of I and Other, about the relation of I and Other to each other.

We have long ago, by now, left behind solipsism.

# We Are One

Then along come other-than-normal experiences. We experience, or we find out indirectly of, experiences that are supposedly those of one or more of those supposedly *separate others!* This might include, for example, psychedelic or other altered-state experience of another's experience, from another time or place, especially. These experiences are not unusual or unique to our times, by the way. These experiences arising spontaneously, through the use of entheogens and psychedelics, or through various psychotechnologies which exist in each and every culture, indeed arise and are accessible in every society known and thus potentially to each and every person.

What this is saying is that there are ways in every culture that one is able to experience one's boundaries of self to have been arbitrary. There are ways to experience biological transcendence, to experience *ecstasy* — meaning, literally, to go out of oneself as a fixed state of being, to go outside oneself. There are everywhere ways to experience one's delineation of self to have been limited, more limited than what one is actually possible to experience. That is, in all potentiality. And that, amazingly, when the barriers around one's self have been removed and our experience expands ... this is why they have been called *psychedelic*, that is, "mind-expanding," by the way ... beyond its former limits, we find that we include that of the Other — whether that be other persons, other planetmates and animate beings, other inanimate "things" (beings? ... at this point we begin to doubt our interpretation of matter as being thing-like or non-conscious), cosmic realities or entities, microscopic and subatomic realities or entities, and even other supranormal realities or entities, such as archetypal ones. We find that our experience of self is *overlapping* of that of what we have called Other. At times we experience something that is more akin to identity, even, with these realities, consciousnesses, entities ... something which is more than just overlapping. And we need to conclude that even our definition of self is arbitrary. We have left solipsism even further in our dust.

At any rate, based on these, we are led to conclude that therefore others' experience is *not* separate from one's own, that that was a mistaken view built up on insufficient experience (evidence). It was a logical or rational deduction but was not a sufficiently empirical one. We conclude that there is a "bleed through" of experience from what was thought to be separate entities/realities, at least ... and overlap or identity more likely.

Other evidence/experiences — such as experiences of being or "identifying with" what were thought to be other "things" or other "species" ... this is how we named those patterns that were supposedly farthest from our own experience — convince us that there is no separation either between what we called oneself and what we called world, others, other species, and so on.

We are led to conclude that we are part of all that exists, as far as we know of things existing, or at least that we are so in potential. That is to say, we discover that there are no definite and impenetrable boundaries where we thought there were distinct separations. The World as far as we know it appears to be characterized by interconnectedness, overlapping identities, and "porous," indistinct, or illusory boundaries, and arbitrary assignments of identity ... with even *collective* identities being possible, along with there being possible identities of "parts" ... of what was formerly thought to be a singular and irreducible self.

It is by this empirical-existential means that I have come to know — and others have come to know ... according to the patterns that have been made known to me through the other patterns in my experience called *communication* — that one's subjective experience is not separate from that of others.

I repeat, the basis of this belief of non-separation lies in my understanding that, first, other people explain their experiences to me in ways that are so much like the way I would describe my own ... and the more deeply sharing and revealing the communication the more alike they appear to be ... that I cannot help but think these others are exactly like me, except for apparently being confronted with different experiential facts. My conclusion is that were I to encounter the exact same set of experiential components, I would experience my world the way they do. My suspicion beyond that is that if I were to match their experiential realities exactly, I would actually *be* that person. That indeed I could be that person. Hell, maybe in some way I *am* that person!

Second, I come even closer to a conclusion that there is no separation between selves because people in certain other-than-normal states are able to experience what "other" people have experienced in different times and places — and this is verifiable.

Third, non-separation is demonstrated empirically, both in quantum physics and in the new biology where the phenomena of morphic resonance and morphogenetic fields point to a sharing of subjective space, or fields, or a Common Intersubjectivity. As the quantum physicist, Schrödinger, put it, "The total number of minds in the universe is one."[3]

Fourth, various other experiences of "experience-sharing" are verifiable — such as the trans-species experience and identification with aspects of the so-called "material" world, both of which have been described by Stanislav Grof in his many works as occurring quite frequently.

And, yes, in this last, for those who are waiting, is where we encounter the consciousness of matter ... "of stones," metaphorically speaking. It is here where we get a peek into the secret life of stones.

# God Exists

So we are part of All That Is ... as far as we know it ... and the boundaries we perceive are only illusory.

## The Universe Is Friendly

The next element in this argument enters with the realization that those supposed other-than-us, separate things that impinge on us do so in ways that lead us positively forward into better and better experiences, even despite our intentions ... and this, if only known in hindsight. Even events constituted mainly of supposedly inanimate "others" — that is to say, actions of the "physical" world — reflect a helpful tendency. Thus we conclude that there is something outside of us that is both helpful to us and higher than us ... in that it knows what is better for us even when we do not.

It also appears to be omnipresent, existing the same in all beings and the "things" of the world. It appears to be the same; that is to say, it is consistent in what we learn from it. It is the same "pattern" that we interact with in different times and places and emanating out of different people and things ... so it is One. We call this unknown, powerful, helpful, singular, and everywhere and always present thing, "God."

We conclude that we are in the normal course of things limited, bounded, and separate, but that we are essentially unlimited, unbounded, and united with all and everything. And we conclude that everything that exists outside of oneself as well as inside of oneself is a singular God with characteristics of being omnipresent, omnipotent, omniscient, normally unknowable hence mysterious, transcendent of us, and infinitely kind and merciful. So Reality is One ... and is God.

# We Are God

But since we have found we are not separate from the so-called Other, the so-called World, we must conclude that we also are not separate from that helpful thing that is part of what we thought was Other, and World.

Thus, the conclusion is

1.  that one, oneself, is part of All That Is ... insofar as one is in any way aware of what is;

2. that one mistakenly concluded at one time that one was separate from that All because of insufficient evidence … and we learn later, also because of fear that caused us to retreat from the evidence for our essential unity … evidence which we did indeed have, if we had wanted to see it

3. that All That Is is beneficent overall … or at least, if this ends up being wrong in the long run, it would be better that we make this mistake than even to get it correct; and

4. that we are part of that beneficence in the All That Is, which we call God.

It is on these sorts of grounds that my viewpoint has come to approximate that of primal, or indigenous, societies — a viewpoint that Western culture has termed *pantheism* — as well as to approximate the mystical teachings of all spiritual traditions and the perennial philosophy on the essentially Divine nature of the self. *These perspectives can be summed up in that all that exists is God, that all that can be seen and perceived are manifestations of God, that all that can be experienced is God, that therefore Experience itself is God, and that I also am God in that I am part of the All That Is (which is God) in that I partake of that Experience.*

# 16

# Invisible Entities and the Universal Game:

## From Transpersonal Reality to the Falls from Grace and Back Again … Life is a Wiki-Novel

*The Fall from Grace: "Development" Is Actually a Reduction of Awareness Through Painful Experiences, Which "Civilized" Cultures Rationalize as Being "Good"*

*Actuality, Potentiality, and the Fall from Grace — Life Is, a Universal Play or Game, with Supranatural Beings, Invisible Entities, and No-Form Observers, and with Rules Decided Upon by all Entities, in Which There are Incarnate, Form Actors (Participants) and Discarnate, No-Form Observers (Spectators, Audience, Witnesses)*

# Transpersonal Reality to the Falls from Grace and Back Again

Let us now add some other — some compelling and interesting — considerations.

## Transpersonal Realities Exist

If subjectivity or psyche is ultimately more real than the material world as presented to us by our external senses, it follows that certain "psychic" realities may exist and even be more real, even though not *manifesting* — meaning simply not able to be sensed by our limited human senses — in the "physical" world. Thus, this position, this worldview necessarily includes the position that psychic or "invisible" realities — for example, God, Spirit, "allies," spirits, and so on ... which are seemingly separate from us but which ultimately we are part of — may exist though in common-sense ... that is to say, anthropocentric ... reality we do not normally concede they exist.

This position can be supported at even the most fundamental levels. In addition to the argument presented earlier about the existence of quasars to hunter-gatherers, at the simplest levels of this debate there are few people who would assert that realities that are not directly perceived, even by our most sophisticated instruments, do not exist, when their existence is compellingly thrust upon us by their effects and by the congruence that their existence has with the principles upon which our world is found to run.

If one could not see the other side of the moon, one would not say that it did not exist. There are those among us who would theorize that it is made of green cheese ... or inhabited by reptilians who spy on us, lol ... but that is another matter. No, even the least dimly lit among us would not assert that the moon ceases to exist when it is out of sight. It is said babies think that way, thinking that something no longer perceived ceases to exist, but that is out of limited experience of the physical world, which is corrected with greater experience. Nor would we say that electricity does not exist simply because we normally cannot see it. Our operations on the world simply would not be possible, logically so, if the world operated like that.

## Our Falls from Grace, in Consciousness, in Awareness

However, I believe that we are not normally aware of these other realities, call them "spirit," or "other consciousnesses," because our past experience influences us to believe, and therefore perceive, in particular distorted ways. These ways are prejudiced by our past experience,

1. as a spiritual entity — we have an identity, and apparently a personhood, even "personality," that is non-corporeal ... call it *soul, spirit,* or who we are when existing in the No-Form State ... and that has its own set of experiences distinct from others;

2. as identified with a particular species form — we exist within a species, with all of its limitations on what can be experienced and what will be perceived as world; and

3. as identified as a particular person — we are a particular form with its own set of unique experiences as an individual.

## And the Prods to Our Greater Awareness, Again

Yet our prejudices are challenged continually, in both lesser and greater ways, by the other realities which we do not see. For these realities impinge upon our experience whether we acknowledge their existence or not. That something is able to do that is a part of the definition of something that is considered "objectively real" as opposed to being "imaginary." Thus in this case they would be "objectively real" subjective, or psychic, or experiential realities. I am saying that something is objectively real if it is true; and by that I mean if it is intersubjectively able to be validated and is replicable, given the proper conditions. It is on this basis, for example, that Ken Wilber (1977) asserts the empirical and even experimental validity of spiritual realities such as enlightenment.

# Quit Looking in the Material World for Psychic Realities!

One aside I need to make regarding this idea of psychic realities that are objectively real has to do with a common misunderstanding, rooted again in those habits of materialistic thinking embedded in our intractable anthropocentrism. This has to do with the assumption that all "objectively real" realities, even when acknowledged to be psychic or subjective, can be detected in physical reality. Psychic realities are sought in the physical world when one seeks to detect them as energy, as scientists do; as vacuum energy, electromagnetic energy, as sound energy (EVP), as photonic energy, and so on; or even as ethereal or plasma as paranormal researchers might; or even as the ectoplasm of fictional ghostbusters!

This assumption is anything but true. For one thing remember that from quantum physics we learn that the physical universe, not only is affected, even determined, by the perceiver of it, but it also both appears and disappears, is there, then it is not, at a subatomic level. What is this saying except that physical reality is a conjecture or construction of mind. It is hardly a good place to be seeking to validate any reality or experience.

If you think this to be far-fetched, just look around to any of the new-age understandings and see how common it is to relate psychic and spiritual realities to vibrations, as in molecular vibrations, to energy, or to light itself. They are not saying that psychic and experiential realities are somewhat detected and/or observable and/or measurable through these mediums, but that they essentially, at base, *are* these things. They somehow think they have made a stronger case for spiritual realities by asserting them to be, at base, physical phenomena! The illogic of that is what I am trying to shine a light on, no pun intended.

Whereas it is silly to look for spiritual realities in a physical world in order to validate them, the reverse of this logic is equally irrational. To discover psychological roots of spiritual realities does not *invalidate* them, rather it gives them a stronger foundation in the realm of the psyche. For example, this is done when religionists with a fundamentalist bent seek to discredit Jung's theories with an assertion that he undermines the basis of religion because his "gods" are "merely" psychological. They would have their gods be some version of a physical reality, you see. Yet, how ridiculous it is that they would think that something being psychological would be any kind of criticism when what they are asserting through their theologies is indeed a psychospiritual reality, an invisible one, not a physical one.

As for the reverse of that, I think it is equally wrong-headed for new-age spiritual sorts, both within and outside of science, to go around assuming that something in the physical world is the basis for *their* spiritual and psychological experiences and realities.

This wrong-headed thinking is also the way of behavioral and neural science which puts forth the idea that eventually for all psychic, intellectual, emotional, or mind events there will be found a physicalist basis, that is, one detectible and measureable by some instruments detecting the physical world we share in common. In saying this, they are saying merely that they know they cannot prove this assumption of there being some physical prior reality for experiential phenomena, but they wish not to be challenged on it on the basis that in some future they will be proven correct. Well, hell, nobody else gets that kind of allowance!

We also know, from quantum physics, of action-at-a-distance, which also implies forces or realities that are not detectible within physical reality, even as fields, as energy, or as anything else. All that remains is what has in the past been called *spirit*, or the *supernatural*.

Furthermore, remember that in Part One I covered how what our scientists detect with their advanced and refined instruments can only be an extension of our senses. For we cannot know to look in areas we do not know to exist. In this sense, our senses as well as the technology extending them create their own paradigms of reality outside of which we cannot see, beyond whose outlines we cannot know anything to be existing. Ultimately, Reality will be mysterious, at some point, as long as we are biologically constituted beings — that is, we are in the Form state, we are incarnate. Logically, it cannot be otherwise. And this conclusion is irrefutable in that is impossible for biological, incarnated beings to know what it is impossible to know when thus constrained to a Form.

# Yes, Invisible Others Exist

Hence, realities that are objectively real by my definition — that is to say, they are realities able to be shared and are in common among beings — probably exist. However, they are impossible to be shared — that is, observed as objectively real — from within *our* biological parameters as humans. It is also impossible to detect them with the expansions of those parameters produced by our instruments. This follows from my argument that there are other conscious perceivers in the Universe of both the known — that is, the species on Earth — and the unknown variety. This last sort would, I will remind, be those unable to be detected with our limited senses at all. Or they would be able to be sensed but only partially or incorrectly — as would be the case of beings with qualities that are only partially sensed by us, and so are misunderstood. This would include the beingness of whatever consciousness or being it is that arises within our perceptions as the inanimate Universe, including those beings whose consciousness — whose experiential reality — appears to us as stones.

So, there are invisible beings and consciousnesses — that is to say, experiential constellations with foci and organization, or pattern — that are impossible to detect as being so within our limited status as Form or incarnate beings. What exists will be ultimately unknowable, hence mysterious, at some point, regardless how deeply we look into the physical universe to detect its essence.

Finally, any venturing into the mysterious beyond what is detectible in the world of Form must necessarily be done using the medium that actually *is* essential to the Universe that we know: It must be arrived at through experience and be essentially psychic, consciousness, and experientially based. The greatest discoveries of a non-physical Universe — essentially quantum, experiential, and rooted in subjectivity — will be unveiled through the research in consciousness and the experiential research, and not through the research into the physical, material world.

I understand how inconvenient it would seem, and even distasteful, for scientists to leave off their research into a detached world with which they have no personal or emotional connection and instead to look to or participate in research that would actually be so interwoven with one's consciousness and personality that it might be life-changing, not to mention emotionally disruptive. One cannot expect to simply come home after a day of such work like one did the day before. But that is where we must go, that is where we must look, as quantum physics has led us back to ourselves as the basis for what is real. Look to experiential researchers, not the technological ones, to reveal the most important truths on our growing edges right now.

Yet to the extent that such realities can be experienced by others, to the extent they can be shared experiential realities, to the extent that they are an aspect of the Common Intersubjectivity of humans and all beings known and unknown, they are .... drumroll here ... *objective* realities. Yes, subjective realities can be objectively true. Just ask Stanislav Grof or any other transpersonal researcher, including Jung.

## And Back Again

So it is that some people, having become aware of this, will allow themselves to be taught by these experiential challenges to their prejudices and will therefore become aware of some of these other "invisible" but "realer than real" realities once again ... such as spirits. This is true despite the fact that ultimately what these realities will be and are will at some point be mysterious and outside of our ken. But then even what we learn from each other is received from persons who at some point are essentially mysterious and unknowable.

### *Leads to Awareness of One's Devolution of Consciousness in One's Life*

Also, it is in the process of being taught by the incongruence of one's prejudices with That Which Is that one can come to learn the roots of those prejudices in one's "past" experience and can come to know that one's experience was less prejudiced "prior" to those experiences — which are often traumatic ones — and that one was oneself more aware at that time of the "greater reality" of which I have been speaking. I am saying that if we follow our experience it will lead us back to knowing that we knew some things — some realities, some truths, some consciousnesses, some entities — earlier in our existences but for reasons having to do with the constraints brought about through biological and cultural experience, we turned from them, got distracted from them, hence disregarded them, so ultimately forgot them. Then, if one is like a normal person in the modern world, we claimed and operated our lives on the basis that they do not exist.

Yes, I am saying that an expanded spiritual awareness is part of our nature and is something we lose through negative experiences which cause us to retreat from larger reality. But that lost awareness can be retrieved by experience … by particular experience, which is positive in its nature of expanding awareness, though it might not be pleasant, and which enables one to reintegrate those awarenesses.

Therefore, a corollary of this learning is the realization that our so-called "development" is actually a process of reduction of awareness through various painful experiences which, curiously enough, "civilized" cultures have come to rationalize as being "good" for an individual in the course of that person's "development." This gradual reduction in awareness in the course of an individual's "development" is what I call *devolution* — the *devolution* of consciousness in an individual's life And I use that term because it carries the meaning of the reverse of evolution and the opposite of forward growth.

## We Remember We Once Knew It All, But Forgot It

We realize that this diminution of awareness over time accounts for our belief in our separation from others in the first place. It accounts for our perception of duality in the Universe. For when we reverse that diminution, all the realities, all the experiential encounters with and overlapping experiences with Others occur. And we realize that we once knew all this, but we forgot it.

## The Devolution From Grace in History, Too

Finally, the startling conclusion arising from all this is that "civilized" societies' distinction from the other ninety-nine percent of human societies that have existed over the hundreds of thousands of years history of our species lies in a peculiar pathology that is a result of a *devolution* — same meaning as above — that occurred to us as a species in that time.[1]

This distinctive mental illness is characterized by reduced awareness, which is elevated, desperately, to an undeserved status in our worldview and is mistakenly said to be a result of an *evolution*. We overvalue our reduced awareness, come of civilization, for reasons having to do with the pain of cognitive dissonance and the need, therefore, to rationalize as good *any* experience, regardless of its true value, in which one finds oneself. In our desperate struggle to justify the pathetic and meager state in which we find ourselves ... and thereby to beat back the pain of realizing how much we have truly lost ... we promote our meager "civilized" state far above that which is *truly* high and good and better for our species and for the experiences of the individuals within that.

Correspondingly, when we are confronted with aspects of that better way of being, exemplified by certain other people in certain other cultures, we feel the urgent and irresistible urge to scapegoat them, lest we become aware of our Western craziness. Thus we project onto them the characteristics of that pathology which is, in actuality, inside of ourselves but which we are frantically, and uncourageously, running from..

This plague, which has arisen and afflicted us in the last one percent of our history, thus creates the "kitty-drowners" and "butterfly-mashers" of the world. These things being true, we are able now to understand how it could be that we would find ourselves, at this point in time, on the brink of a self-destruction so all-encompassing that it would take most, if not indeed all, other life forms on this planet down with us into oblivion.

# Life Is a Cosmic Game

Taking this idea of life in Form being a reduction of a larger awareness or Reality, and based upon new-paradigm and conscious-ness research, we can go even further in our exploration of what is Real — this time regarding the apparent purpose of these processes. Remember that Bohm told us, "Matter is frozen light," and that Sheldrake added that matter is "the energy of light, or light-like energy trapped within a small space going round and round upon itself within fields. So matter is energy bound within fields."

Notice here how even in this description we see that coming into physical form amounts to taking energy that is free and constraining it — thus matter is a "fall from grace" for light. Energy descends into matter in a process where it becomes constrained (bounded). It "focuses," it stays put ... it is no longer free. Though I would say that it is not energy that is doing that but Experience. So the world of physical matter and bodies is actually a world where Experience descends from itself as free and unbounded into becoming specific and bounded and in place. It sets up an "experiment in truth" out of the vast potential of unbounded Experience ... of the No-Form state ... the state of free energy, free experience. Matter is like Mind deciding to write a book, to see what one will come up with, rather than leave itself open to ultimate potentiality.

With this understood, it is possible that what Reality amounts to is a Universe of beings, who are observers or watchers or witnessers but not actualizers. Like, for example, the masses of people in modern society who observe the events on the world stage, but who are not directly involved in any of it. Additionally, that Reality includes actualizers, incarnated beings like ourselves who bring things into form that are then shared and observed and "stored." That the actualizers create a shared reality, like a shared game, an ongoing one, that can be continually contributed to. So it is like we as No-Form beings are spectators; and those who come into Form are, for the time they are in Form, participants.

How this is different from what I said in the past is that it makes physical reality an arbitrary construction, yes, but it is one that was arrived at collectively for the purpose of creating a shared and ongoing endeavor ... for no other reason except that it would be fun to do it ... so that actions, experiences, and events could be made manifest, and not arbitrary, could become actual, and not potential, and could be shared, collected, and stored ... like a common enterprise ... rather than be individual, dispersed, and unfixed.

It is as if we all exist as eyes, witnesses, observers, but coming into form amounts to, when we do it, being part of the construction of a creative shared reality like a collaborative book or novel, which can then be shared among others, viewed by non-incarnate beings, and added to by others. So Reality amounts to a kind of wiki-novel. Which all the universe can read, at will.

Altogether we are led to conclude life is a kind of a game or a cosmic wiki-novel, if you will, involving ever aware and conscious of themselves Form and No-Form entities within a universe of Experience, Itself aware and conscious.

The physical world arises out of mutually confirmed assertions of it by others ... and the more others the more real it is. Reality is simply a set of agreements among those who we think to be like us ... it is a set of rules of the game. The rules of the game are that we agree that such and such will be shared realities... and we call that the physical universe.

We further agree that we will observe a separation of selves. Which means we will hide those elements of our experience of ourselves, for the most part, that involve our direct inner perceptions of and/or experiences of the other selves we have concocted ... the other people in our world.... It is like agreeing on the "tokens" in a board game. Though we could be any of them, in order to have an interesting interaction ... to make Experience better by being more interesting ... we stick to one of them; and we exclude our experience that involves being the others of them.

In other words, one of the agreements is that we are going to pretend we do not know what we indeed do know about others ... and their experiences (which are at base our own).

Yet all of it is an observed, a witnessed event.

The No-Forms are the audience. We are the actors on the stage. That is our only difference. And when beings become incarnate, they become actors. When we die and become No-Form, we become the audience once again.

It is all about actuality and potentiality ... one might say, being and becomingness. Add time to potentiality and you have created becomingness, you have created what we experience as Reality, as experienced in our Form state..

Reality comes down to being a wiki-novel, which those who come into Form, "participants," create, and those who are in the No-Form state, that is, "spectators" ... witnessers, observe as they will.

Reality is a shared creation, an actuality which we as No-Forms create ... for fun....

by incarnating.

# 17

# How "Within" Can Also Be "Outside":

## Demystifying the Link Between Consciousness and Matter … The Map of All Reality

*"Conceptual reality forms our external world and is necessarily relative and idiosyncratic. Yet the reality within is ultimate reality and is the same for all. It has been called World Soul, Mind-at-Large, Atman, and the Void."*

## How "Within" Can Also Be "Outside"

Despite the time-honored traditions and the revered societies and cultures that have maintained the preceding worldview, as described in the last two chapters, Westerner's find it hard to consider such perspectives without getting trapped in the boxes of solipsism, narcissism, "navel-gazing." This last — "navel-gazing" — points to the problem Westerners have in that, with their materialistic bias causing them to equate the self with the body, they cannot imagine a Divine Within or a God as Self or Experience without picturing it actually *inside* that body, and hence separated from the world outside! Then to take the further step of calling the physical world "illusory" has them imagining that world disappearing, leaving only one's body, suspended in a vast and empty space. And having nothing to look at but one's navel … *chuckle* Not very appealing. Not very logical or intelligent either. Yet entire paradigms and philosophies are based on such cognitive prejudices and cultural constructions of thought.

Nevertheless, living in the Western world as we do, the question must be addressed: Is this Experience solipsistic? What is its ontological status? By way of answering and to reiterate, the Common-Sense Realism that is taken as the basis for scientific claims about the material basis of reality is itself overturned by science. Hence on what basis is such a transpersonal reality to be founded as I have described? What is the ontological status of this model of radical subjectivity and how can it fit with and make sense of the elements of our experiential worlds?

Carl Jung attempted to answer these questions with his metaphysic, yet he has been criticized on both flanks, by scientists and religionists. Scientists have called him too mystical in his implications of a higher ontological status to psyche than to matter. But we have discussed how scientists themselves have overturned the notion of *any* ontological status to matter — letting us know that the status of our material world is dependent on the perceiving organism.

Hence that leaves the psyche or subjectivity of the perceiver with a higher ontological status.

Yet from religious circles, Jung's metaphysic has been criticized as being "merely psychological." It is said he has destroyed the old gods. However, one could think of psychological as in any sense "merely" only if one attributes a higher ontological status to matter than to psyche. Thus, that so-called religious people would criticize in this manner displays in them an inherent materialistic, not spiritual, worldview. Woe upon them for criticizing using that which they abjure.

At any rate, Jung has not destroyed the old gods, science did that, physics and astronomy did that. What Jung has done is to give such gods and spiritual realities back to us, although on a more enlightened level.

The old gods were always "merely psychological," but the "merely" part of it can only exist if one underestimates the psyche. And this usually happens when one overestimates the outside world. And here I think Jung sees remarkably well.

# Matter Matters. It Just Ain't Material

Jung warns against the mistake of forgetting that the outside world is experienced as a function of the psyche, that one's perceptions are dependent upon the psyche. So what could be more fundamental than the psyche? It is the only thing that one can ever *really* know to exist!

The outside world is an inference as Jung said, and it is well not to forget that whenever one goes about discussing reality. This is not to say that the outside world does not exist; but merely that if one may legitimately assume anything, then it is that the psyche exists. For psyche is directly perceivable. What we *cannot* assume is that the outside world exists as it is perceived, because it is only indirectly perceived.

If the external world were to exist as it is perceived — which is the theory of Common-Sense Realism — then one would need to assume that the psyche, or the brain, or the perceptions, whichever you wish, is perfect, is capable of sensing exactly what is out there. But then this is ridiculous, and even the relatively limited means of modern "scientific" psychology has shown that different individuals perceive different things according to their mental set, attitude, and so on. That is even before factoring in all the "constituted realities" — biological, biocultural, cultural, and the like — as we discussed in Parts One and Two.

And as to whether or not one individual's experience of external stimuli is exactly equal to another individual's of the same stimuli, there is no evidence nor any means of obtaining evidence that it is, and there is some evidence that it varies at least a little. The same stimulus may be said to have different intensity, and so on. In addition, one can never know if one person's experience of the color red, for example, is the same as another's; and it is most likely it is somewhat if not radically different

The point is that all is ultimately dependent upon the psyche. So what kind of facts could possibly be *ultimately* more valuable than psychic facts? We perceive and experience the world within and the world without, the one directly and the other indirectly. We interpret these experiences and call it reason; there is no rational mind if there has been no experience. Therefore, experience is fundamental and what is experience but that which is the psyche, or, in a sense, "produced" by the psyche. No psyche, no experience, no perception, no outside world. In this light it seems that in relating religious life to the psyche, Jung is closer to building a foundation for it than reducing it to nonsense.

To me, it seems that the reason people shy away from the idea that Ultimate Reality is within is that it seems then so limited. It seems that when a person encounters the concept of a reality within there is a tendency to picture in some way a small world within one's physical body, or at least to imagine that it would be limited to within one's ego. And since one externally views one's body as being a certain size and shape, and, most importantly, separated from everything in the whole world that is not oneself, one gets the feeling that if there is something, some kind of reality within, that it is likewise separated from all else and hence becomes of little value; thus the term "merely psychological." Yet, to me, this concept is not necessary and may be replaced by a new one.

# The Map of All Reality

Allow me to propose an image which, although it makes no claims to ultimate truth, expands the mind sufficiently to be able to imagine a situation in which "within" may also be inclusive. Eastern mystics and psychedelic researchers have frequently used terms such as "planes of existence," "planes of reality," or "levels of experience" in attempting to describe their journey within. The implication is that there are other states of consciousness or of experience at which the body and physical reality are no longer experienced as subject-object;

in other words, that one somehow has access to the Universe, is reconnected or achieves union with it, and is no longer separated from it.

However, for the externally-oriented Westerner, as mentioned, it is hard to imagine how within could also include the without. Mandalas have often been used by the mystics to illustrate this situation where descending into one's self is also a release into a greater reality, and mine will be on that order.

Imagine our reality to be a hollow globe with a cloth material covering the surface. Imagine the center of the globe as the source of all; and from this source extends roots in all directions, "supply lines" which proceed to diverse points on the surface. In the diagram this *source* is labeled the *integral* level, level 1.

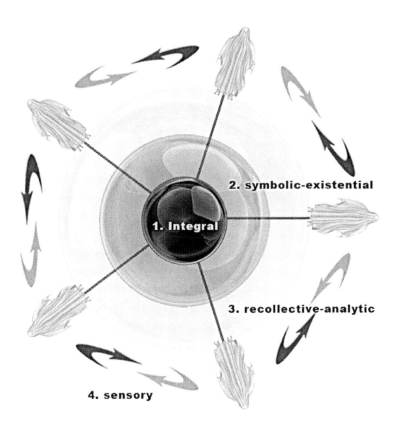

The more astute of you are already noticing that this is an Emanationist-type model … a devolutional one.

To continue, at the surface are figures which have emerged from the center and have protruded with layers of cloth enveloping their self, somewhat like Halloween sheet ghosts. And the sheet acts to filter reality, so that a limited perception is possible. (Somewhat trite, I admit, but it serves to illustrate the point.) This represents the *sensory* level, the outside world — level 4 in the diagrams. It is our world of common-sense materialism, which we perceive through the "sheet," the filter, of individual, cultural, and biologically determined constructs.

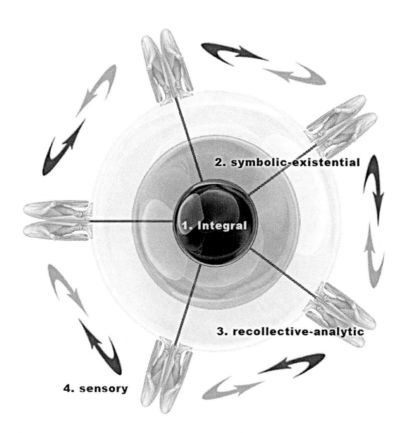

So, in the diagram, we see there are four domains or "levels" of Experience, from the most common or "outermost" to the most fundamental or "innermost." I have labeled these levels in accordance with that derived by Robert Masters and Jean Houston (1966, 2000) from their definitive work with LSD. In their research they did "depth soundings" of the psyche and came up with these levels.

In the list following I have added the levels Stanislav Grof has found in his work with LSD, as well as the comparable terms for these levels from spiritual and philosophical, and other psychological understandings. I have also included some of the classifications I have introduced in this work, for example, biologically constituted and culturally constituted levels. You can see that they line up nicely with each other, indicating the same reality is being looked at from all these different perspectives.

## The Map of the Universal Mind

4. Sensory/ Materialistic/ Common-Sense Realism/ Individually Constituted Realities/ Evidentiary

3. Mental/ Recollective-Analytic/ Psychodynamic/ Rational/ Existential/ Culturally Constituted Realities/ Potentiality

2. Participatory/ Metaphorical/ Symbolic/ Experiential/ Prenatal and Perinatal/ Biologically and Bioculturally Constituted Realities/ Actualization

1. Mystical/ Integral/ Raw Experience/ Ground of Being/ Non-Metaphoric, Non-Interpretive/ Transpersonal Reality/ God-Conscious

0. Beyond Integral: *TOTALITY OF EXPERIENCE/ DIVINITY*

To summarize them:

4. Senses ... Sensing

3. Mind ... Thinking

2. Participation ... Acting, Doing

1. Unity ... Being

0. God

As you can see from the diagram of the globe, an obscure perception is possible on the "surface," or in the outermost layer, of the relative reality of the external world including the other people in it. The sheets covering the individuals in the diagram represent the layers of individual, culturally constituted, and biologically constituted preconceptions through which we try to communicate with others. They explain why we only do so ineffectively and with great difficulty, with only rare real understanding between individuals occurring on that level.

We will leave off for now any discussion of the levels of Experience separating our egoic, materialistic self (level 1) from our self as God at the integral level (level 4).[1]

However, levels 2 and 3, the *recollective-analytic* and the *symbolic-existential* are levels of deeper experience that we traverse on our journey back to Source. For these are levels of Reality. But they are also stages of growth in expanding self-understanding, as I have pointed out (1972) and will publish as The Stages of Re-Membering Series, in upcoming years, and in a book summarizing these four phases of self-discovery ... hopefully fairly soon. So, the full explication of these levels as both levels and as stages of growth is taken up in other and forthcoming works of mine and is not so relevant here. However, see the Afterword of this book for a description of these works that are forthcoming.

For our purposes here, suffice it to say that Source and Ego are connected, and that Source is to be discovered "within."

## Sri Yantra

Thus, it is possible to imagine humans as having their roots in a Source which is likewise the same for all. This cosmological mandala resembles the Sri Yantra (pictured above) in meaning when it is said of it that from the center emanate forces which are manifest on the surface as physical reality, *maya*, or illusion; so that what we see are the diverse surface manifestations of one Source or one Ultimate Reality.

Putting my globe diagram and the Sri Yantra together, we get something like the figure below.

205

So, it is not that the physical/material reality does not exist, rather that it is filtered through the "sheet" of our ego. And this is not to say that external reality does not exist; rather that it is transitory, not ultimate, and that it is also not perceived as it really is, even in its relative reality, for it is distorted by the individual ego, which is language, memory, past experience … in one word — conceptions. Those conceptions are comprised of the biologically constituted, bioculturally constituted, culturally constituted, and individually constituted realities described in Parts One and Two of this work.

## Our Mind-in-Common

Conceptual reality forms our external world and is necessarily relative and idiosyncratic. Yet the reality within is ultimate reality and is the same for all. It has been called World Soul, Mind-at-Large, Atman, and the Void. Remember, I said it is "the same for all" not that it is experienced the same for all. Anyway, in the light of this inner identity of self with all and everyone, one will not, for example, make the assertion that psychic phenomena, because they arise from the psyche, are therefore not valid or real or true. Indeed, in the diagram we can see that we have connections to each other from the inside, psychic links if you will, overlapping Experience, more accurately, Experience in common, another way of saying it; and they can sometimes be more reliable connections with others — as in empathy, for example — than our observable connections of actions and words.

## The Problem of Distortions

Though distortions of this information are easily made, for all the reasons of the constituted realities we have been discussing. Still, the information that is shared this way is of a deeper, meaning more true, more important, more relevant nature when it is not distorted. And it is possible to experience and to verify at times that such information is not distorted. Good psychotherapists do this all the time … both formally and informally. Researchers of consciousness, such as Stanislav Grof, also do it. It is the way we separate the wheat from the chaff of inner views.

The distortions are an entire and huge issue, and problem, in themselves. For these are the things that have given such information a bad rap. Filtered through ego … and all the constituted realities of which it is composed … some pretty nutzy stuff has been asserted. Why, even one surprisingly popular conspiracy theorist currently has it that there are reptiles in government and that they spy on us secretly from behind the moon, as well.[2] Clearly, his ideas have been distorted by information that is currently out of his awareness related to or emanating from the reptilian brain, and the primal pain and distortions that arise from it.

He is being influenced in his understandings and his perceptions by clearly biologically and bioculturally constituted realities, if not other distortions, of which he is unconscious. So he sees these things of reptilian brain and the reptilian-like experiences of cellular experience everywhere, including in his altered state experience on a particular drug, which he acknowledges is where he first perceived this reptilian reality. He perceives their reality all about him, for he is not recognizing it as being symbolic of an inner reality that would teach him a lot if it was addressed and embraced. Hence this problem of distortions needs to be addressed at some time. And that I have done and will continue to do.[3] But not here.

## Our Inner Connectedness and Common Intersubjectivity

Also, if one conceptualizes as I have described, one may think that if a person has "died" and gone back to the Source, it is possible for that supposedly deceased person to visit a relative in a dream and to rise from the depths of that relative's unconscious (being therefore a psychological reality, "merely"), because in the framework I have described we would all be connected at the Source, at the center. Though, again, the veracity of one's experience of such sort is necessarily affected by the layers of unworked through constituted realities. That must be kept in mind when evaluating the status of any information received through such means.

With this model, also, one could easily understand how it would be possible for a person like Edgar Cayce to know things that others know or have known, through having access to the roots of all through the Unconscious. In other words there may be an intuitive link between us all. The Akashic Records — which spiritualists have claimed to exist and which are the repository of all knowledge and all history of everyone and everything — is understandable as Source, or Integral, in this model. And of course the Common Intersubjectivity I have described earlier — with shared experience and overlapping identities — is clearly understandable using this frame, as well. In any of these, naturally, one is wise to guard against all the distortions of constituted realities in making one's assessment.

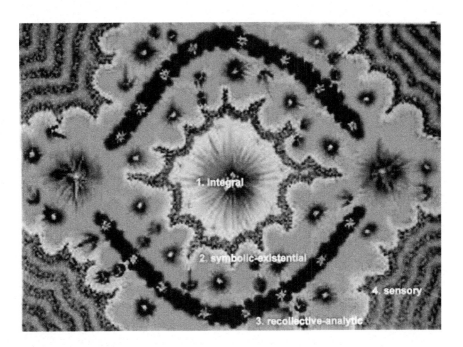

In any case, the graphics above and below show how such a model as I am proposing for the purposes of understanding how within can also be outside has manifested in physical reality in aboriginal art and in a crop circle, respectively. Look around yourself, and you will see the Universe revealing its structure in all kinds of ways, in a myriad of mediums, and everywhere.

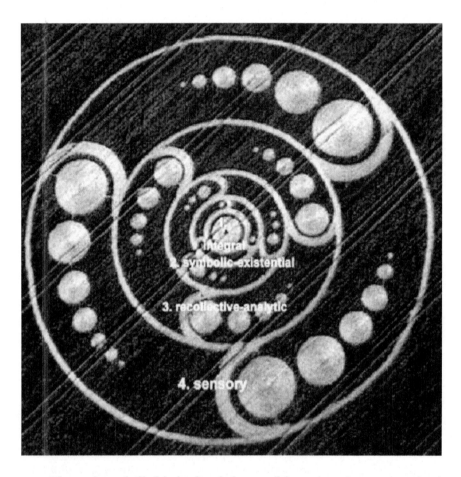

The point of all this is that it is possible to imagine a metaphysical framework ... and one only has to look to the East, as in the Sri Yantra, to see that it has been done ... in which "merely psychological" realities can be both ultimate and inclusive.

# 18

# Experience Is Divinity; Cognition Is Illusory:

## Why We Say One Should "Look Within" … The Highest Reality Is Also the Most Immediate One

*No, Bette Midler, God Is NOT Looking at You "From a Distance." The Divine Could Not Be Any Closer, It Is Identical to Your Very Own, Immediate, Experience*

*"…cognition of something is not the Reality itself any more than a picture of a beach is the actual waves hitting the sand or the feeling of the beach-goer basking in the sun."*

*You cannot have any "revelations" if you only allow in the thoughts you already have.*

*"If 'looking within' does not mean looking into one's direct experience, what could it possibly mean?"*

*Fearful of Looking Directly at Experience, We Defend Against It with Ego and by Creating Time: The Shield of Perseus*

*"A mind all logic is like a knife all blade. It makes the hand bleed that uses it." — RabindranathTagore*

# Experience Is God

Since the terms *God* or *the Divine* are usually associated with what is most real or what is the highest reality, I use those terms (*God* and the *Divine*) to refer to that Reality — that Highest Reality, or to That Which Essentially Is — throughout this text.

So since Reality can only be that which is directly experienced, and we can know nothing other than that, then *Experience is God.* Experience is the Divine, cognition is essentially illusion. I do not mean that the experience of cognition is illusion, for that itself is Experience, not simply cognition. When I say that cognition is illusion, I mean that the *contents* of cognition are illusory; and even more so, the results of cognition or reason are illusion. They are maps solely — reflections *only* of the That Which Is. And reasoning is merely maps derived from other maps.

Now, maps can be useful. They can reorient us and send us back to Experience in a manner that allows us to experience What Is in a different way, maybe even a better way. Experience and cognition can act dialectically to further each other. But cognition of something is not the Reality itself any more than a picture of a beach is the actual waves hitting the sand or the feeling of the beach-goer basking in the sun.

They are like those "communications," from outside of ourselves, of Others, which, though similar in their depiction in symbols (words) to what we might also use, are not the same as our direct experience. They are secondary interpretations of Reality, not Reality as experienced, therefore known.

Yet just as depictions by Other of *their* reality are useful and informative, a picture of a beach, while not being the experience itself, may allow someone experiencing a beach to have the thought of looking around for prone bodies and may open them to a different experience of beach because of that, whereas otherwise one might continue having the same, or similar, experience of beach again and again. It is in this way that maps are part of our experience of the Other, are *part* of our direct experience, which "impinges" on us and leads us, ultimately, into greater beingness.

If, furthermore, that Direct Experience has other characteristics associated with the Divine — let us say, for example, it guides us in living, provides us with values, assists and "saves" us, and basically helps us to grow and be better beings ourselves — then essentially that Reality is acting as God and deserves to be called by that name and worshiped as such.

That is, if one believes in doing such things. Speaking for myself, the only "worship" I consider valid is the feeling and expression of *gratitude*, to all else outside of myself. I see anything more as being sycophantic and demeaning of a self that is part and parcel of God. Also I consider any such worship, including in its form as prayer, to be conducive to and reinforcing of the duality that a path of greater beingness is intending to overcome in its seeking of re-union with Source.

That Experience might have these God-like characteristics of helpfulness and redemption is not something that can be deduced rationally or in the traditional scientific manner — it is outside those domains. But it can be empirically tested on the individual level, much as Ken Wilber (1977) has described that mysticism can be tested empirically on the individual level — that is to say, if you as an individual follow these particular steps, such and such will happen to you, or will be observed by you. It is in this sense that one can say that an assertion such as that Experience provides values and assists us can be tested in a scientific manner. Once that experiment has been accomplished, one can go to the spiritual literature and see if Experience as Divine does not make sense of much of what is found there, indeed much of what is incomprehensible otherwise. This experiment is one that can only be done by each person for him- or herself.

While this conceptualization of God as Experience or of Reality as Experience may seem unusually phrased, I explain that I am meaning the same thing by these statements as I believe is meant by phrases such as "Reality as Consciousness" (Wilber), or "I Am the I Am" (the meaning of *Jehovah* in *The Bible*). I believe it means the same as saying in Hinduism that *Brahman* (the ground of all Being) is equivalent to *Atman* — the "ground" of one's individual being. As explanation of this statement, Sathya Sai Baba explains that the only reality is the "I" or "the witness," which is the watcher and Experiencer preceding all maya or illusion.

But if this is so, then the Experiencer is Experience itself, is Awareness itself, for how can one distinguish the Experiencer from the contents of Experience — a point that is also made in these traditions. And I believe my terms — *Experience,* one's *immediate experience* — bring out the immediacy, the relevance, the fullness, not to mention the excitement, of those possibilities much better than words like *Consciousness, I Am, Brahman, Atman,* or even *watcher, witness,* or *Awareness.* I daresay that my immediate experience in the here-and-now ... equivalent to a slice of Experience ... is much easier to grasp, experientially and conceptually, if one says it is identical with God, than some amorphous *Consciousness.* And *Experience* contains and implies much more than that denuded term, *consciousness.* And I mean to imply all those wonderful things. If for no reason than to give back some appeal, if not downright enthusiasm, to the quest for self and enlightenment which terms like *Void, ground of being, nothingness, the Now, consciousness, awareness,* or some foggy elusive "witness" manage to sidestep.

While words like *awareness* and *consciousness* sound more important and prestigious to throw around, if one wants to impress others of one's advanced state (ahem). If we would be honest we would acknowledge they are simply sophisticated ways folks assert they are smart. Variations on this crude ploy of defending against the pain of being made to feel dumb as a child is acted out endlessly in social interactions, if one notices. In myriad ways, people are professing they are "not stupid, they are smart!" It is telling of how little patience parents and teachers have had with children's gradually growing awareness and competence.

However sad that is ... and such a waste of time to hear ... these terms of *awareness* and *consciousness* are not only sophisticated spins on childish hurts, they are not explanatory, either. Hence they are not very helpful. And they merely contribute to deluding people into thinking that the goal of any such quest is really quite outside one's ken of possibilities. It puts it out there, again, as on top of some pedestal, or mountaintop, especially when we describe it as "higher" consciousness, as something that is unattainable. Which is great if you want to lead people to thinking you are better than them if you have it. Hell, being unattainable for them, you must be quite magical and great if you are able to reach it. But it contributes to that corruption of the quest as described earlier in that parable from the East having to do with that person traveling all over China to find his horse only to discover, in despair, that he was riding it all along.

Contrary to all that, I believe that true enlightenment arises through a process of *descending* more deeply into one's immediate Experience, not trying to leave it behind to get to something "higher." "The fastest way to get to where you are going is to be most fully exactly where you are." "The only way out is all the way through." "A feeling, is a feeling, is a feeling." These are some of the signage on the path I affirm. Or, I might say simply, "Look down to what you are riding upon!"

Also, what else is to be meant by the terms that one should "look within" or "search within" when seeking out the presence or guidance of the Divine? If "looking within" does not mean looking into one's direct *experience*, what could it possibly mean?

This is also no different from what Nietzsche meant in describing the *empirical* basis of all true knowing. He pointed out that what was truly real could only be that which one directly perceived. But he did not mean what one perceived *only* with one's major five senses — that is, seeing, hearing, tasting, touching, smelling — as his famous assertions have been taken to mean in the founding of modern science. Rather he intended a more radical empiricism — one that could be founded only upon what one perceived in the sense of the totality of one's experiencing ... one like I am describing in this book.

# 2. Reality Is Not the Interpretation of That Experience

So here, finally, we arrive at the second of this book's assumptions, shared with the fields of transpersonal psychology, the perennial philosophy, and Jungian thought. Which is that Reality is not the interpretation of one's experience, directly apprehended or perceived.

Remember, raw experience has the status of being the only ontological reality that we can know. Thus interpretation of that experience creates distortion. Furthermore, interpretation brings *metaphor* into existence. By *metaphor* I mean the symbolizing or reflecting or map-making that we do both to explain and share our experience with the Other, as well as so as not to experience Reality directly.

## Interpretation Brings Metaphor into Existence

Metaphors are useful concoctions and unless one has the experience of overlapping Experience ("mind-sharing"), as I described earlier, they are necessary, and are the only way left, if one wishes to pass along one's good fortune on the path to others. However others, receiving them, are wont to live in them and not get to the Reality described itself. They get caught up in looking at the finger that is pointing ... the words *Consciousness, Awareness, witness, I Am*, the *Now*, for example ... instead of directing their attention to what these terms are pointing *to* ... which I submit is their experience *in that very moment.*

Fearful, for reasons I describe at length in other works[1] — these would be our prenatal, perinatal, and infancy pains and traumas, by the way — of looking directly at Experience, often we humans, like Perseus, turn our backs on it and seek to discern its mirrored image in the polished shield — that is to say, psychological defenses — of our egos. We tend to do this regardless how "spiritually" buoyed up in recently acquired metaphysical metaphor and jargon that ego might be.

So with this first gap of interpretation and metaphor, laid upon raw experience, error is introduced, just as a rippled pond distorts the image of the moon reflecting in it. Metaphorical realities then become all that can truly be known in the common sense of "knowing."

It makes perfect sense, then, that if metaphors are what one must use to convey one's experience to another, metaphors that hover closest to the realities they describe, that hover close to the raw experience itself, have the most to say or convey about the nature of the Reality they are reflecting. This does not give metaphors an ultimate ontological status then — as is done in archetypal psychology, where the metaphors hover close to experience. Nor does this assign metaphors an ultimate ontological status when they are furthest and most generalized from experience — as, for example, in the "Platonic" abstractions upon abstractions and the "fundamental" laws and principles of science.

No, metaphors are still reflections at all levels, they are not the Thing-In-Itself — the Experience. Still, there are close-hovering metaphors — ones that, let us say, are reflecting off the least disturbed pond or the most polished, least distorted shields. It is the attempt to seek out better metaphors, more closely mapped on to direct Experience, closer to God ("honest to God"?) metaphors, if you will, that is the intention and purpose of my works.

## Time Is an Abstraction As Well

Obviously then, this Experience that is direct and is not an abstraction must be experienced in the Now. For past and future are abstractions; they can only exist as memories or imaginings that exist in the Now. Thus there is only the Now, and direct Experience in the Now. And it is from this base upon which, I believe, all good theory on the nature of reality is based.

# The Uses of Normal Knowledge

Certainly there is theory based on scientific premises and research that is considered to be real and factual. And the replicability and verifiability of these pronouncements add further to their credibility. But we are always to remember that they are abstractions, generalizations only, of experience. Further, the experiences that they are usually generalizations of are those of an observer of an event which might be happening to another person or thing … which for that person or thing might be a direct experience but for the observer is already one step removed. Therefore such a pronouncement, "fact," interpretation is usually an abstraction of an abstraction. These abstractions of abstractions are then combined and worked together to form higher order theories and laws which are then another level of abstraction removed.

Not that these abstractions do not have their uses and purposes. The point is that we make a grave mistake when we presume that these abstractions *are* the things that they describe and the events whose actions are outlined. It is even worse when we give them a higher status or reality than our own experiences, which we invariably do. They have their purposes, as maps do, in terms of guidance and direction on how to control and predict such events and Realities. But not more than that.

Yet *we are engaged in a completely different endeavor when we seek to understand Reality as opposed to merely controlling or predicting it. We are engaged in a completely different endeavor if we seek to understand people as opposed to merely controlling or predicting them as well.* To do that *we need to reverse the direction of abstractions and look directly into Experience, as it presents itself and not as it is interpreted. Even one tiny step of interpretation removed, one split-second of analysis later we are no longer in Reality, in Experience, we are in abstraction.*

# A Better Way of Knowing

But there is another way of knowing, another way of venturing after Truth. This methodology is radically different from the supposedly "empirical" one of the sciences. I say "supposedly" because this is in fact a more empirical approach — at least in the sense that Nietzsche meant when he used the term *empirical*, which became a foundation stone of modern science, but which modern scientists have apparently forgotten. This methodology involves the *heuristic*, the *hermeneutical*, and the *interdisciplinary* methods of research and of attempt at understanding and discovery.

## Hermeneutical

Truths that are rooted in raw Experience — ones that "hover" as close as possible to the actual Reality and are least removed of their vitality and least refined into abstraction must needs be largely speculative, based, as much of it is, on subjective reports. So the ultimate relation between these experiences and other human cognitive, behavioral, and experiential structures — their degree and manner and direction of influence — will need to remain open.

Still, endeavors such as this next one — in Part Five, "Matter Is Message" — and that of my forthcoming works, following from this one, are in the strongest traditions of the social sciences.[2] This sort of hermeneutic approach is what has been called the "left-hand" of science, and it provides both the exploration of areas that cannot be served otherwise as well as it teases out implications and avenues for further research otherwise unseen.

*Hermeneutics* is the interpretive branch of science. It seeks to discover meanings inherent in events as perceived. And while normally this endeavor is seen as an inferior route of understanding within our dominant materialistic paradigm, and is only begrudgingly allowed on the basis that observers do apparently and irrefutably have some influence on events they perceive and these events are apparently needful of meaning, the preceding analysis should hopefully have made clear why I believe the hermeneutic route makes possible a *superior* understanding of an "object" of study.

For one cannot go into an objective study of something that is not on a more fundamental level a going into an aspect of one's *own* experience. It is by acknowledging, boldly and up front, that inherently subjective and interpretive base of any study that one can most likely turn it to one's advantage in discerning the deepest and most important understandings of what is within one's experiential focus of study.

As an example of how this can be so, take the analogous technique of *participant observation* in anthropology. It is the time-honored and required approach which anthropologists use in studying other cultures. It is based on the acknowledgment that a purely "objective" observation and analysis of a culture is profoundly flawed and that the only way one can hope to have the smallest possibility of understanding another's culture is to participate experientially, to the extent that one is able, in the events of that culture.

So just as one cannot imagine that a detached perspective of a culture could possibly be superior to a participant perspective, so also is this participation vitally necessary and superior to other techniques in various other types of study. I submit that, among other studies, the spiritual and philosophical aspects of pre- and perinatal experiences are one such, as exemplified in my book, *Falls from Grace* (2014a). So also are any philosophical or metaphysical studies of the nature of Reality and the meaning of Life, as exemplified in the next Part, "Matter Is Message."

## Heuristic

In a similar way, the importance of the observer is emphasized in the tradition of heuristic research in humanistic psychology, as described by Clark Moustakas (1990). As he explains it, heuristic

> *refers to a process of internal search through which one discovers the nature and meaning of experience and develops methods and procedures for further investigation and analysis. The self of the researcher is present throughout the process and, while understanding the phenomenon with increasing depth, the researcher also experiences growing self-awareness and self-knowledge.*[3]

Further:

> *Heuristic research involves self-search, self-dialogue, and self-discovery; the research question and the methodology flow out of inner awareness, meaning, and inspiration. When I consider an issue, problem, or question, I enter into it fully. I focus on it with unwavering attention and interest. I search introspectively, meditatively, and reflectively into its nature and meaning. My primary task is to recognize whatever exists in my consciousness as a fundamental awareness, to receive and accept it, and then to dwell on its nature and possible meanings. With full and unqualified interest, I am determined to extend my understanding and knowledge of an experience. I begin the heuristic investigation with my own self-*

*awareness and explicate that awareness with reference to a question or problem until an essential insight is achieved, one that will throw a beginning light onto a critical human experience.*[4]

## Interdisciplinary

The next approach, the *interdisciplinary*, should be self-explanatory. It means simply that approaching knowledge from a number of directions gives one a much better understanding of whatever it is. Yet, it is astonishing in this day and age how little this approach is used. There is a way of thinking that the sciences have fostered that has it that the best truth is one that is arrived at through specialization and through staying within the boundaries of separate disciplines.[5]

How this has come to be is that singular discoveries have come about through narrow focus on a particular issue. And these discoveries and the technology and inventions they give rise to have become the major focus of university knowledge. The major benefit of this is, again, to bring to a capitalist and consumer culture new "things" that can be used, mass produced, and marketed. Hence we have all these electronic "trinkets" today, as one example.

A way of looking at knowledge that used to be the way it was and which is the way it still is in spiritual circles has today become totally foreign to scholars. This way was that of the generalist and the one with a "liberal" understanding of the many ways of approaching knowledge. However, this generalist understanding of things has virtually no commercial value. Certainly it does not lend itself to employment or a corporate career either.

Yet, if one wants to do something more than simply be a producer of things and one wants the richness of understanding, the generalist, the interdisciplinary route cannot be ignored. I am reminded what one great innovator in science, in modern times, said, about the fact that he had often been referred to using the term, *genius*. He said, it is easy to display genius when one simply goes outside one's field to its neighboring field to draw from and feed one's inspiration. He said genius is just a matter of straddling disciplinary boundaries. And I would add, it is easy to appear brilliant, connecting the discoveries of related but separated fields, to those who are trapped within those disciplinary boundaries, enslaved by their jargon, and who cannot see anything beyond them.

In any case, my point is that an interdisciplinary approach, a generalist one, is the one I feel is most conducive to uncovering the kinds of overstandings that are attempted in this work and my other ones. With that, along with hermeneutical and heuristic approaches and research, I am bringing to the table something that is rarely done these days but I believe is critically needed.

# The Best Possible Map: Both Kinds of Knowledge Combined

I use such approaches in the upcoming part as well as in the works following this one in The Path of Ecstasy Series of books, which are forthcoming. Similarly, I present a model of Experience and Reality, a new paradigm, arising from such a methodology in the works already in print in the Return to Grace Series of books.[6] In these works my attempt has been and will be to hover as close as possible to the experiential reality I am modeling. Yet it is aided by other ways of knowing, more traditional, more scientific ones. However, in that these interpretations will have essentially been informed by the participant observer himself, that is to say, me, as well as the experiential reports of others who have journeyed into the same general domain, they seek to go beyond the interpretations that are possible from solely the traditional sources.

That is, that to say Experience is Divine is not to say that it is perfectly true in the way that it is immediately interpreted. Interpretations are one step removed to be sure, and so immediately introduce the element of error in that abstraction. In addition, Experience being Divine does not mean that all experiences are equally valuable in providing us with fertile and useful interpretations or understandings.

It is my belief that all experience is perfect in itself and cannot be otherwise. That is a belief based upon my experience. It is not a necessary assumption for this work, but it is something I share for the purpose of explaining how it is possible that Experience can be Divine in the sense of that word, *perfection*.

Still, we are aware that experience is sometimes called delusional or hallucinatory. This means essentially that it does not fit very well with the experiences of others who report experiences of that variety. But it is possible to think of these experiences as being perfect for the individual experiencer and yet not compatible with others of a similar variety. Then when we say that they are not real, we can be meaning that they simply do not conform to a general map for a particular group of beings — although they are Real for the person to whom they occur — and thus cannot be used fruitfully or to any good purpose by that group ... by any other outside of the individual involved. So we distinguish between Reality as What Is and Reality as what is useful to another.

Since I am *basing* my model and my interpretations on What Is — that is to say, direct experience, as closely mapped upon that as possible — but I seek to create low-hovering abstractions that might be useful to others, I do not simply leave off with the descriptions of experience by myself and others but I measure them against the other kind of abstractions available in the Now — those that are associated with science and with the generalizations of the experiences of others. It is the *combination* of these — much as one needs both particle and waves in understanding light — that I feel comes closest to providing what is helpful, interesting, and yes, useful, in terms of our understanding of our Reality.

So it is that in the following part, the final part of the book, "Matter Is Message," I lay out a great deal of what I think can be learned through the *experience* of matter. I will let you choose for yourself; but offhand, the conclusion I come to, all in all, is that matter reveals itself to us in a way that is astonishing. Further and more importantly, that matter has a message for us that is utterly astounding ... as well as is pertinent and necessary for us in present times.

# PART FIVE

# Matter Is Message

# 19

# The Earth Speaks Out on Love, Death, and Liberation:

## Breadcrumbs from Divinity, and Matter Is Message … One's Experience of Reality Is the Wisest and Most Beneficent of Teachers

*Experience Is Divinity. The physical world is its "Bible."*

## Physical Realities As Messages from the Divine

The modern day holy man from India, Sathya Sai Baba, explained,

> *He who seeks the Guru can find him in every word spoken within his hearing, in every incident that happens around him.* [1]

There is every reason to believe that he meant this literally. And, considering that in this context "guru" had the meaning of God and the cosmic divinity, the statement bespeaks much more than that as well.

Lawlor (1989) tells us how the Australian Aborigines' idea that the world is a metaphor or imprint for a truer inner reality is the essential element in their world view. As he put it:

*All of existence is the projection outward of internal, subjective states into objective ideas, forms, and substances; the Sky is the "dreaming" of the Earth. All life and all energies emerge from the Earth, even those we consider subtle and celestial. There is a constant exchange between the Earth and its dreaming.* The stars in the sky are the spirit energy of beings who were born from, and who have lived on, Earth, *just as all men emerge into the world from the female womb. These ancestral beings* return from the dreaming (the starry firmament) as radiated light and heat, which generate new life on Earth. *The male sperm is analogous to this radiation as it fertilizes the female but, itself, was born from the female.* Our minds and imaginations are always attempting to listen to the voice returning from the starry ancestors and we then reimage them.[2]

In another place Lawlor (1992) phrases it:

*The dreamtime creation myths of the Aborigines guided them to see the physical world as a language, as a metamorphosis of invisible spirit's psychological and ethical realms.*[3]

Similarly, Ronald Laing (1988) tells us, "The whole world was once part of man's psyche, but no longer."[4]

This idea of the physical universe as reflecting and expressing our basic spiritual and psychological realities is a common perception and viewpoint of mystics of all traditions. In the West, the Twelfth Century mystic, Hildegard, wrote about this vision of reality. Of her, it has been said, "Hildegard plainly uses physical laws as illustrations of spiritual truths."[5] And further on: "Physical images are most useful to Hildegard in comprehending the things of the soul."[6] This relates to the idea of physical reality as metaphor for Truth, which I am proposing.

Another quote:

> *Like the Platonists, she understands the world to consist of four elements: fire and water, earth and wind. She employs these pairs archetypically, to describe psychological traits and to create complex analogies for spiritual development.*[7]

The point is that this is the same way in which I am talking about matter as message: That in fact the world as we perceive it gives us lessons in underlying realities which are, in the absolute sense, more true.[8] That, in actual fact, the psychological traits of which she speaks are simply reflected in Nature in the form of earth, wind, fire, and water, and so on.

At this point, I feel it is important to stress that I am proposing much more than that the physical world is a source of metaphors or analogies for expressing psychic and spiritual truths. If this were all there were to it, I would be saying nothing more than that our perceptions of reality are a good poetic source, which is rather close to asserting nothing at all.

## The Spiritual Code Written Into Our Reality

From the preceding sections, it should be clear that what I am saying is that the physical world is our indirect perception — for direct perception, look within — of spiritual and psychic realities. Hence, the physical world cannot help but express the spiritual and psychic. It does not just reflect mind, it reflects Mind, or Divinity, or God. As I said earlier, our experience of life reveals that it is helpful and guides us. Hence our experience of life is God … it is Experience with a capital *E*. In looking at the makeup of the physical world, as well as our experiences of it, we are seeing that helpful Divinity. So of course the world contains messages for us, to help us to our highest good, our most encompassing understandings, and our ultimate destination in the Divine.

What I am saying is: Look around yourself; the world is rife with messages, both personal and universal, relating to your place in the Universe, the meaning of our existence, the meaning of existence itself, and, most importantly, of guidance for getting you and us back hOMe. If one is open to this possibility, the messages/truths are everywhere to be found. And the Universe and one's experience of Reality becomes the grandest, wisest, truest, and most beneficent of teachers.

The physical world and all its events are metaphors for consciousness; they are indirect spiritual perception, as we are seeing; and they are messages from ourselves as Divinity. We are taught in observing the world ... in being aware, in witnessing ... and letting the world and our Experience teach us.

The physical world, as indirect perception, is no different from symbols ... like the symbols of language. As well, they are as symbolic as those of art or of dreams. The physical world is hardly *real* ... solid, immutable, the base, the Source. Rather it is reflective of Source. It is an offshoot of a deeper reality of subjectivity, of Experience. It is an *epiphenomenon* of Consciousness. And, as reflective, as one step removed from Reality, it is symbolic. Its elements are symbols, which we can interpret, which are there to teach us.

# Breadcrumbs from the Divine

## The Mushroom and the U-Turn

When we do take in the world's messages, we see that even the tiniest details of reality — of its architecture and components — are instructive to us on our journey. One example of how such teaching is to be found in even the most trivial of details of the physical world is discovered by "listening" to the shape of the "lowly" mushroom. When we do, and we reflect upon it, we notice it is a breadcrumb from ourselves as Divinity; it is a letter from Divinity, a signpost to lead us hOMe.

You see, mushrooms, in their umbrella shape, are symbolic of the U-turn that is necessary in our spiritual evolution in returning to the ground of existence. They are "road signs" for the way hOME. As Jung explained and Michael Washburn (1988, 1990) clarified forcefully, the path of enlightenment is not a ladder path from no consciousness to awareness, or from low consciousness to higher consciousness. No. Our essence is the most expanded consciousness of all — Divinity. And our sojourn in life is one in which we begin, in the womb, with a relatively enlightened state in which our identity is rooted in the Divine — and we are deeply connected and accessing of Divinity — to one where we are separated from those roots and become a solitary unit. We become a separate entity; we see ourselves as body only. We do this in a stage-like, or ladder-like path of degression or descent … which we erroneously call "growth." This we "achieve" by adulthood if not before.

Truly advanced souls, when they come into life and "grow" towards adulthood, do less of that descent, by the way. Sathya Sai Baba is the best example of doing less "confining of the energy of light" in the best possible way. Jesus of Nazareth was apparently another one. Remember, he said, "Unless you be as a little child, you will not enter the kingdom of heaven." Pretty much what I'm saying, right?

However, it is true in the general sense, as well, related to the degree of forgetting of Divinity that we do in the process of "growing up" (should we be saying "growing down"?) in one's life. Which we achieve by adulthood, I repeat. If you do not think we, as adults, are reduced or constrained versions of a greater self, simply notice, as many astute people do, how we change in going from the time of schooling, as in high school or college in the United States, to the time of engagement into the commercial and "responsible" world of adulthood.

Many will remember how friends change alarmingly within a few years of leaving the nurtured fold of schooling to the initiated world of adult responsibility. Gone are the expansive feelings, the love and drama and trials and openings … the idealism and passion and dreams … and what is left, as a matter of course, is an adult consumed with, prodded by, and directed and taken over by the larger societal world with its more immediate demands around housing, income, career, and the like. Consciousness has been even more reduced down from what it had become as a result of the other constrictions of it caused by the events at the primal scene, birth before that, and conception before that.

Put another way, this explains how most people lose the "idealism of youth," as it is said. It is said folks become more conservative as they get older. And since conservative means more constrained, also more fearful of venturing outside what becomes an all-too-well trod "comfort zone," indeed that is true.

Then, at some time as a fully "grown" ... Jungians say the second half of life, I say anytime is a good time to begin ... one begins a process, taught by the travails, pain, the frustration, and exigencies of life, of returning to Divinity.[9]

Anything good we do or happens to us in our "descent" — and there will always be some, usually a lot, of descent, for even in becoming part of society we lose some of ourselves, of our deep Divinity — which mitigates that process of forgetting means we have less far away to return from. We are less "prodigal." We've got less "returning," less re-membering to have to do.

In any case, we arrive at adulthood. Something initiates the process of awakening, usually some tragedy or huge misfortune or disease or accident ... or addiction.

By the way, in this modern world addiction *is* such a big problem because it is a common way that folks deal with the psychological discomfort of having to be reduced. For we are given no institutionalized ways of regularly going into nonordinary states of consciousness for renewal and growth, as all other non-modern, and more natural, cultures provide, as Grof is wont to tell us. Lacking such a regular release into ecstasy — in its essential meaning of going outside *stasis*, or the severely constrained day-to-day self — many folks feeling that psychic injustice resort to a dim reflection of transcendence in the form of intoxicants that do not release to a greater reality but rather simply alleviate the pain, for a time, of our oppressive and otherwise relentlessly tedious Form existence.

Continuing now, sometime in adulthood that droning status quo is disrupted; it is derailed by a crisis of some sort. We are forced to turn inward for we can no longer go outward in an effective way. Hence we "return to the drawing board" ... we seek answers. We take up the quest. We turn round about, one-hundred-and-eighty degrees, like a mushroom, and begin the journey hOMe. Like a prodigal child we seek out connection with our universal "family." This is the message of the mushroom. This is how matter, as perceived, can be message.

This is interesting, more so, because mushrooms do in fact have psychedelic properties and they do, indeed, return us to the "ground," as Terrence McKenna (1991), among others, so poetically explains.

While this explanation of the message of mushrooms came to me on my own, many decades ago, I was to find confirmation of it years later in the thoughts of another writer as such:

*Everyone knows that a caterpillar turns into a butterfly, and for ages the chrysalis process has been a charming metaphor for transformation. But what does a mushroom turn into, except for the ground?*

*A mushroom, as Alice discovered, can turn us into all kinds of new forms. But whether we shrink or expand, grow as tall as the sky, or become as short as a blade of grass, isn't as important as the process of turning inward — the spiritual conversion of turning toward and into the inner life. What really matters is this inner change, a changing of attitudes, spirit, perception. In this light whole worldviews can be transformed in an instant.*

*The mystical experience has been described as "becoming one with the ground."*[10]

Now, the fact that the mushroom eventually "dies" and actually becomes the ground is telling us, if we listen, that the U-turn eventually ends up returning us to the ground of being at what we call death and mistakenly think of as an end of existence. More about that, coming up.

The point is that not only is this U-turn necessary in spiritual evolution but that physical reality teaches us this; that physical reality, if we notice it, is constantly teaching us and guiding us: Physical reality is metaphor and is as symbolic as the images in dreams. Thus matter has two aspects to keep in mind. It is both metaphor and message, you see. Matter is a message expressed metaphorically, symbolically, like all language and the symbols of dreams and art. Indeed, one's physical reality can be interpreted as readily as dream images in understanding oneself and seeking guidance on one's path.

# Fire and Transformation

Another example is that of fire. Fire is a changing of matter into energy. It is no coincidence that it has become a universal symbol for the process of transformation wherein one goes from one's personal, ego-based, desires and programs to transpersonal concerns and rootedness. For, indeed, is a fire, in changing matter into energy, not also a kind of going from matter (sensory awareness) and ego (body focusing) to spirit (consciousness) and energy (feeling awareness)?

Gurus from India are wont to express this — I am thinking, in my experience, of Shirdi Sai Baba and Sathya Sai Baba here — in the distribution of *vibhutti* to their devotees. Vibhutti is simply ash, holy ash. It is put on the forehead, consumed, and used externally and internally as medicine. What this ash is saying is that all our Reality is ash-like or having no form, ultimately. That our roots are in the No-Form State. That what we need to do to realize our essential nature as Divinity is to "burn up" the desires we have of the physical world in order to be liberated into a No-Form reality. Catholics are saying the same kind of thing in their distribution of ash on the foreheads of worshippers at ceremonies (Masses) performed on their Ash Wednesday, which signals the beginning of Lent, which is meant to be a time of sacrifice in preparation for the "rising up" into the light, symbolized by the resurrection of Jesus on Easter.

Notice here how similar this idea is to that of the Phoenix rising from the ashes, by the way. The fire, thus the ashes, precedes the rising up … of Jesus, of Phoenix. One would not think such "pagan" symbolism and Christianity to have so much in common; but here, as in many other places, they overlap.

In any case, notice that the process of doing this involves *burning*. Many spiritual aspirants believe that the path to liberation is about *detachment* from desires. That is to say, about separating oneself from desires, which, by definition then, acknowledges their continued existence. But vibhutti, the ash, symbolizes a *burning up* of desires, not a suppression of them. You do not get ash by putting out of one's mind the firewood in the forest, though the spiritually timid would wish that were so. No. Rather by gathering it up and engaging with it by setting it afire, that is, activating it.

Whereas, the path of detachment is usually employed in spiritual practices. And this means, for the vast majority of aspirants, that one seeks essentially to *suppress* desires. Sexuality is usually the first target, as we all know. This mistake of suppression, detachment, enforced "relaxation," is one of the greatest boo boos on the spiritual maps that are usually drawn in our religious rituals and our descriptions of spiritual practice. Terrified would-be adepts, alarmed by their desires and hoping that wishing away disturbing psychic-emotional contents can make it so, insist on these erroneous charts.

By contrast, Bhagwan Shree Rajneesh, also known as Osho, described and facilitated, at his communes in India and Oregon when he was alive, processes which involved *going deeply into* whatever desires one had which were blocking one's path. If one was drawn to drugs and alcohol, it was thought the best thing to do was to face that head on, go deeply into it, until one was finished with it. It was not thought effective or good to simply suppress urges but to face them. Those familiar with the twelve steps of AA and narcotics addiction will hear in this advice something similar to what they know to be true in practice, which is that one can never truly give up addiction until one has "hit bottom." I can attest that is true. I can also attest that hitting bottom not only works, but works splendidly; whereas struggle fails miserably, inevitably.[11]

In any case, Rajneesh used techniques of a "primal therapy" which involved getting out one's rage, fears, sorrows, and other inner suppressed emotions. I went through and then facilitated an actual, an effective, primal therapy, to accomplish the same thing, by the way. And along with that I experienced and later facilitated holotropic breathwork for the same end. Regardless, Rajneesh had rather raucous group events for this purpose. Rajneesh's adepts were notorious for their sexual experimentation as well; this was viewed as part of that same process of burning up, not detaching from, desires.

The way this path is metaphorically explained, by Osho/ Rajneesh is that one can seek to grasp sand by holding it tightly, in which case it will seep through one's fingers and will be lost. This is akin to the striving that one finds aspirants usually doing. They try *so* hard; they are left with so little. Or one can hold one's hand out palm-like, and one will be able to hold and be able to receive much more of any sand put into it. Thus it is through surrender, not struggle, that one progresses.

The effective path is not the strenuous ladder-style path from a "lower" state to a more accomplished ability to repress emotions. Rather it is a giving up of such strenuous efforts and a turn round about … that mushroom-like U-turn again … to simply allow the beneficence and guidance of the Universe, which is always around, to come in. And remember, the Universe is God, and Experience is Divinity, so It most definitely will be there to assist and comfort. That one will allow oneself to do that, to do that surrender, is the essence of the idea of *faith*, in that surrendering requires a rather pronoiac belief that the Universe *will* come in to assist one.

To the contrary, those seeking the strenuous route are actually giving rise to the devilish evil they are so fearful of trying to keep out … or the "desires" they are most assiduously striving to push out of conscious awareness. For in seeking to keep out thoughts, feelings, and emotions … to keep them down and under wraps … one is asserting that one *needs* to do that, and one is thus saying the Universe is indeed dominated by evil, which wishes to come in and hurt and destroy one at every opportunity, and not by benevolent Divinity. You see how in believing in a devil or Satan actually creates one? Whereas having faith in a benevolent Divinity allows one to experience that actual reality instead?

Indeed, I once described this as the essence of the primal therapy I went through and later facilitated in others (1985, 2014a). I put it, "Likewise, an important benefit of primal is that it can teach us an attitude of surrender to process. That we can throw ourselves, time and again, into the maelstrom of catharsis and still, somehow, be upheld and even embraced, despite ourselves, gives us confidence in a beneficent universe and allows us to foster surrender in our attitudes to the pushes and pulls of process as it makes itself known to us in our daily life."[12]

The other way Osho explained it had to do with tensing up to achieve relaxation. It is an idea I brought to bear on a technique I used specifically, and regularly, in my facilitation of holotropic breathwork. I would have the group members, or the experiencer, at the beginning of the session, tense up their bodies. I would have them focus on one part of their body after another, then larger parts of their body, and eventually their body as a whole. They were told to *hold their breath* while doing this, as well. Notice that this is the *opposite* of what spiritual questers are told to do — which is to relax and breathe. That comes later in the way we did it, and at that time, as a consequence of the earlier exercise, more easily.

After each time of strain and tension, of, say ten to thirty seconds, they were told to "release," to "let go." They had been instructed to let go totally and completely ... much as if one had allowed oneself to drop out of an airplane. They and I found that it was much easier to reach the relaxed state conducive to receiving the guidance and inspiration accessed in nonordinary states of consciousness not by *striving* to be relaxed ... do you see the inherent irony in that? Rather by going directly into tension to an extreme degree so that, in truth, it could be left behind with little effort at all ... simply by allowing.

Rajneesh (1976), in his book, *Meditation: The Art of Ecstasy*, wrote that this "leftward" path is similar. Again using the metaphor of the fist, he said that if one wanted to hold more of that sand, again, one would do better to tighten one's fist as much as one could and then let go. At which point, the relaxed palm would allow one to receive much more.

Indeed this leftward path is expressed, of all places, in the movie, *Joe Versus the Volcano*. It is depicted as a crooked path, in this movie. A "crooked" way expresses the unexpected twists and turns of a path that is not methodical and regimented but learns from and is allowed to be taught by the exigencies and pain of life through a process of surrender to what is actually fate or a kind of Divine Providence. Similarly, Grof (1990) describes it as a "stormy" path to self.

Naturally it is fire, in the movie, this time the fire of a volcano, that one must allow oneself to drop into in order to be reborn. The movie accurately states that this requires both courage but also a bit of heroism on one's part. It is not easy to go against the pulls of the current of common opinion and social pressure and adopt another path. And it sure as hell is helped by having a compelling reason to do it, which is achieved when one does it for a higher cause outside of oneself, as was the case in *Joe Versus the Volcano*. That is, for transpersonal reasons of love, caring, and desire to serve the world and other suffering beings.

## *The Second Half → A Higher Cause*

This idea of aligning with a higher cause as being the final stage in a path of liberation is something you will see me getting into in depth in the future. In the past I have explored it in the publications, "The Second Half of 'the Cure'" (1995b, 1995d) and "Unconditional Acceptance and the Primal Process" (1993). However, I have much more to say on it, and I will, when I bring forth my work tentatively titled *Primal Spirituality* or *Primal Spirituality and the Primal Process: The Second Half of "The Cure."* For the book describes the stages on the path of primal process, with the final "cure" coming about, and true happiness and enduring joy only to be had, when one aligns oneself with something higher than oneself — a cause, a love, a service, an ideal. You can check out the Afterword of this book for more of what I have in mind for this work.

Incidentally, for those steeped in the literature of Eastern spirituality, especially that of Buddhism, I will note that this has something to say about the concept of the *bodhisattva* — the being who holds off going into liberation until everyone has, so that she/he can assist in the process ... like the leader in an emergency who allows and assists in everyone getting safely out of the burning building before one allows oneself to leave. In the sense I am saying about the true cure for misery, then, it is the bodhisattva, not the one who becomes a buddha by having striven for one's own liberation, who is the truly enlightened being.

## *Pain*

Fires burn, also. Fires are painful when approached closely by humans. What this also is telling us is that the process of transformation is necessarily uncomfortable and requires, to some extent at least, suffering. As Jung put it, "There is no coming to consciousness without pain." And, "One does not become enlightened by imaging figures of light but by embracing the darkness." As Janov told us, paraphrasing here: The unreal self was put up through violence. It can only be overthrown in what might seem a violent way.

Indeed, relinquishing one's ego, going out of one's comfort zone and facing what one has suppressed and repressed, and allowing the emotions and feelings to come up and be dispersed by *feeling* them, not by acting them out, is a painful thing to do. It involves suffering.

When one refuses to direct one's Pain onto the world and innocent others, it wreaks havoc on oneself. One feels anguish … one feels one's Pain … when refusing to use scapegoats for one's "shit." But this is the thing to do to go beyond it. By refusing its projection outside, it is directed inside where it can be "burned up" in a process, which is eventually illuminating, but is uncomfortable in the near term … to put it mildly

But it is a misery that ends. And it is an agony which — despite everything one might think — is not only much less tortuous in the long run than acting out one's Pain on others. (That requires its own elaboration, but here is not the place.[13]). But it is also an anguish that leads to real freedom, real liberation, as the Phoenix so poetically reveals to us.

The point is that all of the above is the message embodied in fire. As in the myth of the Phoenix risen from fire, it is only by going through the "fire" of the pain and discomfort of the loss of ego — which comprises the rigid set of defenses one has in place to block from feeling one's Pain — that one becomes free.

## Butterflies and Change … About Ecstasy

The other potent message about transformation is found in observing the process of the butterfly. It is not about going from matter to energy in this case, but about the process of change and how we misinterpret it and can do better in that regard. Is not the cocoon like our coffin? Yet does the caterpillar die in the process of transformation? Hardly, it becomes better; it becomes "more." I am saying that it is no coincidence that we perceive butterflies as beautiful, for a part of us knows that the change we think is death actually involves going into something more wonderful, more beautiful.

Hell, even the unappreciated moth becomes something that flies. Pretty good for something that was once more like a worm. And by the way, do not moths seek out the light? That is not coincidence. It shows how in the process of transformation, we seek greater awareness.

Butterflies and the process of chrysalis demonstrate something about the greatest change of all for humans. Death is the most profound leaving of stasis, of ecstasy; it is the greatest going out of our "comfort zone" and into an unknown. Our sciences tell us death is like a going into a pitch black nothingness, total nonexistence, because the person ceases to exist *as a body*. Meanwhile our fears ... and tragically, all too often, our religions ... would have it that death is a going into a place that is lesser, maybe even horrible.

Our butterflies want us to know that, like Rabindranath Tagore so poetically explained, death is a process of becoming greater than one was, of going into a better consciousness and experience of existence. As he said, "Death is not extinguishing the light; it is only putting out the lamp because the dawn has come." So death is actually like a dawning of awareness, going into a "lighter" and happier state of existence. It is an ecstatic experience not just in *ecstasy's* root meaning as a change of state but in *ecstasy's* emotional connotations as well. Just ask any butterfly. Don't bother with interrogating the caterpillar however. It, like us, is in a state of ignorance for the time being.

## Snakes and Death ... and Birth

The lives of snakes are potent messages about the essence of death, as well. Once again we see that a process of transformation, which leaves behind a corpse-like thing ... refuse only, just like the butterfly's cocoon ... is actually a renewal. It is like a rebirth into a new, better, "younger" state. Is death how we become better, younger? Well, ask anyone and that is the last thing with which they would agree. Yet that is what snakes tell us all the time. If we but open ourselves to their "communications."

Snakes tell us not only about death, they also tell us about our birth experience. As the snake shedding its skin is like being renewed or being reborn, so also its shape expresses that our birth is like going through a tunnel into the world. And the snakes who crush in order to kill, well, they are telling humans, in particular, that our birth is a crushing experience and is quite deathlike in the way we experience it. It is, too. See especially my *Wounded Deer and Centaurs* (2016b) on birth being experienced as death.

## The Process of Decay and Change as Cyclical … on Entropy and Re-Forming

What about the process of the decomposition of form we observe everywhere around us? We see that things do not stay the same but they deteriorate over time. That things disintegrate into their components over time, or become lesser, is termed *entropy*. It is the gradual movement of the Universe from order into disorder.

However, there is no reason that things have to *decay*, which is the way we normally observe the breakdown of living things. For if we observe the Universe, we see that matter simply transforms. Planets, asteroids, galaxies move about. They change from matter to energy and then back again. As they say, matter is never created nor destroyed. It does not decay. Matter, like the butterfly and the snake, simply transforms, if anything, to energy. And that tells us a lot about the fact that consciousness never ends. There is never a time when it is not. It has just changed.

But on Earth there is this additional thing of decay, which happens to biological things. It is about biological things acting upon other biological things. Bacteria acting upon plants and flesh, for example. It is beings interacting, when you come right down to it. Take out our misunderstandings about decay as being death, and decay is as much an interaction between beings as puppies playing, as cats nestling within the arms of children, or even as supposedly "parasitic" insects feasting upon the waste matter accumulated on the skins of rhinos. Take out our prejudices and what we call *decay* is all just the game play of the tokens in this spiritual adventure we call "life."

At any rate, biological things changing in the way we call *decay* means simply that they change, but in a way that they *seem* to be lesser. Keep in mind, that would be to *us* — remembering what I said about biologically constituted realities at the beginning of this book — and for all we know, *only* to humans.

But are these biological things really becoming lesser? Are they actually destroyed? No. We know that, here also, like the snake and the butterfly, they have just changed their form. They re-form. They *trans*form. They, like the mushroom, also return to the ground. They break down into smaller components, their elements, but they hardly go away. This tells us that life is not about beginnings and endings but about cycles of infinite renewal. Living things become greater, bigger, they add things to themselves ... they *play* at this existing-in-physical-form thing ... which is how all biological things are artists, really, and how they express the aspect of God as Creator. Then they start over again as a different form. They return to elements, then they reorganize those elements in a magnificent and often beauteous creation. Again. And then again.

## Seeds, Their Plants, and Immortality

We get the same message from observing the patterns of reproduction. Let us look in particular at plants and how they "renew" through becoming seeds. Notice I said that differently than what you expected. We make the mistake of anthropomorphizing their process by saying plants die and then new plants are "born" from seeds. As if the seed is not "alive." As if the seed was not a part of the adult plant. We project our own fears about death ... and decay ... on the world of the flora; we look at it from the perspective of an "adult." This time, an adult plant. Again, we see everything in terms of growth in an *upward* direction. Our goals in life we project on the plant. As if its goal is to be the adult plant, bear the fruit or flower, and then go away. Like we think, in our biologically constituted way again, is what our life amounts to.

But from the perspective of the seed, the plant is a carrier of its essence, just as our body is simply a carrier ... actually a physical manifestation, an indirect perception ... of our actual reality of Experience, or Subjectivity. So from the perspective of the seed, it uses plants ... as we use bodies in our process of reincarnation ... to continue its "game" of existence. The essence, the seed, uses plants as part of its play. And we do not have to think of that essence as actually becoming a plant any more than I as a writer think of my book creations as being me. No. My books are created from my essence, and they are no more me than the physical plant is the

242

essence of the plant, its seed. The essence, the seed, just keeps renewing itself; "playing at existing"; God "having fun" again. And it is immortal, in a sense, that way.

This way of looking at it is like we could imagine going from video game to video game to play them. Different games, or the same one over and again. The game ending is not the end of anything, really. It is the beginning of a more interesting game when the game one was in got "boring." We are beings engaging in lifetimes of different dramas, or games, just as the seed, actually its essence, "engages" in different plants.

And yes, that is another thing we notice about Reality by observing physical reality and its changes. The purpose of life is fun, is to be interesting. Why else would there be the energy constraining itself as Form? Why else would you come here? Why else would you reduce yourself? If not for fun? The only thing that is really like death is boredom, from the Universal perspective. Remember that the next time you are bored, by the way. For as Abraham Maslow had it, "The capacity for growth is equal to the capacity for boredom."

## Gravity and the Omnipresence of Love

Yes, physical reality has messages to us about life related to fun, interest, and … even sex! Love, actually. By that I mean the patterns of the Universe tell us, with the gravitational force observed throughout … from planets and stars and galaxies to the attraction within atoms … that the *intention* of the Universe is to seek to come together, to unite, to re-unite, to attract, to be attracted.

I am not saying that love is like gravity. I am saying that the entire Universe *is pervaded by Love*. And we, looking at it indirectly, from our biologically constituted perspectives, our perspectives in the reduced Form State, or physical state, see it as gravity. In this way we not only diminish a profound revelation of the nature of the Universe into an abstract force with only one characteristic to it — attraction of matter to matter. We also separate ourselves from experiencing its deeper dimensions. This is how in splitting off from the Divine and Nature we diminish our experience of and appreciation of Existence. Oh, what a tragedy we do in seeing only as gravity the Love that is everywhere around and compelling everything in the Universe.

Yet it is really love we see in observing the force of gravity. So, yes, the world loves us. Yes, gravity is the world in love with us. And why not? Do not we, in our actual *experience* in relation to it, the Earth, experience the compliment of that gravity in the form of our love for the Earth?

You say you do not love the Earth? Oh, you're one of them. However, if you did not love matter, why do you fear death so much? Yes, even our appreciation of being immersed in physical reality, our bliss of existence, of interacting with "things" is us being in love with the Earth. So there! Lol.

# 20

# The Universe Speaks Its Intention for Existence:

## Matter Is Message on Time and Existence, Being and Becoming … The Intention of the Universe … Is Fun

*"The river tells us that Being and Becoming are one in Reality…. The ocean, adding to that, tells us that separation is ultimately an illusion."*

## The Big Bang

Concerning the intention of the Universe, the Big Bang has something to say about that, as well. In the Big Bang, we see the pattern that exists, at its most encompassing level of Universe, in the process of the Universe's changing and evolution through time. The Big Bang speaks the Universe's intention to manifest and return, endlessly; it reveals eternity to be cyclical and dynamic, not static as it is usually portrayed.

Since matter reveals Ultimate or No-Form Reality, however distorted, it has something to say about human spirituality, as well. It tells us something about the processes of spiritual existence ... about spiritual reality and, yes, even God. It also says more about the essential nature of the Universe being love.

The processes of the Big Bang and its return ... to another Big Bang again ... expounds on our cycle of descent and return to Divinity, our cycle of forgetting and remembering, of separation from Divinity over lifetimes and our return to identity with God over lifetimes again. I will elaborate on this in the forthcoming.

# Water and Time

Water speaks to us of the intention of the Universe, and its process, as well. It tells us much about the process of life through time. It is all right there in full view. And rivers flow into and merge with the sea, which tells a profound much more. This time about the Universal Project ... about the motive and design of the All That Is for entertaining and glorifying Itself through manifesting in reduced states in which parts interact and play.

One of the major teachings of rivers and streams has to do with the nature of time ... as well as the pattern inherent in process over time.

First, it reveals there is no such thing as time as we think it. The river exists at its head, at every point in its journey, and as it merges with the sea, simultaneously. One could visit it at any point and it remains the same, unchanging, yet it is ever new with each new advancing point on the journey. So it has Being, in that it is always at every point the same, yet it has Becoming, as well. Being and Becoming, stasis and change, seem separate but are actually united in a way we have no word for, in our dualistic Universe with its polarized language. Yet Nature speaks such a "word" in its manifesting as river, as stream.

This word has other connotations, too. Rivers and streams tell us there is one constant Reality, a beingness, which is unchanging but which participates in an illusion of change, a becomingness, for the sheer, blissful, bubbling delight of it. The stream, especially when it is "younger," is the most delighted, effusive, and joyful, bubbling and frothing up and around and over everything and anything. Of course, as Old Man River it shows us it is somber, spent in some sense, more able to be useful and helpful, in another, but, regardless, ready to return home to the sea.

And it speaks these revelations by means of discrete entities. It is composed of individual drops of rain, the atoms of water, too. Yet neither raindrop or water molecule are separate from the river, the stream, the ocean. They are one, yet separate. Just as we are separate yet one with Divinity.

This process of manifestation through time … as water drops, creeks, rivers, and oceans … never changes, yet it is always creative. Every journey of every driblet of rain is different. Any water molecule, or drop, is potentially everywhere, for it can show up anywhere on Earth and eventually does. Yet, though eventually it manifests globally, it is for periods of time limited to *regions* of water, and to geographical areas. These can be likened to regions in our experiential pools wherein we continue to encounter life after life many of the same people.

Water, for another thing, tells us about how to live life through the process of time. The water encounters obstacles in its journey, as do we. Does it fret? Does it give up? Does it get angry? No. It bubbles up blissfully … giggling … as it goes forward in any way possible … around, over, under, and eventually, in the course of time, through. Yes, the river laughs as it encounters obstacles, frothing and churning over them … playing and pointing at them, gleefully. We imagine it teases and capers in interaction with the other "beings" in its world, those of its streambeds and boulders. In any case, seeing this, we could transform our life profoundly if we truly wove merely that one teaching about how to deal with obstacles into our experience of living.

The stream shows us much, also, about the necessary exigencies of life. It acknowledges the way life is full of *crashing* down to the depths, to scour its gritty underlayer; and then alternately, and often suddenly, being tossed up joyfully into the air. There is a reason we use *turbulent* to mean both troubling and fast moving events as well as to describe the quality of a stream at times. For that matter, it is no coincidence that *bubbling* describes both an effusive feeling of humans as well as an activity of water. Consider, as well, the dual meanings — of the characteristics of water and the qualities of human feeling — expressed in the words, *sparkling, effervescent, shallow, turgid, deep*.... All of these express a water's and a human's contrasting moods and experiences, their motility, their tendency to change suddenly. Water is often a symbol for emotion, in fact.

More than that, water shows again, like the Big Bang process, the intention of the Universe to "enjoy" Itself by transforming again and again ... ever renewing and ever creative ... in the way water flows to the sea and the way all water rises eventually into the atmosphere, only to begin the entire process again by "descending" to Earth — no coincidence there, either, just like the "descents" from Divinity we make in coming into Form, into vessels, into bodies. And, why? Because it is fun.

Rivers and oceans also tell us a lot about merging and becoming more encompassing ... having more participation, one might say, in a larger reality, ultimately in the Universe. The song, "Old Man River," expresses this quality of becoming broader, sounder, more persevering, more constant and steady, more unaffected, less dramatic, but more helpful and able to provide service to others, as the river, "fully grown," gives so much to us in terms of passage, beauty, habitat, ecological niches and sustenance for the living, and more. A river broadens and swells with each merging of river or stream just as a person serves more as one grows in time, embracing and including in one's existence more and more of the real experience of life.

Creeks show also that it is the experience of life that purifies us. By which I mean that just as water in its ebullient journey is purified of its detritus and infused by life-giving oxygen and thus continues on its path in joy, light, and sunshine; so also we see that it is by action, not stagnation, that one stays bright and bubbly, fresh, and ever inspired. Ever moving forward, encountering and interacting, learning through such and becoming wiser, but ever more longing of our hOMe, just as the river yearns for the sea.

# Oceans and Knowledge ... Enlightenment and Service

And water as telling its tale through seas and oceans? It has quite a narrative prepared on that, as well. This time it expounds about universal experience and knowledge.

Old Man River gets wiser through experience and service but yearns to become one again with the ocean, to merge, to get a rest of sorts, to be home again. Yet it adds the wisdom of its experience with that of all waters, all raindrops. In this way we have a collective consciousness prevalent in the Universe. Not so esoteric as Akashic Records, still we enjoy and are part of a grand morphogenetic field, a collective unconscious, a depository of knowledge to which each of us adds.

The ocean is serious and strict as a storm, refreshing as a rain shower, emanating beauty and majesty in its clouds, and teasing as a drizzle. Importantly to us, it is playful on its shorelines, lapping and interacting festively with all of life. And the ocean is full of secrets in its darkness. It is ever more mysterious in its depths.

It tell us there are deep reaches of revelation, of insight to be had, as well. As knowledge alone, the ocean tells us there are depths of experience ... we usually say of knowledge ... which are dark and normally inaccessible to us ... unfathomable in the usual Form State.

In another facet, the ocean, like a mother, comforts with the sound of its waves ever crashing and receding.

What does all of this tell us? It tells us about the state of advanced awareness through experience of life ... of enlightenment in a sense. It tells of that quality as being homelike, as being both origin and destiny, as being eternal, yet dynamic. As encompassing much, but being little understood. It is alone, yet embracing. It'll bust you with a thunderclap if you get too far afield, this majestic teacher, this enlightened one. It'll also embrace you as a mother and allow you to find comfort in the rocking waves and the soothing waters that are ever greeting its warmer beaches.

We as drops or atoms of water participate in a reality larger than us. And when we identify more with that larger reality, as creek or stream, as river, and eventually as ocean … not merely as raindrop or molecule … we are more risen up and out of our egoistic buffeting with life's experiential elements, as shown by the molecules as they collide with their surroundings of rock and froth. We are more blissful and ebullient in our expanding our identification to ourselves as stream, even as when we identify with family, and species, and as planetmate, and thus we are removed from insular misery.

Identifying with our larger identity as ocean brings to us its characteristics as well: Knowledge, service, teaching, contentment, nurturing, and yes, occasionally scolding, we come to embody them. In this we are identifying with all of life, with all of history, with all beings who live and who have ever lived on Earth. I'll talk later about identifying with our Divinity when we muse upon the message of the Cosmos, and its array of infinite lights, of stars.

The ocean is the giving and soothing mother of all; it is the misunderstood teacher or guru with depths no one less constrained can fathom and so it is ever misinterpreted. It is ever dispersing gifts which are not seen for what they are and are misapplied; yet ever giving, still, is the ocean.

Nevertheless, the ocean reveals Beauty just by being there. It makes artists of us all. It inspires in random ways that in total are part of just a much grander awareness and Beauty … a perfection.

# Free Will and the Wave

The river tells us that Being and Becoming are one in Reality. Now, the ocean, adding to that, tells us that separation is ultimately an illusion. As the Buddhists say of Buddha's death, "The dewdrop slips into the shining sea." Ultimately our identity is not a separate one but is an expanded one … Atman is Brahman.…

The waves approaching the shore are one of the ocean's lessons about separation and unity as well. It has a "chapter" in it about the illusion of free will, too. For the illusion of free will is as ludicrous as the wave believing it is of its own power that it reaches the shore. The wave shows that we think we are separate, but we are all, as my wife, Mary Lynn, once put it, "a movement of the Universe" … just as the wave is merely a movement of the sea.

Indeed, everything that happens is just a movement of the Universe, no more. No less, either, keep in mind. So all our actions, like those of the wave we see rolling, are actually movements of "the ocean" itself. That is to say, they are Divine ones. As Sathya Sai Baba put it, there is only one Doer and one Actor in the Universe and that is God. And he noted that each of us is God. Schrödinger said something similar when he pointed out that the grand total of the minds in the Universe is one.

Sathya Sai Baba taught that there is free will only from a particular perspective, but not ultimately. That from the perspective of the separated and singular entity there is the appearance of free will, just as the wave thinks it is deciding to go to shore, just as the raindrops think they are deciding each of their movements in the stream's journey downstream. Yet the truth is that both of these are components of movements far larger and more powerful than that single unit boasting its achievements. We are all a product of an infinite number of events, none of which we as singular souls decided. So is there free will?

No. Not in the sense of individual choice or decision. As solitary units we are compelled in every action, regardless how tiny. As is recorded in *The Bible*, there is not a movement of a blade of grass that is not an intention of the Divine.

So, how do we reconcile this feeling of having the ability to choose with this idea that we are, regardless, always and in everything, determined?

Well, this is hinted in the fact that the wave does not get to shore by its own power or will ... but the ocean does.

So free will for the wave? No. For the ocean, well more so. Though the brightest of you are already realizing that the ocean also is a product of all the forces that are in play to create and move it. So, ultimately, it is, as well, as Mary Lynn said, "a movement of the Universe." And thus it is only the Universe that has free will.

But remember, Atman is Brahman. Our ultimate identity is God ... is the Universe in toto. So it depends upon where one's identity is fixed ... what position amid the infinite possibilities one "embraces" at any particular moment. As Divinity, we have free will. All the Universe and every movement of it, regardless how tiny, is an intention of the One.... Since we are that One, everything is our intention, then.

Yet we descend into separate form, as I keep repeating, and in doing so we forget that Ultimate Identity, ours. Hence we also forget that Divine intention, our own.

What I am saying is that everything that happens to you and everything you decide is decided by you as Divinity, and so everything in the Universe contributes to that decision, and participates in its enactment. But you as singular particle, as ego, because of your forgetting of your unity with All That and as a kind of compensation for all you have lost, will attribute it to yourself as ego — as self, not Self.

This explains why you cannot get or do anything but what you are meant to get or do. It reveals why what you choose has consequences other than what you intend. It says something about why you end up in a different place, almost all of the time, than where you are trying to go. For we are all unfolding in a process intended by ourselves as Divinity. We do not know that. (We, as Divinity, do not let ourselves know that ... well done! ... for those of you who just thought that.) For the source of our decisions we have obscured from our awareness for the purpose of making this a game that is fun, an adventure that is engrossing.

Yet this script we have written as Divinity relentlessly comes about in our lives. Regardless the trivial decisions, pronouncements, strength of will, affirmation and intentions and notes to ourselves on mirrors, repetitive patting ourselves on the back in self-congratulation for a vainglorious ability to "create our own reality," it unfolds. Regardless the strenuous and counterproductive efforts to "change" one's thoughts (in actuality to deny the thoughts one is having) in a voodooistic attempt to conjure ... or whatever, of our singular egos — that is, of ourselves as actors on the stage, as those units acting out the drama — what we decided in our highest, through normally inaccessible, part of ourselves comes about.

Why you inevitably fail at creating your own Reality? It is simply that you already have and are refusing to know that. You have already created your reality. But you have forgotten that, and are now, in your prodigal state and in an act of rebellion against your deepest Divinity fearfully attempting to keep it from unfolding.

So the correct attitude to embrace about everything that happens to us? Well the river shows that, as well. It is best not to resist. Does the water resist? It is best to embrace it ... the events of life ... to contain it, move around it, or jump over it ... but in any case to continue rolling forward.

Roll with it, one might say. Spin it positively is another stance of worth. And always always make lemonade out of lemons. Don't try to create your own reality, instead take the reality you have already given yourself as the raw materials to build of it that which you have already decided, that which at one time you have already intended.

Your goal should not be to create your own reality. Rather to discover it. And to the extent one sees it to align oneself with it. To get in line. To manifest it. To be a conduit of it. To become it.

There's a difference, you see?

But very few of us do that. We struggle. We fight. We resist. However, it is good to come to the realization that we can let go of continuing in that.

Incidentally, this is how from the perspective of Divinity we are wonderful comedy in our diminished identifications. Shakespeare knew this well and expressed it beautifully.

*Life's but a walking shadow, a poor player,*

*That struts and frets his hour upon the stage,*

*And then is heard no more. It is a tale*

*Told by an idiot, full of sound and fury,*

*Signifying nothing.*[1]

Yes, as Divinity we are great fun to watch. Shakespeare elaborated.... No doubt he, as identifying so much with Creator in his writing, had a Divinity's glimpse at us. "What a piece of work is man" he laughed. "How noble in reason," snickering now.[2]

Nevertheless, and as I just hinted in speaking of Shakespeare's perspective, at later stages of spiritual evolution one's identity is not limited to ego but expands to Self, to Divinity, to God. I believe we can approach that in life, in the Form State, only to some degree. But it is our ultimate potential in the No-Form State to realize that. For it is in fact our essential reality, our only and true Identity.

So, free will for humans versus Divine intention, or some would say predetermination? They are one and the same. The one is a Reality; the other an actually existing and common *illusion!* So does free will exist? Yes and no. It exists for you (and me) as an illusion we share, an illusion we collectively experience and we experience virtually every day of our lives. But ultimately, no. It does not exist. Meaning, our will as egos is not free.

Why bother to know that? Why not just continue with this illusion of free will? Well, in practice we do. However, knowing the Truth of all that brings with it potent and wonderful rewards. It brings with it magnificent comforting reassurance, Divine comfort, purer and better actions in one's life which can henceforth be based on an attitude of surrender, not will power. And so on. Yes, I will keep bringing up the rewards of knowing all this as we go along. I will elaborate in full as we continue our journey together. For Truth is God. And Truth is thus profound, wonderful ... but also rewarding and comforting, helpful in its guidance.

To continue, however, separation and identity, well, they are one as well. We see that in the wave in relation to the ocean. Is the wave just a wave? Is the ocean just an ocean? Are they both not wave and ocean at the same time? Are they both not separate as well as identical at the same time? So separation and identity are not opposed, as logic would tell us. Nature is wiser than our logic and has better class materials, too.

Thus, in a manner similar to the way Nature and Divinity tell us of the unity of Being and Becoming in speaking the stream, the river, so also does Nature and Divinity have words for this identity of part and whole. As I have been saying, one of them is *wave.* Another one is *tree.* They grow or move and are both separate and apart ... oceans and raindrops tell us this, too. The tree in its configuration expresses unity and separation, like the wave, but more than that.

So let us now consider the tree.

# 21

# On Separation and Identity and How the Universe "Feels":

## More Letters from hOMe — Trees Speaking on Infinite Identities and Being God, and the Parable of Participation

*The Universe Tells Who It Is and Who You Are ... More Communiques from Divinity ... More Emails from "the Lord"*

## Trees and Unity ... Separation and Identity

How can we possibly comprehend such a grievous contradiction as that we are separate yet one? Of disunity and unity existing simultaneously in the same reality? What possibility have we of approaching such an unfathomable reality and Truth? Well, here again we are taught if we listen. Listen to the sight of the tree.

## Leaves and Branches and Limbs, Oh My!

One of the greatest teachings is revealed in the anatomy of the common tree. It tells the same tale everywhere, hence it is no wonder that the Universal Tree is a worldwide symbol, most important in natural cultures, and recorded by humans from the beginnings of time. It speaks of the simultaneous reality of both separation and unity; it explains the conundrum about identity.

The tree demonstrates to anyone with the ears to hear it that it is one ... one tree, yet it is many leaves, many branches and twigs as well. Each leaf, like the wave, is a discrete entity. And the leaf has its goals, its beginnings and endings, just as the wave. The leaf is born in the Spring. It grows up, experiences pleasant sunlight, battering rains, annoying caterpillars, lady bugs, and other imposing beings who come right in as if they own the place and walk all around and over without so much as a by-your-leave. Annoying, yes.

But Leaf is ever serving. It gives of its beauty. Ever the gracious host, it gathers up carbon dioxide and serves up delicious repasts of free oxygen. That's its job; rather, its play. That's what it "enjoys" doing ... what it takes "delight" in being a part of, that process.

Then, at the end of its life, it "dies"; it falls to the ground; its "body" is just of the soil soon enough. But while the leaf has a beginning and ending, a job, a function, a goal, a service to perform, and is a happy contributor to "the cause," is it the only consciousness aware of itself and its doings? Does not Tree itself partake of the inner life of Leaf, just as Ocean participates in Wave?

Of course, it does. This is a different kind of idea of overlapping experience, but in this case it is experience that is identical, not overlapping. One is just subsumed within the other. So when Leaf is no more, Tree still retains all that Leaf experienced. Indeed, being Leaf was just an entertaining diversion that Tree engaged in amid its other diversions as Branch, Trunk, Limb, Blossom, Fruit, Nut, Seed.

This is much like the way in which Seth, as described by Jane Roberts (1974), says we all have oversouls. Rather we are subsumed within larger selves, larger entities of being, oversouls. We are all part of souls that are greater and more encompassing and include other souls like ourselves.

Grof agrees. And he says so, too.[1] Indeed if, for example, Gaia is an aware being, as Grof and others have put forth, then what are we? Are we not part of that awareness? Yet we are separate, or at least we think so.

So Tree expresses how we are separate and yet we partake of a larger reality and that the only difference amounts to a kind of switch in where we choose to place our focus of identity — in a leaf, in a branch ... in an individual person, in Earth as a whole as Gaia ... in soul, in oversoul, in the All That Is, in God.

How can this possibly be? This changing of focus? Ever have a cut or an abrasion on a part of the body? Well, it is hard to think that one is anything *but* a Mister Stubbed Toe when that happens. Wait long enough, however, and it is like a close relative hurting… one is fully aware of it, yet separate in a way, too.

We are ourselves and Mister Stubbed Toe, that pesky neighbor now, who keeps his stereo too loud so we are ever distracted to him. And our consciousness subsumes both within it at the same time, switching between one and the other, as well as being some confused and motile amalgamation of all sensations and aspects of our experience. We never bother to think of it, but we are a mix of many things, the boundaries of our experience are ever varying in size, conscribing and re-conscribing different items and combinations of things, and persistently changing in boundaries, size, scope, and contents. The arena of our consciousness along with our point of attention are continually on the move.

When that is worst and the most confusing, we call it ADD (Attention Deficit Disorder). When we can slow it down, we say we have *focus*. We can pay attention. We are in the Now. And the boundaries of our Experience proceed more river-like, less fire-like.

Then, in another moment, and sooner or later, one has forgotten Stubbed Toe Self and is oneself again. Just as Leaf in time falls away from Tree. We do this kind of switch in perspective all the time. I as a writer am constantly jumping around in the worlds I create and inhabit. Yet after the fact, I am still me. And the experiences I have as my many characters … or books … are part of me, yet separate. Yet at one time they filled my consciousness completely and I had forgotten that I have a body others call Michael Adzema and I call sillymickel.

So, notice that the example I used involved pain, the stubbed toe. Indeed, is not that very often the thing which determines where the attention is brought, where the identity is placed for each time one chooses one? The dramatic part gets the attention. And in the Universal Mind, just like the Universal Tree, I imagine we as No-Form "beings" find ourselves "drawn" to notice what is most engaging, most dramatic, most fun, most "entertaining. And since Time is infinite, well, eventually that includes Everything. We as No-Forms tend towards noticing what is most interesting, just as we are Tree noticing its blossoms in Spring … for that is the most interesting thing … or the damage to a limb … for that is the most dramatic … or its feelings of pain in a clipped leaf. And yes, we now know there is a "secret life of plants," where they also feel pain and even "scream," in a sense.

You see, identity follows drama and interest. Our attention is drawn to the center of the activity. You might say higher and more gripping events draw larger audiences. Damn good thing the venue is unlimited and there is no gate fee … 'cept the level of one's awareness.

So we, as Universal Mind, are all these things, but only one thing, one Subjectivity, One Experience, One Mind.

We do this moving of identity, this transfer or repositioning of the center and boundaries of identity all the time. We do it repeatedly in watching movies and other dramas of stage and screen. This example of the cinema is particularly illustrative. You tell me you are not forgetting you are in a theater when you shriek when the bad guy appears suddenly behind you with a weapon. You see, at that moment, you *had* thought you were the character on the screen, not you. You drifted into identity with her and out of identity with you.

When you cried out, it was as if the creepy guy's attack had been perpetrated on you! Yet, when we come back to ourselves we forget that we *actually were* that character at that moment. We have become ourselves again. Shortly, then, in watching the movie, we are

259

somebody else again. When we leave the theater we might find ourselves moving in a way or talking in a cadence and tone that mimics a character with whom one had identified. We could very well be looking at events or one's reality from a perspective that character embodied. It's a damn good thing we have a body to act as an anchor. But then, when we do not, in the No-Form State, what is that like, I wonder.

Certainly there are differences in us in the degree of our ability to do that — that is, to transfer identity. We call folks empathic who are able to do that readily. Believe me, as a psychotherapist of many years, that experience of merging with another's emotional subjectivity, in a moment, is not in the least alien to me. Yet I never *lose* myself. I consider it an additional richness of my experience of life to feel myself to be both me as well as the other. I imagine Tree feels much the same richness in his experience being all the leaves.

Such expanding of one's boundaries is great practice in life in terms of many things — including expanding one's enjoyment and richness of being, broadening one's scope or expanding one's identity beyond the ego, identifying with consciousnesses, realities, causes, and powers beyond oneself.... I believe such exercise of one's boundaries and focus is helpful for the purpose of having greater ability to be that One, or at least to be better able to surrender to the All That Is.

In the same way, those in the No-Form State participate in our lives, I reckon.

Employing this perspective, is death merely a re-conscribing of the boundaries of one's being? I think it could be. Along with that, could there be a shifting of focus, just as Leaf repositions its consciousness as Tree? Perhaps. In the No-Form State could one temporarily re-gather the components of a Form once adopted — that is to say, a person one once was in a life — in order to communicate with someone in Form one was close to then? I believe that to be possible. It is the one way, at this time, I have for making sense of some of the events and communications of which I am personally aware. Most of these were not direct communications to me but occurred by way of another person. Which adds another provocative element to this meditation on identity and shared experience.

In any case, certainly, at its ultimate, the Universe is all activity, narratives, scripts, and stories that a single entity, a one Divinity, chooses to do. Furthermore, that One Mind of the Universe is doing the focusing on the smaller, the larger, the part, the greater whole, and the Whole, alternately ... and since there is no time ... simultaneously. Since simultaneously, it makes one all those identities as well as the all-encompassing identity of the One, or Divinity, at this very moment. So, you are God right now.

Just let that last one go. It'll break your brain to conceive that.

I know you are thinking, so who is the real being? If God is all of us, acting in all of us, and experiencing an infinite number of beings as well as kinds of beings ... well, which one has She chosen? As if the tree has to *be* just one leaf.

No. It is time which causes that dilemma. For we all know in life that we cannot "do it all." It is overwhelming to think of it — One Mind "doing" all that. And we certainly cannot imagine such a God any more than we could, at a certain age, understand how Santa could come to everyone in the world in one night. Remember, *one night*. There's the time part. It is time that causes the problem.

And as we have said, time is an illusion. It is a construction, a convenience, we have fixed in place for ... exactly what? For enjoying the aspects, the parts. Time is an arbitrary construct we adopt, then intentionally forget it can be otherwise, for the purpose of "the game." Actually, I prefer to say, "the play," "the drama," or "the story." Regardless, as I have heard in many places, "Time is what we create to keep everything from happening at once."

More than that, Time is the way God gets to savor and enjoy manifesting as each one of us. More even than that, Time is the way the Divine manages to enjoy, to appreciate manifesting in every single aspect of Creation, as every single thing — all of which are conscious and experiencing, and essentially Divine — from the tiniest molecule to the largest galaxy or dimension of existence. There's that glory of God again.

It is at that brink, in looking out in awe at the expanses our minds cannot comprehend, that we are left with only *awe* and *mystery* to describe it, and only one word for motive — *glory*. Though I daresay, *fun* is the way we, in our experience as humans, can come closest to a feeling of how that motive might be experienced by a Divinity.

Therefore, taking down the illusion, the barrier to overstanding, of time we see that identity is not a problem. In an infinity, one has an infinite capacity to be infinite things, to be whole and parts, in infinite combinations creating infinite wholes, from the supremely tiniest and subatomic to the majestically largest, the Universe, or one of its dimensions. For, it is not like God has to hurry up to pull it off. This is the mystery. For the sake of the glory of the Universe, we as God manifest infinitely. Hey, if you can write one good book, well, in an infinity of time … or more exactly no time at all … would not Divinity want to create an infinite number of books? Of stories? Of dramas?

And for what?

## The Intention of the Universe

Well, this is where we get into the intention of the Universe. And we had a taste of that when thinking of the stream, the water drop, and such. Here again we notice, using Tree as an example again, that it unfolds in precise, symmetrical, poetic movements of growth that bring forth wonderful productions, terrific art forms in blossoms, spectacular complexities of limb and branch, fulsome and aromatic offerings of fruit, and all the rest. Why? Well, why not? Is that not more of God having fun being Tree again.

# You Are Not Superior, for You Are Not Separate

The intention of the Universe … fun. Interest. Drama. Adventure. Experimenting in Truth. How do we know? Well, what do *we* desire? And are we not part of the Universe? How do the scientists get it that we could be the crown of creation, as they so egoistically assume, but somehow we, of all species, would not have a clue as to the intention of existence? They are wont to say when we think we are understanding the motives of Nature, whether in fauna, or in the case I'm using of flora, that we are anthropomorphizing what is happening. They have a habit of saying we are projecting our own feelings, desires, and understandings into the processes of animal or vegetable we observe.

But why would we *be completely, totally, and utterly unable* — as scientists claim we are — to understand a reality that we ourselves are part of? Would they say, as well, that when they think they are understanding a colleague's theories or participating in the birthday glee that their child experiences at her party that they are anthropomorphizing ... or projecting ... when doing that? No, of course not. For that would leave a figure of a human who truly *is* solitary and alone in its reality ... truly solipsistic.

Yet they would poo poo the idea of solipsism as well. For more than anything they wish to hide the hubris, the egotism, they feel. And acknowledging the solipsistic basis of their belief that they can somehow understand humans but be totally bereft of the experience of Nature would hint at such egocentrism.

Would they at least *try* to be consistent?

By this you can see that scientists, and humans in general for we all partake of the dominant paradigm of their common-sense materialism and anthropocentrism, are a lot like religious true believers and new-age consciousness "athletes." Religion-minded and positive thinking types are intent on pushing out of their minds their desires and "inappropriate" thoughts and feelings, making them bad that way. In doing so, they actually create the devil and evil, or the "negativity," they say they are doing that to combat.

In a similar way, scientists — in claiming it is ridiculous to think that we are solipsistic and not understanding of the feelings, thoughts, and motives of other humans — somehow would have it that we cannot do that same kind of understanding of another, although admittedly less well, with the rest of Nature. Yet, if it is similarity that allows us to understand another human, how can it possibly be that we can be *completely clueless*, as they would have us to be, of the inner experience of the rest of Nature, which we emanated from, are still a part of, and with which in some cases are so alike that we share over 98% of the same DNA? For we are composed of DNA that is exactly like 98.4% of those of gorillas, and an extraordinary 99% of chimps and bonobos.

Thus in seeking to not project humanity into reality, into Nature, and to stay above that distortion of Reality called anthropomorphizing, scientists create a much more blatant distortion of understanding by proposing a separation from Nature for humanity that does not exist. The current scientific paradigm remains infused with the assumptions of a dualism of man and environment, of man versus beast, of human versus Nature. Thus in presuming that separation and superiority they are in lockstep with, as we saw earlier, those tired old Judeo-Christian notions of dominion over Nature and human superiority. That is not too surprising in that science arose out of a bed of rabid religious fundamentalism in the Middle Ages.

Still, even at its beginnings, science laid a claim to be apart from religious bias. Yet, out of egoistic reasons clearly, rooted in the presumptions of religion about dominion over Nature — which they would, oh so self-servingly, deny, by the way — scientists are at the very least not being consistent. In point of fact, they are being blinded by their ego and species-centrism.

So yes, we understand and partake of the inner experience of Nature, in at least some way that is not so much less than we partake of and are able to understand the experience and inner states of other humans. The degree of similarity is what accounts for the degree of accuracy in our abilities to do that, in the normal sense. Though in the sense of it occurring in a nonordinary state of consciousness, well even the degree of similarity, or difference, is not such a barrier. More later on that.

## How the Universe "Feels"

So trees bloom for the joy of it. Bees delight in their tasks. The ocean is deep, wise, and comforting. And the Universe is pervaded by love, which we erroneously label gravity. This is what we know because we are part of Reality, part of Nature, part of Divinity and not superior to it as the Judeo-Christian religions presume... or fallen from it like we are some kind of alien fruit that was somehow projected out of a tree, a Nature, that we have no part of.

They say that the fruit does not fall far from the tree. Well, somehow scientists have concocted this strangest of notions that not only has it happened but that we do not even come from a tree ...

metaphorically speaking … literally speaking, from the Nature we see ourselves at least immersed in, if not a part of.

The way they view us, you would think we are from another Universe and are totally unrelated to the life forms on this planet. It is because so much of the alien DNA conspiracy theories are even more built atop such arrogant presumptions that I see them as incredibly laughable, as ridiculous as the outdated notions that the entire Universe has Earth as its center and everything revolves around it. Only now, with these scientific and conspiracy notions, it is our human form that is the prized commodity and the focus of interest of beings far away.

You don't think we do that? Remember what I am saying here the next time you see a *Star Wars* or *Star Trek* movie. It is not uncommon to see in them this grandiosity as if all beings … all infinite numbers of them … look to us as center … or at least as part of their reality. Next time, notice how virtually all the "intelligent beings" are some version of a two-armed, two-legged human. Which assumes that all the Universe puts forth its life in roughly the same manner that humans evolved on Earth. Hell, even in looking at the beings on our planet that is not true. There is such incredible variation in species. What arrogance for humans to presume some special, higher status for our shape, our consciousness, over against that of a grasshopper, or a bacteria for that matter. Not to mention something that would be completely unimaginable for us, but would have evolved on another planet, or … even wilder … in another dimension.

Do you see how in denying our ability to understand the inner life of Nature and Reality — as well as failing to see "the secret life of stones" — for the reason, which we give, of not wanting to anthropomorphize upon it, we end up doing exactly that, and more egregiously? It is not the poets and mystics going around saying that life forms that exist on other planets or in other realities would need to have "the building blocks of life" as they appear to us for the humanly knowable beings on our planet. Which scientists do. Nor are we philosophers and transpersonal psychologists going around trying to communicate with "higher" lifeforms or "other intelligent life" in the Universe by sending out messages, sometimes in human languages, and music composed by us *humans*, of all beings, and leaving messages of invitation to aliens for contact on our Internet, worldwide. All of these and more the SETI (Search for Extraterrestrial Intelligence) and the CETI (Communication with Extraterrestrial Intelligence) programs of science indeed have done and continue to do.

We earlier saw how anthropocentric that is, but do we not see how in our imagining beings who would understand us how *anthropomorphic* we are being? I mean, they say that we are probably wrong in thinking that a dog with its tail wagging and its mouth open with tongue lolling out has an experience anything like we would call happy, though we spring from the same branch of the tree of Nature. Yet somehow the "intelligent life" — meaning folks like us, ahem ahem — in the Universe — far far removed from the life on Earth which we are connected to, indeed whose web we are enmeshed in — would somehow grok our words of human language and our tones of humanly pleasing music. Maybe even google us on our Internet.

## We Are Not Superior to Nature, for We Are Not Different from Nature

The point of all this is that laying our species blinders to the side the way that scientists say they are doing in ridiculing "anthropomorphizing" hardly gives us an "objective" view of our relation to the rest of living reality on this Earth. Rather it assumes something not proven and only egoistically supported: Which is that we are some special status of species, as some religions have it, and in that case that we are, for some magical ... and usually some conveniently pompous or laudatory ... reason separate from Nature. Which makes us not only separate, special, and no doubt "superior" *sarcasm*, but we are then necessarily and magically alien. That hardly seems to me to jive with the intentions of science that they claim of being neutral and objective in their proclamations.

Rather, this bogus, we see now, "objectivity" of science which asserts that we can only *project* our own human experience into reality in trying to understand it and correspondingly that we have *absolutely no way* of comprehending Nature and its beings, or parts actually gives rise to, which we also see now clearly, a prejudiced, a slanted view. It is a view that is wrought of innate human arrogance, species-centrism, abnormal estrangement from a Nature that somehow spawned us but we are alien from, and a wonderfully self-congratulating superiority to Nature … in which we are alien and separate, in which we are separate and superior. This is true regardless that they label it *science* and slap each other on the back for being the most "objective," dispassionately reasoning, least prejudiced ones in the room.

One the other hand, in assuming simply that we are a part, in a way, of Nature, or any other conceivable being or entity that contains us, we reverse that Tower of Babel wherein we found ourselves unable to communicate with each other, but also, as extension, and even more powerfully, with the rest of living beings. We need to drop our arrogance and assume, instead, that we are part of Nature, as much a part of the forces of Nature as the tree, the stream, the ocean, and the gopher. In doing so, we once again can realize that we *can* understand and even overlap in feeling with the consciousness and feeling and exuberance and sorrow and joy of Nature and all beings and movements in it.

If you think that is just a supposition, remember what I was elaborating on earlier about what Grof (1998) has demonstrated to us … indeed revealed to us! Which is that our consciousness partakes of the consciousness, not only of all living things, but all non-living things, of all scales of Matter, along with that of all entities, all archetypes, and all "suprahuman realities," as he calls them, up to Divinity Itself. There is no way to explain his discoveries, some of which I have been describing or jumping off from above, in the old ways. In the old science. In the old paradigm. But rather, only in some way akin to what I am laying out here … and throughout this book.

## Okay, Then. Just What Does Divinity Want?

So, yes, trees bloom, which is an outward expression of their joy. And in every place you look in the world … in the Universe … is a creative … a fun thing. Full of exuberance, delight, awestruck wonder, dramas, intentions, and all the rest.

As I once expressed my experience in a holotropic breathwork training group in which I experienced myself as a tree … and later, in this haiku framed it as a plant in general:

A strong plant blossoming…

Digging deep, and casting high.

'Tis bliss to exist.

# The Tree's Parable of Participation

So trees tell tales of separation and unity being not different, as we think, but coexisting in All and everything. Trees tell us experience is a shared one and that identity is multiple yet singular at the same time. They want you to know that all of life and Reality, which is Experience, overlaps in some way, at times large and often including us, our experience. At other times in ways distantly removed from our individual experience, as one leaf's experience is distantly removed from another's. Yet both awareness of Experience greater and encompassing of us as well as that seemingly separate from us — i.e., other beings — are intimately connected, through Tree, and ultimately accessible … yes, indeed, experience-able. Remember the exposition about the Sri Yantra, from Chapter 17, "How 'Within' Can Also Be 'Outside.'"

All of this happens in the only Reality there is, which is the one of our infinitely blooming and in the moment experience, with its feelings, perceptions, thoughts, emotions, awarenesses, and unwordables — all elements combined, melded, and only separate for the sake of talking about them. And that All and Everything partakes of that one thing that is not a thing at all, but is indeed no-thing, which is that Experience, comprised of the same realities of consciousness and experience we once arrogantly ascribed only to ourselves.

Trees tell us something else. Something about growth. Something about the natures of consciousness and the unconscious. Something about the processes of forgetting and remembering and the cycles of birth, death, renewal, and immortality. Let us address this next.

# 22

# The Structure and Purpose of the Universe?  Answer — "Tree":

## The Map of the Universe and All Its Beings and One Divinity Is Told Us by the Tree

*And Roots, oh my! ... The Tree's Roots and the Map of Personal Awareness and Growth*

*"I slept and dreamt that life was joy. I awoke and saw that life was service. I acted and behold, service was joy." — RabindranathTagore*

Notice that all plants, and trees especially, tell us something about above ground, and below ground, about roots and branches and their relationship, about sustenance and service, about the observable and the mysterious, and about the way in which we grow and for what purpose. Let us look at those.

# The Tree and the No-Form State

## The Structure of Psyche, and of Reality

Trees tell much about the structure of that psyche we include as our individual domain, which we carve out of the infinite expanse of Experience. Trees are saying that we have a known part of our selves, an observable part. It is a part that we identify with. Trees also explain that there is a part of ourselves difficult to see. It is "in the dark," it is underground. It is something we do not identify with, often do not want to know, and/or have forgotten. Regardless, it is part of us and plays into everything we think and do, just as roots predetermine the tree and continually feed into it.

Consider how we grow. We grow — physically, mentally, emotionally, and in all ways — by allowing what is below us to "feed" us, to give us what we need, in exactly the same way that the tree and all its parts, and all its actions in the outer world (the above ground) are fed and facilitated by its roots reaching deep down into the darkness.

Along those lines, the tree explains the structure of all Reality. The tree tells us there is a knowable us and a mysterious us. In reflecting the nature of Reality and the Universe, it lectures to us about the Universe having an observable part "above ground," so to speak, and a mysterious part — unknowable, always in the dark, "under the ground." Philosophy, psychology, spirituality, consciousness studies, metaphysics, and physics — indeed, all these fields of knowledge and more like them — are rife with explanations echoing the tree's underground and above ground message. They describe Reality and/or Psyche as being in two parts — a conscious and an unconscious, an implicate and an explicate order, a beingness and a becomingness, an individual consciousness and a ground of being, a body and a soul, and many similar ways.

Our arboreal guru tells us, also, of the nature of muses, of Source, of Divinity: They, rather "It," for they are the same, are "below ground," in a sense, below our conscious awareness. It is in the dark and has its abode firmly in the mysterious. Our teacher relates how we, at our roots, are deeply in this mysterious, just as our soul exists in the No-Form State while being with us always here in Form.

## No-Form "Personalities"

Yet, says Tree, there is a subtle boundary between ourselves and even larger personalities. Our teacher reveals … "take notes, class," she says, "there will be a 'quiz'" … that even in the No-Form state, while ultimately the roots by extension are parts of the ground embracing them, they maintain a boundary. Again, God having fun. Maintaining a seeming separation.

Like you as Divinity say to you as everyone else, "Hmmm. Let us see, even in the No-Form, what this Experience, my Experience, will be like if I draw a line around it, a boundary, an arbitrary and insubstantial one, and call the inside 'entity….'"

Meaning, by *entity*, a soul, oversoul, or some other "No-Form configuration." Yes, I am aware of the seeming contradiction in that juxtaposition of words. Call it a "no-thing form," then. lol….

Anyway, "…and call the outside, 'the ground of existence,' 'Divinity,' or 'God.'"

Why? Again, for the fun of it. Exactly this way do we distinguish between a tree's roots and its surrounding earth.

Of course we as Divinity already know that answer … as to what it will be like to maintain a semi-separation, in No-Form Reality, into entities, into No-Form "configurations" (lol) — our souls, our oversouls, and the like. But again, we frisky Divinities suspend that awareness — much like we as playful humans pretend that the stakes of board and card games and competitive sports are real in order to enjoy them — so as to frolic in No-Form as well as Form. For the reason: Why not? Again, interest, drama, fun, creation, play are central to everything that happens and exists. The Universe is a Divine *leela* … a dance of God.

Those roots of us, as Tree, which we see are entities or souls/oversouls, engage in the pretense of interaction with the Universe and Divinity, though ultimately they are no different. For the molecules of root are no different from the molecules of ground and indeed they exchange those elements continually. There is only an arbitrary line … indeed, it is even a *moving* perimeter … between when a molecule is "ground" and when it is called "root." In the same way we are only "playing" at being person, planetmate, planet, and No-Form being, when we are no different — ultimately and most truly — from the Divine.

# The Way We Grow and For What Purpose

In any case, "fed" by, "inspired" by, and arising into Form from those roots — those No-Form identities of ours — we give back to All and Everything in the best way we know how. We grow. We stretch out our limbs. We blossom in our youth; we give shade in our adulthood; and we bear fruit in the autumn of our lives … and again, just like a tree, for All and Everyone around, without discrimination.

Professor Tree speaks to us on the nature of the psyche, also. This provides guidance for our existence. For the roots are roughly the same in depth as the tree's height above ground. Hence, deeper and higher are connected; the deeper we go, the higher we can reach.

Tree wants us to know that the deeper into Reality, and our reality, we reach — the more of our experience into the mysterious, the dark, the unconscious, the No-Form State, into nonordinary states of consciousness, into our repressed Pain and hidden memories — the greater is our growth. Hence our capacity to give … and to reach out … are determined by our willingness to open ourselves to both our Shadow and our Mystery.

## The Tree Mirrors Itself

We see also that the above ground of the tree is much like the shape of the below ground. This tells us about within and without. As they like to say, "as above, so below" … as below, so above. This is the true meaning of that saying: Inner and outer reflect each other in so many ways.

In the tree's connection to its roots … and by extension, to the ground, to the Earth … it tells us we are a part of that which feeds us, that we are God. Essentially, inevitably, (occasionally?), most truly, you are God. Roots, existing "in the dark" or the Mystery, tell us that our muse and our strength are given to us and it is our only job to bring it up, forward, and out. The reaching limbs and branches of Tree tell us to *express* what is inside, just as the tree expresses itself in its blossoms and fruits.

## Sustenance and Service

Tree says that one's expression is not a vain or solitary achievement but is actually — mirroring how Root is in perpetual exchange with Ground — intimately and inextricably related to the beingness "outside" ourselves. It tells us that any "fruition" we do — any expressions of ourselves — are seeds, extending beyond ourselves … grasping to connect and offering freely with the exact same palm … or fruit, as it were. That, like a pebble in a pond, we send out ripples into the Universe from everything large and small we do. That we benefit the All just by growing. But that our worth in It All is greater to the extent we create and we share. To the extent that we connect and we offer.

We are fed by and connected to the No-Form realities, and we feed and connect to the Form realities around us. We receive sustenance as well as we serve to sustain in our sphere of activity in Form. The degree to which we serve is mirrored, as well, in the degree to which we receive. Count on that as on some kind of universal law. From each according to their willingness, to each according to their needs.

# The Tree and Fruition

The tree's blossoming speaks to us of the bliss of simply existing. Service and living are not hard, except at certain limited times of storms and the buffeting of winds. For the most part our job is playful, fantastic, interesting, and creative. It is more than downright bliss to exist; it is in the surface moment engrossing, delightful, and entertaining.

When we observe the tree giving of its fruit, we see the tree enjoying itself, having fun. These events are hardly mechanical and consciousness-less. We are witnessing, in Tree's fruition, the outward expression of a tree's feelings of fulfillment; its love for the All and Everything and therefore wanting to contribute to it; its expansiveness of caring in its non-discrimination as to who will receive its blessings; and its joy in belonging, in being a part of a process of creation much larger than itself. Perhaps nicest of all, because Tree in bringing fruit out of its very self is identifying and therefore resonating with Creator Itself, in our perceiving its producing its magnificent offerings, we are witnessing the outward form of its ecstasy. The tree is ... yes ... blissful, giving, nurturing, selfless always, ever content, resilient, persevering, generous in its provisions of shade, food, material, and fuel, and much else. There are few gurus greater.

Yes again, earth-rooted beings — those plants and trees — experience "fun" in their growing. Indeed, it is only because of a religious tradition, a patriarchal one, which promotes work and overexertion as virtuous, that we fail to see its play. Perhaps we see only its utility. It is only because we are indoctrinated into a capitalist system where everyone must fend for themselves — where competition rules, "there is no free lunch," and instead struggle is required — that we fail to see its giving bliss, its joyous generosity.

It is only because we come into adulthood and all the world around we are emotionally assaulted to make us embarrassed by our childlike qualities of playfulness, emotion, silliness, exuberance, giddiness, that we fail to notice the passionate and shameless outpouring of Tree in its Spring times, with its hippie-colorful adornment, its incense-like aromas, its bohemian-like scattering of its creations everywhere, and its lusty insistence on drawing and attracting everyone to it — all planetmates.

Yes, in its expressing itself as flower and fruit, Tree is festive, alive, shamelessly having fun, being generous, and doing service. And in doing that it is telling us that we can and should, too.

# And Immortality, and Promise

Furthermore, that sage old tree expounds on renewal and immortality. Spring is a message with a promise about the cycle of life … telling us nothing dies. Everything gets renewed. That even out of the depths of sorrow and the winter times of our lives there is awakening and new life again.

Ah, yes, Spring is a promise to us from the All That Is that things will be all right if we just hang on through the stormy times — the times of coldness of feeling, of buffeting by the icy winds of misfortune and loss, of scarcity of resources, and of the darkness and persistent cloudiness of depression, despair, and the monotony and tediousness of life.

For there is always a Spring, somewhere in our futures. There is always, sooner or later, a return of life, light, new growth, and happiness.

In the same way, after difficult, "rainy" times appears another promise, also a reward for persisting despite difficulty, a rainbow. Let me reveal that to you, next.

# 23

# The Universe Says It Is Friendly … and Funny:

## More Scripts from the Universal Playwright … The Universe is Helpful as Well as Fun

*On Rainbows, Divine Providence, Pronoia, Birth,*
*Change, Hope, Faith, and Promise*

*"Clouds come floating into my life, no longer to carry*
*rain or usher storm, but to add color to my sunset sky."*
*— RabindranathTagore*

# Rainbows ... Hope Amid the Turmoil of Change

## Pronoia

Rainbows occur after showers. What is that saying except that life is positive, even in its changes and seeming negativities. It is the pronoiac pronouncement of God — the Divine proclamation that the Universe is out to do us good. This one is so easy for we know it instinctively. I do not believe there is a culture that does not equate rainbows to new beginnings. For Western culture, remember the rainbow that Jehovah caused to appear for Noah and the survivors after the turmoil of the Great Flood.

## Birth

Concerning new beginnings, rainbows show up again, just like halos and angels do, in BPM IV imagery.

*BPM IV* (*Basic Perinatal Matrix* IV) is part of the matrix of experiential constellations around birth which Stanislav Grof has found to create one of our most fundamental templates through which we view and experience Reality. His *Basic Perinatal Matrices*, *BPMs*, as he terms them, are a centerpiece in our species' biologically constituted realities in that it is our birth which is unique in all of Nature and which constitutes the biggest difference between us and the rest of Nature. For that, look especially to my works, *Planetmates: The Great Reveal* (2014b), *Falls from Grace* (2014a), and *Prodigal Human: The Descents of Man* (2016a)

Our uniquely configured human birth, with its prematurity and secondary altriciality and fetal malnutrition[1] ... none of which occur anywhere else in Nature ... causes us to see everything in the Universe, and to interpret everything in the Universe, differently than the rest of all of Nature and, indeed necessarily, the rest of the Universe, with all its beings. A curse. But something we are able to fashion into our singular blessing, if we choose to.

I have plenty to say about these constellations and matrices — these BPMs — in other works and for that a good place to look is in my *Apocalypse NO* (2013a), especially as in its describing the "emerging perinatal unconscious." Also, you can check out *Falls from Grace: The Devolution and Revolution of Consciousness* (2014a), which lays out in elaborate detail the characteristics of this traumatic imprint on our consciousness, as I relate it to the "Second Fall from Grace: Birth."

Most recently these early imprints are brought forth for review in *Wounded Deer and Centaurs: The Necessary Hero and the Prenatal Matrix of Human Events* (2016b). In that work I rely on Grof's work about birth matrices as part of the structure of my model which then goes in great detail into explaining how the no-exit characteristics of BPM II are further seen to be able to be expanded and in doing so create a fundamental matrix for, not the entirety of life experience, as Grof's *Basic Perinatal Matrices* do, but specifically for the uniquely evil characteristics of humans. All of human darkness, atrocity, war, bigotry, greed, domination, submission, revolution, racism, torture, murder, and so much more is rooted in a specific time in our lives that occurs to us in the last month of gestation, just before our entry into the world.

## Halos, Angels

Then there is birth itself, described as having experiential components, by Stanislav Grof, of release, exuberance, peace, euphoria, freedom, joy, and many other positive feelings and experiences. Some interesting things about this experience of birth are that the painful constriction of the pelvic ring around the head at birth, which is then … along with considerable relief … released at birth, shows up in our understandings of spirituality as a halo. Additionally, the factor of release and freedom alongside the light of coming out into the world shows up in our depictions of angels, who characteristically are free, hence wings, and abound in a white-themed heaven of light, notably in clouds and in the sky. These last relate to the experience of coming out into the light at birth, being in the air now, not in the liquid medium of the placental surround.

278

I have added to that, in several of my works and most especially in *Funny God: The Tao of Funny God and the Mind's True Liberations* (2015), specifically in Part Two: "Breaking News" and in Chapter 20, titled, "Jacob's Ladder and How It All Began and What It Means Now ... Something Wonderful Happened," how birth imagery shows up in framing our near-death experiences, our NDEs, which are occurring increasingly frequently because of our modern medical advances related to keeping folks alive but also bringing them back once death has actually been pronounced. The imprint on our perceptions occurring as a result of our traumatic birth experiences shows up at death, in an NDE, as a re-creation of what we experienced at birth, which was metaphorically similar to going through a tunnel into the light.

What I am saying about rainbows has several of the elements of the above, which are related to birth, combined. A rainbow occurs after a time of discomfort and "negative" experience ... a rain storm. It involves coming from a darkness into a light ... as clouds disperse after a downpour. And it is tunnel-like, as in the curve of the rainbow. A rainbow creates a halo effect as well. Both rainbows and halos are related to that euphoric time coming out into the world.

So, rainbows have plenty to relay to us about Divine Providence (if you wish, please enter your own preference, or nothing, for "Divine"), about faith, about trust, and about reliance.

Rainbows remind us we are connected to something beyond us that wants to reassure us. They brighten our mood. I have never heard of a single soul who was not lightened in mood, at least a little, by the sight of a rainbow. Indeed, some people respond to this heavenly antidepressant with sustained euphoria.

## Blessings

Coming directly after a storm they are telling us to hang on through the bad times, of course; but also that in doing so there are rewards. Notably these are not necessarily rewards like the ones that one chooses and strives to attain. These are *blessings*.

Rainbows explain to us that we can expect, at any time, and even in the darkest places, to be blessed with a break, a beauty, a lightness … a hope.

So they say to have faith when one has lost all hope. Have faith that things change and eventually for the better. Trust that things will at times be put in one's path to aid one, unexpectedly; that, like manna descending from heaven, at times one will have laid upon one's person ease and blessings, seemingly from out of nowhere and totally without one's intending it.

They tell us to rely on the goodness of the Universe, or the beneficence of God. And they contain one extremely helpful message, for those so attuned to receive it. That message is that Universal Reality will never give one more than one can handle. That endless suffering is a concoction only crazy humans would come up with and that no such thing exists in any of Reality. For all Reality is change, and involves contrast. There can be no sun without rain, that is true. But also there can be no rain without the sun shining through eventually and a rainbow popping in to put an exclamation point there. The rainbow arrives to reinforce the message that hope abides … and that blessings are gifted to the persevering and the gentle of heart.

# Snowfalls Say … Beauty and Comfort Are to Be Found in Adversity

By the way, snowfalls have a similar message to rainbows. They stress the teaching about the beauty that lies even in adversity. That, as I have elaborated upon elsewhere, even in the darkness there is a seed of light.[2] That in the midst of dreary desolation one might often discover beauty, even a kind of maternal nurturing.

Why is a white Christmas so appealing? Well, there's nothing too charming about rolling around in the snow putting chains on one's tires. However, in the center of a season where nights and darkness are the longest and chill is a constant reminder of nearby discomfort and difficulty, we crave the surcease of worldly activities in a holiday where we can be cozy inside, with family surrounding, ideally a cheery fire, and looking out on what, instead of cold and wet, is artfully blocking out the world in blankets of brilliant wonder. The havens we create in the midst of snowy weather are the way we tell ourselves that even in the coldness and difficulties of life there is the possibility to find the center of the storm. One readily creates a cocoon of comfort inside a snowfall, which is a place of silence, withdrawn from the world.

## A Calm and Steady Eye of Comfort

Snowfalls tell us there is a calm and steady eye in the center of the storm, so to speak ... that one can always find, in any situation, a place of nurturing and comfort, something to focus on, a pleasantness to get us through. That might be noticing the coolness and smoothness of the pans one handles endlessly when working in a factory bakery ... or focusing on the pleasant and varying aromas of baking goods wafting always around one throughout such a tedious day. It might be the coldness, the pleasant hardness of the bathroom floor one embraces, in suffering through the excruciating and feverish agony of a withdrawal. It might be simply noticing the homey warmth of one's breath blowing upon one's face as one hunkers one's head inside a scarf on a cold and rainy day, waiting for a bus.

Then again, it could be the perfectly pixelated high def of the images on one's computer screen one enjoys in trying to make it through an endless time, a monotonous day at the office. Or the smoke one enjoys at the ten-minute break (but no more!) one gets every couple hours. Or the pleasurable and satisfying comfort of the chair one sinks into while enduring the arrows of disapproval flung at one from a boss's eyes throughout that workday.

It might show up as the cool refreshing drink offered and the pleasant air-conditioned insides of the cabin of the tow truck one sits in, having just blown the engine of one's auto, hundreds of miles from home, in the middle of nowhere on an Interstate, on a ninety-some degree sweltering day. It might be the pleasure, euphoria, and fulfillment of a creative passion one basks in, while suffering a painful disappointment in love. It might be the vision of global peace and worldwide brother-sisterhood one keeps in one's mind and shares on Facebook, while enduring an endless war, with death always around or approaching, having painful effects upon one's health and one's ability to provide food for one's children

Or the message of cocoon-like comfort in the midst of a snowfall and the beauty within adversity it is speaking of might be reflected as the company of a one good and dear friend one keeps in mind, going through the loneliness or bullying or difficulties of adolescence. These are the things we do to get through the difficult times of life. We hang onto these things like a mantra inside a meditation. There is beauty ... and comfort ... in adversity. There is a place to stand, a rope to hang onto ... a solid rooftop to stand upon and be deeply grateful for in a flood while waiting for the helicopters to arrive.

There is even a solemn pleasantness, a poignant beauty in the longing for a final end to pain one is reminded of while stopping by a quiet woodside on a soft-falling snowy evening.

## Life's Necessary "Snow Days"

So it is also a message that difficult times *do* call for withdrawal, for inner vision, for restraint from action until the timing is right.

And it says that moment will come, without fail, in time. It tells us of the serenity that comes with balancing action with inaction, or outward activity with inward vision. It says that the Universe, unlike society's and economy's demands, does not insist that one push oneself beyond the point of breaking, like the overlords do to their field slaves, and the foremen whip out of their pyramid-makers. No. It says that rest is a part of life. That life is not *just* about action and moving outward. It says a lot about keeping one foot in the world of action and one in the world of stillness and calm. I don't have to tell meditators about the value of that. Nor, for that matter, the children hearing they will have a "snow day" and be home from school. One might learn far more and it be more memorable, such a day.

# The Structure of Atoms, Solar Systems, and Galaxies … The Universe Is Dynamic, Playful, and Loving

So, the Universe is loving, nurturing, guiding, and reassuring, as well as being fun and helpful … as we saw earlier. The Universe reveals that it is dynamic and playful, too. In that planets surround and circle stars. In that electrons surround and circle the nuclei of atoms. In that galaxies swirl and rotate in a manner that has a center and is ever expansive as well. In that hundreds of millions of sperm are attracted to and surround the human ovum. In that moths are attracted to a flame and a lightbulb. These are due mostly to gravity, or in some cases desire or other factors. However, remember, as we saw before, gravity is merely the outward perception of the Universe's true nature as Love.

But what of this circling, Not just the attraction but the surrounding and the "playful" … one might say "worshipful," though I would prefer "respectful" and "honoring" used instead … dynamic of a center and an outer that are separate but intimately connected. As in the movement of moths, we are always separate yet attracted, enjoying the duality and yet honoring the unity.

But why? Well, if there would be only attraction, we would have, in our Universe, about all the "excitement" of one magnet and another coming together. One instance, and end of story. Bo-ring, right? That would be like a Divinity dividing itself for fun, then, snap! Clicking back together. That would be one no-fun boring Divinity. A movie no one attends. ½ star. 1% on the Rotten Tomatoes scale.

Rather, God is greater and more entertaining than that. He is great fun on a "date." Each and every one, on every single calendar. We see that in the fact we have this thing, taking a planet's orbit for our example, of something attracted, yet swirling and on its own away from its focus of honoring, of respect, of Love. It draws toward, yet pulls away from. It spins away from out of its individualistic desire to be other, with its own kind of movement, of orbiting. It seeks to be united, re-united, but yet it does not. It wants the fun of separateness, not just merger. It wants, we might say, the *poignancy,* of a love that is ever experienced but never consummated in a way that would end its dance, that would end its existence as separate.

So, the Universe shows us it *wants* duality — even though it is not our essential nature — for *playful* reasons. For fun. It wants duality *so that it can experience* attraction. If there is no separation, there is no *experience.*

Do you see here again, over and over and over, how the Universe is telling us it wants to be planet and star, wave and ocean, tree and leaf? And for what? For the joy of it. For the fun of it. For the drama and story of it. Because, as we say, it is "a trip" to do so.

Yes, all of the Universe is God having its "current fantasy." Like how trippy it would be to manifest a physical reality out of myself, oh and to become multiple, and then having those units wanting to re-unite. Of course, for how can things not want, ultimately, to return to being what they are… in the long run, to be "other" is *exhausting* *chuckle* if nothing else…. Wanting to re-unite but keeping that from being able to really happen in any way that would end the "relationship."

Yes, it is why we both push and pull in our relationships. Why we seek to love and unite, but we wish to be solitary and alone and not bothered either, allowing ourselves to be angry at the impositions of closeness that we have chosen … and unfortunately and wrongfully blame our partner for bringing about.

Yes, you brilliant readers are seeing I am already lifting this veil. There is love pervading the Universe; but the Universe intends for there to be separation and for there to be a dynamic interaction or play between these "opposing" elements. This says something about opposition not being conflictual but harmonious … if we could but get it right. It says something about the Universe being playful in its interactions.

And again, as the Universe tells us in its rivers' ever "rolling with it," downstream and around obstacles, it tells us another feature of that advice in the planet's orbiting: It is also always moving forward, yet facing and being drawn to the object of its "desire," and then "rolling with it," in its spinning. In doing so, it says, "I will love you and I will never leave you, but I will continue doing my own thing …

I will do my own 'spinning' you see ... and I will experience feeling free in doing that. But I will never forget my inner lodestar, you. I will never let go of longing and attraction for the sweet alive poignancy therein."

Oh, yes, it says something about handling our relationships with each other. It also says much more about handling our relationships with God, with our Inner Divinity. As the most illuminating spiritual literature tells us, the answer to how to go about our relationship to the Divine is not sycophancy, not a self-crushing worship, but rather a simple "facing" of the Divine. Keeping Divinity in one's consciousness is all that is required. Aware of this, some adepts will focus on a saying, a mantra, or the name of God that appeals to them, so as to keep their minds ever fixed on the center of existence, on Divinity. It is called being "God-conscious." And it, like the beautiful poignant profound and meaningful "behavior" of a planet toward its star, is as simple and easy as spinning and orbiting ... then also facing *towards* it, in the same way a planet's face is lit up by its sun.

And it says so so so much about the intention of the Universe to be, not just Beingness, but Becomingness. For the purpose of Existence to be Story. To be a Play. To be as Sathya Sai Baba put it, playful ... a Divine *leela* ... a Divine play. It shows the Universe as the Divine scriptwriter, the Universal Poet....

## The Divine Comedian

And look in some places and you will see its hidden, its well-kept secret, its reward for those who have journeyed far on the way hOMe ... to continue their interest, to refresh them, to inspire them, to bless them.... Look without judgment or prejudice and you see revealed the Divine Comedian. You will see laughter, and play, interaction and *entertainment* as central to Divine Intention. Yes, we are here to glorify the Divine, but also to magnify interest, fun. The Universe's entertainment value is one of its central reasons for existing.

You do not think God funny? Just look to the platypus. I know, what was She thinking? I can still hear Him laughing. And the land crab, what the hell? You ever see them scurry across the sands like manic ballerinas in flight or pursuit? Sideways, no less! And, c'mon … *chuckle* … how goofy are the peregrinations of the seal and the penguin! As funny as any Charlie Chaplin, as silly as a *Sesame Street* script.

You do not think Divinity playful? Turn your attention to our planetmate relatives, especially their young. You will see how they play. Humans learn by working, for the most part. But the Universe shows us that awareness is best arrived at through play … and I might put in that category *adventure*…. For the Universe is saying that it is through trying out ourselves in interaction with everything … playing and adventuring … that we manifest the purpose of existence.

## Revolving … the Night and the Day … the Peek-a-Boo Nature of Reality

The Universe reveals one of its deepest secrets in the night and day alternation created by its "individuality." Notice that it is the desire to be dual … and thus to play … that creates the darkness and the light. For stars are just light, they do not emanate darkness. No. We as individuals, just like the planets, make our own darkness through our being discrete, separate. And by dancing our own dance of spinning while orbiting.

This alternation of day and night is the teaching of the Universal Peek-a-Boo. It is daily telling us that light always exists, there is no real darkness. But we create a seeming darkness through our actions that are separate from Divine action, just like the planet's actions are separate from the spinning of its sun.

Every night there is darkness and the world is saying that light does not exist. Like the handkerchief put up by your Mama to hide her face, we tease ourselves by hiding our Truth. The veil will be lifted, the handkerchief pulled aside, but there will be tension in the meantime. Like wandering in a "haunted house" at Disneyworld or attending a creepy horror film, we juice ourselves up with tension. To feel the release, you see. It is dynamic. It is playful. It is sport. It is fun. It is God dancing, God teasing … God laughing all the while. And when we realize it, it is the Cosmic Giggle that wells within us, reverberating and shaking down the rafters of the illusion we created in our absence, of Mind.

And the stars, during that fitful and foolish night, are reminders that light does exist, even in the deepest and the darkest of those nights. Indeed, on the darkest, most moonless of nights, we see those seeds of bright in the midst of blackness that much clearer.

And the moon. It is the most blatant constant reminder of the light and love of Divinity… its happiness in its light, its love in its gravitational pull. The moon is the comforting mother, cradling us terrified infants, wracked with fear in the illusion of our own making. The moon is hope, ever saying, "Do not despair. I, your Mother, the Light, am here. I'll be home shortly, you'll see."

Sure enough, at dawn, unexpectedly amid our foolish distractions of foreboding, and out of the deepest dark comes the brightest and most beautiful of lights. In the same way as a rainbow, the sunrise speaks to us of the rewards of persevering through adversity, through the illusions that torment us, to persevere against, and ignore as ultimately weak and inconsequential, the little demons of the night with pitchfork thoughts.

It also encourages us to laugh at our foolishness, born of our self-created darkness. The darkness we create all on our own, through our decision to move separately from the All, or the sun. Yet, even in our continual movements, we are inevitably blessed and taught, just as the sun brings its light to us at dawn. In this way we are taught that our foolishness is itself part of the Divine Dance and thus the Infinite Wisdom. "In spite of ourselves, we're gonna end up a sittin' on a rainbow," goes the lyric of a song I love. In the same way, regardless our dark insanity and foolish wickedness of thought and fearful unwarranted foreboding, the dawn comes, the sun rises, the mind clears, desire for goodness expands in us, hopeful optimism rolls out from us, just as we roll out of our beds.

So each night we pull the veil across the sunlit daytime of joy and strength and beauty and optimism and productivity and creation and activity. And we tell ourselves they are no more. They are gone forever. We stew in this frightful illusion for reasons which we hide from ourselves. For the darkness is like the "penalties" that we build into our sports and games. They are the things that keep us "in line," that keep us grateful, that magnify the drama of The Game, or the entertainment value of The Play. It is like the conflict that is placed at the center of every script, creating the tension that will be resolved, released at the end. Giving both participant and observer alike a delightful journey, with a peek-a-boo hollywood ending, which makes the journey worth it overall.

Yes, the dawn is the peek-a-boo brought to us by our mother the light, not reflected now, as it was as the moon at night. "Peek-a-boo, I love you" appears the day, telling us it never really left.

And the world begins anew, every morning, with a big joke, a huge relief, a promise that all is well, and a reminder that all darkness is illusion for it is temporary, often fleeting, and in any case it is not stronger than the light any more than any devil or Satan we concoct can be greater than the highest angels of our Divinity.

# Stars and the Darkness of Space

If planets and moons show the style of the Universe in movement — which is playful and fun, teasing and nurturing, desiring separation and unity, through orbiting and attraction, at the same time — what then of the stars, themselves, in relation to the darkness of space?

Easy enough, for are not light and darkness, a lot like figure and ground and therefore a lot like Root and Ground? As we saw with Tree?

But more than that, I wish to "point" out the quality of a dot of light. It speaks of individuality, of separation, of being a unit, of being solitary. It tells us also of its relation to a ground that is mysterious and dark, just as the ground is for the tree.

Yet that stardot is itself light, showing the quality of awareness of these conscribed experiential units we call beings and entities. And again like the tree holding out for us its fruits, the star emanates its offerings, this time in the form of light, to all and everyone around, indiscriminately. It is most helpful to those in its immediate surround, of course, just as we are most influential on those in our most immediate "orbit." But like the pebble in the pond, again, its happy and energetic waves of bright extend infinitely, and forever, in all directions simultaneously. There is nothing in existence to which we are not connected, at least in some small way.

Stars as spinning within galaxies show also their relation to the All and how it is playful, too. Wishing both to be separate and united. So necessarily dynamic ... playing. Dancing. The Cosmos is highest art. It is no wonder we are in awe of it; no wonder that so many of our human artists try to re-create its messages in their creations.

# 24

# The Nature of Everything:

Matter Is the Map of God, Direct and Indirect
Perception, Form and No-Form Personalities, the
Afterlife, and You Are Me and I Am You

*You keep saying Reality is ultimately nothing. I keep insisting it is no-thing. My Reality is lots more fun.*

*Experience is a one thing ... that is no-thing, by the way ... containing all that is felt, sensed, and thought in any and every discrete Now.*

*Experience is the no-thing you are riding on, while looking for your horse.*

*Seriously? What else did you think it meant to "look within"?*

# The Physical Universe Is the "Map" of God … The Nature of Matter

Now certainly, many, including and maybe especially scientists, have taken their clues from their observations of physical reality (matter). You hear it all the time in terms of what these thinkers say in describing their ideas but also in terms of what observations inspired their thinking. But I am claiming there is more to it than that. I am saying that these features of the world have an *intention* behind them. These are — a metaphor I use often — "breadcrumbs from ourselves as Divinity."

## Matter Is Message

I am not saying that randomly, coincidentally, or even serendipitously we can see these parallels or metaphors. I am saying that they *are* the messages of consciousness itself, which are accessible "within," as well (and more directly), which are manifesting materially as these things and processes of things. They do not merely *point to* these Truths and realities inside us, though of course they at least, and at first, do that.

No. Matter is more than metaphor, *matter is message*. Matter is message in a way similar to the way there are two sides, but of the same coin. It is similar to the way we can perceive the exact same energy of the sun as light and as heat. So, yes, I am saying that if we could view the physical world with the same clarity as we perceive the sun, we would see that looking outside of ourselves at a world of matter is just another way of perceiving our insides, of feeling, emotion, wisdom, thinking, awareness.

# Inner and Outer, Direct and Indirect … The Nature of Perception

Let me make that clearer. It relates to our direct and indirect perception — the former being our subjectivity, that which we directly *feel*.

The other, the indirect, has to do with our *perception* of a world we consider to be "outside." We consider it to be "not us."

Of course, as I continue to point out, that which we perceive as outer is actually ourselves, but it is the part of ourselves we have separated from, and put into an unconscious, so as to have The Game. The game of duality.

## Easier to Access and Veiled Truth … Self and Other

It being unconscious, having been "forgotten" in our coming into the world of Form, does not actually make it other than us, or outside of us … not really, not in actuality. So we maintain, for the purpose of duality's dance, an illusion of inner and outer, of direct and indirect perception. The only difference is that a huge part of our Reality we have hidden behind a veil of illusion — the illusion of there being an Other.

So, the difference between inner and outer perception, between feeling and five-senses perception amounts only to this:

The one is easier to access — "the inner." We have not "forgotten" it is us. We "feel" it to be us.

Whereas, the other is harder to access — "the outer." We have separated from it, called it "not us," then forgotten it, and it sits behind the illusion of separation and is therefore blocked from clear perception as us. We perceive it as Other, and we call that perception "outer." We relate it to five senses of "outward" perception.

But when we close our eyes and we "feel" our "inner" reality, our "direct" perception, does it exclude the messages from the outer? Do we feel any difference between what we feel "inside" and that which we are sensing in its being heard, its being felt as up against our skin? As being smelled? Of course not.

You see you cannot distinguish between inner and outer perception in any moment. Not in any fundamental way, though humans like to break things apart and create categories. But experience is a one thing. And if we break it down at all what it amounts to is that things are "felt" inside and other things "impinge" on us.... You see we have already decided beforehand that they are outside of ourselves, so we are only confirming an assumption.

However, the fact that they seem to "impinge" reveals a clue. *Impinge* versus *feel* has to do with whether something is thought to be "of us" or "not of us." Which is repeating what I just said. But what is instructive is that *they impinge* means they are things that want to be felt directly. From the dictionary, the definition of *impinge* includes "to have an effect, to make an impression," as well as "*encroach, infringe.*" These are "things" outside that want to be "inside," in a sense.

And sure enough, they *will* make themselves known endlessly throughout life until their true nature is revealed and their message is gotten. Yes, the only difference between inner and outer, between subjectivity and World, is that between a letter you write yourself (inner messages and signals) and one from another that you do not open, that you are afraid to open, that actually you wrote yourself *to* yourself at one time, then purposefully forget, so as to experience the *pleasure*, the joy, of reading it again as if it is for the first time (outer messages and sensations).

But that is an illusory category itself. For at its base, we cannot distinguish between thoughts and emotions (the inside) and the sensations (outside) that are components of them. We "think" with our body ... too. We even imagine with our sensations. When you "imagine" you are on a beach, say, you might have sensations, however, mild, sometimes not so mild, of warmth from the sun, a breeze in the air, perhaps some spray from the surf. So, sensations are an integral part of our "inner" world, including our thoughts and our imagining. Indeed, imagining itself is a form of thinking *with* sensation for is it not a visual sensing, hence a visual sensation? And in dreams, an "inner" experience, do we not have sensations, smell, touch, sound, especially sight? Experience colors? Lucid dreamers know we do, even if you think you, because you forget after the fact, think you do not. We cannot stop sensing the outside world. That is true whether or not it is there, in your shared and constituted reality, at that "time." Meaning only that we say it exists physically for you at that time.

On the other hand, inner is not separate from our outer, either. What we think and assume *determines* what we "sense" ... too. That last was one of the main points of the first part of this book, where I established all the different "constituted realities" and showed how we create the external reality we "sense" out of our inner assumptions, past experience, biological makeup as a species, and so on. So in sensing our physical world, we are essentially creating the sensations of it out of our assumptions ... and our prior decisions, collectively arrived at, for what it will be in this life, and at that time. Remember, quantum physics and the particle-wave paradox, the uncertainty principle, and so on.

So, Experience is a one thing ... that is no-thing, by the way ... containing all that is felt, sensed, imagined, and thought — in any and every discrete Now. And ultimately it is irreducible into those parts. There is no such thing as pure sensation or pure thought, for example. For each has aspects of all. Though we create categories to point out different qualities of that one experience. And for reasons we will look into next.

## A Feeling Is a Feeling Is a Feeling Is God

So what is the difference? What is the difference between inner and outer, direct and indirect perception?

The difference is we have divided It, that one Experience, into two. Into that which is experienced inside and that which we experience outside. And the one we cannot doubt: Our "inner" experience; indeed, it is what we call "I." To deny the existence of that is to deny one's own existence. And if you do that, by the way, then it hardly matters whether you understand what I am saying for you do not exist. Buh bye.

And the messages we get from self cannot be misunderstood; they are what they are. A feeling of doubt, of unhappiness, of joy cannot be a "symbol" of something else ... it is what it is! It is the symbols that point to *it!* That is the nature of Reality Itself ... it is Experience, it is *feeling.* And a feeling is a feeling is a feeling. Is God.

# The Secret to the Quest … The Nature of Change

This does not mean feelings cannot *lead* to things beyond themselves. For in fact they do. And therein is the secret to the quest, the journey. Work that one out on your own. That is the only way it can be done.

You see, though they — your feelings, your immediate experience — are not symbolic of anything else, when focused on, they go deeper … as well as expand. And when they "go deeper" … or go further back in time … or forward in time … or into other times, as in past or future lives … or out of time, as in the No-Form State … they stay the same. That is, the circumstances in which a particular feeling arises changes over time, but it remains a constant. It is the thread passed through time, never leaving, just as the feeling of being you … the "I am" is currently a popular way that is being referred to … is always there. Feelings are the rock of Reality that are always the same in any reality, and thus they constitute self. They constitute "you." The feeling is the "core" of experience, is one way that is phrased. The fact that it is fixed is how we know it is not the symbol, but the Reality. That is how we know Experience (what one "feels") is God.

But do not think that means that feelings do not transform and morph, just as you do. For in fact they do that, too. Indeed, they are the only way we can evolve. The only way we can move into states more optimal. Feelings transforming … processing, refining, distilling … is the only real change that occurs in beings, for all else is smoke and mirrors … moving the furniture around on the decks of the Titanic … trying to "create one's reality" by "changing one's thoughts."

This mistake is made in an obvious way by Jungians who think the archetypes are a higher reality of some sort. In point of fact, they are merely a better "map" for Reality than others. But what they are pointing to, as well, along with all the other words, symbols, icons, and maps, is one's direct experience. And a huge error is often made by Jungians, then, in their focusing on the symbols and the archetypes and ignoring that which they are pointing to — one's experience, one's feelings, one's subjectivity. Which is the same always — like God. But is ever changing, like Time. Mind and motion, again.

So feelings do change, rather they morph ... like a river they transform with each second. However, feelings change and evolve ... you change and evolve ... in the way opposite to what is normally assumed. Feelings do not change by attempting ... through some aggressive effort of will, some battering upon one's feelings through desire and intention ... to change one's thoughts. Indeed, that is *exactly how* to be stuck in them. Our thoughts no more change that way than our children and friends change when dealt with that way. Consider that our thoughts, our feelings ... essentially our self ... are as worthy of nurture, patience, and care as are one's children. Being our Divinity, though often in disguise, even more so do they merit such honoring of their integrity.

Feelings evolve ... and we grow toward our Divinity, we evolve ... by going deeply into them. By being the river, not trying to detach and be the bird flying above it. As they like to say, "flow with it." "Go with the flow." So feelings transform and the path of actual ecstasy occurs through embracing them, embracing feelings, embracing self. Facing toward Divinity. The planet with its face lit up by the sun. One way this is phrased: "The only way out is all the way through." My favorite, however: "The fastest way to get to where you are going is to be *most fully* exactly where you are." Oh, and there's that "Now" thing, again, that everyone likes to talk about. But perhaps "now" it makes more sense to you?

So it is futile to attempt to change one's thoughts and feelings. Truly they will change themselves. You need only wait. Watch them. Observe them. Do not act them out. Do not let them drive you into action, unless that action is a good and desired one, a dharmic thing to do. In which case, do. Otherwise, wait. Senses wide, notice. This is called identifying with your Witness Self. Watch and wait and notice how they change. See how they do. Let yourself take in the way they do. There is the lesson for you; your next play in The Game. A peek-a-boo is not far behind, maybe even a Cosmic Giggle.

I would like not to have to mention, but I "feel" I must, that the reason this secret is not known is that, sadly, folks engaging in spiritual quests are often trying to *get away* from their inner realities.

They would rather be that bird hovering above than the flowing river they are. They like the ideas of heavens and nirvana and Voids and Nothingness, Cosmic Consciousness, and all the rest. For they are living a difficult reality from which they are trying to escape. Enlightenment sounds to them like a place they would like to move to, far away from where they now are. So they take to paths that tell them to *strive* … do "practice," "work" on oneself, do inner "work" … eventually you will get *there*. They are weak-kneed before maxims involving mastery, which implies a duality of dominance and submission, upper and lower, better and lesser. They are suckers for aphorisms connoting struggle, and they expound precepts enjoining one to reach elsewhere, to change their thoughts and habits. As if liberation can be worked to attain like getting a degree. Anything but let it be.

So the last thing these folks want to hear is that their answers lie in the center of their uncomfortable feelings and that the only way to change them is to go deeply into them. 'Nuff said, take it from there.

# Coo Coo Ca Choo … The Nature of Me and You

So the inner is direct experience and is true. One can only get it wrong by trying to make it other … denying or detaching from it … which therefore projects it *outside*, by the way. And makes it indirect perception.

Which brings us to that "other," the "outside of ourselves. This other half of our Experience — that which we see "outside" ourselves — *can* be misinterpreted. For it is the reality that not only we have split off from and have put behind a veil of illusion, but it is the part that is *shared* with the other entities in our lives — usually, people. It is the reality, conjured physically, that we collectively have concocted for the purpose of playing our "game."

## I Am You, You Are Me

Of course, those "entities," those people, are only part of the illusion, as well. We are not separate from each other any more than we are actually separated from World ... or Universe. In Truth, I am you and you are me and we are we and we are all together.

Coo coo ca choo, by the way.

But for the purpose of the Drama, the Play, we, as Divinity have multiplied ourselves into many out of the One.

And we put those others behind a veil of illusion, too. Again, for the purpose of The Game. If we did not keep anything out of our awareness there would be no dance, no game ... no fun. In order to enjoy solving the "problem," we have to keep the answers hidden at the back of the book, until we are done. Until at death, when No-Form again, they are revealed.

We return to being who we are in essence. That is to say, we as Divinity have nothing that is hidden, or not in awareness. But it would be boring to stay endlessly that way. You might say that existence, and especially humanness, is the way we as Divinity recreate. We "tie one on" getting physical. We get "stoned," get dense, we take our unbounded energy, the infinity of Experience, and draw a line around it to conscribe it, which becomes our personality. We are drunken divinities, needing eventually to sober up. In the meantime, though, we gods just want to have fun.

## You Are God and Not-God ... Right Now!

And as I have been saying, that experience of Total Awareness is reputedly possible for us ... that identification with God. Though as I also shared, I believe it is possible to be only approached while in Form. However, in No-Form, in a Universe without Time, it is an actual realized experience of ours, for our game-playing in the No-Form State happens in No-Time, which means it happens *simultaneously*. All at once you are you as you think yourself to be; you are you as you are in a "past" life; you are you as this planet, this stone, this galaxy, this goddess, and as Divinity Itself. Which means that we both experience ourselves as Total Awareness along with experiencing ourselves as lesser awarenesses, like those of us in Form as well as those "No-Form configurations" again.

As I explained earlier, the one way I can offer as to how that kind of awareness of all and part at the same time is possible is to imagine ourselves playing a video game or watching a movie. So doing, we are aware we are ourselves … analogous to being Total Awareness or God in that No-Form State. Simultaneously we are aware that what we are engaged in is a game or story — the movie or video game. We know, by contrast, the plot or script is a lesser awareness, with parameters and rules arbitrarily decided by us … which is the metaphor for our life in Form. Nevertheless we immerse ourselves in the drama or play of them … for fun. So also do we as Divinity come into Form, we focus away from our No-Formness … for fun, for play, to magnify the glory of Existence, for the "hell" of it.

# Total Forgetting or Not … The Nature of Humans and No-Forms

So, the difference between No-Form and Form personalities lies only in that in Form we create a most intense game of being completely unaware of our essential Identity, as Divine. I have compared it to bungee jumping and after leaving the bridge, forgetting we are attached to it by that elastic cord. I have pointed out how that makes for the most extreme and intense kind of Drama for we can truly believe that all the stakes are real, that death really is an end of existence. We have totally sold ourselves on the ideas that we are limited, and that our survival depends on our competing and our taking care of ourselves as if we are an unassisted, separate being needing to take full responsibility for itself. None of that is true. But it makes for a great movie!

## Being Human. Divinity's Reckless Trek in Darkness

It makes for the most intense game of all with the greatest degrees of contrast within that duality … of there being the most horrible evil as well as the most awesome heroism and goodness. Along with all the other dualities: The most devastating feelings of loneliness alongside the most intense feelings of love, and belongingness. It is analogous, using the metaphor of planet and star as standing for us and Divinity, to the planet deciding not only to not re-unite with the star, or sun … which is the way we might imagine of No-Form and non-human planetmate entities … but to turn her back on that light of Total Awareness, creating a night, creating a darkness, a place where there is only reflected light, like the moon….

Indeed, in that description I have just exposed the difference between our human reality and that of our planetmates and assumedly all other beings. Which is that all other beings are separate yet aware of their essence being Divinity. Like a planet orbiting a star, they are aware of the object of their attraction and are enveloped, as well, in its light. However humans, metaphorically equivalent to our being cast out of Eden where we "walked with God," are the dark side of such planet. For we have turned our back, so to speak, on the light, on the sun, on the awareness of our Divine Identity

## Our Moonlit, Reflected Awareness

Keeping with that analogy, we humans, living in the nighttime of having turned from the reality we are orbiting, see reality, that light of the star or sun, in reflected form, a moon. That moon with its reflected light is our world of matter. And sure enough, since our world of matter only reflects the light, of reality, or truth, of wisdom, of the sun; we spend our entire lives in darkness, in something that is an endless night … in comparison to what is true, and is possible to us, as possible as it is to other beings, and planetmates.

So most truly that moon-like, reflected light is that indirect perception … the "outside" world.

# Separation and Symbols … The Nature of Human Interaction

However, all those entities "outside" of you are describing *their* direct experience, and we have forgotten they are us. Actually we are keeping our direct experience of their experience out of our awareness for the purpose of The Game. So, when we are told what they feel, we have to use symbols, their words, to try to uncover those things — those feelings and experiences — inside of ourselves that they are pointing to inside themselves with their words. When we do that accurately, we unveil that part within us of the Soup of

Experience they are talking about as their experience in that moment. Empathy happens; overlapping identity is possible or not far away. We have had a peek at our true nature as One … One Divinity, One Experience.

I want to add that this is not a common experience, this empathy as I am describing it. We say we "feel" for one another and claim we are empathic, too. That we are even more than merely empathetic, and that we can actually feel another's reality. We need to ask ourselves how much of other people's experience we are actually feeling, can actually feel, alongside that powerful one of ours of vanity attendant to our claiming such an ability.

For it actually to happen, this overlap, it is my opinion that it might actually take an experience of a nonordinary state of consciousness, or an entheogen, a psychedelic, or much inner experiential work to get to the place where you actually actually *hear* another as to what they are really saying … and line up with their actual inner reality. For we are, in our beta state — in our normal awake state, that is — so distracted with myriad thoughts, obsessions, compulsions, and erratic sensations that we rarely hear another. This is what is essentially being referred to in the myth of the Tower of Babel.

## Human Babbling

In this myth of Babel, men wished to reach God by erecting a tower to heaven. For that, you can read the way we "developed" our Ego … actually *devolved* into it, in our early early evolution (see *Planetmates* and *Prodigal Human* on this, by the way). We built an Ego, an outward reflection of our inner reality, our inner Divinity, and tried to make it as large as the Divinity we had split off from, inside. This is a lot about the way we project the world of Form out of what we split off from in our identity as Experience and made it unconscious.

In any case, the main part of the myth has to do with how that caused us to not be able to understand each other anymore, which is symbolized in the myth by the different languages we split up into adopting. This myth expresses a very true and common reality and experience that we rarely are aware of unless we actually do have an experience of sublime hearing and understanding of another. In which case, however — that is, if and when we do — we can grok what I am saying about us having the same inner reality ... being suspended within the same Sea of Experience ... and so being able to experience overlapping experience and overlapping identity.

Though we rarely attain that experience of actual hearing of each other, we are desperately driven to attempt it all the time. We talk talk talk and we comment comment comment and we make update upon update in our social medias, desperately. For we are compelled by an inner knowing, felt but not remembered, that true understanding of each other, indeed actual identity with each other, and merging, are possible. We seek that in our friendships and especially our love relationships. The fact that we so rarely achieve that actual overlap, at least not mutually, has everything to do with our repetitive disappointments in love.

So we attempt to communicate in our feverish desires to re-experience our true identity again as One. We wish to be heard; but we rarely have the experience of actual "hearing" of others. They also rarely "hear" us, so we are ever disappointed. That Tower of Babel.

# The Puzzle of Existence ... The Nature of The Game

We do it, this communication — necessarily, since we have split the world into inner and outer — through symbols. Through pointers to our inner experience, mere indicators of it. And that is a pretty indirect way of accessing what for them — the others — is their *direct* reality of their Experience. Remember their direct experience is our own, too, but we purposefully put it out of our minds to create the Puzzle of Existence we want to enjoy trying to solve in our Form States.

So, the difference between the outer world and the inner world, between indirect and direct perception ends up coming down to only one thing: It has to do with the degree to which one's Reality is able to be correctly understood or interpreted. We have put half of our reality behind a veil, and that veil creates distortion. That is the nature of The Game. The Game is, become ignorant of a huge part of yourself and see "how long" ... and this is where we put the part about there being a Time in, as well ... *how long* it takes you to figure out your true nature ... as One, as Divinity, as being non-separate.

## Finding hOMe

It is similar to the games in which we start somewhere and have to find our way "home." Parcheesi comes to mind. Or like those films and TV series where the character wakes up somewhere, with no memory and no clue who he or she is, but she or he must find their way home and discover their true identity. Which they do by noticing all kinds of clues around them, often ones they put there themselves for themselves beforehand, or by having flashes of perception that open onto their "true" reality. Both of which they need to notice and reflect upon. Meaning they need to see what realities for themselves on the inside those outer clues are indicating, or revealing.

They need to make a "connection" with it, just as in our experiential psychotherapies we need to make a "connection" between our present feeling ... our present patterns of events, and our present patterns of behavior in response to those events ... and the feelings and pattern of experience and of event we went through at a time in the past, which we pushed out of our awareness, which is now appearing to us in the present in the manner of our feeling and present experience. We need to make the connection in order to stop those repressed experiences from showing up continually in our present experience.

In just the same way, we need to make a *connection* between what we perceive outside ourselves and call *world* — matter, people, and the patterns and processes of them — and the actual realities directly experienced on the "inside," for which they are projections. We need to do this to find our way hOMe ... to reintegrate once again our Mind. To *re-member*.

## Clues and Connections

Anyway, in these dramas, the character has to notice and reflect on these clues or rays of actual reality breaking through the clouds of forgetting and make the "connection" to them in one's reality — that they have to do with what one has forgotten and needs to know

303

again … indeed are the very things left "out of mind." *John Doe* is one series like that, a television series. *Memento*, the film, has a similar plot, with additional provocative insinuations. *Vanilla Sky* is illustrative of this, as well.

So we focus on our "inner reality" for advice on The Game for it gives us "direct" access to our Truths. Meanwhile we have this grand expanse of "outside" reality which gives us "hints" about our actual Truths, outside The Game. It gives us hints, flashes of light, or veiled messages, about our ultimate Reality and guidance on getting us home. It does this "indirectly," meaning the "breadcrumb from ourselves as Divinity" has to be noticed, then reflected upon, so as to have the messages, the Truths, that are within it … actually that *are* it, in its truest and direct state … be allowed to come *back* into our awareness once again. I am saying that matter, all of physical reality, is a projection of the realities we have direct access to within. That when we see these breadcrumbs and bring awareness to them, they point to the realities inside you that they truly are. Therein we make the *connection;* with that we are further hOMe.

This process of noticing, reflecting, processing, and connecting for the purpose of arriving hOMe is what I have been unveiling for you in the last few chapters.

## Bounded and Unbounded Perception

Thus indirect perception is only of *harder to realize* … notice, *realize,* to make real … harder to realize Truths. Direct, or inner, perception is of *easier to realize* Truths. That is one reason why meditation, experiential psychotherapies, holotropic breathwork, and entheogens are so valuable in pulling the curtains obstructing Reality to the side: These experiences expose us to inner realities that are *direct messages* (inner ones) of the messages around us we see all the time as our physical world, that we mistake as being "objects" and not messages, and within which we have our drama of temporary limited awareness for the purpose of regaining True Awareness all over again at some point, in some lifetime, in some Form or No-Form beingness. And then to do it again. And simply for the fun … or the adventure of it … all over again.

So, why indirect is indirect is that direct means anything can be accessed at any time, requiring no specific place or time. This is that "unbounded energy" again that Bohm talked about. This is not the limited energy, the bounded energy of Form. It is energy in the singularity, the infinity. Whereas physical reality is the creation of obstacles to the direct access of experiences or knowings, truths and Truth.

# Anytime and Anywhere ... The Nature of the No-Form State

Hence, what is the No-Form State except the ability to have everything and anything at any "time" ... without the obstacles of Form?

## Exquisite Sensitivity

Think about that one for a minute. The closest thing I can imagine to that is a state like a lucid dream, only where there is more than just lucidness: There is awareness of one's essential identity as Divinity. Something far more aware than our normal waking state in Form, also. Indeed, one No-Form personality — who I knew personally when he was in Form, he was a colleague and friend — conveyed, through another, to me and her, that the No-Form State is one of "exquisite sensitivity."

## Mind and Motion

In any case, consider, it would be a state of No-Time, yet movement and change. Where there are events, but they are all happening simultaneously. I can only imagine something like that as like having a book, say a novel, that has all the events in it, all right there existing already now. But we as Divinity pick it up at some point and create a kind of movement, if not actually "time," for the purpose of reading the story, savoring an event through focus, not *all* events unfocused ... unbounded.

I am reminded of one philosopher who once said that ultimately the new physics is going to determine that all that really exists is "Mind and motion." That is something along the lines of what I am thinking here.

## Set and Setting

Getting back to those breadcrumbs, which are *actually* the inner realities inside us, projected outward ... again, like I mean, is this how Divinity does it in the No-Form State, too? Might Divinity "project out" a time, that is, create "motion" within Mind, so as to have "events" in No-Form Reality? Which unveils a startling observation about us as well: Is it that we, in this Form State, this dimension, are "projecting out" space, as well as time, so as to further spread out, so to speak, Reality? So it can be taken in, in some more engaging, ultimately more "enjoyable," at least more "fun," way?

And let us "spread that out" to savor it! I mean, we can assume that any "motion" in No-Form reality involves a creation, or a projecting out, of time from the essential reality of No-Time. Thus, No-Form personalities experience dynamism — that "fun," or interest, again. Indeed, it allows Divinity to *be* multiplied into No-Form personalities. Is it not true that we do a similar thing in creating space in our Form reality? Can it be that we "project out" space, out of what is no-space or no-form, to create the physical world so as to "spread out" — for enjoyment, for to savor — the multitude of aspects contained within that no-form, that no-thing state?

Does God project out of Herself motion — a kind of no-form "time," a time that is self-evidently arbitrary, non-linear, modifiable — to create No-Form personalities? Then additionally does Divinity project space out of Himself to bring about the Form State? And along with projecting a space — whose parameters we mutually decide and collectively abide by — does the Divine, then, make that pseudo-time of the No-Form State linear? By linear I mean taking the "time," actually the "motion," of the No-Form State which is arbitrary, modifiable, "individually"-decided ("individual" as in a No-Form individual or personality); and making it invariable and uniform. Is that what Divinity does? That would be like creating a time that is not individually decided, rather, collectively, mutually decided upon for the purpose of interacting, "playing" together? Hence making it to be time as we know it. Is that what we as Divinities do in coming here in order to make Time?

If nothing else, that conceptualization fits with the facts. For in going into nonordinary states of consciousness, not only do we experience No-Form realities where we can find ourselves being other entities — people, planetmates, plants, planets, cells, stars, and so on. This is by definition "no-form" experience for we are not bounded in any particular form, ourselves, but can experience ourselves as different "forms": Our boundaries are mutable, modifiable, arbitrary, variable. In the same way, in these nonordinary states of consciousness we experience "motion." That is to say, there is a process in our experience. It moves along, time-like. But that time is variable, arbitrary. We may find ourselves in a past or future life, or in a different time in our current life. What connects it all, by the way, is the *feeling* — which is what I said earlier is *us*, oneself, the "I am."

So how to explain this paradox? Everything is already being … there is Beingness … it is already complete in Itself … and along with that, correlated with that, there being No-Time.

Meanwhile, becoming also exists, thus time. How can this be?

A good way I have of thinking about that is to imagine it as like having a board game in a box. Except consider that all the possible games that can be are already contained within it. For example, when I play Free Cell on my computer, a game of solitaire, there are thirty-two-thousand different games possible with the particular number and constitution of cards it uses. By analogy there would be thirty-two thousand lives, Stories, Plays possible for a similar beingness existing within similar parameters or rules and having a specific constitution or makeup. Particle in relation to wave. Configuration in relation to environment. Set in relation to setting.

In any case, imagine opening that box or opening that card game application, and spreading out that game, to savor the experience of it, in order to enjoy it … and all, merely for the fun of it.

Is that what we as Divinity — in both Form and No-Form realities — do?

# Life in the Infinite ... The Nature of the Afterlife

Reality is ultimately *no-thing*. So the No-Form State, the after-death state or the afterlife is basically no-thing. That is to say, outside of this life, outside of this space and time, Reality is *thingless*. You might see how that follows from this idea that "things" (matter) are merely Experience (consciousness) that are not recognized as such and therefore are projected, while here in Form. So in a state where that is not done ... nothing denied, nothing projected, matter not created ... how can there be "things"? Well, there can't. Outside of this Game, Reality is matter-less, thingless, for all is in awareness, potentially. There is nothing intentionally blocked from awareness or inaccessible (which creates "things")

The conclusion, then, is that Reality is no-thing, not nothing. That makes a big difference. For being no-thing and not being nothing hardly makes it boring, nothing, worthless. It simply makes it that it can be anything, and variable, and changeable in accordance with what one wishes to experience. It is only "nothing" if we have the assumption — and we do, by the way, and that is another problem — that this reality is the only one possible, so anything else must be "nothing" ... and if existing, certainly not *real*, meaning not consequential, insignificant.

Outside of our lives in Form, also, time does not exist ... *in common*. It does not exist *as an absolute*. That does not mean there are not experiences to be had which unfold time-like. It is just that *that* time is not one in common ... in common with other beings.

These are the mistakes we make in thinking about life after death. These mistakes have us thinking life after death is pretty unappealing. And we dread death like we are going to go into an unconsciousness, like a coma. We say "rest in peace" as if someone is going into a deep sleep. Or we think it amounts to going into a pitch black non-existence.

These ideas could not be further from the truth. In fact, No-Form Reality is exciting, wonderful, fascinating. Imagine having meta-human abilities to go back to any time, to any place — including other planets, galaxies, and other dimensions — and to interact with anyone at any time to do virtually anything. No appointment needed. No mapquest required for directions.

I know, I know. You're thinking, what about taking pictures and doing status updates? And how would you be able to tell everyone? Okay, it has that one ... that *one* ... drawback. But for all I know, there is something else — something like that or overshadowing it — which is far more engaging and interesting! I can hardly lol at the moment, with my tongue so deeply in cheek.

Seriously, though, imagine your reality as being able to choose any experiences and events to have, like as if you had access to infinite virtual reality games and could choose any one of them.

The reason we think this must not be true is because we have been brainwashed by religions, which at base are tools of very human societal elites. Tools whose intent is to make us behave and keep us in line, for purposes of social order. Social order which is desired, ultimately, because it protects their status, their holdings, their investment, their wealth. We have been taught to fear death ... hell, and all that ... so as to make us to apply ourselves more diligently to their ends while in human form. We have been told death is about judgment, about punishment, about paying a price for the bad things one has done in life. All of this regardless those same religions claim God is *good* — the *goodest* actually. So the inconsistency between a wonderful God and a horrible afterlife could not be more of a mind-fuck.

However, why do you think we have this idea of heaven, too? Where does that come from?

Well, an afterlife of heaven is much closer to the truth, in my opinion. I believe the afterlife is, actually, far more wonderful than even heaven is imagined to be. This is a big part of the *something wonderful* that is going to happen that the planetmates predicted in 2014, as I see it (see *Planetmates: The Great Reveal*, 2014b).[1] Their last message to us, in the last paragraph of the book, reads, "As in your Jacob's vision, there is no separation any longer 'between heaven and Earth'; there is a going to and fro between humans and all the angels in Nature and the Divine, which you have so long excluded. Know that this experience of inter-being consciousness, this Unity, is the most exquisite experience and is unimaginable; you might liken it to

Love expanded infinitely. Yes, that particular plot is available to you. And if you, as a species, take up your role in it, life on this planet will go on. This Earth will continue in alliance between all planetmates ... and something wonderful is going to happen...."

So, this vision of an afterlife I am presenting here is consistent with the *coming together of heaven and earth* they describe — in "their" words, "there is no separation any longer 'between heaven and earth.'" Actually, it would be just *one* of the "something wonderfuls." As the paragraph points to much more beyond even this, particularly in how it would manifest on Earth, in this Form reality, in *this* space and time, as well as what it has to do with a continuation of life on Earth congruent with an "inter-being consciousness" that brings humans and planetmates together again, brings humans and Nature together again. Indeed, that last part of the prophecy is being manifest in this work, which stresses the consciousness of everything, including humans and planetmates, and puts them on an equal footing once again.

The "something wonderful" is brought forth again ... this time in much more detail ... in my book, *Funny God: The Tao of Funny God and the Mind's True Liberation* (2015). And while the planetmates imply more, even, than is revealed there, still, in that work, *Funny God,* you can see a great elaboration of "something wonderful" and a "coming together of heaven and earth." And it is made absolutely clear how it has to do with this new vision of an afterlife, as well.

By the way, *Funny God* points out not only that there is a coming together of heaven and earth happening now and gives evidence for it. One of them is the increasing incidence of Near-Death-Experiences (NDEs) brought about by incredible medical advances which are able to bring folks back from death. But it points out that NDEs, along with evidence from entheogens and psychotechnologies like Stanislav Grof's *holotropic breathwork* and a few other developments — increasing visitations and communications with the "dead," for example — reveal the after-death state to be much like I am describing it: More heaven-like. Hardly nothingness. And characterized by incredible abilities to experience wonderful, fascinating realities. See *The Afterlife of Billy Fingers,* by Annie Kagan (2013), for a sample of what I mean by that.

In any case, with all these possibilities in the No-Form State, do you see why No-Forms (dead people) rarely check in with us here? They could be experiencing anything, anywhere, anytime, with anyone, in any life. What are the chances that here is where they would decide to be, to experience and interact with us?

Not only is time and space not existing *as an absolute* or a *shared* reality, in the No-Form State, which means space and time can exist as individually chosen and temporary ones instead, but one's identity is arbitrary and flexible. Be a planet, be a mountain, be the evolution of the Universe, be God, be you in one of your past or future lives.... And anything else you can imagine.

I mean, why do you think they call it "the infinite," "the singularity"? They don't call it the *subfinite*, do they? It is *everything*, not *nothing*.

# The Bottom Line

One way of looking at all this, then, as it relates to the nature of the physical universe, is that we, as Divinity, and having "agreed" on the parameters of our game of life and the physical components and timeline we will collectively create in which to play that game — that is, the universe of space and time — have also agreed to "place" these messages within physical reality, in our "remembered" or aware state, to guide us when we are in our "forgetting" or diminished state.

Better yet, that these elements of actual, not reflected or projected Reality, which are kept out of consciousness for the purpose of the Game, cannot help but make their way into the game play, this time as an Other or an unconscious reality, and one that is projected out and reflective of what one is not noticing inside. This would be similar to playing a board game, yet being aware of the events going on in the room one is in, the temperature of the air around one, and the sounds of the bird chirping outside of the window of that room, for example.

Another way of keeping in mind the view I am presenting is that, as I repeatedly say, matter is the indirect perception of Mind. So it is like the "map" of mind. Better said, it is the Mind itself, in reflected view. Matter is the map of God.

So by observing physical reality we can see what corresponds or correlates with it in the realm of Mind. That is the bottom line.

Okay, in the next chapter, let us kind of do that. Let us see what the process is like of looking into reality and seeing what it really *is*, in the realm of Mind. I have been doing that in the previous chapters. But let us see how another author — a brilliant philosopher and novelist — has done that exact same thing.

# 25

# Truth, Lives, and Ecstasy:

## From Divinity's Perspective, All Experience Is "Fun" … or at Least "Interesting." Thank You for Your Service, by the Way

*All Beings Are Equal, Varying Levels of Participation:*
*Have You Also Learned the Secret of the River That*
*There is No Time? Everything Has Reality and Presence.*

Hermann Hesse (1951) gives us a charming story of just such teaching from the "outside" world. We see how Nature, how That Which Is guides us in opening ourselves to its nature, our nature, and our true Identity.

# All Knowledge Is Accessible from Any Point

In *Siddhartha*, Hesse relates how his character left the sensory world of business and marriage, and became a river ferryman. Siddhartha's inner voice draws him to such a life and guides him to listen to the river:

> In his heart he heard the newly awakened voice speak, and it said to him: "Love this river, stay by it, learn from it." Yes, he wanted to learn from it, he wanted to listen to it. It seemed to him that whoever understood this river and its secrets, would understand much more, many secrets, all secrets.[1]

Notice that Hesse says "all secrets." All secrets are revealed peering through the same portal of river. This idea itself opens on a number of revelations we can explore now. They have to do with all experience being the same, all selves being equal to each other, all experience being potentially equal to Experience.... Finally, it leads to knowing that all truths (personal wisdom) are collective Truths (Infinite Wisdom), if one is observing from the same perspective as another. That is, that within the infinite expanse of the Universal Soup of Experience, there is Truth, only one, one Reality. So it is exactly the same for any of us when viewed from the *exact same* point of all possible foci, or the exact loci.

Confusing? How about that everyone in the Universe would see everything *exactly* the way you do if they were standing in your "shoes." Meaning there is no essential difference in beings (there is only one "God"), there are only different perspectives. So what constitutes, or creates, different beings? C'mon along; let us take a look.

## One Truth, Infinite Variety of Limitations of It

There is only one Truth, but there are many limitations of it, many "bounded," "constituted" realities. Just as all entities, as we have seen, are bounded experiential units, restricting Experience down to some subset for the purpose of experience ... and ultimately fun. The difference in these limited truths lies in the extent of their boundaries, with the more encompassing truths (individual truths) being *truer,* in a sense, for they are more useful in journeying further. They are better "maps" for our path, if for no other reason than that they "cover more territory." They encompass more of what is real, so are better aids on the path. Although no map (no truth) can ever constitute the experience of the journey itself.

So all truths are bounded "maps," relative to different experiential units. Each being, or experiential unit, has a truth, a "map," coincident to it. Our experience of life creates each of our understandings of reality, none of which constitute our understanding of Reality, as long as we are an entity or a limited experiential unit.

But there are degrees of usefulness in these truths or maps. The greater ones have greater experiential boundaries.... But since we are talking about experience, we have to say they have greater experiential *participation* in the Whole or the All That Is. Greater participation is equal to more expansive boundaries and more useful "maps," or truths with a small t, *coincident* to them.

Notice, not *arising*, but *coincident*. For the experience of map or truth is also part of experience ... and Experience. They are not separate, truth and experience, map and subjectivity, ideas and feelings; though we create dualities out of singular realities all the time. The *experience* of maps ... one's thoughts, insights, understandings and overstandings ... is also part of one's bounded experiential unit that is called self.

# Varying Levels of Participation ... Equality of Value, Worth

## All Beings Are Equal

So, though all beings are equal, we have different degrees of participation. Since all are equal, there are no goals, ultimately. But since there are differences, along with our experience or enjoyment or fun of life we can create goals for possible greater participation in the future — that is, for down the "line" in our "story" or "play."

All beings being equal, ultimately, means expanded experience is equal to more confined experience: Being a bacteria is equivalent to being a human; being a kidney is equal to being a person; being a cell in the kidney is equal, in value to Divinity as the Whole, to being the entire kidney. And being an atom is equal to being a galaxy.

If that last idea results in your mind jumping its track, I understand. It is practically unfathomable for humans to conceive it. However, let me continue, and I will show you how one can understand this idea of all "lives" or "games" being equal ... thus no goals, ultimately ... and all beings being equal, ultimately. Then hang on, and we will explore the vision related to that idea: the revelation which more directly addresses exactly why we have such incredible difficulty with a perspective like this.

Spoiler alert, it has to do with a deeply rooted assumption of ours involving humans having, within all of Nature, a superior awareness. How can that not be true, correct? And related to that, that beings are ranked lower to upper, regarding their awareness, according to their size and complexity ... in *Form*. That is, we think larger entities, like galaxies over atoms; and more complex beings, like humans over amoeba *has to* result in greater awareness as you go "up the scale." I will address that specifically two chapters on, in "The Secret Life of Stones," Chapter 28. I believe you will be surprised at what we see there.

## All Lives are Equal

For now, though, let us look at the first of those issues. Let us explore this idea of all lives being equal. Using the metaphor of games again ... and to use a modest example ... from Divinity's perspective playing a child's game of Go Fish is equal to participating in an Olympic event. Similarly, playing Tag, a children's pastime, has equal value to participating in the "game" of a political campaign. That is to say, from the point of view as to their value to Divinity. Do not we desire ... at different times and for different reasons or to accompany varying moods ... do not we desire one or the other equally?

I can tell you, for one, it was just as engaging in the past, depending on my mood, to get wrapped up in Pong, Tetris, or even further back, flicking the flippers on a pinball machine or making break in a game of 8-Ball with friends, as one of the newer video games like World of WarCraft, or Grand Theft Auto. It all depends on what you want to experience at a particular moment.

For humans, that might have to do with varying our experience over time. An example might be wanting to unwind with a simple game of FreeCell after writing a book of philosophy for seven hours, say. Or someone else might desire a "mindless" game of Tetris — where one enjoys "flexing" one's "muscles" of reaction and intuition, and enjoys the feeling of increase in ability on a preconscious level. That same person might on another day, after some more routine activities of life, say, want to spice it up by visiting friends, seeing a lover, watching a basketball game, having a philosophical exchange with friends on Facebook, or, going back to the metaphor of the "game," engaging in hour upon hour of Dungeons and Dragons or Rise of the Tomb Raider.

Even the game of a seeming no-game is "fun," when you think about it. In the midst of life which is often felt to be tumultuous, many want an oasis of stillness at times. They might meditate. I might stare out the window or simply close my eyes with no intention, no desire, no goal. Allow myself to be given to, by the All, and not giving.

We desire, indeed require, variety in the "games" of life, both tiny and all encompassing.

For Divinity, since there is No-Time, that choice of making all choices might be more related to, not varying experience over time so as to magnify interest in life as humans do, but more like varying experience to manifest in Reality a more magnificent Universe, with more grandeur ... that glory, that fun, that finest of all paintings with the incredible variety in color, stroke, and texture each highlighting and adding to the rest ... and again, equally.

And if all experiences — large and small, simple and complex, "light" and "dark," "good" and "evil," wise and ignorant, fun and seemingly boring — were not desired equally by such Divinity ... who would by definition be capable of choosing anything ... why would not that Divinity bring into actualization only those experiences desired? That is to say, only those serving to further its intention of magnifying the glory … the fun, the entertainment value … of Existence. And why would not He leave out the one's failing to do that or of lower priority in augmenting Existence? And perhaps She did. It is not like Divinity needs to learn any "lessons" by enduring crappy experiences, either.

## All Experience is "Fun" … from Divinity's Perspective. Or at Least "Interesting."

In either case the conclusion is that all movements in the Universal Pool of Experience are equally valued by Divinity. And they all magnify … glorify … the All. Divinity only has "fun."

Of course it nearly breaks our brains to think that Divinity is having fun through all the horrible things we see happening in life. But that is from *our* perspective. Bear with me. We are able to have a glimpse of Divinity's perspective, we are able to go outside of ourselves and our biologically constituted realities, we are able to experience *ex* (out of) *stasis* (form, state, or status quo) … that is to say, *ecstasy* … with a few modifications, corrections actually, of our biologically constituted beliefs about reality.

I get into this more in other places. I touch on it in *Planetmates* (2014b), explore it in *Experience Is Divinity* (2013c), and lay it out in considerable detail in *Funny God* (2015). And I will say more about this further along in this book as well. However:

### Death Does Not Exist

For one thing — just as a "taste" here and now, though — consider the fact we are immortal. Death does not really exist, as there is no such thing as an end of existence, or consciousness, or experience, there is simply transition from Form into No-Form. And back again, of course. Remove the "fact" of death from all the horror in the world, and we might glimpse a Reality that is exciting and interesting, however "reckless."

I know, I know. I can scarcely do it myself … evaluate the atrocities of history and the tragedies of life with the factor of death set to the side … without pulling a "muscle." It is nearly impossible to imagine Reality outside of our biologically constituted assumptions of death, since we are "in" Form. And our human compassion, wrought of our own very personal and excruciating experiences of pain, especially when coming into this world (*Falls from Grace*, 2014a, and *Wounded Deer and Centaurs*, 2016b, for that) is extremely difficult to set to the side when, indeed, we don't *want* to. Why would we ever want to take the feeling of compassion off the table? If even for a minute? We feel it even borders on the unethical, perhaps even the dangerous, to think this way.

Believe me I feel that way, too. However I am asking you, for the sake of *ecstasy* — of getting a glimpse in a Divinity's way, a No-Form's way, that is "out of Form" — to temporarily push that compassion to the side and put that assumption about death on the shelf and take a peek. I assure you, you will not "lose control" of yourself and go around acting upon others as if there is no death, or no suffering. It is important for this game we have in Form *to* believe that and to abide by it. It makes for a shitty experience for all, if we did not. Have faith that you are not someone to go nuts that way. If there were such a soul, it is highly unlikely, perhaps even impossible, that they would ever see these words.

Besides, this perspective has woven into it, inextricably, that there is no difference between you and another, between you and another human. So greater compassion, not less, comes of it, naturally.

So, knowing that it is only you and me here. And trusting yourself that this peek will not upset your morality … you are Divine after all, essentially. And Divinity does not want needless suffering either. I trust you. Now you trust yourself. And doing this, let us take that peek. Let us continue. We don't have to tell everyone, or anyone, what we will see.

So, to continue….

## Suffering Cannot Be Meaningless

Now, about suffering. We *assume* suffering is evil. Yet we know we learn more from suffering than anything else. And if suffering leads us eventually hOMe, in a way that no other type of experience can, then is it an evil? Or is it part of a "Divine" plan … "our" plan, you see, though "forgotten"? So remove the seeming meaninglessness from the fact of our suffering. Next:

## Suffering Cannot Be "Endless"

Remove also our fear that it is possible for it to be unending. That is a fright nearly impossible not to have. For it is a most definite fear, arising from our prenatal experience in which we suffered and were unaware of time, or of the end of the suffering coming with birth, so it *seemed* endless. We also suffocated as part of that, and we know how that involves a terror of it not ending, a panic, even, where every second is immense.

This fear of a pain, unending, is the basis, of course, of ideas of unending suffering, as in hell.

So these are just horrific thoughts and feelings rooted in a misunderstanding we had at the very beginning of our lives. But in actuality, unending suffering is not possible in the Universe. For one thing, we are Divine, with the only actual "free will" in the Universe, so why would we choose it? It would not be fun. Unvarying experience is boring, from any perspective, including the Divine's.

How do I know that? Well, because look around in the Universe and the one thing you cannot doubt is that infinite variety, infinite experience is desired by Divinity for that is what exists! That is the quality of the Universe, if nothing else. Evil and suffering are at best the spices of existence, not Its goals. It is ridiculous to think the Universe as an ever recurring Big Bang or a spinning galaxy is experiencing *suffering* in doing it.

For another thing, since there is No-Time, how can there be *anything* that is endless? We are everything and every"one" doing all things and experiencing everything and all at the same time.

Finally, if we as Divinity would find it unfun to have an experience of "endless suffering," well then who would be enforcing such an existence on another? Here we see how this assumes a duality in the Universe which, in practice, we do not find. Not at the level of Consciousness or Experience we are talking about here.

Which is the level of Ultimate Reality and Divinity. The place beyond illusion.

So immersing oneself in this hard to accept notion that there is no such thing as either meaningless or endless suffering, you catch a glimpse of how one could, at a later time ... though rarely when one is within it ... look back on that suffering as more like comedy than like tragedy. *Like* comedy. You see, some of our past suffering is readily seen that way ... and "oh what a piece of work" it is ... and we are.

And why? Put it this way, comedy masquerades as tragedy to bring about the most joyful peek-a-boo of all when its true face is revealed. That is a perspective I take up at great length in my books, *Funny God* (2015) and *Experience Is Divinity* (2013c). For now, though, consider this.

## Tragedy Is Veiled Comedy

In order to see as "comedy" some other of the horrors we know about — at any time, sooner or even far later — we have to assume some kind of perspective way outside of our bounds. But rely on the fact we are limited, will you? As well as that as we have more experience in life, when we look back we increasingly can see its humorous if not hilarious parts, which were once horrible to experience. I believe it was the famous American comedian, Carol Burnett, who said, "Comedy is tragedy plus time."

And I know it is virtually impossible to contain this overstanding while here in Form. But just take it, based on this explanation, that it is possible to see everything, all of the Experience in the Universe ... all of God's "events" ... that way. That is to say, with corrections of our mistaken assumptions about death and suffering — arising out of our humanness, in Form — it is possible to get a glimpse of All Events as being "fun." Often as being "funny." And again, here is another alley where the Cosmic Giggle lies in wait to pounce on you. To wrestle you to the ground and tickle you.

There are many, probably most, who are absolutely iron-clad unable to consider this. To go outside such grooves of terror laid down in us before birth, even in thought or imagination, is impossible for most. However, it is unlikely they are here right now reading this. They live in a world my words can never enter, let alone can they be comprehended. Certainly no "glimpse" for them. For outside of Form, for ecstasy. So this is only for you. Here and now.

I know I had to address that, at least a little here … seeing as how it was on your mind and you could not hear anything else beyond it. Unless I addressed it. Just know that a fuller explanation is had through checking into the works, of mine, mentioned.

In any case, this vision is one of a Universe as Divinity having fun, "enjoying" HerSelf. Glorifying and magnifying the All Existing through a process of motion, thus Time … and forgetting, thus Form.

Hopefully now we can continue.

## Greater Participation and Overstandings

Thus, part of Divinity's desire … which is what creates that movement in Beingness, that "time," that "motion" within Mind … is to experience the possibilities of greater "participation" in It All. Not greater in the sense of "better," but merely in the sense of more expanded. Greater participation leading to greater "overstandings" (better "maps") is one but only one desire of Divinity. It is one if for no other reason than that experience of greater participation opens upon the possibility of having the experience of being the Whole, or at least a greater expanse of the All.

However, enlightenment, this way, is just one existence, desired by All and Everyone, at a particular "time." There is no big deal about it in the Universal scheme to have the experience of being God. It is one experience that is desired alongside all the others. Why would it be a greater desire? It is already attained by Divinity (everything happens simultaneously). It is not like that experience "improves" anything or makes God's "life" "better." It is only we in Form that might want, in any particular life, to get a more expanded "peek." Perhaps if only for the reason of getting a break from the oppressive elements of existence, the suffering, one had earlier chosen. God is not trying to become enlightened. She already is. The only "desire" of Divinity has to do with magnifying the glory of It, making a more awesome "picture," increasing the "entertainment value" of Existence as a whole. God just wants to have "fun."

And, what follows, this is like saying that at times we choose lives where we loll around on a beach, so to speak — metaphorically we are playing a card game akin to Gin Rummy, or even the simplistic Slap Jack — and another time we wish to participate as an athlete in a decathlon, metaphorically, in a life.

A different life involves a different experience, not in terms of its having more worth, or importance, or more "entertainment value," than another; but merely in its degree of participation. And along with that greater participation, a greater overstanding of Reality, accompanying the greater immersion in experiential reality it involves — the greater complexities, the more refined perspectives on Truth unveiled.

I and another are not different in that, hypothetically, one of us lives a life of ease and pleasure and has little interest for Truth or one's essential Identity and the other of us chooses a mix of both difficult and fantastical experiences, agonizing and euphoric ones, for the purpose of checking into that Identity, raising the curtain on that larger Truth. So, you and I are not different, not just essentially in our identity as Divinity, but also we are not even different in terms of the value or importance of the lives we choose, the games we decide to play. This means no one's life is more important than another's; no one is more important than another.

Why? For I want your life as well, in a sense. And I *have* your life as well ... as you are experiencing mine. We are one Divinity having simultaneous lives for the purpose of magnifying the wonder of Existence and the interest and overall value of It All.

## Thank You for Your Service

So my experience of life is equal to yours and yours is equal to mine. For there is no time, there is no separation, and I am you and am doing that, too. Whatever you are doing, and whoever you are, I am doing that, too. And you are doing this, too. Aren't you having a great time writing this book, right now? We know we are. *happy face*

323

There is no difference in the value of Divinity's infinite lives any more than there are differences in the values of the many different colors that go into the beauty of a work of art. The colors of blue, and black, as well as yellow and orange, are equally important. These each contrast with and magnify the value of the others. And together contribute to the magnificence. God's glory again.

Thank you for your service, by the way.

## The Only Goals Are Non-Goals … All Glorify the All

So differences in degrees or levels or participation create the only goals that exist, which are non-goals, from the perspective of Divinity … which is us at our base or ultimately. For Divinity wishes *all* experience. All experiences manifest It. They all glorify the All.

So greater truths, closer-to-Truth truths, and greater participation in the All are the only goals there are. If one is living an experiential unit which includes having goals, that is. However, the vast majority of lives of entities or bounded experiential units have only the goal of experiencing and expanding the fascination of movement in the All … in other words, fun. Or adding to the glory and magnificence of the All, which contributes to the fun and enjoyment of each of us, all beings, all entities, all bounded experiential units. For each partakes of the All. So, experience at all levels of participation are equal in that they all add to the "glory" of the All.

## For "What a Piece of Work"….

Now, this is how we distinguish between this way of looking at things and all the other tendencies of anthropocentric humans to put their Reality at the pinnacle of every pyramid. How can humans be so stupid as to not give a damn that they are destroying all the life on the planet they inhabit and still be the brightest bulb in the pack?

# Being and Becoming

To continue with *Siddhartha*, then,

*But today he only saw one of the river's secrets, one that gripped his soul. He saw that the water continually flowed and flowed and yet it was always there; it was always the same and yet every moment it was new. Who could understand, conceive this?*[2]

Since I have already elaborated on this point, at great length, earlier, in Chapter 20, "The Universe Speaks Its Intention for Existence," I will leave it rest for now. If you remember, this characteristic of the stream explains how there can be both beingness and becomingness at the same time, in the same reality. Let us continue.

# "The River Knows Everything"

## "Seek the Depths"

Further guidance about the river is provided by Siddhartha's friend, the elder ferryman, Vasudeva. Concerning his remarkable ability to listen, Vasudeva tells his protégé:

*"You will learn it," said Vasudeva, "but not from me. The river has taught me to listen; you will learn from it, too. The river knows everything; one can learn everything from it. You have already learned from the river that it is good to strive downwards, to sink, to seek the depths. The rich and distinguished Siddhartha will become a rower; Siddhartha the learned Brahmin will become a ferryman. You have also learned this from the river. You will learn the other thing, too."*[3]

"Seek the depths"? "Strive *downwards*"? There is not a thing I wish to add to that. I suggest here you just savor it and, like the river, listen to it for what it reveals to you. I already have, yes. It was profoundly illuminating for me in terms of my life. Thank you for asking.

## The River Tells Time

Later, Siddhartha's education progresses. He speaks to his mentor, Vasudeva:

*"Have you also learned that secret from the river; that there is no such thing as time?"*

*A bright smile spread over Vasudeva's face.*

*"Yes, Siddhartha," he said. "Is this what you mean? That the river is everywhere at the same time, at the source and at the mouth, at the waterfall, at the ferry, at the current, in the ocean and in the mountains, everywhere, and that the present only exists for it, not the shadow of the past, nor the shadow of the future?"*

*"That is it," said Siddhartha, "and when I learned that, I reviewed my life and it was also a river, and Siddhartha the boy, Siddhartha the mature man and Siddhartha the old man, were only separated by shadow, not through reality. Siddhartha's previous lives were also not in the past, and his death and his return to Brahma are not in the future. Nothing was, nothing will be, everything has reality and presence."*[4]

This also I have elaborated on in that previous chapter, where I spoke about brooks and rivers revealing that time is an illusion. But it is interesting to see how Hesse (Siddhartha) includes past and future lives into the mix. Fascinating, also, is his pointing out that even return to Oneness is already attained. *Everything* happens simultaneously. You are already God.

## Overlapping Identity and Shared Experience

Further on:

*Often they sat together in the evening on the tree trunk by the river. They both listened silently to the water, which to them was not just water, but the voice of life, the voice of Being, of perpetual Becoming. And it sometimes happened that while listening to the river, they both thought the same thoughts, perhaps of a conversation of the previous day, or about one of the travelers whose fate and circumstances occupied their minds, or death, or their childhood; and when the river told them something good at the same moment, they looked at each other, both thinking the same thought, both happy at the same answer to the same question.*[5]

What joy it is. Isn't it? At those moments when we realize experience is shared and our identities overlap. Synchronicity, not merely. We feel ourselves not alone in time but immersed in an Experience beyond ourselves. Embracing us. Caring for us. When we merge for a moment with another. And the boundaries between personalities collapse, revealed to be imaginary. We experience belongingness in All. We care about everything. And everyone as us.

# 26

# The Greatest Teaching:

## Unity Is Divinity, A Blessed Possibility, Coming hOMe, and the Nature of Divinity … "Listen Better"

*Looking Deeply Into the Message of the World: Taught by Nature, by That Which Is — The Heights of Learning and Transformation Possible in Wide-Angled Contemplation of the World*

## The Greatest Teaching of All

Such teaching, in contemplation of the river, continued for a long time. Until one day, Siddhartha was to learn a teaching surpassing all others.

# Oneness

Once again, it is his mentor Vasudeva who directs him to look more deeply and listen more intently to the message of the World:

> *"You have heard it laugh," he said, "but you have not heard everything. Let us listen; you will hear more."*
>
> *They listened. The many-voiced song of the river echoed softly. Siddhartha looked into the river and saw many pictures in the flowing water. He saw his father, lonely, mourning for his son; he saw himself, lonely, also with the bonds of longing for his faraway son; he saw his son, also lonely, the boy eagerly advancing along the burning path of life's desires, each one concentrating on his goal, each one obsessed by his goal, each one suffering. The river's voice was sorrowful. It sang with yearning and sadness, flowing towards its goal.* [1]

Among the rest, notice in this how it is the feeling, loneliness, that is the same. It is central to all the Forms, to all the persons and their diverse and varying contexts of personality and place. Consider how this relates to what I had been saying in the chapter before last about the feeling as being the Reality. The feeling being equivalent to Experience, to being Divinity, to being the thread woven through time connecting everything. The feeling being related to the "I am" or the sense of self. Or in this case Self, or approaching Self (there's a hint for you). For it plays into what comes out of his reflections. As so,

> *"Do you hear?" asked Vasudeva's mute glance. Siddhartha nodded.*
>
> *"Listen better!" whispered Vasudeva.*
>
> *Siddhartha tried to listen better. The picture of his father, his own picture, and the picture of his son all flowed into each other. Kamala's picture also appeared and flowed on, and the picture of Govinda and others emerged and passed on.* [2]

Notice here how he is learning the teaching, from the river, that we are all One Being. This is especially taught by the river's flowing into the ocean or, as a Buddhist might say, the "dewdrop vanishing into the shining sea." He explains in what follows. Notice again how it is feelings or felt experience that unites us, rather is the thing we share and out of which we only "think" we are separate.

*They all became part of the river. It was the goal of all of them, yearning, desiring, suffering; and the river's voice was full of longing, full of smarting woe, full of insatiable desire. The river flowed on towards its goal.*[3]

## I Am You ... Coo Coo Ca Choo

In this we see how all goals, desires, intentions, pains, and strivings are identical. We all participate in the same Experience; we all "swim" in the same pool. Where we *are* in that pool makes all the difference. Different locations create different beings. And no other thing. There is no separation, just different, and temporary, reorganizations of Universal Experience ... usually called "God." Continuing, now....

*Siddhartha saw the river hasten, made up of himself and his relatives and all the people he has ever seen. All the waves and water hastened, suffering, towards goals, many goals, to the waterfall, to the sea, to the current, to the ocean and all goals were reached and each one was succeeded by another. The water changed to vapor and rose, became rain and came down again, became spring, brook and river, changed anew, flowed anew. But the yearning voice had altered. It still echoed sorrowfully, searchingly, but other voices accompanied it, voices of pleasure and sorrow, good and evil voices, laughing and lamenting voices, hundreds of voices, thousands of voices.*[4]

I am reminded how Yoko Ono sang, "We're all water from different rivers. That's why it's so easy to meet. We're all water in this vast, vast ocean. Someday we'll evaporate together."[5]

### Matter's "Personal" Message ... and There Is No Problem in That!

In Siddhartha's vision, notice that the messages are both universal ... *and* personal. These thoughts, found in Nature and the world of matter are *ideas, cosmic truths,* as well as personal insights. Also, remember that there is no strict dividing line between cosmic and personal truths as the boundaries of self are self-constructed and ultimately there are no boundaries and self equals Self. Meaning the personal and the cosmic are identical, the self's boundaries expand to be identical with the All That Is. Or, as is said in the East, the personal world and the Universal Soul or Word Soul are identical … that is, *Atman* equals *Brahman*.

## You Are Me … Diddeley Diddeley Dee

What this means in a practical sense is that what I learn about myself in the course of my experience of life and my observations of the world are *identical* to what another learns in exactly the same situation. Put another way, we are all foci of consciousness in the same experiential soup, or ocean. We are in different places, we have different locations and thus "perspectives." But it is of the *exact same Reality!* This means that were I to be in the exact same position in the experiential soup as you, my revelations, truths, insights would be *exactly the same as yours*. This is indeed what is meant by I am you, and you are me, and we are we, and we are all together.

### And We Are All Napoleon

We express this when we say, "There but for the grace of God go I." But it is much broader in scope than that. For this means that we are all not just kings and slaves in some metaphorical way. We actually *are* Napoleon, in a sense. That means that we, having had the exact same experiences, over the course of lives, would see and feel everything *exactly like* Napoleon. So, essentially, we are all Napoleon. So, yeah, we can all wear our hats sidewise and they will cart us away together to the looney bin. lol.

By the way, often people fall into these revelations through some unique and socially different or aberrant sort of events and then when they express them, society labels them "nuts." There was a time when there were lots of folks going around claiming to be Napoleon. Granted, *they* probably *were* "nuts," lol. But it reveals something to us. For, interestingly, this was at a time after Napoleon had been exiled and then after his death. Is it only coincidence that an essence of him popped up in people's minds once he had been "repressed" in physical form?

Is it coincidence how much the ideas of Lincoln and JFK arise continually, even today, with more power perhaps even than when they were alive? How many people quote Gerald Ford compared to quoting John F. Kennedy, for example, both of whom served less than a full term in office at the same relative time in history? The same can be said for the inspiration of Martin Luther King and John Lennon. And most powerfully of all, the words of Jesus have lived on after him. What these figures all have in common is assassination. Their physical forms were repressed out of existence. Indeed, they were obliterated.

I can tell you in fact that many of us devotees of Sathya Sai Baba feel that his death marked the beginning of his manifesting more powerfully in our lives, from the inside out. Not the outside in, as was the case for many while he was alive. These books are a manifestation of that, in my opinion. It might be relevant that Sai Baba also, in the last decade or so of his life, experienced a "repression" — a slandering akin to a character assassination. Not quite the crucifixion that Christ suffered, but there is a parallel there.

By the way, I am not saying that all important people who are murdered pop up in our inner lives. Certainly, not that all show up in the form of inspiration. But only in the form of something that is needed in reality at a particular time but was repressed forcefully out of it. In this sense the ideas and inspiration of the leaders I mentioned are what are needed, though they were forcibly pushed into No-Form.

As for Napoleon, I do not believe it is his inspirational ideas or any message of his that needed to come out, but there is another thing. It might be that he represented the power that people were lacking in their lives at the time. For at a time of huge conformity such as that, still somewhat stuck in medieval ways — in the late Eighteenth and early Nineteenth Centuries — people's sense of individuality, let alone self, had to have been practically obliterated. Perhaps his reputed smallness of stature — however untrue and propagandistic — as married with his largeness of power had something to do with it; that might have made him identifiable for folks severely lacking confidence, or any measure of self-esteem.

Though individual power had risen up during the French Revolution, preceding him; it was suppressed again in the years following that led up to and continued after Napoleon.

As often happens, when a new development is meant to arise it often comes out flagrantly and with great force — the French Revolution, the Sixties. Subsequently it is repressed. But the vision, the ray of light that shone through gives a taste ever after of where society, the world, needs to go from there. The route it should take. The ideals of the French Revolution burned even brighter in a Russian Revolution a hundred years later. However distorted those ideals became over the years after those revolutions and however much they were sometimes reversed, they refuse to die, continually seek expression.

Fifty years after the Russian revolution, we saw a worldwide revolution, an awakening, a counterculture, during the decade of 1962 through 1971. Most recently, Sixties ideals, themselves repressed, want also to come alive, again. The Sixties resurrected itself in Occupy activities worldwide, beginning with Occupy Wall Street in September of 2011 and continuing worldwide with outpourings of mass action in eighty-two countries, including Brazil, Romania, and the Ukraine, and across all continents except Antarctica. Earlier that year its spirit emerged in the Arab Spring in the Mideast. Even earlier, in the spring of 1989, it arose in China, around the seven-week occupation of Tiananmen Square, in Beijing, which spread to four hundred cities in that country. A few years after Occupy's high point at Zuccotti Park, it showed its colorful, ebullient self throughout Turkey over the euphoria around the events of Gezi Park and Taksim Square in the summer of 2013. Though repetitively slapped down, this vision arises in a Millennial Generation whose values grow from and embellish those of the Sixties. Who knows where it will stir and take form again?

So these repressed aspects of consciousness, once arisen, are powerful and move societies. For they provide an unexpected vision. They open upon vistas that once seen can never be forgotten. Once known, they can never be unknown, regardless how many John F Kennedys, Martin Luther Kings, Abbie Hoffmans, Robert F. Kennedys, or John Lennons are pushed into No-Form before their "time." These spirits can never be undrunk; they can never be put back in the bottle. These inspirations can never be uninhaled; they will find expression somewhere.

They work, on the societal level, in much the same way that entheogens do in the personal arena. Entheogens, formerly referred to as *psychedelics*, are capable of opening one to a reality far beyond one's self. Thus they give a "taste" or a "peek" into a larger Self and a more expanded, less onerous, reality ... which can only be realized over time afterward and only through much more Form-ly experience. However, suck a peek provides both a direction and a confirmation of the validity of the understanding. Both of these are invaluable for personal growth; visions and catalyzing events are equally helpful in social evolution.

They say it is because these inspirational figures were martyred that their ideas are strong. But where is the mechanism for that? I know of no such psychological rule or law or observation from Nature. Except that is, along the lines of what I am relating here of inner and outer, awareness and projection. In which case, is the "martyr" explanation simply a convenient, a common, indicator, not a real explanation, of something that can be explained in the manner I am presenting? That what is repressed in consciousness manifests in matter and the world of Form, we know. But perhaps what is repressed in Form arises within consciousness as well. That is something to think about.

## Thank You for Being You, Though

In any case, we are all Napoleon; we are all Caesar; we are all Jesus. We are all God. We are all you. We are all me. And I want to thank you, by the way, for your taking up the being of you. Somebody had to, and I was already engaged; rather, I was interested in something else right then.

You are doing a heckuva job, too, by the way. We thank you, again, for your service.

("And you, over there. Yeah, you. Talking over me. Thank you! Somebody had to be the pain in the ass." lol.)

And nowadays there are lots of folks having pseudo-experiences of past lives in which they *are* Caesar or the like. You find them at the

New Age gatherings in suburbia and those of bohemian artsy elites in urban centers. They come forth in interactions that have intentions to entertain, where past lives are invoked to impress. Or these faux past-lives come welling up in the dead of one's night, when one's esteem is ebbing low. However, it is Ego that causes such folks to find, amid the vast potential of all experience that ever was, is "now," or ever could be, the experiences or set of events that most embellishes themselves ... themselves, you see, as small self, as ego.

Actual past-life regressions ... Roger Woolger (1987) and Stanislav Grof, in my opinion, uncovered them best. Authentic past life experiences reveal that we were all kinds of lives, including the most despicable and painful lives imaginable. In fact, it is those kind that play most into the issues we bring into our current lives. They are far more important to real-ize, to re-member.

# A Blessed Possibility

But if we are creating all these small selves down from the All Self, are we not then just saying that God multiplies Herself endlessly and we are all parts of Divinity? However true that is, what I am adding is that we are not separate and that both potentially and at times in actuality we can be each other, we can be even another species, the consciousness of the planet, of a galaxy, or of the All. One need only look to any of Stanislav Grof's books to grasp the immense range of possibilities of that. So that is quite a huge modification of that more pedestrian understanding of us being parts of some gigantic machine, as commonly thought.

## Divine Gift of Our Times

No, then, the truth is not as simplistic as the ideas that we are like individual cells in a Universal Person, or sparks of thought in a Cosmic Mind. For both of them imply boundaries. The astonishing discovery of modern times and current science is that the boundaries of self are arbitrary and mutable. Modern consciousness research has revealed the possibility, once again, through psychotechnologies such as entheogens and holotropic breathwork and modern forms of shamanism and deep experiences in experiential therapies as in expanded forms of primal therapy and past-life regressions, that we are not just the All, in potential, as in an experience of "becoming one with God" or an opening to the All That Is. Along with and more easily than that, we can take up one of the infinite foci of consciousness anywhere, potentially, in the vast expanse of Experience and actually *be*, for a time, another entity … be it an insect, a star system, a single celled animal, a sperm or egg cell, a planet, such as Gaia, the Earth, and anything in between..

And we do, indeed, have the potential to expand our boundaries to the point of No Boundaries, too; which is that experience, and for humans that *fleeting* experience, of having the experience of God, being God. I am not saying I have achieved that ultimate no-boundary experience, though some of the other things I mention I have. But I am told from mystics throughout the cultures that this potential exists for us as humans.

And yes, this means that we are potentially even Hitler and Genghis Khan. Remember that the next time you want to "get on your high horse" and bask in the mirror of your own greatness. But the next time you want to slither around in worm-like self-loathing, remember also that we are all, in essence, Jesus, too. Or Sathya Sai Baba, Sitting Bull, or Chief Seattle. Or Confucius, Mohammed…. Einstein, Jung….

# Coming hOMe

Such is The Game while in Form. There are infinite bounded, limited selves and the potential to experience many of them. However, one of the experiences of Form, which happens to everyone, is of tiring of it. At times we wish a surcease in all that experiencing we are capable of and do. We long to return to the unity we emerged from, to go back hOMe. Our nature is that Oneness, that non-duality; it calls to us, in time. By way of the river, Hesse continued his teaching,

> *Siddhartha listened. He was now listening intently, completely absorbed, quite empty, taking in everything. He felt that he had now completely learned the art of listening. He had often heard all this before, all these numerous voices in the river, but today they sounded different. He could no longer distinguish the different voices — the merry voice from the weeping voice, the childish voice from the manly*

*voice. They all belonged to each other: the lament of those who yearn, the laughter of the wise, the cry of indignation and groan of the dying. They were all interwoven and interlocked, entwined in a thousand ways. And all the voices, all the goals, all the yearnings, all the sorrows, all the pleasures, all the good and evil, all of them together was the world. All of them together was the stream of events, the music of life. When Siddhartha listened attentively to this river, to this song of a thousand voices; when he did not listen to the sorrow or laughter, when he did not bind his soul to any one particular voice and absorb it in his Self, but heard them all, the whole, the unity; then the great song of a thousand voices consisted of one word: Om — perfection.*[6]

## Dialectic and Divinity's Nature

While expressing the yearning come to us in time, notice also the identity between the personal and the cosmic truths. We are separate as well as All, both Form and No-From simultaneously. Our truths and Truth Itself merge with each other and dialectically give rise to each other.

Notice also Hesse's identification of self with self's experience, self's feelings — merry, weeping, lament, yearn, indignation, groan, sorrow, pleasure. He calls them "voices." He uses the metaphor of music, of songs, to portray them. He was aware he could not reveal his personal illumination in words so lame as *consciousness, thoughts, knowledge,* or *awareness* ... or even *jnana* ... thereby taking all the "poetry" out of existence, out of spirituality.

Illumination is a feeling experience, not a cognitive one, or some empty nothingness of blank still consciousness or aware Voidness. However intellectually true those concepts are in some sense ... yes they can be applied ... they misdirect one from the path. They mask its goal in a cosmic greyness bespeaking comfortable numbness — unappealing to say the least; hard to be motivated by, to say more. It makes it attractive, if anything, only to those seeking escape through such striving. Yet Hesse was supremely aware that the bright light of an illumined soul arose phoenix-like only through the fires of worldly experience, by engaging in life, not retreating from it. This misconception and its correction we will look at in the next chapter. However, Hermann Hesse knew Experience was Divinity.

He also had no doubt that enlightenment was not a retreat from life but an embracing of it and of action in the world. This is another exposition coming next. Hesse's character, Siddhartha's experience of ultimate unity and perceived perfection leads him *into* not away from "the stream of events." It integrates and focuses him, yes. It resolves his conflicts of soul and desires. And it frees him from a prison of fighting himself so he can fully immerse himself in his destiny in life.

*"Do you hear?" asked Vasudeva's glance once again.*

*Vasudeva's smile was radiant; it hovered brightly in all the wrinkles of his old face, as the Om hovered over all the voices of the river. His smile was radiant as he looked at his friend, and now the same smile appeared on Siddhartha's face. His wound was healing, his pain was dispersing; his Self had merged into unity.*

*From that hour Siddhartha ceased to fight against his destiny. There shone in his face the serenity of knowledge, of one who is no longer confronted with conflict of desires, who has found salvation, who is in harmony with the stream of events, with the stream of life, full of sympathy and compassion, surrendering himself to the stream, belonging to the unity of all things.*[7]

## Listening Better

This is, of course, an elaborate illustration, from Hesse, over these last two chapters, of the ideas I have been expressing in the six chapters previous to them. Matter is message. It teaches us everything, and it will tell us everything if we attend to it reflectively. Hesse's example of Siddhartha's illumination, taught by the river, with Nature Itself as his guru, then, expresses the heights of learning and transformation that are possible in wide-angled contemplation of the World.

If we but, "Listen better."

# 27

# Identity and the Sea of Potentiality:

## Our Soulular Constituted Self, Multiculturalism, Staying Afloat and Navigating Amidst Overwhelming Possibility, a Modern Curse, a Modern Opportunity

*"First there is a mountain, then there is no mountain, then there is" — Donovan, from "There Is a Mountain" on* **Mellow Yellow***, 1967*

*"Before enlightenment, chopping wood and carrying water. After enlightenment, chopping wood and carrying water." — ancient Zen proverb.*

# Our Soulular Constituted Self

As mentioned in the previous chapter, we have access to all lives, potentially, with their infinite varieties of darkness, as well as light. And porosity and mutability of personal boundaries makes for a truer, more authentic constitution of self, more deeply rooted in the All That Is and more open to direction and assistance from that All, from Self.

Still, the Universe is an experiential sea of infinite potentiality that we are immersed in and interconnected with. Though we potentially can access all of it, we do not *wish* to be all these things. Not while in Form. I don't believe even in No-Form, for the most part. I do not think our Soulular Constituted Self — including the movement of the Universe we call "I" as existing in both Form and No-Form Realities — wants to be All … or even "a lot." Where's the fun in that? Except maybe at times, which I do not need to point out we are already doing even while limited for it all happens simultaneously. It appears, when you look at the infinite variety of It All in the Cosmos — even the limited part we can see as our Universe — that we as Divinity desire diversity. As always, we gods just want to have fun.

So, we — each "I" of us and at all levels of beingness — are an intention of the Universe … each of us, individually. As Jung said, each of us is an "experiment in Truth." That is to say, we, as essentially God, *wish* to limit our perspective, to limit our *range of vision*, to create all those constituted realities described in Part One of this book. Reality limitations which now, we see, include even the soululary-constituted realities we create in the course of our experience over lifetimes.

Indeed, this fact of existence — our Sea of Experience which we all have access to, our identity as Divinity — we *must* limit to something … it cannot be everything … *especially* while in Form.

# Paddling the Sea of Potentiality

Swimming in a sea of potentiality. Staying afloat in a sea of potentiality.

## Pitfalls and Problems

This conscribing of the Sea of Experience is sometimes a problem in youth; sometimes we carry it through our lives. I wrote about this pitfall in the first book I ever wrote, at the age of twenty, which I titled *The Dangers of Mysticism for Modern Youth* (1970). There are dangers herein, for at our identity stage of life, in youth, we are necessarily open to many potentials, and it is from them that we need to choose. We have to choose something to actualize — at least temporarily, even if we change course later, and maybe often — out of that Infinite Sea of Potentiality.

## Rites of Passage and Identity

In many cultures, this "problem" is "solved" by forcing the youth into a straitjacket role decided upon by the culture. This is done through an initiation ritual, specifically, a rite of passage into adulthood. Because it is such an affront to the psyche, these sorts of rituals — particularly the patriarchal ones — tend to be brutal, assaultive ... damaging of both body as well as mind.

In other societies, some primal ones, the role is not enforced ... "inflicted" upon the youth ... but is arrived at through some kind of experience within Reality and Nature. The Native American vision quest is the penultimate example of that. It is the ideal way to handle this, for then the "experiment in truth" that one actualizes in life is decided not by another but by the individual him or herself and in actual collaboration with the All That Is. Which is the way it was "decided" before this life ... in the very decision to come into Form (again), to incarnate, in the first place.

Of course, brutal initiation rituals, rites of passage, are seen in their worst form in the indoctrination a youth must go through to be beaten into the mold of a military member. All over the world, youths with access to all of the potential of the Universe, are shunted into narrow tracks of other-decided action for the purposes of murder and war. For the purpose of others, their minds, reflective ability, decision making, desires, dreams, and visions are blasted out of these young ones. They are whack-a-moled into utter quiescence, which is called training, lauded as being "obedient" and conforming, but is indeed a murder of soul. In carrying out the depraved desires of folks higher on society's scales, mindlessness is instilled in such underlings. This is the antipode of one's Divine Identity. One cannot get further away.

An aside: Still, all lives are equal. Divinity wants that, too. Murderers. Warriors. Hitlers and Genghis Khans. These represent those darker colors demanded of the Divine Masterpiece to manifest its beauty. The thing to see in this is that it is hardly what society purports those lives to be. Though such warriors and soldiers are Divinity, too, I never thank them for *their* service, yet society does. Society values its sanctioned controlled murderers and puts to death its uncontrolled ones. Both are equally removed from Divinity, and perhaps the military member even more so. Society tells he or she that they are great, are heroes. They are, thus, further from realizing the diminished quality of their lives. So they are an unawares evil. Much harder to see the Divine from that place. Yes, they are part of Divinity's Grandeur and Glory, too. But one should not make a fucking religion out of them.

In fact, their actual role in the Magnificence? More exactly they are the darkness the light is seen as much brighter by. They are the black frame setting off Divinity's Portrait. They are the percussion woven through the Heavenly Opus, marking the beat against which one composes one's own song of simple kindness and yearning for unity, quavering though it be with poignancy.

## A Modern Blessing

Back to my "story," there is still another aspect to this process of configuring a Form-ular self. What I am getting at is that, in terms of the pitfalls of configuring one's identity in Form, at that stage of life called youth, in modern times we have a situation unlike any other time in history or in any other culture. Modern youth are exposed to a vast ocean of information and possibilities for being and existing throughout their childhood and have, usually, an incredibly large array of possible paths to choose from in continuing their lives, as adults.

Nothing wrong with that. That, in itself, is a wonder of our times, with its multiculturalism. Such multiculturalism makes possible a better fit between one's soulular and one's Form-ular selves than ever before in history. It is important, as well, in that we need to access and align with our Divinity more than ever, in these times. It is our natural inclination to grow toward that, toward Divinity. Just like a flower grows to face the sun. And while most people will not take that path of expansion of self into Self, still with the potential for it to happen being there more than ever, more folks *will* be inclined along their truer soulular way than ever.

That makes the modern situation to be bringing out, ideally, the beneficent results similar to that which a vision quest does. That is to say, a youth's role and path, in modern times, can — more possibly than any time we know of save that of those Native American and similar cultures — be a collaboration between her or his real self and the Divine, the Ultimate Self. It may be why so many have chosen to incarnate now.

## A Modern Curse

However, there is a tendency to feel overwhelmed in such a situation — during youth. If, on top of that, one opens up to even greater possibilities and potentials through mind-expanding drugs or the occult or mysticism, one can feel even more overwhelmed, unable to integrate, and one can feel like one is drowning in a sea of potentiality. Difficult to come into Form when flooded with such No-Form potentiality. This was a common occurrence in the Sixties among the youth of my time. Of course I felt it as well. How else could I write insightfully about it?

Importantly, we see a reflection today of that which happened considerably in the Sixties — that paralysis and terror in the midst of overwhelm. It is important to note that the Sixties was the first postmodern era. It was the first one characterized by multicultural-ism, with the disintegration of staid personality and ego constructs come of it. That is something to keep in mind as a huge factor, as well, in contributing to the paralysis and overwhelm, which often at the time was termed *alienation*.

We see that arising again today. Understandably, for we remain in a postmodern world of overwhelming possibilities; of ever increasing multiculturalism, catalyzed, more so, by the Internet; and of collapsing cultural barriers alongside erosion of national, religious, familial, and community identity.

Not complaining. I see those to be wonderful things, much needed now — at a time when we need global and universal identities, not ethnocentric or national ones, for peace. Veritably, just to survive. However, this expansion of identity — this establishing of one's sense of self in identification with larger units such as humanity, all life on planet Earth, or the Universe, the All That Is — comes with its problems. Nothing less than that, it requires a period of adjustment, which is necessarily turbulent, difficult, tricky, and could use some help from culture and society.

And just as in the past — those glorious days of worldwide awakening, just past the midpoint of our previous century — we see such a problem, today. Interestingly it is coming about after the huge push by the elites, the filthy rich and their social programmers, in the Seventies and Eighties, to bring conformity and traditional, strait-jacket roles back to youth, and to the adults they would become. Certainly, these societal helmsman and manipulators were alarmed, if not terrified, to see such radical change in the world they had invested in and helped to create. They sought to and unfortunately succeeded in bringing this about, this return to traditional roles, through a massive reorganization of society begun, in America, in 1971. (See my *Culture War, Class War*, 2013b.)

However, something is arising, now, in reaction to that abysmal repression of potential during the mid-Seventies and the Eighties, and continuing. Yes, that campaign of societal reorganization and massive misinformation for the purpose of reversing the clock on the evolution that was occurring in the Sixties did reverse the tendencies toward alienation of the previous lot, the Sixties generation, for the one following it, Generation X. But at what cost?

For alienation was truly only the expression of the liminality naturally arising in a transformation to greater selfhood. That is to say, these youth of the Sixties were manifesting the kind of inner looking that is the necessary borderland, the liminal, of society ... indeed, the field of potentiality ... that one must cross, prior to arriving at the oasis of self-actualization.

This was strikingly represented by the peace symbol that was manifest everywhere at the time and continuing directly into today. This symbol, said to represent peace, but also moratorium, is a cross within a circle with the cross's "arms" pointing down. These downward arms, compared to upward arms, which indicate expression, symbolize withdrawal from the world and into self. The peace symbol means cessation of activity, hence peace, when action is clearly counterproductive, or meeting with horrific results. Thus, retiring from action, "moratorium," is what was being advocated by the antiwar movement of the time.

Correspondingly, in their personal lives, these youth of the Sixties were going inward to seek out better solutions for self and society in radically changing times characterized by overwhelming cultural, personal, and historical input. They were evolving perfectly in response to the first ever situation of a sea of information allowing for the most optimal alignment of self with *atmidharma* (one's spiritual duty in life), with Self, with universal intention.

At any rate, subsequently, during the mid-to-late Seventies and Eighties, there was the response of repression to this "frightening" (to the elite) evolution. This repression of potential was instilled all too successfully in the crop of youth designated Generation X.

Since then, however, another movement arose. It emanated from a cohort populated predominantly by Millennial Generation folks and the most disaffected, and oftentimes abused, of Generation X. So that today, we see this disaffection, formerly called alienation, arising in the fascination these youth, and their older compatriots, have with occult conspiracy theories.

To be clear, I am firmly in the camp of those aware that there has been some massive hocus pocus on the national and world scenes in the last half century, convincing entire populations of blatant lies for the purpose of manipulating mass action. I have just pointed out my version of one of them, having to do with the retaking of society by the elite beginning in 1971, exemplified by and manifesting the twisted "findings" of the Trilateral Commission in July, 1973.

The Trilateral Commission was a non-governmental think tank, or discussion group, founded by David Rockefeller, and intended to bring together, for cooperative action, the interests of the major Western powers — throughout North America, Western Europe, and Japan. As Noam Chomsky said, summing up the purpose of its "findings," The Trilateral Commission

*was concerned with trying to induce what they called "more moderation in democracy" — turn people back to passivity and obedience so they don't put so many constraints on state power and so on. In particular they were worried about young people. They were concerned about the institutions responsible for the indoctrination of the young (that's their phrase), meaning schools, universities, church and so on — they're not doing their job, [the young are] not being sufficiently indoctrinated. They're too free to pursue their own initiatives and concerns and you've got to control them better.*[1]

It was said that the problem with the Sixties was there was an "excess of democracy" and folks were "too free." The times were "suffering" from that problem. Not real problems, you see. Nothing to be concerned about — like wars, hypocrisy, environmental pollution, or social and cultural issues, such as racism, inequality and the like — but just too much attention to them, too much action on pressing and vital concerns ... too much "democracy." As for "too free," well, hey, folks need always a certain amount of enslavement, right?

So this is hardly speculation, what I am unveiling — this effort by the powers-that-be to repress the growing edge of the world's societies. Indeed, there was even a memorandum distributed widely to the wealthy elite at that time describing the reactionary path that these societal controllers should take ... in detail!

Still, this effort was effectively a conspiracy. The media did not inform its populace of this massive reorganization of society underway. Indeed, the media participated in its cover-up, claiming a "conservative backlash," at the time, which did not exist at all, except in the hopes and intentions of the societal orchestrators. The media, indeed, colluded by putting a virtual stop on coverage of protests and demonstrations, thus bolstering the false argument that there was a backlash. And they contributed by producing and promoting books and other media, such as news reports, that hammered this lie into American minds. Still not dislodged. (See my *Culture War, Class War,* 2013b.)

Furthermore, I am fully aware of the legitimacy of some other conspiracies for control and manipulation of the people, in particular the American people. The most obvious ones of those being the JFK assassination and the Twin Towers massacre — both of which were brought about by forces other than what was announced and promoted publically. And both were perpetrated for the purpose of wrestling social change along avenues contrary to what was naturally unfolding and instead along roads the elites could profit from.

But we also see currently many young and not so young adults, disaffected, alienated, awash in the immense sea of misinformation mixed with information which characterizes the current scene. We see them drowning in satanic, illuminati, Rothschild, anti-Semitic, Alex Jones–style, Glenn Beck murkied, climate-denying, New-World Order conspiracy thinking that is driving an ambulatory insanity in many cases. Which in some cases is tossing aside all rationality and concern for life and ethics as they act within an imaginal world, a world of delusion, built of the girders of quotes from Revelations and painted with the dispensations for all wrong doing of an imminent Rapture.

We have already seen eruptions of some of this in mass murders in recent years, by people taken over by these ideas. Turning their particular illness, and their individual suffering, into contagions of insanity affecting us all. These folks are no less insane than ISIS sympathizers like Omar Mateen who just a few days ago massacred forty-nine people, seen to be gay or somewhat "pink," in an Orlando nightclub, The Pulse.

Examples of these include Jared Lee Loughner, who killed six people, wounded thirteen, near Tucson, Arizona, in January, 2012, and grievously wounded Congressperson Gabrielle Giffords. And Timothy McVeigh and Terry Nichols, who murdered 168 folks in the Oklahoma City bombing in April, 1995 for "anti-government"

347

reasons.[2] And in Oslo, Norway, there was Anders Behring Breivik, who on 22 July 2011, massacred seventy-seven innocents, perceived by him to be leftists, in advancing his right-wing, admittedly fascist, agenda.

These unthinkable massacres typified several others, of recent years. They all have typical right-wing motives — anti-government, anti-liberal, anti-women, anti-"socialism," anti–gold standard, and so on. They speak of New World Order and illuminati conspiracies and receive inspiration in the writings and media of right-wing ideology of various sorts. These atrocities were perpetrated by right-wing, *Revelations*-misunderstanding, conspiracy-mired folks infused with the ideas of the likes of Alex Jones, David Wynn Miller, Glenn Beck, Rush Limbaugh, and the like.

Loughner's motives are revealing. In describing his political positions, I quote, they were a,

> hallmark of the far right and the militia movement." In the aftermath of the shooting, the Anti-Defamation League reviewed messages by Loughner, and concluded that there was a "disjointed theme that runs through Loughner's writings," which was a "distrust for and dislike of the government." It "manifested itself in various ways" – for instance, in the belief that the government used the control of language and grammar to brainwash people, the notion that the government was creating "infinite currency" without the backing of gold and silver, or the assertion that NASA was faking spaceflights.[3]

Further, part of his motive for going after Giffords was misogynistic. He believed positions of power should not be held by women. He was involved in a message board that discussed conspiracy theories. Loughner espoused theories about the 9/11 attacks and a New World Order and believed in a 2012 apocalypse.[4]

The reason these are not true or legitimate conspiracies, by the way, is because they are concoctions comprised of many promoted yet fraudulent ideas, seeded by right-wing elements, propounded by filthily moneyed interests for the purpose of keeping the active edge of the masses, the youth, paralyzed with misinformation....

Who the fuck benefits from a return to a gold-silver standard, for example? You? With all *your* huge stash of gold? Think!

Who benefits from reduced taxes — another right wing theme — you? With your huge income? And investments?

Who the fuck benefits from Agenda 21 misinformation — which is an environmental program of the UN, not even being implemented (and I wish it were) — you? With all your land, your holdings, and your investments and your profits depending on despoliation of the environment. Are you the Koch Brothers, then?

Who the fuck benefits from chemtrails misinformation, which takes the incredible destruction we are doing to the stratosphere through one million air flights a day, worldwide, and misdirects the environmental awareness required for our survival into a government conspiracy? Think!

For that matter, who the fuck benefits from denying the reality of climate change except the huge polluters? *cough* Are you going to benefit when the oceans rise sixty to one hundred feet, city-leveling storms are unleashed on the planet, and there are mass migrations and food shortages? And that contributes to worldwide virulent epidemics. While the temperatures rise, making Maine the place to live, Florida unlivable, and the oceans die off, taking away our primary source of oxygen for the planet. *gasp* You? Are you then a plant who needs no oxygen, doesn't live in a city, doesn't need to eat food or get human diseases?

Who the fuck benefits from a belief in a fakery of NASA space flights except flat-earth believers. lol. Is that you?

So there's "my" conspiracy theory! *snicker*

I want to add that opening to one's "unconscious" in this way, risking overwhelm from both information and misinformation, is tricky. Be clear that in all this it is one's unconscious that one is opening to, for the unconscious of one's self, and Self, includes everything that is not in one's consciousness. It is everything that is not part of the area of identity one has staked out for oneself at any particular time.

Remember, the unconscious is the other half of our Divinity.

Unfortunately, it also includes these tsunamis of misinformation, for they also are "facts" in that they exist as lies. Lies which must somehow be forded or dealt with successfully. Misinformation and lies contribute to overwhelm even more than the truth does, for there is cognitive dissonance involved in it. Lies inevitably conflict with the truth that also exists. This creates confusion. This is a responsibility, demanded. This puts a burden on those seeking to find a foundation of understanding to stand upon from which to fashion one's life.

In addition, opening to this sea of possibilities also means opening to one's personal Pain in this life, for it also is part of one's unconscious. Indeed, it is for this reason it is so easy to understand how folks overwhelmed with misinformation might also act out violently, as was done in the horrendous killings I have mentioned.

It includes opening, even, to traumas carried over from other lives. For they, too, are the "unconscious," now. So, opening to the unconscious happens in the same way that Arthur Janov says that opening to feelings is an all-or-nothing thing. That opening to one's Pain, as in his primal therapy, means opening to one's ability to enjoy life, means opening to one's sexual feelings, means opening to one's love, but means opening to one's frustration and anger, too. Opening is simply opening, for all are part of existence, and life.

The same thing is true for the unconscious as a whole. Indeed, the repressed Pain that Janov speaks of *is* a person's personal unconscious, and the feelings a person is accessing have been split away from and constitute that unconscious personal self from this life. But it includes as well, out from that, everything else that one is not conscious of in all of Reality and the Universe, including one's Divine Identity, one's soulular configuration, one's dharma, one's duty, one's fate.

Now, that is a beautiful, a wonderful, an eminently rewarding thing to do: to resolve those issues. That is why we come into this life. Still it can be paralyzing in its being so overwhelming when it arises along with the other potentials one has to choose among within Reality. It can seem a veritable opening of a Pandora's Jar.

The fact that such overwhelm is prevalent today is indicated by the rise in demand for and usage of all kinds of antidepressants and pharmaceuticals to deal with it. Overwhelm is a close companion to depression. It afflicts youth, but many throughout society. The mid-life "crisis," or, optimally, "adjustment," is another of those times when one opens to vast potentiality and is in danger of overwhelm.

At mid-adulthood *and afterwards*, I should point out. For oftentimes the crisis is not resolved at the time it occurs. Indeed that is one of the drawbacks in the usage of pharmaceuticals for dealing with events, "crises," that should be worked out psychologically, spiritually. Drugs keep one stuck in the problem. The problem is put in abeyance, unresolved and ever ready to reoccur.

In any case, here in mid-life, and afterwards, in people's lives, oftentimes there is a flood of drug use of all kinds — legal and illegal, addictive and not so much. I had a front row seat on this sad mass development during my years as a psychotherapist.

However, in reaction to the suffering of paralysis come of that overwhelm, some folks can make even worse decisions than merely repressing it with drugs. They can make these wrong choices even more readily when there are — as indeed there are now — outside interests actively seeking to manipulate them for their own benefit. And you better believe that moneyed interests are benefited by a massive misinformation that gives them, among other things, a paralyzed populace for the most part; a radical edge ostensibly insane to point to in discrediting accurate and legitimate dissent; and points of explosive violence to motivate repressive measures, overwhelming furies of prison punishments, draconian and violent responses, societally condoned, of police and right-wing citizens — all of which are "instruments" in the societal philharmonic they are orchestrating to bring forth the music sweetest to their ears. And their ears alone. Which not coincidentally has the same snake-charming tones that conjures enlargements of their bank accounts.

In any case, this all brings us back to this point that one can have access to the entire Universe, but while in Form, one not just *should* but has actually come here to do some aspect or part of that. One has one's dharma, one's duty arisen out of who one is, and not anyone else's. This is called one's *atmidharma*.

So it is good, in fact imperative, to open oneself to all kinds of potentials. But if one does not express it, does not bring it out, positively, creatively — and in a fulfilling and socially satisfying way... like a tree does in taking the nutrients it sucks out of the soil to manifest in leaves and blossoms and limbs — one is like a drowned plant, underwater in a swamp ... unfulfilled, depressed, unhappy. At best, one is in an oar-less rowboat, directionless and drifting, in the middle of an infinite sea.

This peek into immersion in the Cosmic Soup is instructive. It says something about the spiritual process, the primal process, and the identity processes of life, especially in the places where they all overlap.

It says it is not enough to bring down the limitations of self, constructed of pain and trauma, through feeling and integrating one's Pain, alone, for example. For that expands one's potentialities, yes. But that is a state of non-actualization similar to a No-Form state. But here in Form is where it is our purpose to experience Form. Meaning it is our *duty* to limit that ultimately infinite potentiality down to something small and *doable*. And it is in this sense that the dangers of "mysticism" are not just for "modern youth" but for all. There is the danger of "swimming in a sea of potentiality" and thereby losing one's enjoyment of life in a Form state.

One must limit in order to enjoy. The Game can only be fun with established parameters. Otherwise, not so fun. That too — such "unfun" suffering in the soup of potentiality — is a valuable experience of Experience necessary in the glorification of the All. However, in a practical sense, one would do well to know that one has the potential to enjoy life and have fun by engaging in actualization.

# "Promises to Keep"

Yes, eventually we long for hOMe, but it is unwise to embrace that path before its proper time. Earlier I had paraphrased Robert Frost's poem, "Stopping by Woods, on a Snowy Evening." I was making the point that even in the cold and bluster of a snowstorm, we sense a feeling of calm and longing. Frost's words are, "The woods are lovely, dark, and deep."

In this chapter, however, we reflect on the truth he expresses in the rest of that: "But I have promises to keep. And miles to go before I sleep. And miles to go before I sleep." We need be aware that actualization of self is why we came here, not just to leave it

Yes, we want rest amid the turbulence of life. But if we seek that before its time, this longing turns a spiritual quest into a cowardly escape from life. At its worst, it becomes suicide.

But retreat has nothing to do with spirituality, as I was saying in a previous chapter in referring to its requirement that we be purified by the fires of life, and action. This is a common, sadly, a prevalent, misunderstanding. However, a clearer look at what is entailed in a spiritual life reveals something quite different from retreat. One need only look to the *Bhagavad Gita*.

In the *Gita*, Arjuna *expresses* this desire to refrain from engaging in his duty. Whereas Krishna, as deity and guru, guides him to take up his task. To fulfill his destiny. A parallel development is narrated in *The Bible*, when Jesus prays in the Garden of Gethsemane to be relieved of his duty, his destiny. We don't know what the Divinity said back to him, but right afterward, Jesus takes upon himself his purpose and fate.

You see, we come into Form for a reason. We choose to do it; our fate is involved in it. Our only goals in life, really, are to discover, to re-member our reason for arising in this collective Game and then to actualize it. We are a singular tone brought into the symphony of existence and if we do not express it the Universe is a less beautiful harmony for it.

Still, many folks fail in that in life when they jump the gun on that seeking of an end to the drama of one's existence. We are actors on a stage, and they would refuse their lines, and make their exit before the script says to. Certainly then they are fulfilling their "destiny" to fail in life and to have a life where one learns from that, from failure. Perhaps that soulular self is having a life somewhere else that needs to feel the consequences of cowering from one's destiny here in order to actualize one there.

However, if you are reading this, there is a good chance that kind of learning through failure is not what is meant for you here and now. I do not believe anyone hears words such as this, or Hesse's as in the last chapter, unless they are meant to.

Naturally, we cannot expect not to wish a surcease of experience when our life is characterized by pain and difficulty. When we suffer, we long for an end to it, and often that takes shape as a desire for an end of our existence. In these cases, we might be attracted to paths that express that return to nothingness as their goal.

Yet, especially when we are younger, it might be that in taking those roads, we are ignoring or running from our reason for being here. Sometimes our fates are difficult; often they can seem overwhelming. And always are we here to learn and grow and we only do that by moving out of our "comfort zone," which means discomfort; it means suffering.

This does not mean a spiritual path has to wait till the end of life, either. How else could it be that Krishna was an aid to Arjuna. Certainly, the *Bhagavad Gita* is a pillar in the spiritual edifice because it brings such wisdom about the necessity of pursuing one's duty, of actualizing the potential one has brought into existence.

Furthermore, notice that in Hesse's story, Siddhartha's illumination results in his taking up his "destiny" and participating in the "stream of life" and events, not splitting off from it into cave-like and mute inaction. In his own life, Hesse clearly adhered "religiously" to his dharma, his duty, to write the wonderful things by which we can learn at this very moment. That is telling us something about that mellifluous Universal music to which we are asked to add our own song, in coming here.

Such an inner journey can be part of one's awakening, as it was for Siddhartha. In the same way that the hero's journey, as described by Joseph Campbell (1972), is a necessary retreat from the world, in order to disclose what light one needs to reveal to oneself that one needs to bring back to the world. Just as on a vision quest or walkabout one retreats from ordinary activity in order to open self to the potential the Universe wants to actualize through one. Indeed, that is the "discovery" part of the quest I mentioned. One needs to actualize, but first one needs to "discover" what that unique thing is that one is to do.

And therein is the problem on that end. For too often that period of discovery is not done and one finds oneself to be unhappy throughout life, having taken up roles not meant for one. Hence, one is learning in this life, through failure again. Through losing one's way, one impresses upon oneself the knowing, helpful later in this life or in some other, that one must seek self in life — one's true identity

— and not go along with the ego insisted of one by others, which is the socially constituted self.

Spiritual wisdom comes in to teach us this as well. We are told that "First there is a mountain, then there is no mountain, then there is," as Donovan expressed it in song. Out of Asia it is expressed more clearly in that "Before enlightenment, chopping wood and carrying water. After enlightenment, chopping wood and carrying water." What is implied is the time of enlightenment, while seeking self-discovery, where one necessarily desists from worldly activities. The time when "there is no mountain."

What these quotes are expressing is that there is a process of normal life, then retreat from life, and then return to life with a higher calling ... with more composure, more direction, more peace, but no less adherence to one's duty, in fact more. For now it is felt as one's dharma, one's duty in relation to self, Self, and the All, all at once.

Notice that Hesse phrases it that "Siddhartha ceased to fight against his destiny." After he experienced oneness, Siddhartha embraces "the stream of events." His soul finds harmony with "the stream of life, full of sympathy and compassion, surrendering himself" to it. That describes anything but an escape from life.

Remember also that at the time when Krishna advised Arjuna to go into battle, Arjuna was delaying and doing his best imitation of Hamlet. Mired in questions of acting or not acting of "being or not-to-being," Arjuna was despairing at the karma that action inevitably brings.

In the same way that Krishna advised Arjuna to go into battle, to do his duty, and not to refrain from life out of despair at the karma it inevitably brings, Sathya Sai Baba pointed out about karma that it is inevitable that while in Form there is action, hence karma. In a teaching he gave to hundreds of thousands of us at Puttaparthi, India, in 1989, he said that even the action of the heart's pumping has consequences.

He related how in a body, movement is unavoidable, hence karma is unavoidable. He then explained that the accumulation of negative results from such actions can however be prevented by offering one's actions to God, to Divinity ... to one's higher power, in whatever way one wishes to imagine it. He gave examples such as becoming a doctor but dedicating that work to the Divine by giving those skills over to the service of the poor, freely. For, he pointed out, those skills do not come of oneself, of one's efforts, either solely or predominantly. He pointed out that all that goes into making a doctor involves the efforts of thousands and millions of souls that came before, giving rise to the knowledge that is put into practice. Further, that even the instruction received through both primary and secondary education, as well as that of the university, are products of society and the efforts, sweat, thoughts, and skills of many others. Society creates and maintains those institutions. One benefits from all those, so one should not think ones' skills to be one's own. To do otherwise is to be that wave of ego, again, thinking that it alone gets itself to shore

On the contrary, a dedicating of one's efforts to the Divine is, analogously then, using the metaphor of the planet and the star again, represented by the planet, separated from and orbiting its star, but with its face to its sun and lit by it. This — being God-conscious, Divinity remembering, higher power acknowledging, muse attending — is how we, while still in Form, can be freed from the dark sojourn fitted for humanity. This is how we can be liberated from our lives on the dark side of the moon.

# 28

# The Secret Life of Stones:

Is a Life Most Divine. "It's All Fucking Magic"
… The Greatness of Us as Our Assumed
Universal Law and God's More Likely Address

*Animate and Inanimate … What Is Life, Really? The
Spirit of Statues, Consciousness, and Practical
Panentheism*

## What Constitutes Aliveness?

At this point in this discourse on matter being message, I want us to
turn our attention to our planetmates — to all of them. This includes
the living — the animals, plants, bacteria, and such — as well as the
supposedly "non-living." We share this planet with all that. And if all
is Consciousness, all is Experience, including the physical world, then
we have to reconsider the vast terrain outside us, on this planet, to
which we attribute varying degrees of awareness.

In this chapter I want us to survey our understandings and assumptions about the inanimate world. In the next, "The Other Is Our Hidden Face," I would like to take a journey through the forest of our relationship to the world of the animate — which I refer to as *planetmates*. That is, all nonhuman "life" with which we share this planet, Earth.

## Inanimate? From Whose Perspective?

First let us address the elephant in the room, inanimate … "life"?

I know. I know. But let us continue.

Notice I said, what we "label" life. For I have been establishing that consciousness … Experience, more exactly … pervades the entire Universe — both the most obviously (to us) *living*, or animate, but also the seemingly (to us) non-living, or *inanimate*. Indeed, this is what I mean by the title of this book. There is a secret life in the Universe. It is found everywhere and even in the most unlikely of places. When you look at a mountain you are seeing Experience, in some indirect way. There is a secret life of stones.

## The Inanimate Is Animate

When you think about it, even considering the way our indirect perception of the world perceives matter, as revealed by our sciences, there is activity in the inanimate. So the inanimate is animate. *chuckle*

But do think about it. We say matter has vibration; that there are fields of moving energy pervading it. Most fundamental of all, we see the atom as a field of electrons "circulating" or existing as potentiality around nuclei. Slightly above the atom, we see atoms coming together to create molecules. That's movement, is it not? Well, how much more animate do they have to be? Hell, if gravity, including that of an atom, is actually love manifesting, then are not molecules little "marriages"? (omg)

I'm going to have to stop cracking myself up here. And probably that is too much for most to take in. But the Universe is delightfully funny when truly revealed. That is much the meaning of my work *Funny God* (2015), in fact.

In any case, slightly below the atom there is the subatomic. With "things" that both exist and do not exist, as if they are turning off and on. Of fields of activities, quasars, that are not physical... Perhaps like those no-thing Forms? Those No-Form configurations?

## Determined and Unchanging? Or Simply Harmonious and not Rebelling

We claim the Universe is operating according to immutable laws of physics and the like. We say that part of it is *determined;* it is predictable, unable to be otherwise, and abides by established unchanging principles.

However, could it be merely that the part of the Universe that is like that, which we call *matter*, is merely the "beings" of the Universe who have simply not descended from identity with Divinity? Earlier I was making the analogy that the duality in our Universe is like the planet orbiting the star — both attracted and separate. Later, I likened human life to the part of that planet existing on the far side of it, away from the light.

Now, is it possible that we can think of the consciousness of matter itself as like entities who would be analogous to that planet, rather the matter of it, that *does not* orbit its sun? Which means that it *is* the star or is contained in it; that it *participates* in it, the sun. This couldabe planet does not become dual, separate, and orbit. Which is metaphorically being separated from Divinity, yet attracted by and aware of its Source, the star, in the analogy. Neither, of course, would it be like that part of the planet turning its back on the sun, or star, which is the analogy I have used for describing the state of humanness.

So, in terms of the metaphor, what about the consciousness, the beingness, which does not split off from or separate from star or sun at all but participates in it? The consciousness that is most like Divinity for it is not separate from it, does not split off, indeed participates in it? Is matter merely the unrebellious aspect of the Universe, of that Infinite Sea of Experience happening — the part of it visible to humans, anyway — which remains harmonious with Divinity? Do you see where this is going? Are you opening to the implications of this?

Well, there is no way of knowing that this is not the case. The status of matter just might be Divinity; in which case aliveness is irrelevant for it is beyond that. It is the embodiment of Consciousness and Experience.

## Definition of Life: It's Stuff Like Us

What it comes down to is that what scientists — and us by extension living within its paradigm, the scientific one — are saying when we make the distinction between living and non-living "things" is that certain things ... and here we go again ... are like us. They are composed of molecules that are carbon-based, as we are.

Whereas the rest of the world is not like us. It does not live and die like we *seem* to. So in that category, notice, it is immortal. Further, it does not *seem* to have intention.

But then it was not long ago that we thought "animals" did not have intention and were merely mechanical. Like they were machines, "things," directed by instinct, operating according to immutable principles ... soon to be discovered! ... and not like us free-thinking free-wheeling humans, the guardians of Earth and the masters ... indeed, devourers! ... of Nature.

Think about it. Some even in this day, consistent with such ideas of dominance in and dominion over Nature continue to deny intention to those aspects of Earth deemed animate, that is to say, our planetmate relatives. At least they allow them that they are considered living. But only that, and only in that they seem to die.

## Does Free Will and Intention Distinguish Us from Matter?

But if there is not free will even for us, as I explained earlier, where is the *intention* in anything? I can tell you that I, as a psychotherapist among many other things, often see my clients, and people in general, as inexorably *driven* to do what they do, much like machines. That they do not have intention, are not able to choose.

Indeed, my experience has taught me that people are not at all able to change except through experience, not by thinking. That thinking and deciding actions, as we *insist* we can do, is about as much helpful in what happens as the field of electrons deciding the fate of its nuclei. Or the flies buzzing around a cow determining what grass it chews. It is as much full of air and non-substance as the immense area of the atom, comprised of absolute space; being all puffed up on itself, "signifying nothing."

## Well, We're a Legend in Our Own Minds, Aren't We?

And its major function, this thinking, appears to be continual, compulsive, repetitive rationalizations for actions one has already done or will do. Again, more smoke screens of delusion telling us we are great, superior, above the rest of Nature in having free will, and are able to choose and direct our lives, despite all the evidence to the contrary. Are we not as determined in what we do, operating along the lines of laws of physics, or some other, as is the supposed inanimate world?

Some scientists, notably behaviorists, would think it to be possible to totally determine a human's actions based on certain laws, if they were known. And I would agree with that, for the most part, in keeping with this stance about the non-existence of intention and free will. However, I would modify that by adding that there is as much determinism in human, and personal, individual events, as there is in that card game which only has particular outcomes in accordance with its components, which I was describing in a previous chapter. With that, I believe, they would concur. What that means is that Becomingness is limited by Beingness. What happens is determined, limited — all events are — by the constituents of the actors or beings involved.

Where the scientists and the behaviorists and I would part ways, no doubt, is at the point where I would include in those factors — those constituents of those actors or beings, which are determining all of us beings — all this woo-woo stuff regarding experience and consciousness. For it seems to me that the fundamental principles are spiritual and psychological ones and the actual "elements" of the Universe are the infinite fractals of experience. In my conception of this, it is experiential and consciousness (and awareness) elements that constitute The Game and factor in to its unfolding. Just as that card game I mentioned is constituted of elements such as the number of cards used, the "abilities" of the individual cards — the way they are able to interact with and move in relation to each other — and the rules of play of the game.

Such rules in "our" game ... that is, the game of all of the existences of all experiential units like us, or beings ... and the "constitution" of that game — the makeup of it which determines our human lives and their unfolding — include, for example, all the principles of karma, psychological action-reaction, the factors involved in forgetting and remembering, of separating and re-uniting, of veiling and then joyful peek-a-boo revelation, and of attraction-love vying with separation-individuality; along with a multitude of spiritual, metaphysical, and other principles, most of which we are not able to know and probably do not need to know.

## The Vanity of Free Will

However, for the most part, despite mountains of data that would convince us of our suspension within forces that move us despite our intentions ... to which we only need surrender, having faith in the goodness of All ... we fabricate more rationalizations and explanations congruent with our greatness of will. Or at least its potential. As we "decide" this, "affirm" that, "focus our attention" here and there, and assert "control" of our lives. Some take it even further in the spiritual realms to claim a possible mastery of their souls. Which, amusingly, is in direct contradiction to the unity that is the supposed aim of those spiritual efforts.

In truth, free will is only a concoction we have because we are so terrified of the Universe. It is a derivative of the lack of faith we sink to in going dual, splitting severely from Divinity. We do not trust the Universe; we do not believe the Universe is "friendly," regardless how many gods we proclaim. Free will is a delusion defending against our fear of uncertainty. When we realize the supreme goodness of the Universe, God, and that we are one with it, free will is ludicrous.

The delusion of free will also gives us allowance to punish people, with a clear conscience. It allows us an act-out of our rage and frustration, giving us a road to run away on rather than taking in the lesson come of frustration and tragedy and achieving the soul and personal growth that is trying to be catalyzed through it. We can unleash ourselves freely in casting judgment and inflicting harm on others. For we can tell ourselves they could have done differently and so they deserve it!

The worst part of that is when we concoct our gods, saying they — like little demons — made us do it. "We are only carrying out God's will!" "We are simply enforcing Divine Justice!" It is actually this loving God's desire to torture, persecute, murder, and enslave, we tell ourselves, not mine! We proclaim Heavenly support for our smaller frightened hateful selves, or we say He is doing it. For that awards us even greater freedom from conscience, for having "blessed" ourselves with even stronger sanctioning — that "from above" — of our decisions to stay small.

In any case, humans are ever conjuring delusions of grandeur and god-like powers congruent with such supposed free will.

## Is Death a Real Dividing Line Between Living and Non-Living?

Regarding the nature of life, continuing now, if you consider what I have been saying about the immortality of ourselves, along with everything else, and how death is only a seeming end, and is actually a transformation into something, into some place that is not observable from our place or our status as a Form entity, then what is it really meaning to say that there is a living world and a non-living world?

If the differences have to do with *intention* and *mortality*, and we can see that at a deeper level or a higher overstanding they do not really exist and are only part of our illusion — that they are only components of our Game — then is there any difference between living and supposedly non-living?

# Is Movement the Dividing Line?

The other thing pointed out as a difference between, say, a grasshopper and a stone is that one moves (grasshopper) and the other *does not seem* to. Yet, just as we see that assuming all life is carbon-based, is it not possibly also a prejudice of ours ... one of those emanating from our biologically constituted realties, sprung out of our humanness ... to say that one form of activity is living and the other one not?

Since atoms vibrate, moving fields pervade everything, hell, even rocks break up and disintegrate, mountains rise up and are worn down ... is it not merely that we think we can understand the "forces" making those particular events to happen? The events in the world of matter? Whereas the forces pushing around the animate — the so-called "living" — are harder to understand, more complex, and mostly hidden or unknowable? But how does being better able to understand the forces moving something make it indisputably not living?

And by the way, what are the forces that are moving *those* forces? What is the cause of those elements and forces scientists fashion their laws of physics out of? You see, scientists pile one explanation upon another, never acknowledging that the cause of their initial "force" is unknown. For that force moving everything in the Universe is gravity, from the subatomic up to the cosmic. And scientists have no idea how to account for gravity. It is something — a force, something with "power" and potential — that just is. Give it a name, "gravity," and then go from there. Never looking back.

But remember again what I said about gravity really being the external or "unfelt" manifestation of Love?

Newton saw the apple drop. He said "gravity" was responsible, being the materialist fuddy duddy he was. More poetic or more bohemian, he could have said he discovered that the Earth *loved* that apple ... loves *all* apples .... and me and you. Our loss.

Oh, I dunno, maybe if he had acid he'd a seen it.

In any case, *gravity is attraction when viewed in the physical world. It is love when felt inside.* If we were to grow to encompass the entire Universe — if we were to be like God — we would feel those forces moving everything in the Universe as the Love moving within us. Think about that for a second, the next time you teeter on the edge of pessimism.

At any rate, if, as the behaviorists would have it, even humans, every activity of ours, could theoretically be able to be determined when we understood all the factors contributing to its occurring, does that make it that we no longer are living, that we are in a sense, like moving stones? Or as aliens are reputed to have said of us, that we are "bags of dirty water" ... but moving? lol.

## Is Complexity the Dividing Line?

Think that silly? Remember that all this talk about artificial intelligence has it that activity of "things" can be thought, at some level of complexity, to be "alive." Specifically, it is considered possible that supremely sophisticated machines can be conscious, at a certain point. These machines — called, artificial intelligence, robots, androids — are moved and directed outwardly by the subtle and near infinite variety and complexity of electronic movements in a silicon-based environment within them — think *computer-like*, for that one. And supposedly intelligent scientists and technological wizards somehow are mesmerized into thinking that at certain level of complexity ... note that as the determining factor, *complexity* ... they can be considered to have awareness, to be capable of intention, hence to be alive.

Okay. Well then why the problem with reversing that to lower complexity, indeed down to pedestrian simplicity, such as in uncomplex matter? Stones, say? Why cannot there be consciousness in that? Well, it has to do with the level of complexity, they would say.

So they would have it, more and more complexity added, and at a certain point, poof! consciousness out of a hat! I mean, I think the Universe is "magic," but that is not magic. It is wishful thinking substituting for more thorough and more astute inquiries into the nature of life. *Complexity* is simply a blanket term to allow one to ignore the irrationality of that assumption.

The point is that if in describing life the only difference is a level of complexity, is that any defining dividing line at all? For again then, are we not saying that something that is more like us — it is complex, in this instance — is alive and that what is not complex, what is simple, is non-alive?

Do you see how our biologically constituted realities infect the way we see everything? And cause us to misunderstand everything?

Do you see that our division of a world into animate and inanimate is just another extension of the same tendency in humans to say that planetmates are not conscious, are not alive, are merely mechanical? As was the common thinking in science for hundreds of years and right into our modern era.

## The Greatness of Us as Our Assumed Universal Law

This relentless, unwavering tendency of ours is incredibly hard for us to see or understand. Hell, we embody it. For our egoistic and anthropocentric bias is ever putting ourselves as an end point of some grand drama of evolution whose sole purpose was creating us. Some of us even going so far as to think the entire creation of the Universe with its billions of galaxies was for the main purpose of pushing out the human form. It is this delusion of grandiosity which blocks our view from the perspective I am presenting, this revelation of the aliveness of matter. And intellectuals take that bias even further by putting their thinking abilities at the top of that peak of supposed universal "achievement."

However, God is not trying to "better" Him or HerSelf through the human experience. And intellectuals or philosophers like me are not some better attainment of humanness that *all* others would do well to try to be. No. I repeat, God manifests as an infinity of beingness for the purpose of magnifying the glory and the fun of Existence. Being human is not an "achievement," it is a variation. At best we add a spicy element of recklessness in descending so far into ignorance of our identity as Divinity, in coming into Form.

## God's More Likely Address

And at worst, since matter and Form Beings are restrictions of Experience, hence awareness, larger and more complex entities are greater constrictions, greater boundedness, of awareness, Experience, spirit. Hence, humans are among the *least* aware … yeah, the stupidest … of entities on the planet. Bacteria are better at being aware, then. And look for a vision of God somewhere past when you are experiencing your reality as being an atom, or a subatomic particle.

No, I'm not funnin' here. I am serious. Greater mass, greater density of Form, and especially greater complexity, as in our larger and more convoluted brains, makes for more of that "brain as reducing valve," which limits reality down only to what is useful, hence narrowing our awareness. We can look to dolphins, whose brains have less "convolutions" in them, to be more aware of the real deal. It is possible trees … I think it is true actually … are groking the big picture magnitudinally. And much more than we are.

## Matter as Magic

Stones? Well, they might be akin to archetypes, titans, gods, or powers, watching over us ever. For all we know. Perhaps even participating in our events, experiences, and lives, are they. And if they are, as matter, as physicality, simply the part of our awareness we have separated from, then of course they do! Of course they participate in our lives based upon many of the principles arrived at so far. Interconnectivity of everything for one. Innate Divinity for another. Consciousness and Experiencing as being the only Reality, another. Unity not duality, another. Innate friendliness of the Universe, because it essentially *is* us, another. And so on. Perfection, another, and coming up.

So perhaps matter, stones, mountains, clouds, planets, stars … perhaps they *are* the invisible watchers and helpers — *invisible* in that we do not see them for who they are — that we sense as part of our Existence. They could just be the kindly forces we feel moving us, directing us, helping us, guiding us, blessing us. Consider that the next time you are blessed with a rainbow. Or, as happened to me a few days ago, a huge double rainbow within the most glorious orange sunset, creating a magnificence I had never seen before.

Perhaps consider them to be like angels, as they guide our lives along paths of increasing awareness in the way they perfectly construct our reality. Just as was that rainbow appearing as a message to me ... telling me sunsets, deaths, are the transition to the most wondrous beingness imaginable ... with that double rainbow indicating such a tunnel, such a blessed passage to the beyond at the end of life. Or the way matter and things observably line up in the course of our lives to contribute to our greater understanding, to leading us along in our dharma, or fate, or in contributing to some other blessing or lesson or confirmation or message. Something as simple as the computer that won't work, when you really should refrain from saying that to someone. That auto that breaks down mysteriously someplace, which we find later has had major consequences for one's life ... either good (guidance, blessing) or so-called "bad" — which is just another word for "lesson," teaching, or best put, "blessing not yet" ... "grace delayed" ... for perfect timing, of course. For perfect readiness, perfect synchronicity. From the small to the large: The movement of autos on a freeway causing you to miss a flight, which in retrospect was perfectly what needed to be.

Traditionally, religious folks acknowledge these things, but they imagine God to be some hugest of all kings, rulers, or directors of everything. As if he is the wizard behind the curtain, only more so, directing everything. ... and all for *their* special benefit, each and every one of them ... the football bouncing just so, to allow one to make the play. And somehow we put out of our minds that if we are so blessed, and god is just a Grand Phantom Santa, how is it that we get blessed while the one who becomes the goat on the other side of that play does not?

No, I see it as happening — that phenomenon of perfection married with blessedness — but based upon the principles I have put forth: That All is One. That the Universe cannot help but be perfect, precise, and orchestrated along the lines optimal to each and every being — every conscribed experiential unit — within it. For the Universe is you. And it is me. And we are not separate, you and I, nor is It from us.

And, indeed, yes, some of this magnificent perfection of the Universe including all of the matter in it we do label *synchronicity*. And we can thank Jung for opening our eyes to that occurrence in our lives, helping us that way. (Thank you, Carl, by the way.) However, I am talking about much more.

I am talking about a perfection, an awareness-consciousness-experience that exists in every moment orchestrating everything perfectly right down to the sounds, feelings, sights, matter around one, the very movement of the electrons involved in everything around and in one ... in any specific ... and each and every ... Moment ... of Existence. *The Bible* refers to it as the will of God, as it says there is not a blade of grass moving outside God's intention. I would add, not an electron moving to the contrary. However, will of God? Big Guy pulling all the levers just right? An infinite number of them for each and every of the infinite beings in Existence? Within a Universe that is somehow dual, a Creation and a Giant Building Contractor, and a world of matter that She/He would have no part of?

No. Divinity we can feel. It is part of our Experience. The feeling of wonder is God, not just the wondrous giving rise to it. So, the cause behind perfection?

I prefer to call it *magic*. All of it.

Fundamental principle of the Universe: Indeed! It is all fucking magic.

# The Secret Life of Stones

## Brain-as-Reducing Valve, Again

Or consider this, on the secret life of stones ... and Christians'll crucify me for this: Reflect on this idea that the Universe is Experience, thus everything existing in it is Consciousness, even physical reality. That larger, more complex beings, like humans, are limiting that vast expanse, of Experience, of Consciousness, to greater degrees than Infinity in its more simple forms. Simple forms, like stones, like matter in general, are less "reduced down," less "bounded" than more complex forms, like humans, whose greater complexity involves eliminating more of Reality from the consciousness, the experience, the beingness that humans will have. That makes humans less aware of the All, the Important Thing, than the less "bounded" beingness in the form of simple "inanimate" matter. Got that?

Refer again to what was said earlier in the book about "brain-as-reducing-valve." What this means, then, is that it is possible, indeed, if all that I have been saying — if this paradigm I am introducing has merit, at all — it follows that there is higher consciousness in simpler, inanimate matter. There is consciousness in stones, not just. There is greater awareness, conceivably.

## Calves and Cows and Nature

Now, take all this and apply it to the common notions Westerners have of folks from India, in particular Hindus, seeming to "worship" statues. Now again ... and here is where I will get strung up for saying it ... how about the "worshipping" of that golden calf? Now I'm totally in the camp that golden calves are symbolic of worshiping wealth ... the Bible calls it *mammon*.

However, I see a reverence for Nature in a reverence for a symbol of it — a calf. In exactly the same way I see an honoring of Nature, and the Mother, the Divine Goddess, in the reverence for the lives of cows, of cattle, in India.

## And Statues and Consciousness

And then the "graven" statues. Oh my! But here I can lean on Sathya Sai Baba. Go ahead, Try to crucify him! He's already dead! Ha!

I remember Sai Baba's explanation for the reverence allotted the statues of Divinity is his native culture, that of India. It was an explanation I never really bought. Not that it "mattered" *chuckle*. Seriously though, it was a little off-putting, kinda confusing, so I set it to the side. Divinity within statues? meh. I filed it in the same category as the weeping saris I had read about in the stories about his life. That, for another time; I have to get to the point here.

# Is the Divine Life

Sai Baba's explanation is that when Hindus are seeming to worship statues of Divinity, they are quite aware that it is not like the statue itself is a god ... or something similar that prejudiced and mean-minded Westerners have concocted to rationalize their fear and hatred of folks with seemingly different beliefs. No. He explained that Hindus are aware that the entire Universe is Consciousness, as I have been saying, which includes all the matter in it, which I have been saying, too. Therefore, the granite, matter, stones, that you see in a statue, are an aspect of that Consciousness.

## God Ruling or God Pervading ... Transcendent or Immanent

Remember, we think of God as some controller, like an authoritarian father figure, a dictator. That creates our misunderstanding of the Hindus' beliefs. We see God as being a kind of boss, the Lord of the Universe. A king. Whereas Hindus are not seeing God that way, as some kind of Jehovah, rather something closer to a principle. A life force. A personal one; one, indeed, that is so close to us that it is closer than our breath. For it is our higher Self.

Easterners see God as a life pervading the Universe. A World Soul. A Universal Soul. And as I have been repeating, it is a soul that is within and encompasses All That Exists and so also enfolds us. But it is also identical with us, with our essence, or soul. Atman is Brahman, again.

Thus, when Hindus craft that granite or marble into a form of a Divinity that touches their hearts — say, a Shiva, a Ganesha, a Vishnu, a Rama, a Krishna — they are taking that vast illimitable Consciousness pervading all the Universe, including the living and the reputedly non-living of it, and fashioning it into a shape, an appearance that is appealing to them. Something which they can relate to as Divinity. So essentially what they have done is take the Infinite and — while aware that God is immanent in all of matter — make "an affirmation" of it (my words) in stone... when they craft the image.

So when they "worship" it, they are not bowing down to *that* statue. Granted some do, but then so do some Christians of their statues and images of Jesus. But both of them are equally mistaken of their religion's beliefs. It is not the actual plastic Jesus on your dashboard that will save you in an accident.

As for Hindus, the majority of them, they are not honoring that statue so much as they are reverencing the Divine principle in the Universe pervading all of matter in a way that reduces all that down to something relatable. And like the holonomic principle, in our holographic world, the part is contained in the all, the all is contained in the part.... Each and every part ... smallest to largest ... in the Universe.

Or you can take it this way, closer to Baba's words, that, paraphrasing, when the Hindu is seen to be "worshipping" (reverencing) a statue, she or he is honoring the "spirit," the consciousness in it, which is the same as the spirit, the consciousness, that pervades *all* of matter. Indeed that pervades the Universe. Indeed *is* the Universe.

## Pantheism and Panentheism

Remember, this is not so far removed from pantheism, which is the belief that God is immanent in the Universe, which is so pervasive in primal beliefs and wisdom.

It is not much different either from the panentheism, the belief that God is both immanent in matter as well as transcendent of it. Which, I explained earlier in the book, once had a staunch proponent in the West, in Europe, in Karl Friedrich Krause. Not to mention that I have been dinging that triangle throughout this work myself, practically like a soundtrack. Which intones that matter is Divinity, yes, but there is also an invisible, a No-Form Reality in Existence. Congruent with panentheism, one might say even that it is a "transcendent" one ... in that it can exist when not in Form, when not in matter. And as I have said, which No-Form realm is the one of our souls, of No-Form personalities, of the actual consciousness of stones (not just the stones themselves), and of the highest "personality, " the embodiment of all of Form and No-Form, of God ... of Divinity.

372

## Practical Panentheism

In which case, the Hindu belief and worship involving their forms is a variation of primal as well as sophisticated understandings that is being put into practice. You might say the religions (there are more than one) of Hinduism are a kind of practical pantheism. Or a pantheism … or panentheism … in practice.

Whew. We done yet?

One last thing, before continuing.

So, the secret life of stones? It is the Divine one.

## Matter's Magnum Opus

Again, though, in that the purpose of it All — that Universe of "living" matter now, as well as the acknowledged to be living beings in it — is the Story, the Game … even outside of human form … then the entire Universe with its ever recurring Big Bang is its magnum opus, you see. Its *War and Peace* novel. Its grand and unending theatrical production.

So, in relation to this, humans? Our story? In the Greatest Story Ever Told? Well, we at least have the distinction of being the nuttiest bunch, making for the greatest comedy for All to enjoy. Perhaps it is titled, *The Jerk,* "out there." lol.

Anyway, you've caught my wave: In order to transcend our biology, our Form, in order to go *ex-stasis*, ecstatic, out of Form, the first and most fundamental thing we need to do … it is imperative! … is to stop thinking we are the cool kids in school, the sharpest pencils in the pack.

Got that? Okay, as I was saying….

# 29

# The Other Is Our Hidden Face:

## How the Planetmates Tell Us About Our Inner and Our Supranatural Worlds … Angels in Nature and a Planetmate's Garden of Play

*How Planetmates Speak to Us about Psychology and Human Emotion. How They Are Our Angels in Nature and Give Us a Look Into No-Form "Personalities"*

## Planetmates Are What We Are Inside

Next let us consider the other beings on this planet to which we do ascribe the category of living. We are intimately connected to them. Far more than to river, planet, star, dimension, or leaf; we are related to that which we label "life" on Earth.

Of course I have already written about the meanings of snake, butterfly, caterpillar, plant, and tree. They are all included in the category of all things we call "living" that is on this planet — they are all *planetmates*.

However, what message is there — adding to that of planet, atom, galaxy, river, and ocean, and beyond that of snakes and butterflies, as we've seen — for the likes of dogs, cats, lions, crocodiles, cows, chickens, birds, and so on.

Some of this is easy. All cultures the world around see freedom in birds, delicacy in butterflies, docility in cows, gentleness in deer, nobleness in horses, pride in lions, and so on. What else? Well, for that matter, peskiness in insects, busy-ness in bees, ferocity in alligators-crocodiles and sharks, sneakiness in snakes, motherliness in bears…. You take it from here.

Such universal perceptions have to do with the way planetmates, especially, are projections of the feelings and emotions that we have split off from inside and denied and repressed in ourselves.

In terms of planetmates, for example, kittens *are* our playful self … our playful self as Divinity. In playful interaction with a kitten, then, we are not merely interacting with another being. For just as when we are interacting and "hearing" another human we are connecting with a part of our selves that *is* them, which is inside of ourselves; in playing with a kitten we are not merely "accessing" our playful part within. We are *actually* interacting with, opening up to a part of ourselves inside, of which that kitten is a projection. You see the difference?

It is reversed. The things outside are not the real things that we have symbols to express and feelings about on the inside. No. The things inside are the real things that, because they are denied within, are projected as symbols, which we call "things," in the physical world. These manifestations of our inner lives, which are cast in the world, we call the different planetmates … and we saw earlier, we call the different material items and material events in "the outside us" (matter) — as in, stars, rivers, rainbows, and so on.

Anyway, that is a huge difference in our understanding. The outside is not the real world for which we have symbols within. The inside is the real world for which we have symbols for without. If you do not believe me, just wait till after you die and the "real" world of matter "disappears" and instead of being left with thoughts, symbols and feelings related to that physical world, you are left with a realer reality, one that is directly experienced, of everything — wisdom, awarenesses, feelings and emotions, that you then realize you were projecting outside as matter. How else does it make sense that we are immortal? How else does it make sense that our awareness is expanded at death?

Considering the No-Form State has *no form*, that is, no matter, and yet it has a characteristic of "exquisite sensitivity," how can it not be true that what we experienced as Form, during life, is not more directly and more accurately brought into our awareness, after "life," as the inner realities they always were. How can those knowings and feelings that we saw outside as a physical world of stones and rivers and kittens and lions not be a part of that exquisite sensitivity that is part of our after-death experience, which is a conscribed pool of experience within the infinite ocean of Experience.

It is a huge difference in our understanding, as well, when we get that the outer *is* the indirect form of the inner, and the inner is the *direct* form of the outer. For it means we have removed the cover from myriad techniques of accessing *ourselves* through interaction with the outside world of "inanimate" matter, yes, but also through interaction with the other "animate" beings in that world as manifested in the planetmates.

As example, who would think that in interacting with a ferocious being, an angry bear, a crocodile, we are doing "inner work"? We do not, so we miss a huge opportunity.

Consider: We traditionally have placed these beings outside of the sphere of things we consider conscious. This corresponds to our own state, when doing that, of putting out of our mind those parts of our inner experience which they more than merely symbolize, but they actually *are*. Another way of saying this is that when we deny consciousness to another species, or another being, we are denying the existence of those parts of ourselves that they are. Hence we are denying ourselves access to them inside us. Our response to these parts of ourselves which we have projected outside of us is to assert they do not exist within us. Nope, "No anger in me," we think. "No way I'm weak," as a kitten. "I'm not like those *beasts* who hunt down and kill and eat each other," in full-on idiocy of the hunters and hamburgers before us. Denying consciousness to huge parts of the conscious reality around us amounts to, *is the exact same thing as,* denying awareness for ourselves of those parts within.

Thus, in denying consciousness to "animals" in the past, we denied awareness of those aspects of ourselves on our insides as well. The implication of that is that societies who denied the conscious awareness of animals were less consciously aware themselves. And does that not seem to be the case? Did not such societies make possible the atrocities of Western and Judeo-Christian history?

Do you think it only coincidental that a European culture in the Middle Ages, dominated by a Catholic orthodoxy that had the world of Nature to be not real, could put to death so many, during its "burning times," thought to be associated with that Nature? We recall that the belief at that time was that only the life in heaven was real. A huge step below it, they had humans on a pinnacle in Nature with dominion over it, as if Nature was a world of things and resources only, with even the animate life in it considered not to be conscious. Planetmates have no "soul" is the way this was put. Not like humans who, curiously … though having been ejected from Eden for a crime … still end up in God's eyes with such a blessing over the noncriminal elements, the "animals," left behind in Eden. *guffaw*

Undeterred by logic during the period of Catholic hegemony, and with people having such little connection to their own consciousness, and denying it as well to all of Nature, there was little regard for human or other life on Earth. Consequently nine million women, many called "witches," and those associated with such beliefs of having connection to Nature could be tortured horribly and burned to death.

Does it not make sense that a society with cultural values that denied Nature and the parts of it inside themselves — like their severely repressed sexuality, or like birth, which was associated with women — could then "severely repress" — kill — that which outside of them represented that? That is, they could murder the so-called "witches," and women? That they could burn at the stake, indeed torture as well, those who represented the things inside that they themselves were diligently struggling to repress — those feelings they were ferociously torturing and trying to burn up within?

Similarly, do you think it only coincidental that a culture embodying a scientific paradigm that denied consciousness to all planetmates, awarding it only to humans — as was true even from its beginnings within the Renaissance and is hardly let go of even today — could also invent a bomb capable of destroying all life ... and consciousness ... on this planet? Is it only by chance such a consciousness-denying culture would invent methods of industry for the production of edible portions of flesh in a way that would house planetmates like things, in boxes, to be stacked upon each other, with the beings within forced to walk over their dead companions and even feed off them? Or, as cows to be attached ignobly to machines to have fluids drained regularly from them, like one was draining honey from a hive?

This is why we tend to attack and beat upon those people who represent the parts of ourselves that we have repressed. If we hate and wish to blast away at hippies as we see them as impudent, ill-mannered, and uncivilizedly free it is because we have already, by the experiences and influences of our lives, been forced to repress and beat back our own feelings of being free.

Similarly, denying the aggression, hatred, anger, and rage inside ourselves results in us seeing, not just aggression in the folks and family surrounding us, and in our society — which is why such folks buy guns, for example — but also in Nature. That "wild" Nature, which similar folks, again with guns, consider it admirable to kill. For they do not acknowledge that in their pearly white personas they have any such darkness such as the ferocity of "beasts."

In the same way, if we wish to drown kittens, we are only doing to the playfulness we have projected outside, as kittens, what we are continually doing to our playfulness within. We drown our playfulness. And when we see that playfulness, drowned within, appearing outside of ourselves, we drown it there as well.

(lol. I'll certainly be "drowned" for some of the things I've said in this book! Let's hope those kind don't read it. *wink*)

So, the practical thing that comes out of this is that in changing our interactions with those entities outside us, in this case planetmates, we *are actually* working on a different relationship with those parts of ourselves on the inside. I am saying that, literally, when we play with a kitten … not drown it, lol … we are interacting with the playfulness within us. We are gaining better access to it; bringing it more into the sphere of our awareness and out of the domain of unconsciousness, where many of us were taught we had to put it so as to be a "real" adult.

Similarly, when we react differently to the rage of a lion, or the aggressiveness of a crocodile, we are interacting differently with the rage and aggressiveness within us. We truly and actually are doing "inner work" in doing such outer work.

And I know, you are thinking well how differently can one interact with a raging lion, a snapping crocodile, a pesky insect, a stinging bee, or a charging bear. For there is only one way, correct? That way is to shoot the lion, shoot the bear, shoot the crocodile, and slap and kill or put out insecticide to kill the insects.

And that tells everything about what one is constantly doing with the rage, aggressiveness, and irritations within oneself: One is seeking to kill them. One is seeking to not feel, to become numb, though one would never admit it. Yet, like a knight slaying a dragon, we are continually, for we have been taught that is the only thing to do, engaged in pushing down and repressing inside ourselves, hence "killing," the feelings that are appearing outside of ourselves in these ways, as things and creatures.

Which brings up the law of reality that whatever you deny or "kill" within yourself will show up outside yourself to be dealt with.

You're right; those "bastards" just won't go away! It is the whack-a-mole nature of Reality and Experience. Or the many-headed Hydra whose heads keep growing back, even if they have to show up outside you.

Thus it is the person who is repressing his rage who will confront an angry lion … if living in such a setting where there are them. But it is the person in that same locale who has that rage woven into a personality which gives it a place, a use, and a function, who is not just enjoying inner peace, but also who does not have encounters with angry lions!

379

You're still wondering how differently one can react to these threats outside us, seeking to hurt or kill us, aren't you? Well, that's understandable. How about this? Run away, for one. Leaving the scene in the face of aggression is lots more conducive to personal growth than what we have been taught.

Not saying one should not assert oneself, for that is important, too. But once done, once said, or when in a situation where it would be impossible to be done or to succeed at being "heard" when doing it; then backing away, not getting caught up in the struggle are the ways, foregoing aggression, one can better handle that.

But the surprising thing is how often one does not need to have a reaction at all! Like George W. Bush, we engage in "preemptive wars" all the time, similarly based on faulty or made up "evidence." Whose only merit, those actions are, is to follow through on what was already decided for selfish reasons or to have the pleasure of "anger orgasms." Those momentarily orgiastic releases wherein one gets revenge, on innocent others — unfortunately for them — for all the wrong done us in life. Or we have a passive-aggressive response, hiding even to ourselves our aggression, but in this sneaky way unconsciously feeding the beast of vengeance within.

How differently to act? We can often deal with these outside unwanted drama in a way similar to the way we should deal with our negative and unwanted feelings within. That is, as I've said earlier, to refrain from action, watch, perhaps at a distance, observe, and learn what we are trying to be told by the Universe though that event.

Not that killing is *never* warranted. For those interested, and to get a better understanding of how one can work with our attitudes to our own discomforting feelings by acting differently, and more harmoniously, with the beings that confront us, see this book's Epilogue, titled, "The World Is Out to Love You." In it you will see how I dealt with my own feelings of irritation regarding people by opting for a more harmonious response to some very irritating insects who had surrounded me. I not only did the "work," and received the peaceful reward that comes from such "work," but I had the "connection" to my inner life. I had an insight about people and some uncomfortable feelings I often feel in response to them. Acting differently with annoying, "pesky" wasps had me feeling more harmonious and understanding of people who make me feel similarly.

And I want to stress that all kinds of "work" like this results in positive feelings — harmony, joy, euphoria. And it did in my situation as well.

So this kind of perspective on inner and outer, on feelings and planetmates, has immense practical significance as well as explanatory power for our understanding some of human atrocity.

Now, to continue....

# Planetmates Are, Indeed, Our Angels in Nature

Remember, however, that what we call the "living," on Earth, has a special characteristic of relationship to us. I spoke at great length about these living beings, these *planetmates,* in my book, *Planetmates: The Great Reveal* (2014b). In that work, consistent with what I have been saying here about there being biologically constituted realities for humans, as well as some bioculturally constituted realities that are unique for humans and create a special separation from Divinity for us, I advanced that planetmates are less separated from Divinity.

Oh, and I know. You think I am expounding on how "innocent" these beings are … cute furry little things in their simple, limited little havens of mechanical instinct. And by this we assert our human superiority again; we place ourselves on that too comfortable pedestal of intelligence. Basically we are condescending to all of Nature, and beating our chests about being the true "king of the jungle" and the ruler of it all, thus, having "dominion" over all of it.

I am not asserting that at all but quite the contrary. I say planetmates are less descended from Divinity in that they have not the traumatized beginnings we do … so they are less dumb and numb. (See *Planetmates,* 2014b, and *Prodigal Human,* 2016a.)

Planetmates do not need language to communicate, because they are better able to do that sharing of experience, that overlapping in the pool of Experience than we are. They do "mind-sharing" as I have said.

In these ways they begin to sound a lot like the entities I have described as existing in the No-Form state. Remember? Those configured No-Forms (lol), those forms that are no-thing?

I believe, indeed, that they are akin to each other — planetmates and No Forms. For all we know, they are alike or overlapping in some way. As I said, in *Planetmates*, they are our "angels in Nature." Consider, if matter is the explicate or the Form-ly aspect of Divinity, which is thus, No-Form Reality in disguise, might not planetmates be the next step down from that? Like we think of angels in relation to God, in our traditional understandings? Which is that angels are one echelon removed from Divinity and attendant upon God? Might planetmates be the explicate or Form-ly manifestation of those helpful beings — angels, archangels, titans, gods, gopis, higher powers, or whatever your culture uses to describe higher beings? This would make them, indeed, angels in Nature. And they would be more akin to the power animals and potencies and forces that Native American and many other aboriginal cultures saw in Nature.

I think it fruitful, indeed, to actually consider their lives as being like those video games of the gods I have been describing. Like No-Forms interacting within Form, for whatever reason — for fun, for adventure, for variety ... just to magnify the All. What makes them different from us is that in being like gods playing video games in Form Reality, they would be, and I think they *are*, Divinity that is still aware of itself as Divinity. Again, using the planet-star analogy, we are on the dark side, ignorant of the light of our Divinity. They would be on the light side of the planet, facing and undoubting of their essential nature as God. Would that not be the conclusion wrought, even, of a traditionalist understanding of them from their role in the *Genesis* account of Eden? We are cast out of the "sight" of God ... the dark side of the moon; they still live in God's presence ... the light side of the planet.

I think that explains their ability to be so free in their adventuring in their lives. So fearless in a way. It seems death is not such an inhibiting thing to them, as it is to us.

# A Planetmate's Garden of Play

I once had a dream that explained this…. And in it, I was let in on a vision of Reality as it would be for us without that onerous dread of death we suffer. And think, if death is only a re-conscribing of an experiential "pool" that never "dies," actually, for it is really all that exists, then death is the biggest illusion of all, and it keeps us from seeing all of Reality with any clarity.

In the dream I was observing a number of primate-like beings. Earlier in the dream, I might have been with humans; and we might have been traveling, like along some mountains and cliffs. But what stuck out overall was this sight I observed, near the end of the dream, of this number of beings … let us say there were twenty of them.

Well, they were delightful. They were walking all over and around the setting. They were jumping and scampering and darting, more accurately. What distinguished the setting was there was a part of it that was like a path on the side of a steep cliff face. It was very narrow. That is significant, for I am afraid of heights. In a real setting of that kind, I would never walk that path for fear of falling. Not these guys!

No. They played; they "contended" with each other. They advanced, retreated, and tumbled; sometimes in a light-hearted play of combat, but not really. They had great fun moving around in that setting, in all parts of it — on the floor of the setting, along that path, in various nooks and crannies along parts of the cliff face and adjoining or nearby canyon walls or outcroppings of rock. Imagine monkeys playing, though they were more humanlike than monkeys and they did not have the advantages some monkeys do in climbing. Think of them as monkey-like, in other words, playful, baboons. Or chimps. Though they were "handsomer" than either of those.

They had absolutely no inhibitions. No fear! I watched them scurry along that path in their play, jump to nearby spots on rock faces, charge and retreat, spar and chase … and laugh. I was entranced at their absolute fearlessness, especially in regard to their movements through the air, in regard to heights. They seemed literally to "throw" themselves into anything and everything. As well as *over* everything and anything … and around. Fearless this way, their

383

"play," their mock "battle," was intricate, fascinating, alive with stunts that expert gymnasts would admire.

Then, at one point, one of them failed to negotiate that path along the cliff face correctly and fell. I was alarmed. I was probably the only one, though; and that's important. Concerned, worried that he might be dead (you'll see in a moment why I use the masculine pronoun here), I swiftly moved over to him and looked down. He had fallen hard, so hard that it was as if his body had softened and was melting, becoming a kind of a "pool" of liquid, but still retaining a primate's form for the most part.

Just as an aside, it only now dawned on me the significance of him becoming a "pool" of liquid at death. Death meaning losing one's Form boundaries, perhaps? Anyway, considering my chorus throughout this book of all beings being conscribed units within an experiential pool, you know what I mean.

Well, and this is where it got fascinating and, in fact, woke me up with a start. For his face, well it was in the form of a smile, definitely. It was as if he was laughing, while ebbing from life.

And then the primate's face morphed into that of Jack Benny! Jack Benny, smiling. Smiling and then you could almost see that thing Mister Benny would do — his right elbow held in his left hand, arm across his chest. Then, putting his right palm up cradling his cheek on that side, little toss of the head, roll of eyes, and saying, "Well…" as that comedian's way of disparaging or showing incredulity of some person or some event happening in front of him.

Well, this was hilarious. I don't remember if I woke up laughing my ass off at the time, though I did come to consciousness right then. I don't believe so; I was probably too amazed. But I am laughing now, and continuously, in remembering it!

Oh, I must say, what a sight it was, that primate-like planetmate laughing and joking as he was "dying" … or, as he knew, simply going to another place. Smart-alecky to the end. If you fail to see the humor here, well, imagine how Bugs Bunny would do it. (Benny, Bunny, your choice) With a "eh, what's up, Doc?" or some other wisecrack upon meeting the angel of death.

I have thought about this dream often over the years. It was clear these "planetmates" had no fear because there was no death, not really. It was just another wrinkle in the game, when that would happen. They would be as little concerned, maybe less so, as a basketball player fouling out and being taken out of the game. Knowing there are always others.

Simply reviewing that dream is so freeing to me, whenever I do it. Its message to me is clear: Take risks in life. Do things big. Throw yourself into things. Do not be so concerned about what will happen to you. Enjoy. Participate. Be uninhibited. Be jovial. Play. And by all means, at every possibility ….

laugh.

Life?

It's just not such a big deal.

Hahahahaahah, as I think that right know.

To this day, it teaches me. If ever I should ask, should I put another lol into my writing? Should I take a long journey in a rickety car? Dare I say that? Dare I write it that way? Should I throw myself into love again?

I think of that primate and ask myself, "Well what would a planetmate do?" And I laugh....

And I throw myself in.

If it is love, I ask myself if it is true, do I feel it. Since it is, and I do, then I do.

If it is writing, I ask myself if it is true. What would the No-Forms say? If I know it to be true, and important, or helpful to say, then I do.

If it is a risky journey, an uncertain move to another place, a radical change in occupation, project, or path of learning, I ask myself, Is it fun? Is it an adventure? Do I want to do it? Would I dig it? Does it make for a great and interesting life? If yes, then I throw myself forward, tossing myself over any hurdle of unease.

If it is a service, a gracious act, a generous offer, a burden lifted to relieve another or others or to bring some needed ease to the world of people or the Earth, I ask myself, Is it helpful? Is it loving? Do I feel my heart opening about it and a feeling of unity with them? Is it needed? Is it demanded? And if it is a service to people or planetmates, I picture who might be affected. And if my heart melts, and yes marks the beat for all these inquiries, then I do.

If I died the next minute, would I regret not having done it? If yes, then I do.

If it is my style of writing, I ask myself, is it fun? Yes. For anyone else? I don't know. Can you picture someone else digging it? Yes. Will I get a kick out of doing it? Yes. Then it's as good as done.

When posting online, or repeatedly. I ask myself, is it helpful to someone? Yes. Am I laughing when I do it? Yes. Am I crying when I do it, thinking of the tragedies of people's lives, as they continually bring suffering upon themselves, imprisoned in their faulty, fear-rooted beliefs and assumptions? Yes, sometimes.

Will someone be jealous? Will someone think I am egotistical for beings so bold? Will they judge me? Will they criticize me? Yes. But is it helpful to someone ... or many? Yes.

Then fuck the rest of 'em.

And I do.

I laugh.

I throw myself.

I'm leaping from ledge to path and back again. I'm rolling. I'm tumbling. I'm free.

I know I'll fall someday, indeed I often do, though not yet fatally.

And luckily I've gotten better at not looking back.

or looking down.

# Intelligence? It's Someone Like Us.

In any case, getting back to the topic of death, this dream affected my understanding of it ever after. I think now that, most of all, death contributes to our misunderstanding of our planetmate relatives. For it makes them seem, well, beastial, animal-like. That that is not true is my point. Hence I refuse to call them beasts or animals, rather planetmates, only ... those beings with whom we share this planet.

Furthermore, in keeping with all the anthropocentrism we do, an outgrowth of our egotism, we are wont to lift ourselves up in relation to them. And part of that is to say that we are above them in consciousness. Though how the hell would we know that? That is much the kind of prejudice that persisted in the White world about Blacks for hundreds of years. They also were thought inferior to "full humans," i.e., Whites. As was Jews to Germans, as they were thought to be less intelligent. But based on what? Based on the tests that Whites created out of the things that were important in their culture.

In the same way, we can only determine the intelligence of planetmates in relation to our human intelligence, which is merely measuring the degree to which they are like, or not, to ourselves. Well, this says nothing about awareness or intelligence in the absolute, at all!

Better to use the word "awareness" and in that case, they have every right to be considered as having more in that category.

Take the ability of birds to migrate, seasonally, over thousands of miles; of birds to perfectly synchronize their movements in the air, with split-second precision; for salmon and Monarch butterflies to know routes of travel through memory passed down from previous generations; for some planetmates to be able to find their way, with no previous experience of it, over thousands of miles to a desired destination; the miraculous abilities of the smelling capacity of canines, said to be up to a million times better than ours and able to detect events that happened in the past, in days prior; and so on. The list is endless. Such abilities of planetmates are wondrous, unfathomable by human intelligence. Some of this I touched on earlier in this book.

What I am saying is that planetmates might be reflections of No-Form entities existing within the boundaries of our available perception. You don't have to convince me of that very much after my experience with my own cat, Muff, over the course of eighteen years.

About the experiential concomitants of the life of planetmates? Well, in any bounded reality, in any being, in any conscribing of Experience, there is separation, into inner and outer, though perhaps not Ego. Ego is that severely conscribed and limited beingness of humans. However, all conscribed experiential units have a degree of separation, which would include planetmates. And separation implies possible duality of intents, as well. Thus frustration of will, unsatisfaction of desire. As long as there is Form, or limiting and configuring, there is conflict, delayed satisfaction ... and so on.

So about the experiential concomitants of the Form of planetmates? It is perhaps that planetmate Forms are like No-thing Forms in that both might be connected (to Divinity) in a sense and ever aware of their essential identity as Divinity but playing at being separate. Much like we are aware it is only a game when we play a sport or a board game, but play it, nonetheless.

Planetmates are our angels in Nature, I believe. Furthermore, I am inspired in thinking of them as being, not just aspects of No-Form realities, more blatantly obvious to us than the No-Forms otherwise, but as clearer reflections of other psychic realities we meet on the inside ... specifically our emotions. I am inspired in this way by aboriginal thinking. In particular, Australian aborigines have the belief that animals are projections from the Dreamtime of the emotions and experiential realities we feel. They are not alone in that belief.

Evidence the fact that delicate as a butterfly, noble as a horse, proud as a lion ... are universal symbols. That means the Earth tells all of us the same thing. And it is telling us the same things about ourselves through the appearance and behavior of its angels in Nature, its planetmates.

This worldwide impression we get from our closest fellow beings on Earth is not a subjective thing, then, or a cultural thing. The same can be said about the meanings we attribute — I would say the messages being told us — from Earth, Sky, Ocean, Water, Tree, River, and Stream, in addition to Butterfly, Snake, and so on.

The wonderment to take away from this? Nature, the World, the Universe is telling us the same thing ... is broadcasting the same message ... the world around.....

If we, but listen.

# 30

# Universe Calling, Says It Wants to Help:

Splitting Apart, Crisis, and Reunion … At the Portal to a Quantum Jump — Crop Circles, Mandalas, and Gates … The Universe Reaches to Guide Us

*Splitting Apart … a Time when Evil Is Ascendant … In Observing the World, We Are Observing Mind … What Occurs in Psychic Reality Manifests Physically. On Crisis and Reunion, Moratorium and Unity*

# Brain Is the Tip of the Iceberg of Consciousness

It should not be surprising, considering the foregoing, that when there are changes in psychic structures, there will often be noticeable physical changes which correspond to the psychic ones.

## Morphogenetic Fields

In a way, this is the implication of Rupert Sheldrake's *morphogenetic field theory*. On the simplest level of this, scientists tell us that when learning takes place, evidence can be found of corresponding changes in the physical brain. That is not surprising. However, scientists are not able to *reduce* learning to physical changes in the brain: They cannot locate specific learning, knowledge, or memories in specific parts or cells of the brain. And they will never be able to do that, if we are not completely mistaken here.

The best that scientists can come up with is that memory is contained everywhere in the brain. Think of that as memory and knowledge contained within a field woven through and encompassing that brain. Less exactly, using an analogy from the Internet, information and memory in the brain resembles The Cloud. It is scattered everywhere. There is a difference in that The Cloud is everywhere and many places in particular. Whereas what we know about memory and information in the brain is that it is everywhere and nowhere in particular. Meaning that a piece of internet information can be tracked down to an actual physical location, more than one, actually. Whereas a piece of mind information cannot be found to exist in its entirety in *any* single place in the brain, let alone more than one.

More and more, then, memory and learning in the brain sounds like Sheldrake's theory of information being contained within morphogenetic fields. It is more like knowledge is related to patterns of undetectable waves than that it is related to particle-like things making up atoms and cells.

You might say the Universe is hip, groovy, and wave-like, storing what it knows in dance-like patterns … or in the rhythm of Reality's "soundtrack" — a music that is ever playing somewhere in the background. It is not conservative, plodding, and mechanical, storing information like song books in a storage locker ... song books that are rarely opened or sung from. Or like books in an Akashic library, never read and easily destroyed. No. Information and memory is not thing-like and perishable. It is wave-like and alive ... pulsing and ever fresh.

While information and memory is not contained in any area or set of cells in the brain; still, information and memory results, physically, in brain changes that are spread throughout it, manifesting in some areas of the brain more than others.

What we can take from this is something astonishing. For another way of looking at this is that the physical changes observable in the brain are merely the tip of the iceberg of the phenomena of learning-memory. The real stuff is going on "below." Or more correctly, the events of learning-memory-consciousness go on "inside" or "within" — which is, actually, *even more correctly*, the true "outside," the true "without" or "objective" reality, though not all of it is observable to us perceptually limited humans.

One might say information-memory is held and is processing unrelated to Form. For fields are not contained within matter; they are immanent and transcendent of it. Stop for a sec and have a thought about what I said about the Divine, in a panentheistic Universe, being both immanent and transcendent of the physical Universe. Provocative, no?

Continuing, then: Fields are found beyond, extending out from, where matter resides and are independent of it. In case your mind is going there, I want to confirm for you that, yes, Sheldrake notes how these things (no-things, actually) begin to sound more and more like what in the past were called "spirit."

## What Occurs in Psychic Reality Manifests Physically

On grosser levels of physical reality — other than brain — in the world, this is also true, according to Sheldrake's theory of morphogenetic fields. For every physical form ... in the *explicate order* — borrowing from David Bohm's terminology, now — has its morphogenetic field or pattern in the *implicate order*. And since this implicate order is identical with what we normally call "consciousness" ... as we have been establishing ... a subset of which is *thought* or *psyche* or *the mental*, then what occurs in the realm of the psychic will often manifest (to us) in physical reality.

## On Thing and No-Thing

One observation arising from all this is that there is a clear distinction between the "old" science — physicalist science — and the "new" science, which includes that of quantum physics and the new biology and psychology. The rut the old science is stuck in is its obsession with thingness. In old-paradigm science — what Thomas Kuhn (1970) would call "normal science" — the aim is always, regardless the claims on the growing edges of it, to look for "thing" explanations for everything. They expect everything to be able to be reduced to changes in some particles, atoms, molecules, elements, cells ... to "some" thing. They deem everything could be reduced to the laws of physics relating to the movement of objects in space as determined by momentum, mass, and forces like gravity.

Whereas, the "new" science begins talking, not in terms of "thing" explanations, but in field-like and wave-like terms. I would have us go beyond even that and begin using experiential terms for the ultimate explanations of even waves, energy, and fields; for the ultimate "building blocks" of Existence, the foundation of all Reality. I believe it is much more helpful and evocative to use terms indicating how close at hand is Ultimate Reality, how we are not separate from It, by using terms like feeling, emotion, awareness, consciousness, being-becomingness, and inspiration — terms that are closer to or have connotations similar to the old-fashioned, "spirit" and "soul" but are even more explanatory and useful.

Nevertheless, our science is beginning to see beyond at least the thingful causes and elements. In the new science an electron no longer is a thing orbiting the nucleus of an atom. Rather the orbit is a field of "potentiality" wherein that electron "is likely" to show up to exist. In the new science, contrary to the normal laws of physics, at the subatomic level there is "action at a distance." Inexplicably, there is change of rotation in a subatomic particle dependent upon, matching and mirroring, a change in rotation of its complementary subatomic particle in another place ... with absolutely no contact between the two.

This happens outside the laws of normal physics, for there is no interaction of thing with other thing ... there is no force, collision, or momentum involved. There is simply complementarity, or one might say symmetry or resonance in the real world that cannot be explained except by resorting to categories like "fields," which, since undetectable, is as good (and is less honest) than saying that there is spirit involved.

These events occurring to supposed "things" exist in invisible patterns. They operate within non-thing patterns only detectable through their effects. Such fields are assumed; they are demonstrable but not detectable. As Sheldrake pointed out, the new science begins to resemble primitive science in that these no-thing patterns are impossible to distinguish from what in the past was called *spirit*. And, I'm sure you are recollecting, at this moment, how often in this book we have stumbled across stuff just like them, which I have been calling no-thing forms, or No-Form configurations.

## Thoughts Manifest as Things

To review then, what is repressed inside of us manifests outside of ourselves. What is beaten down or killed outside of us might manifest inside of us. Finally, what happens in No-Form Reality, on the implicate order, often is observable in Form Reality, in the explicate order. It has its concomitant in Form as well as No-Form. Thoughts are manifest in things ... emotions and feelings even more so.

This perspective is fruitful for understanding many common but otherwise unexplainable events, such as synchronicity, as we explored a couple chapters ago.

## In Observing the World, We Are Observing Mind

Further, the idea that psychic events comprise physical reality means something astounding. What this means is that Reality has the same substance as do dreams: Material Reality has psychic substance. And literally, as the mystics say, life IS a dream. When we look at Reality we are observing the workings of Mind.

Or as some people would say, the workings of God.

# Crop Circles

This perspective also brings a whole new interpretation to many of the current unexplainables on the world stage: Crop circles and UFOs are two I would like to deal with. What they reveal is nothing less than astounding.

## Crop Circles, Mandalas, Wholeness

Crop circles are indisputably physical: They remain in place and persist through time, until they are physically removed or grow over; we can all see them; they are not hallucinative; and there are many photos of them. Yet their manifesting in our physical reality is so far unexplainable. Some attempts at explanation sound similar to that movement and direction of changes in matter, described above, that can only be explained by resorting to terms implying no-thing causes, such as *fields;* which is a kind of scientific legerdemain (sleight of hand) to avoid terms that might sound spiritual.

Strange that crop circles would be found in "fields" — agricultural fields — also, isn't it? Is that a hint? Everything is indeed interconnected. And when you see that enough, it appears that it is that way even regarding "matters" (pun intended) that appear to be trivial, inexplicable, and even humorous. We often see a whimsical — playful and teasing, even — quality in our messages from the Universe.

At any rate, to think of crop circles as representing fields you might imagine how energy fields are traditionally demonstrated, which is, by showing the pattern of iron filings around a magnet. However, in crop circles, these fields (within "fields" lol) show up in far more intricate patterns than that seen in magnetic fields.

Another common explanation — from those who still operate within old-paradigm understandings of events requiring actors doing things to things, a rather fundamentalist view — is that aliens are using some kind of apparatus or machine to create the patterns. Apparently they would be accomplishing this from some sort of equally physical spaceships. Though they would have to be invisible spaceships since this has never been observed. The closest we have come to these events being witnessed is folks who "heard" it happening, though there was no "actor" involved that was visible.

Granted, some crop circles, only a couple actually, are acknowledged hoaxes, perpetrated by all too human agents. However the vast majority of them cannot be explained away so easily.[1] Debunkers can no more explain away all the many thousands of crop circles in their unbelievable complexity and art by pointing to a couple jokers who went in a field and made a simple, crude circle by pressing lumber down on grain stalks, than all of No-Form Reality, NDEs, and spiritual reality, Atman, and Brahman can be debunked by referring to a few fake mediums. Though the skeptics — lacking imagination and wielding like Thor's hammer a logic constructed of limited understandings and leaving out any evidence not fitting with their prejudices — would love to think they can. And ever do they try, demonstrating their beliefs to have more sanctimonious sounding motives … that of belief and faith in a religion of materialism… than anything like hard facts.

Nevertheless, getting back to the tens of thousands of unexplainable crop circles, in these instances circular or somewhat symmetrical images are found written large in fields of cultivated plants. Often, these circles have elements of mandalas included in them. These mandala qualities underscore the interpretation I am making, which is that they are manifestations, symbolic, of a pressing modern-day need for psychic integration and spiritual-emotional wholeness.

## Our First Split from Grace — Agriculture, the Agrarian Revolution, the Neolithic Era

Consider this: These crop circle formations are clustered around Neolithic sites — that is, they occur in proximity to ancient structures that are related to the time when we began subsisting on farming. Of the over ten-thousand crop circles discovered to date, a staggering number of these, forty percent in fact, were found within a forty-mile radius of Stonehenge. They line up with magnetic and electromagnetic lines on Earth as do Stonehenge, Avebury, the Uffington Horse, and dozens of other sites these crop circles are found near. Note that these sites are Neolithic in origin, which is to say that they are from the time of the agrarian revolution when we made a major split from Nature and began controlling Her as opposed to being in harmony with Her as were our ancient gatherer-hunter forebears.

I have pointed out elsewhere how this agrarian revolution was a fall from grace in Nature (see *Planetmates*, 2014b, and *Prodigal Human*, 2016a). It was a setting up of a duality, the first major one, pitting humans against Nature. It represents the beginnings of the radical mistrust and fear of Nature, hence control of Her, that we are seeing the dire consequences of today with the environmental collapse we have set in motion and of which we are beginning to feel the effects.

All this together lends itself to a fascinating conclusion about crop circles' possible meanings for humanity: Is it possible that these agricultural circles are the way our innermost psyche, our inner higher unconscious reality, is trying to tell us to "get back to where you once belonged" by placing a sign back at the exact place of our original detour?! Metaphorically speaking, these sites are the Gates of Eden. They represent the spot in human history where we left Eden or were "kicked out of it." So, is it possible this phenomenon is saying, "Okay, here is where you screwed up. Go back to GO, go back to wholeness and integration — the circles, see? Uh, do not collect any two hundred dollars though."

Another way to frame this, complementary to the other explanations when you think of it, goes like this: Is it possible that crop circles' coincidence along magnetic and electromagnetic lines of Earth indicates this is what the Earth, what Gaia, is "texting" us? Inasmuch as her life is at stake, why wouldn't she?

Keep in mind that mandalas, as found in crop circles, represent wholeness of personality and integration among all our dualities, including Nature and human, human and the Divine, soul and body. I would venture, also, primitive and sophisticated, animate and inanimate, spirit and science, past and future, ancient and contemporary (see my *Primal Renaissance: The Emerging Millennial Return*, 1995c, and *Primal Return: Renaissance and Grace*, scheduled 2017). Hence, because crop circle mandalas are found near sites related to our supposed agrarian "revolution," might they be telling us, "Here is where you lost your wholeness. Here is what you need to look at. Look back to this time for ideas on how to get back your peace of mind and harmony with the rest of Nature and the Universe."

Maybe also, "Here is your doorway. Welcome back. Welcome home."

"Here are the gates back to 'Eden.'"

# Mandalas as Gateways, Portals

For, mandalas also are gateways; they are like doors between existences. The traditional style of the mandala from India has four gates, one coming from each of the four directions. We saw this depicted, exactly, in the ubiquitous mandala, the Sri Yantra, in a previous chapter.

However, mandalas also, viewed in their entirety, are gateways or portals. Whether in the form of the Christian cross, the wiccan circle, the satanic pentagram, or the Sri Yantra, mandalas are places within which you place yourself or your focus of attention for the purpose of moving to or connecting with another dimension of existence or another "frame" of mind. They are places of accessing higher power; attaining more expanded perspectives; shifting to more inclusive, more powerful and useful stances in relation to Reality; and moving between dimensions of existence.

They are places, like our personal tablets, perhaps, where we receive "text messages" from Divinity, like the crop circles. Or reversing that direction of communication, where we can phone E.T., not home. They are like psychic wormholes between dimensions and between varying levels and times of existence, just as wormholes are between points in space.

They are symbolic representations of a coming together of dimensions, also, that I have been expressing using the symbolism of a Jacob's Ladder — which is a metaphorical ladder enabling the going to and fro of angels between heaven and Earth.

This aspect of the mandala, as portal, is used to maximum effect in many current movies, the prototype of them being *Stargate*. Consider also, as being related, the tunnel said to occur in the NDEs I mentioned in Chapter 23, "The Universe Says It is Friendly … and Funny." Remember how I pointed out that the same symbolism, a tunnel, shows up in rainbows. I explained that they mean the same thing: transition … going from one state or dimension to another. For both are related to the first major transition of our lives, the one at birth. So birth tunnels are NDE tunnels and are symbolized by rainbows.

# Tunnels

Now, we see, that mandalas are forms of tunnels, too. More accurately they are gates and portals. However, at birth we went through the portal of our mother's pelvic opening to arrive in physical form. We went through a portal, though we call it a birth tunnel, or birth canal, and we think of it that way. There are reasons why we conflate portals and tunnels, having to do with even earlier experiences we have all had, earlier even than birth. That's coming next. Regardless, at birth we went symbolically from relative No-Formness into Formness — the mother's vaginal opening was a portal, going from relative No-Form into Form-ly life.

Now then, consider that even earlier than birth, around the time of conception, we have experiences of tunnels as portals between states of existence. We went through a tunnel to get into Form from No-Form in that we were shot through the penal canal, as a sperm, to get to the egg. As a sperm, we came upon a huge mandala-like circle, the egg, just prior to another change of consciousness at the time of actual conception, or fertilization of the egg. On the other side of that experience, as an ovum, as your mother's egg, you descended through another tunnel, that of the fallopian tube. Do you see why we conflate tunnels, portals, and mandalas?

It goes the other way, too. Even more so is this a template for our experience at the end of life of going into a tunnel to get to a light. The tunnel opening to the light, in an NDE, involves a going from Form into No-form, at death.

So tunnels, mandalas, gates, rainbows, and portals are related. They have the meanings of transition, birth, death, accessing higher power, "phoning hOMe," and moving to other dimensions or states.

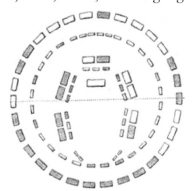

And now this, crop circles. Ostensibly mandalas. Anything portal-like or gate-like or transition-like about them?

# Crisis and Reunion

Well, consider that the rock configuration of Stonehenge is observable from above as a kind of mandala or gate. Consider also that the individual parts of it are gates as well. The stone structures at

Stonehenge resemble crude doorways — two vertical stones with a "header" placed across the top of them, joining them. They quite resemble

the Chinese symbol for *gate*, by the way. Remember also what I said above about it being conceivable these are, by being placed at Neolithic sites and in farmer's fields, placed at our metaphorical "gates" of Eden, at the portal from which we passed from wholeness, in Eden, to our fallen, separated state.

## "Splitting Apart"

Furthermore, in the *I Ching*, from ancient China, such a gate-like representation has a meaning with the most negative connotation of all sixty-four hexagrams, and it means "splitting apart." It is five identical broken lines lying horizontally atop each other, creating something like two pillars, with a solid line at the top, like a header. It is hexagram 23, and it is said it represents a cataclysmic realization of illusion. Which makes it like the idea of *awakening*, currently going viral. It is like waking up from a dream. In the hexagram, it repre-  sents a house collapsing, a home collapsing. It is the end of a familiar and comfortable delusion.

And it results, eventually, though not until after a process of great difficulty, in a new birth. It is a death-rebirth where for a long while evil and evil people gain power and stealthily engage in actions to bring everything down. Consider for comparison the meaning of the Kali Yuga, in Hindu mythology. It is a time in which those of noble intent can only wait. However, the ultimate result of this process is the return of better times.

While writing this, a few nights ago, I had a dream that I just now, in reading back over this passage, realize symbolically and powerfully expressed this situation of "splitting apart," evil ascendant, Kali Yuga.

# Petty People, Petty Lives

I dreamed there were people sitting down and having interactions, negotiating, sitting across tables, about enterprises that were pretty lame. They were impressed by their own importance, clearly. I watched these mini-Trumps, and I was thinking that all that negotiating, wrangling, having people sit down to work out details, and endless delineation of detail was totally unnecessary. If they wanted to do it — it occurred to an annoyed me — they should just get on with it already!

They didn't really need to make everything about it a transaction, as if one were to commoditize every idea and activity of one's life. In pricing, marketing, and trying to get paid for everything they did, they would not actually do very much, ever. It would be like trying to copyright every idea and get credit for it and funding for it instead of just doing it and having more of them. It slowed everything down; they accomplished little in trying to own and protect the things and ideas that came to them. They were always thinking about money, you see, so they always got mired down in what were just the beginnings of things.

Even more consequentially, they were not engaging in valuable, exciting, or useful endeavors in their lives but in substitute ones. These small and petty undertakings had become all important and crowded out any real activities or truly far-sighted, creative ideas. These minor matters they engaged in mechanically, almost ritualistically, and their only real purpose seemed to be to allow them to put on a show of importance, for others, but also to fool themselves.

This went on for quite a while. I left. Though I observed it from an adjoining, a smallish and dark, foyer, where I might have conversed with another. We seemed to discuss the activities we watched. Perhaps we metaphorically shook our heads. But then I went boldly into their room, again. Indeed, they were negotiating over tables that extended from wall to wall, like lines, like solid lines in a hexagram, one behind the other, before me. I wanted to get to the far side of the room from where I was at that time, near the entrance. These tables with trivial activities ensuing upon them blocked my way, like row upon row.

I proceeded forward, nonetheless, and I remember crawling under one table in particular, somewhat halfway to where I wanted to go, having to get past the legs and such of the metal folding chairs they were sitting on, and to bypass the legs of the "negotiators" themselves. They continued their needless activity above me. I could hear them talking, without missing a beat, per my presence. And I got through, undetected and inconsequential to them and their doings.

The solid lines of tables were all yang lines, using I Ching terminology. Yang lines are male lines. Remember patriarchy as we go along. And though yang lines indicate creativity, especially with six of them together, as in hexagram 1, this was creativity in trivial matters, matters of no consequence which only took up time from more important and crucial endeavors. You might say this was activity from the world of commerce and one's Western material existence in modern times. And what I was noticing was how it distracted one, nonsensically, from the more important purposes of life, such as the spiritual quest, the seeking of wisdom, the pursuit of authenticity, and the euphoric participation in the creative flow of self-actualization and self-fulfillment. Not to mention, that of real love and immersion in *its* mystery.

## Important People, Powerful Harm

Later in the dream, there were people, many of them, lying on the floor or stumbling about in a darkish room, similar to the other one, but much larger. It was the next room over from the room with the tables. There were others walking about, not lying down, but much less of them. There was someone here or there, and they were coming over to the ones lying down and were looking down into the prone persons' faces. Doing so, they began "breathing" the very life force out of the ones lying on their backs. It was like a holotropic breathwork workshop but in reverse. For instead of breathing in life force energy and being supported in that, the "participants" were having it taken from them. And the ones who should have been facilitating were instead disabling, killing actually, these people. The upright ones would suck in the energy of the prone ones, then would leave the room. Whereupon I would notice another one or two of them doing it to others who were similarly prone and helpless.

The ones doing the sucking of life force would live. The others were left to die. There was one in particular, of the ones meant to die, who managed to stand up and was stumbling around and trying to keep from losing consciousness and having someone take his life force. His name began with a K, Kevin comes to mind, and Keith, rather some combination of the two that I can't quite remember.

Regardless, I think he represented myself. As indeed I have been bucking up against burn out, over the last several months, stumbling, as it were on the inside, to accomplish the practical things of life, as I have made my work, this book in particular, my focus, my priority. Clearly, I, in the darkish room, was stumbling and unsteady because I was not engaged in the trivial matters about which those in the room with tables were engaged. Now that I think of it, stumbling yet still trying, while trying to avoid the unfortunate fate of all others around me, in such times as these of soul robbery, is a pretty good metaphor for all of my life, as well … as I perceive it.

In any case, you might think of the darkish room of the prone people as being one in which they were lying halfway between the Form and No-Form existences and were being creative channels between the two dimensions. However, we were being sucked of our life forces in this realm by those with only practical matters of concern to them … selfish matters, material ones, family ones … by those who conceived of their activities as all important, mindless of their blithering insignificance, even at the expense of someone else's life.

But more than that. For the sucking of the life forces was the most remarkable, in a horrific way, aspect of that scene. And this is what I related to this time of evil ascendant, with people of selfish and unempathetic natures — sociopaths, we are calling them these days, while pointing out they are in power everywhere, currently — doing exactly that, sucking the very life breath out of the rest of us.

## Ascendant — Evil and Trivial

So, the first room represented much ado about nothing among people thinking they are negotiating important things, which are actually trivial. These are the ordinary folks of modern times.

And the second room was folks who were sucking the life breath out of the rest of us. I liken that to taking up our money, our time, our energy, just as the filthy rich elite in these times keep us all bogged down in trivial concerns, red tape and nonsense, and keep sucking our life breath, our money and resources, energy and time, merely to add more to their already prodigious, bloated and obscene, holdings. They keep us involved in endless ridiculous things — mountains of forms, never ending meaningless hoops to jump through, forever attacks on our meager resources, tsunamis of ads to pull away the little power we have and fill all mental spaces not otherwise engaged, and barriers to the horizon obstructing our ability to just subsist, however meagerly. Which purpose, this oppression of the masses, is essentially just to keep their egoic defensive systems alive … at the cost of our lives and energy.

This dream is my understanding, on an unconscious level, of this splitting apart — symbolized by hexagram 23, which looks like a Stonehenge "gate" — as it is occurring in these times. This is an era of evil ascendant, with good work being difficult or impossible. For they are blocking the way with their trivial activities; and they are sucking our life breath, those of us who are despite them trying to engage in truly important endeavors. So it is a time when the best we can do is refuse to engage them, go under (the table), around, or over it; but not get hooked, like tar baby, into dealing with them and thereby losing one's way.

## Reincarnation and Falls from Grace

I must say also that dreams mean things on various levels, all at once and integrating them. And I have to note the quality of the symbols in the second room as representing the time of no-exit in the womb, when we are getting less oxygen from the placenta and it seems the placenta is an evil entity sucking our life breath. (See *Wounded Deer and Centaurs: The Necessary Hero and the Prenatal Matrix of Human Events*, 2016b.) Indeed, that is the symbol that precedes all evil ventures, like wars, oppression, and bigotry, for it is a feeling that someone wants to take our life breath, which induces folks to attack those others violently. This is something I explain at length in *Wounded Deer and Centaurs*, and it is something I gleaned initially from the work of Lloyd deMause (1982, 2002), who found such blood-sucking symbolism to precede wars and other atrocities of violence and oppression against others. So this sucking of life force is the veritable image of the splitting apart symbolized by hexagram 23. For paranoia and greed lead to the kind of aggression against others and Nature described in it.

Furthermore, my leaving the first room and going into the foyer was undoubtedly reflecting my leaving a former existence and contemplating the pathetic goings-on here on Earth from an after-death state, a No-Form existence. In concert with others, symbolized by the person I shared my observations with, I witnessed the events here and decided to go back to life … "boldly," as I put it … and I went back into the room, back into the womb.

Indeed, the fact that I had to crawl under the table was a symbolic reflection of birth itself. Notice how the dream had it down, including the need to go between legs — chair legs, negotiator's legs — just as we need to do in coming into life through our mother's. Additionally, the rows of tables blocking the way are the barriers, the traumas, the falls from grace one must go through — sperm struggle; conception; fetal malnutrition; birth itself; the horrendous time afterward, still in hospital separated from mother; infancy and its deprivations; the primal scene at four or five; and so on (see *Falls from Grace*, 2014a, for more on this). Notice I said that birth itself — going under the table and through the legs — was one of the middle rows. In the middle is pretty much where the trauma of birth lies in the sequence of sufferings we endure to be here, in Form.

The prone people and the stumbling man was reflective of the groggy state one endures during the last month of gestation — termed *fetal malnutrition* — when one is receiving less in the way of oxygen and nutrients than previously and than optimal. And one, like in hexagram 23, must only wait. Change will come, times will shift, help will come from both inside oneself and outside oneself. For one will be supremely motivated, inwardly, just like one was at birth, when the crisis reaches its peak and is the most painful. One will finally be willing to risk more rather than have to continue on in such suffering. And assistance will manifest from without. Just as the mother ideally assists at the time of birth, and as the Universe, the Divine, Gaia, aliens, and No-Forms are coming forth to help currently.

So rebirth happens eventually. But until then, one can only wait — fortifying and preparing oneself through personal growth in the meantime — till a shift in the tides of change. At which time outward action is paramount. And one will be ready for one's role in midwifing, leading, or being part of it.

## Moratorium and Unity

Hexagram 23, then, is similar to the peace symbol in its meaning as moratorium. It represents a time in which all is going wrong and all one can do is retreat and re-evaluate. To continue in the same course is disastrous. But the process is one that ends with the positive forces once again on the ascendant, overseeing all, determining all.

In the peace symbol, the hands-down cross in the center, meaning retreat or desisting from action, results in greater wholeness, as in the circle that surrounds it. In hexagram 23 of the *I Ching*, resembling the Chinese symbol for gate as well as the doorway-like structures at Stonehenge, the splitting apart, the duality, of the two vertical sides is integrated by the header at the top. It symbolizes duality manifest horribly, as in conflict, war, environmental destruction, apocalypse, and such; but eventually integrated and brought together — the header — in unity. It represents our extreme estrangement from Nature, our severe and apocalyptic duality, coming to an end in a union, or a reunion with Nature, the Divine, the Universe.

# Rebirth

Furthermore, there are stones in the shape of circles associated with Neolithic sites similar to Stonehenge. It has been suspected that these might have to do with rebirthing rituals that were done there at that time. Again, we have the theme of portal — going through a circle, through a ring, through a tunnel (through a rainbow-like thing) to get to another state of being. Stonehenge in particular is thought to be related to death, to burial. We see over and over the same themes: death, birth, rebirth, transition, crisis, access to higher power, opening to another dimension, then union or reunion.

A conclusion arising from all this is that these mandalas in the form of crop circles might be saying all of that: That we are at such a crucial time in the history of our planet and our species where we are on the verge, we are standing at the portal, to a transition where we will either be born, as a species, or we will die, as a species. Who knows, maybe both. Remember in this respect the Chinese symbol: It is a gate.

When you think about it, birth is a transition — a gateway or portal — having the dual meanings of both crisis and reunion. For after birth, the baby is reunited with its mother in a different relationship ... a higher one, in a sense ... where both can better perceive and understand each other's nature. And is birth not also a "splitting apart," of mother and infant? In the same way is the emanation as sperm through the penal canal and the journey to the egg both a crisis and eventually union, in the process of conception. Is that not also a "splitting apart" of father and sperm? Similarly, the ovum's descent inside the fallopian tube is crisis and ultimately union. This ovum excursion was preceded by a splitting apart of egg from its sisterhood of cells inside the mother, in particular her ovarian sac; and it culminates in the uniting with sperm at conception.

Notice also that all these former states were homes; they were comfortable circumstances that needed to end, or come down cataclysmically. And the necessary changes came about through the most extreme kind of "going out of one's comfort zone."

However all resulted in greater growth, greater beingness. Keep that in mind as we continue. Life in general is a series of crises, of painful splittings apart — one leaves one's father's body; one's mother's ovarian sac; one's womb; ones' childhood; one's school friends; one's family; one's college mates; various love partners as one grows through that process of learning through love; and eventually one after the other of one's friends and family members, in ones' advancing life, perhaps one's spouse, as they pass on before you do. Each is a crisis and is painful. Each previous state was a sort of home. Each needed to end, to come down "cataclysmically," in order to move to a larger home, to be able to realize a greater belong-ingness.

So, also, we humans now. We are in the midst of a transition to a greater embrace by the Universe. Current times are apocalyptic and are bringing down our familiar ways of life. Our attachments to things and people are threatened or in disarray. We are losing our home, and we can only wait and prepare ourselves. But like the birth into life, a belongingness of a different nature awaits us, one in which we are on a different footing with the Universe that is birthing us.

Let us look a little deeper into that transition, that liminal in-between time. What can we learn about it that might be helpful, even encouraging, during our trying times?

# 31

# Transition, Belongingness, and Spherical Experience:

## The Gods Are Crazy and Spheres Unify Dimensions; Analysis Versus Experience, Unity Versus Reunion, Integration Versus Being hOMe; and "The Sounds of Silence"

*Yes, the "Gods" Are Crazy. But Not to Worry, for "Many Others Have Taken This Journey Before You"*

*"You can't cross the sea merely by standing and staring at the water." — Rabindranath Tagore*

# Transition

## Liminality and Leaving One's Comfort Zone, My Dream

Going out of one's comfort zone reminds me of a dream I had a long long time ago, which is related to this idea of going between dimensions, going through a tunnel, or tube, and rebirthing, or birthing, into greater consciousness. It provides perspective and guidance for us during these times of splitting apart, of crisis, where we are standing at the gate to a new beingness, which is a difficult and scary prospect.

In my dream I was on a higher plane, above the Earth. It was a gigantic field, flat and with very little vegetation on it, and I could see, off in the distance, a few structures, which were reminiscent of ancient Greek architecture.

## Celestial Adventure and "The Sounds of Silence"

The plane had a celestial quality to it, but I subsequently found out it was flawed. I went to the structures with enthusiasm as to the wise beings who might be there. Upon arriving, sure enough, there were folks who were like ancient Greek intellectuals or philosophers. The setting had Hellenic features — columns, stone benches, wide stone steps, pillars, and so on. I approached a few of the men there, who were sitting on or hanging out around the steps and stone benches, and observed their interaction.

It was as though these "wise" men were mentally checked out, not quite "all there," from my perspective. One in particular, I looked in his eyes and they were not focused; he was clearly "out of it." More obviously, he looked emotionless and detached. These venerated paragons also seemed not to be really hearing each other. Another man with beard and a Greek-like white gown was standing and expressing himself, and I came to see he was as if pontificating. Yet, he was not quite clear in what he was saying and the others were not quite hearing him; nor he, they.

These men all had a high status, clearly, and they conversed with authority. I was disillusioned, immensely so. And this was a dream that happened a long time ago. This was about fifteen years before my time in a doctoral program at a renowned major university, when I witnessed an exact parallel to this and had a similar reaction.

However, in the dream I removed myself from the "civilized" area where the men were and went back to the area I had come from, in the middle of that scruffy field, on that plane high above the Earth. I could look over and still see the structures where the respected ones were, off in the distance.

Now, in the middle of this field was a hole, about the size of a typical manhole. It was the end, the opening, of a narrow tube which connected that plane in the sky to the lower plane of Earth. I knew that in order to get to Earth I would have to let myself drop through that tube. I was anxious, afraid I might get trapped on the way, be stuck there and unable to get out.

## "Many Others Have Taken This Journey Before You"

At that point, someone appeared who was helpful and encouraging to me. Smiling and affable, he explained that I was not to worry as, "Many others have taken this journey before you." And they all made it through and were just fine. With his encouragement in mind, I let myself drop. It is only now, by the way, about forty years later, that I realize the tube was not about being born, going through a birth tunnel. It was *exactly* the way I would imagine dropping down through a fallopian tube.

At any rate, I made the descent; I kept falling. I was in fetal position, and I could feel the sides of the tube as I went. It was that close. At one point the passage seemed to be getting smaller, and I was afraid I was going to get stuck. My anxiety began to spike.

The next thing I remember was being with a group of people on Earth. Somehow I went from the tube and the distress about getting stuck, to being in the group without any events in between describing a transition from one to the other, or any memory of what happened. This had all the earmarks of the kind of forgetting we do of the traumatic elements of our entry into life. Which is something we all do, and which is why so few of us remember our births and infancy, let alone conception and womb events.

## Belongingness, Becoming One

Being in the group I was engaged in on Earth was enjoyable. I was surrounded by friends who I was actively interacting and conversing with, like we were having an ebullient and friendly philosophical discussion, in appreciation of each other. It would be similar to a gathering of student friends sitting and standing around a table at a pub. I was sitting and was one of the figures in the center of the activity.

It occurs to me now, recollecting it, that the intellectual discussion, with friends in the pub setting, was a mirror image of the conversation being had by the ancients, the academic-types back up on the plane. Both groups were having a philosophical exchange, but they were starkly contrasting in terms of the mood and level of actual mental intercourse that was going on: The academic types failed to hear anything but the echoes of their own words and were morose, kind of numb, or else puffed up on themselves. The discussion on Earth was earnest, affable, and the participants engaged with each other in an intense and penetrating way, fully hearing, fully interested … enthusiastic, light-hearted, but intent on understanding rather than merely being heard.

I realized at the time, and now again, how the dream was saying one cannot get to wisdom through mere book learning but one had to "descend" into worldly experience. It has meanings on so many levels. It seemed to be saying that I had decided to come to Earth, just prior to my current existence, so as to learn and teach in a way more "grounded" than others, or myself previously.

I realize, now, that the dream was also saying I had to switch my style of writing away from the pedantic and academic, which indeed it had been previous to the dream, to something more convivial and light-hearted, and accessible for folks in general, not just scholars. That is a message I did not learn until the Universe gave me a house fire in 1999, which took away all my books and my ponderous notecards. So I had to learn to say it in my way, and from my heart and joy, not my head and notes. It wasn't till 2008, after another crisis in which we lost that house to foreclosure, that I truly got the message and allowed myself to be free.

The dream also said that I needed, at that time, to go into primal therapy in order to continue on the path of wisdom; and that college and university study, which I had been passionately involved in, was limited. That such learning was like the blind leading the blind. Indeed the dream came to me in my early twenties, prior to my beginning primal therapy at the age of twenty-five and after having left my college studies at the age of twenty-two. Actually, the dream might have come to me at the end of those studies, in the spring of 1972, my final semester, when I was contemplating going through primal therapy.

The field-like place I had to traverse, in both directions — both to and away from that "academia" — is reminiscent of that wasteland or borderland of society, the liminal, we all need to cross to attain greater authenticity ... as I mentioned in the chapter, earlier, on identity and the sea of potentiality. The dream was saying that the roles of society no longer suffice; but one must take the scary route of authenticity to oneself and must discover, through experience, one's path, one's identity, one's duty or mission, and one's Divine role or atmidharma.

## The Gods Must Be Crazy. No, They Really *Are*

The dream was relating not just that the "gods" must be crazy but they *are* crazy. By that I mean that the leaders and authorities everywhere about in this Kali Yuga — from academics to politicians to corporate leaders — are full of themselves, blind, and do not know what they are talking about. And that in any case, they echo "in the sounds of silence," with no one listening, no one really hearing. The dream experience was telling me that my Jungian route of growth, represented by these ancient Greek archetypes, was ultimately futile and fruitless, also. It showed that those further along on it — those Jungian academics and professionals — had only become steeped in an increasingly deeper muck of cognitive obfuscation and sophistry. Something which led only to greater numbness and self-delusion, not greater wisdom.

And right now the dream says to me that the portal between dimensions, to a better beingness, is tube-like, tunnel-like and that it does not necessarily go up but might go down. That it is scary, as well, but that it is ultimately not only necessary but eminently doable and ultimately successful. That many others do it and have done it and there is nothing to be concerned about.

Finally, that the path we all need to take at this time in history is an experiential one of opening ourselves to risks, going outside of our comfort zone, taking up a spiritual quest and an experiential journey, not a cognitive one; and that the answers will not be found through intellect alone. The dream was a message to us that the traditional smarty pants way (lol), with its academic, pompous, know-it-all delusion, is what, indeed, has led us to this dark pass. For it is a consciousness that is separate from real feeling, real compassion and fellow feelings, real empathy, and real unity — which are the essence of what we need more than anything else right now.

## Let Oneself Drop in Order to Rise

Summing up, I think these messages from this dream are not only messages for me at that time of my life, but are, right now, wise proclamations and advice for all of us as we find ourselves at this portal to the greater Universe. I believe it is of immense importance to realize that this quantum change being required of us has nothing to do with the overweening ego and its rationalizations for hubris masquerading as rationality. As we see again and again in previous chapters, the change required of us is a change in our attitude toward Experience. It is an embracing of feeling, emotion, and not a splitting off from them. For they are our link to Nature and the acknowledged life on our Earth — the planetmates — as well as the unacknowl-edged life around us — the living, though seemingly inanimate, Universe.

Let's put it this way. Do not expect to see college courses or programs on this shift. Do not look for self-help books specifying the eight great and essential steps to quantum consciousness or the like. Do not think anyone can do it for you; do not pay any societal professional for it, thinking it can be bought. Do not think you can think your way into it or decide it, either. You cannot do that anymore than Siddhartha could, and as Hesse said through him, one needs to "seek the depths." One needs to experience life, learn from it, and gain wisdom, not merely more and more information or technological knowledge. You cannot strive toward it. You can only surrender to it. The more you seek to achieve skills for control of your world and yourself and the more you work to "master" your self and your emotions, the further away you are. One needs to "drop down," to let oneself fall "back to Earth," to Nature.

Not to worry, there are many others who have done it before you.

And when one does, when one allows oneself to "fall apart," to put one's faith in what the Universe and the Divine will have of one and will heal and make of one, one finds there was never anything to fear, and that all the mental machinations of ego and mastery were built on a fear that one could not trust anything outside oneself. When one has the experience that the Universe truly holds one up and is on one's side — however one gets that — one feels a palpable nobility, in connection with It All. More importantly, for the first time, one has a profound feeling of belongingness in the Universe, and in Nature, and with the community of souls on Earth among humans, as well as among planetmates, and even among the No-Form personalities constituting the Universe. More on that last one, next chapter.

# Spheres Unify Dimensions

Which brings us back round again to the message of unity, contact, and meeting coming out of the crop circles. We also might be seeing, represented by these crop circles, the coming together of dimensions, as for example, the Form and the No-Form, and/or humans and the rest of the Universe. Remember, these crop mandalas are gateways and portals as well as symbols of integration and harmony.

## Circles Integrate Parts

Jung emphasized the integration of polarities in the harmonizing of up-down, left-right aspects of these symbols, the mandalas, but he missed an obvious, and profound, insight on them. For he saw them two dimensionally, represented on a flat surface. Thinking two dimensionally, as well, he saw them as integrations of aspects of the person, such as feeling and thinking, spirit and body, intuitive and rational, right-brain and left-brain, and all the rest. This is all well and good if one wishes to see it as a psychologist, like Jung, does.

But an individual is also at odds with its group, its environment, its culture, its place in space, and its situation in time. Theodore Roszak (1992) addressed part of this when he did a thorough review of psychology's evolution from its beginnings to its present state — one in which we do not have an idea of the psyche that includes the world, and we suffer the consequences of that in environmental destruction, for one thing, he says. He points out that psychology has focused on the individual as a separate entity and on that entity's inner workings. In his book, which makes a case for an *ecopsychology*, he notes that the most done has been to see humans in their context of society, family, and groups.

Yet, he writes, psychology has not gotten beyond assuming a person who is primarily urbane, modern, and divorced from wilderness and Nature. What he professes changing is predominantly the same as I do in this book. He also proposes getting the inspiration for this new understanding from the same place I do, which is our primal origins — humans who still live or have lived in Nature. And the kind of psychology he proposes has all the features of the one I am proposing in this book — which basically is one where we see ourselves in the context of the world of Nature. Of course, I have done more on those lines — of presenting a comprehensive paradigm of ecopsychology, with humans in their context of all life on this planet — and quite specifically, in my *Planetmates* (2014b) and *Prodigal Human* (2016a).

My point is that Jung's ideas coincide with all other psychologists up till this time in seeing the individual as a solitary and separate unit — one who is much like a machine that can be worked on … however much Jung might have a "ghost" in the machine he proposed. This machine model of the human is consistent with the medical model, from which modern psychiatry and psychology have sprung. And that medical model grew out of a Newtonian-Cartesian model that saw the Universe as separate "things" in interaction.

Psychologists see humans two-dimensionally, therefore, as left-right, up-down, conscious-unconscious, higher-lower, and so on. Therefore remedies are thought of in terms of *balance* of things already existing, which are relatively static … and "thing-like" in being separate and categorizable. Whereas an ecopsychologist, such as myself, views the individual not so much in terms of how its parts are working together on its insides so much as how it is integrated and interacts within the vast context within which that person exists, extending out from that person in all directions, three-dimensionally.

With these things in mind, and with forgiveness for Jung, considering the historical context in which he arose and the intellectual context within which he thought and wrote, it is understandable that what Jung failed to see was the three-dimensional characteristic of the mandalas he wrote about. For when one thinks of mandalas as being cross sections of spheres — as individuals might be considered cross sections of worlds, or at least, of contexts — inside our mind is opened a portal to thinking other dimensionally. We stand upon a doorstep to thinking fifth dimensionally, to seeing an integration beyond the individual, and in which the boundaries of individuality and of time and of space all disappear. Thinking of mandalas as spheres, we integrate, not just with oneself and one's "parts" within but with all else outside of ourselves, with Other.

## A Sphere Is a Merging of Circles

I am reminded of an analogy regarding circles and spheres and human relationships. It is said that in a traditional love partnership there has been a coming together of opposites, or a merging of personalities that complete each other by bringing into each what the other lacks. This can be likened to two halves of a circle coming together to make a complete circle. By contrast, in a contemporary or postmodern relationship — post–feminism awakening — where there is a coming together of equals ... both of whom are whole human beings, in and of themselves, and not requiring someone to complete them ... it is like a coming together of two circles to create a sphere.

Similarly, in the two-dimensional thinking on mandalas as representing wholeness, we have the integration of the "halves" of the personality coming together. This is symbolized by a circular mandala. But thinking spherically, it becomes an integration of self and other beings, other dimensions, other selves in other times, other worlds. And not just two circles, but multiple, indeed, infinite circles. Consider that a sphere can be cross-sectioned into an infinite number of circles, depending upon where one makes the cut.

You can see a sphere as a coming together of two dimensions or *all* dimensions. It is not just a bringing together of two worlds, like a gate, a door, a portal, or a wormhole. Hypothetically it is the bringing together of *all* worlds — all "circles" ... or wholes ... in existence.

For connections between entities in a circular world, think phone-to-phone connections. For that in a spherical world, think Facebook, think Twitter.

For circular realities, think maps, drawings, pictures, paintings, diagrams, words. For spherical realities think holograms, virtual reality, music, and telepathy.

## Spheres Are Whole, Experiential, Not Cross-Sectional, Analytical

With this in mind, it is no wonder that paths that see things circular-like — they see mandalas as circles, for example, as in the Jungian way, the ladder-style Wilberian efforts, and many Eastern-style meditative paths — are so cognitive and so futile. They are ultimately so downright Sisyphean — mimicking the kind of positive thinking of pushing boulders endlessly to the top of a hill only to watch them roll down again. For circles are two-dimensional, cognitive, thought-based, black-and-white, nothingness in contrast with thingness, and dual.

Meanwhile experiential routes are the spherical type: They are multi-dimensional; they integrate person and Other, not merely opposing aspects of self. They are felt, colorful, humorous not ponderous, trickster-like not pompous, and light-hearted not serious. They cosmically giggle at the vain and futile efforts of circular folks trying to empty their minds or impress some kinda big guy in the sky, serious man speaking to the group, or colorless fella behind the podium. They are No-Thing as opposed to nothingness, crooked and irregular not linear and plodding. They are expanding in growth outward in all directions at once, with the past incorporated into one's being for a foundation of a greater wisdom; and they are not about trying to cower in some haven of Nowness, sans a painful past and feared future. Neither are they step-wise in a singular direction, leaning toward goals always in front of one, with the past left behind forever, forgotten, useless as a source of wisdom.

Spheres are whole, experiential routes, in which one is one's fully embodied self, with all senses open to the outer, and with full access to the inner, as well. They are about engaging reality by moving in it not merely analyzing it from a mute and timid place. Yes, these experiential approaches are full and whole, like a sphere. They are not analytical and forever testing the waters; not timid, taking a cross-section of reality to try to understand it. Rather these spherical approaches seek to understand by jumping in, both feet first and fully immersed. Concerning knowledge they are the hermeneutical and heuristic approaches described in a previous chapter.

Furthermore and thinking spherically, the circular mandala, gateway, portal becomes a three-dimensional transition space bringing worlds together. This is where these mandala gateways begin to resemble spherical vehicles, transportation devices bringing together self and Other, self and all other worlds. Think of the sphere that transported Jodie Foster to another world and to contact with other beingness in the movie adaptation, *Contact*, of Carl Sagan's novel of the same name. Thinking spherically these mandalas — crop circles and otherwise — represent far more than integration of sides of anything. They construct entire worlds where all elements inside as well as outside are integrated. So circles imply communication ... of symbolic information; spheres imply movement ... of persons between worlds.

Think of the mandala in three dimensionality as like a space elevator; a Doctor Who's phone booth time-and-space straddling machine, except spherical; as well as any UFO or space ship. For all we know the "flying saucers," the "spaceships" from other worlds, might be physical manifestations or physically conceived mental constructs — that is, human biologically constituted realities — of mandalic spheres that are portal-like vehicles between worlds. They might be flickering and peripatetically moving space elevators.

# Pyramids Versus Spheres ... Dominance Versus Egalitarian

Compare, also, the sphere with the pyramid. You will notice, for one

thing, that circular mandalas tend to have triangles within them. The triangles are integrated within the mandala, which is represented by the circular elements containing them. Yes, that is true, but they are triangles nonetheless. Think, for example, the Jewish Star of David; the symbol on the dollar bill, which is a pyramid within a circle; the satanic pentagram; the Catholic pentacle; da Vinci's Vitruvian Man; and others. Why would triangles and circles so often be seen together, however integrated the symbol is claiming them to be? It is because circular understandings (notice the inherent futility that bespeaks), cross-sectional ones, analytical ones, represent a duality needing integrating. They imply a higher and lower, so necessarily give rise to hierarchies, thus to pyramids.

In pyramids, there is hierarchy manifest. There is an all-seeing

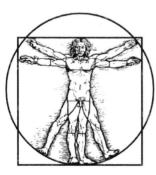

eye above, and there are levels of reality related to levels of importance from the top down. It is our traditional world of the last five to ten millennia since the agrarian revolution. It is the way we view ourselves in the world of Nature, with us at the top of the "food chain." It is the patriarchal world of dominance-submission, leader and follower, boss and slave, father and family, king and pawn. Pyramids involve lines of connection and influence between points — one that is above and one below. And the pyramid is expressed most forcefully in ancient Egypt which had, indeed, such an extreme social stratification.

When you think of it, it is clear that the insignia on the dollar bill is telling us that we are an oligarchy, with those with wealth at the top, like in ancient Egyptian society, and all the rest below and controlled by the all-seeing eye, the elite. And the circle surrounding the triangle? Well, that is merely the aspirations and affirmation of the elite that such a hierarchy is some kind of whole and integrated unit and reflects some kind of "natural order" of things. Which is simply another expression of the divine right of kings, and the nobility of old claiming their elite status and overweening power to be an aspect of some kind of Divine order … meant to be, don't you know?.

The circle surrounding the pyramid is both a christening of one's elitism as sacred and Divinely ordained, as well as a barrier, or a moat surrounding, to deter any who would come from the outside to disrupt this obscenely unjust unity. In a crude sense, this circle enclosing its pyramids implies that such an unjust hierarchical arrangement would necessarily come under assault, regardless one's claims to Divine ordination. So the circle is the military and the police forces of the society, which are embedded in place to protect those of the all-seeing eye, the elite, from the forces necessarily arising both outside as well as within it, within that society.

Whereas the idea of a sphere is a democratic one, where anyone can be a point of influence within it, with power equal to that of any other point, emanating out wave-like to whatever is in proximity to it. The connections are not line-like, but wave-like, they connect not just two, but each and every one potentially with each and every other.

For pyramid, think traditional king- or pharaoh-ruled societies; traditional families; any modern employer-employee relationship, whether corporate-controlled or individually-directed; or any organizational structure, whether governmental or civil. Think humans with "dominion" over planetmates. Think the modern oligarchical form that has superseded democracy in modern societies and nations.

For sphere, think democracy, think leaderless tribe, think Occupy movements, think Gezi Park, think egalitarian gatherer-hunter societies, think hippies, think friends, think transcending species-centrism for a vision of humans and planetmates as equal ... think Eden.

For lines of communication that are pyramid-like, think newspapers, major media, and communications and speeches to audiences and to masses of people such as presidential addresses. For spherical lines of communication, think Internet, think Twitter, think thoughts in one's mind, think The Cloud.

# Unity Versus Reunion ... Integration Versus hOMe

Keep in mind also that mandalas represent an integration of conscious and unconscious selves, as well as all the polarities in our personalities. Jung stressed that aspect of it.

However, in thinking three-dimensionally, as spherical mandalas, consider what that means in terms of the unconscious beyond the personal unconscious, that of what Jung called the collective unconscious and what I am calling Divinity, Experience, and Consciousness ... and matter, for that matter. For, as I have been saying, the unconscious is *all* that we are denying, which includes our Divinity, along with the life and consciousness of beings outside of us — including planetmates, No-Forms, and any aliens that exist.

So the unity implied spherically is not merely the creation of the harmonious person, but the harmonious world — including and embracing self and Other. Not only the peaceful person, or the person at peace with her or himself, but the peaceful world, the peaceful Universe, and the harmonious ecosphere, with all beings having a place and an importance. It is in spherical engagement with life where one seeks not merely enlightenment or advance for oneself but engages in activism as a higher calling to bring such liberation and peace to the world as well. Circular is Buddha-like, sitting lotus-like, thus pyramid-like, both unmoving and unmoved, with higher controlling lower, mind controlling those "nasty" instincts.

Spherical liberation, on the other hand, is Bodhisattva-like. Not controlling one's body, rather letting oneself ever weep, like Kwan Yin, at the suffering of the world and the deluded choices of normal humans. It is participating, like Mother Theresa, Shirdi Sai Baba, Mahatma Gandhi, and Sathya Sai Baba, in the sufferings and destitution and squalor of the masses, in order to lift them up, or at least to shine a light of example to mark their way.

Spherical is not just ego or self-integration, or even individual enlightenment. It is not just self-unity. It is unity with the Universe, hence re-union. For we are and always have been immersed in Universe and Nature and are part of It and Divinity, but we have simply not thought of ourselves that way. Preferring instead, we have, to stand above everything that we deem to be not us, to lay it out like a project, two dimensionally, on a table, or like papers on a desk to work on it.

I am reminded of my dream where they negotiated over tables, spreading things out on it, symbolic items, separate from themselves … things that were split apart, dissected not whole, not in context … that can thus be analyzed, manipulated, controlled, used … not engaged with. In this way controlling and fashioning the things of the Other, the world, we wish to make it something other than what it is by nature, so it can be used by us. Thus we usurp the roles of the Kingly Fatherly and Creator gods, seeking to rule over everything which we needed to separate from and take ourselves outside of — separating from Nature — in order to do so.

So the unity with the Universe implied by the spherical mandala is reunion. It is coming hOMe. It is not some kind of creation of peace within ourselves or even that between individuals or nations on Earth but much more than that. It is a realization that we *are* hOMe, always have been, that we are no longer separate, no longer prodigal, and that in terms of the Universe, we not only connect with it, we *belong* in it. It is the difference between having an achievement and gaining something, versus realizing one already had it and that going after it was a diversion from knowing that. It is the difference between struggling up, ladder-like, versus surrendering and falling back, throwing oneself into the arms of the Universe, to discover that one will always be caught and lifted up. It is the difference between joining together with others versus realizing one lives at home, always has, and that the beings one sees around oneself are not merely friendly, they are family. And one belongs with them.

Essentially, our actual evolution of consciousness or Experience is one of advance beginning from our dim awareness in the cultural matrix, being a cog in the machine, being an element in a hierarchy, symbolized by a triangle. We grow to a state of greater psychological wholeness, having achieved an integration of self ... not necessarily as yet an authenticity, which requires an Other ... a harmonization of one's "parts," which is symbolized by a circle, a mandala. Eventually, and finally, we return hOMe to immersion in the All That Is, to reconciliation with Other ... with all beings on Earth and otherwise as well as with Nature and Divinity as larger entities of awareness ... and to authenticity, meaning a harmony with All and environment, with no separation, thus no dissembling, and connected to Everything — all of which is symbolized by a sphere. Triangle → Circle → Sphere. And to get from Circle to Sphere, one needs to go through a "gate," a splitting apart, a "breakdown" in which one loses temporarily all that one had "acquired" as circle. For this is followed by a greater integration with All, not just one's singular, circular self — one's ego.

Put all this together, integration as reunion; and interrelationship as transition, implying vehicle, implying a change of state, a movement from one place to another, not merely a communication between states; and you have what I have been predicting in several of my works — in particular *Planetmates* (2014b) and *Funny God* (2015) — as a "coming together of heaven and Earth." Or, as *Planetmates* phrases it, "Something wonderful is going to happen."

What might be this "something wonderful"? What might be this coming together of heaven and earth? Well, is that not what I have been trying to show throughout this book? For example, what do we think the "path of ecstasy" is if not a going beyond our anthropocentric and egocentric biases in attempting a stance outside or our biological determinedness? What do you think I am alluding to in telling you there are messages, from Divinity, from God, that are manifest in Nature and the Universe, if not that it is our way of integrating our Form realities with our No-Form, or Divine, visions and overstandings?

I will say more on that last part in a bit, but let us take a look at a related phenomenon to the mandalas of crop circles — that of UFOs.

# 32

# "Something Wonderful" Is Already Happening:

Reunion with The Universe — UFOs and the Coming Together of Heaven and Earth, Jacob's Ladder, Contact Between Form and No-Form … a "Family" Reunion

*"… we are at the doorway to a transition of immense importance — a shift as epochal as for an individual it is in being born from the womb, in dying and going from Form into No-Form, or coming into Form out of No-Form around the time of conception."*

## UFOs

Might we also, in observing UFOs, be seeing another phenomenon where No-Form or unconscious or implicate order stuff is making its way past that barrier, that gate — remember the mandalas again, as gate or door — which separates it from our Form Realities?

## Jung and "Flying Saucers"

Let me back up a second. There is a famous explanation of UFOs by Jung (1978), in which he stated that UFOs were a representation of our modern need for wholeness. In *Flying Saucers: A Modern Myth of Things Seen in the Skies*, Jung attributes this perception of glowing circular images to a psychic need for spiritual and emotional wholeness, which he claimed was particularly lacking in modern times. In this way, his interpretation of UFOs overlaps with mine regarding crop circles. Which is, as I said, that crop circles, like the glowing circular "saucers" — according to Jung at least — are psychic phenomena expressing themselves physically, and symbolically, which represent an urgent need for spiritual re-union and psychic-emotional integration. And then I added, as well they are manifestations of our need for reintegration with the Universe and represent that we stand at a portal to such.

It is interesting that Jung never, in that book, clearly states whether he thinks UFOs are "real" or hallucinated, and, considering the inconclusiveness of our understanding of these sightings, one can see why. But there may be another reason.

As pointed out earlier, Jung's perception of reality was very much in line with the premise of this book: That is to say, he believed that psychic reality — what I call Experience and many call Consciousness — is the fundamental reality. Thus, it may be that Jung could not help but foresee the implications of that viewpoint, as I will set forth here: That is, that UFOs might actually be a "physical" manifestation — a collective perceptual reality — of that collective psychic need.

## John E. Mack and "Alien Abductions"

More recent understandings of the phenomenon of UFOs also bring us to conclusions such as these. Psychiatrist and UFO abduction researcher, John E. Mack — deceased, 2004 — was insistent about the radically new view of reality that comes out of our encounter with

UFO abduction phenomena. In his work with treating the trauma caused in abductees by such "alien abductors," he discovered consistent affronts to our common-sense views of reality.

A little background on John E. Mack is called for. He was an M.D.; he taught and was a tenured professor at Harvard; he was a Pulitzer-Prize winning biographer; and he was a graduate of Stanislav Grof's program — the Grof Transpersonal Training program — which I and my wife, Mary Lynn, also attended, for training holotropic breathwork facilitators. In his private practice, Mack took individuals who had thought themselves to have experienced an alien abduction into a nonordinary state of consciousness for the purpose of trying to retrieve and reconcile with what had happened to them. For these folks are characteristically, and understandably, rather shook up, troubled by their experiences.

The movie, *Intruders* (1992), which he worked on, portrayed some of the characters from his work. Another one, *Touched* (2003) is a documentary featuring Doctor Mack and is about his work. He worked on another, *Crossovers from Another Dimension* (2005), which is a TV movie about the crop circle phenomenon; and there is currently a documentary being produced on him and his life, titled, *Dr. John Mack: A True Story*.

Now keep that incredibly varied and substantive *curriculum vita* for Mack in mind as you read what he has to say on this phenomenon. He writes,

> One man, for example, says, "When we witness their coming it is like scrim [a piece of fabric used in a theater to create the illusion of a solid wall or backdrop], or a movie screen. When they arrive you are looking at ordinary reality as a movie screen in the optic nerve. When they come it is like someone shines a bright light behind the movie screen and obliterates the scene. What we perceive as the movie screen, what we call reality, they burn through, proving it's only a construct, a version of reality."[1]

That strikes me as a pretty good visual of what I am asking of my readers in this book: Through the words in this book I am attempting to shine the light behind the "scrim" — which would be what I am calling the various constituted realities we create for ourselves in coming into Form. I am hoping to stimulate a vision of something like what Mack describes, unveiling itself at the point when the scrim, or all the constituted realities imprisoning our perception, are seen to be relative and ultimately false. Rub a little philosophical Windex on the doors of perception. Turn on the lamp in the place ec-static, out of Form. Sing the body ecstatic, and there will simply no longer be one. No longer a Form-ly or biological screen; no longer a scrim in the away.

I know it is not easy to do that, to see outside the constructs we create for the purpose of our game here. Still, just knowing it can be done allows one so much more, in terms of vision, awareness, and insight, than if we concede the field to our anthropocentric prejudices, not to mention *collude* with such biases, as is usually the case.

Let us look a little further into this to see what is revealed. Sara Terry (1992) is a journalist who spent time with Mack and wrote insightfully and provocatively — and rather poetically I might add — about what she gleaned from this Harvard professor cum holotropic breathwork facilitator.

Regarding Mack's findings and viewpoint, Terry explains,

*Mack argues that abductees' reports point ... to a world that exists not somewhere out there in the physical universe, but in an entirely different dimension.*

*"In the experience of the abductees," he says, "the aliens seem to come from another dimension. They seem to break through our sense of the reality of this space-time physicalist world, to come from some other place. Abductees will describe the sense of space and time collapsing, or of coexistent multiple time dimensions.*[2]

Need I remind of what we have been looking at in terms of No-Forms and the No-Form State? Terry continues,

*"They have the feeling that they have been introduced to another universe which is just as real as this one, but which is other-dimensional," he says. "It's as if it's a dimension that seems to enter our physical world but is not necessarily of our physical world."*[3]

Hmmm.... Seems to "enter our physical world but is not *of* [it]." Is this not a familiar refrain in this work? We have Divinity and No-

Form beings entering our physical world in the existence of matter itself. And possibly planetmates as being somewhat more No-Form — being like the tip of a No-Form beingness operating in our Form Reality.

Bring to mind what I said in Part One about how a being, who we are only partly or minimally able to perceive within the limited ranges of our senses, might be perceived by us. And remember that metaphor of the many blind wise men who tried to discern what was the elephant they were touching and concluded, depending upon where they touched it, that it was a rope, a tree branch, a pillar, a hand fan, a pipe, and so on.

Let me refresh your memory. In Part One, I wrote, "Would we perceive their existence as human changes in pressure, sound, touch, smell, sight, taste? As atmospheric or environmental "ambiance" changes? As solar activity or astronomical phenomena? As change in mood state, or thought pattern? Or hypothalamic or metabolic or heart or respiratory rate change? As *nuemenon*, "aura," Words of God, Music of the Spheres?... Indeed, as leprechauns, ghosts, or elves? Or perhaps as forcible elements in dreams? Inspirational thought or feeling? Poltergeists, angels, "allies," aliens, psychic phenomena?"

At any rate, it seems we are bucking up against another reflection of that dilemma of attempting to conceive Reality with limited abilities of apprehension. While finding that realities that we do not and cannot understand, because they are only partially overlapping into our "field of vision," show up nevertheless. In this work, have I not been saying that such realities show up in major and important ways in our reality — as matter, as planetmates, as rivers, stars, and galaxies, for example — and that we are only partially understanding them for we are only perceiving aspects of them, not them in their entirety?

Anyway, we seem to hear this refrain chorused again by Mack. Well, let us see. Terry writes on, concerning Mack,

*Although he admits that such possibilities have yet to be proven by the physical sciences, Mack laments what he calls "the unwillingness of the official intellectual community to be open-minded about a reality that doesn't fit their world view." As he sees it, the abduction phenomenon could ultimately present mankind with a "fourth blow" to its collective ego. The first, he says, was the Copernican blow, which proved that man and Earth were not the center of the universe; the second blow was administered by Darwin, whose findings on evolution proved that man did not spring from "some higher level of spiritual biology"; and the third blow was delivered by Freud, whose explorations of the unconscious revealed that man's conscious mind was not all that was in control of his life....[4]*

Once again I am compelled to interrupt! Another blow? To what? To "its collective ego." What is that collective ego except the anthropocentrism, the species-centrism, wrought of our biologically constituted realities whose drum I have been beating from the beginning here. And what does this not imply except that we may be on the verge of going "outside of" it, becoming ec-static once again … venturing outside of our comfortable illusions.

# Reunion with The Universe

Okay, okay. You want to hear what else he had to say before I ramble on. *chuckle* Got it. Terry writes,

*...Mack sees a more transformational element to the abductions: an attempt to alert humans to the need for change in their lives.*

*Abductees frequently report that during their time on alien spacecraft, they are shown powerful visual images of environmental destruction on Earth. Many return with a passionate commitment to protect the planet. Mack interprets the warnings, and the increased awareness among individual abductees, as an attempt to reconnect humans with a heightened sense of spirituality.[5]*

Sorry, I simply must. "An attempt to reconnect humans … with spirituality"? Was I not just talking about the mandalas being related to this? And that both of them — UFOs and crop circles — seem to be calling for an integration of the dualities which have plagued humankind and led to our dire state, characterized by such a one, where we have for so longed denied consciousness to the physical world, to Nature, that we are on the verge of destroying it, and us, our physical bodies, along with it?

Continuing, now, about that spiritual reconnection being required of us now,

*It's a quest, he says, best summed up by the poet Rainer Maia Rilke, who wrote:*

*"That is at bottom the only courage that is demanded of us: to have courage for the most strange, the most singular and the most inexplicable that we may encounter. That mankind has in this sense been cowardly has done life endless harm; the experiences that are called "visions," the whole so-called "spirit world," death and all those things that are so closely akin to us, have by daily parrying been so crowded out of life that the senses by which we could have grasped them are atrophied. To say nothing of God."*

*Other civilizations, including Eastern and native cultures, have been far more fluent than the West in communing with experiences that defy understanding in terms of physical reality, says Mack. He argues that the Western world of the past few hundred years may have reached a dead end of sorts — and that the abductee experience may be part of a move away from the strict confines of materialism.*

*"It may be that we're on the brink of some kind of major opening to our proper place in the universe," muses Mack. "I think, in this society, we're involved in a major epochal shift. I don't know what the purpose of all this is, but it certainly is some kind of profound connecting of us beyond ourselves."*[6]

I need comment no more on her words. For they are clearly another voice that harmonizes with the chorus of voices I have been singing all through these chapters.

## Coming Together of Heaven and Earth....

What I will say, however, relates to a provocative possibility arising from Mack's considerations: Is it possible that in all these ways, UFOs, alien abductions, crop circles, and many many more — some of which I touch on in my other works — we are receiving an invitation to a "family" reunion? Are we, us prodigal humans, mired in physicality to such an extent we can barely lift our vision above the muck, receiving a helping hand to raise us out of it? Are we on the verge of a reunion with the Universe?

In other places I have said as much. In *Planetmates* (2014b) I mentioned a coming together of planetmate and human beingness as representing a coming together of heaven and earth, whereupon "Something wonderful is going to happen." In *Funny God* (2015), I described a meeting of Form and No-Form Realities and of Form and No-Form beings along the lines of a metaphorical Jacob's Ladder, with a going to and fro between heaven and earth, between No-Form and Form realities, of angels and humans. These were metaphorically angels; however literally I called them No-Form personalities or "No-Forms." I described interactions between Form and No-Form personalities, communications between them, and I laid out some of the messages we are receiving from them about ourselves, about them, about the Universe beyond them, and about the meaning and purpose of it all, as revealed by them.

## "The Family"

Here, I will reveal — for like primate-like planetmates I'd sooner jump and risk falling than not enjoy the freedom and fun of it *chuckle* — that, through another, I had ongoing contact with some personalities of that sort, over the course of about six months and happening about two years ago.

The No-Form personalities who communicated to me were mostly folks I had actually known in physical form in life, who had passed on. Except for three. Of the three I did not know, in Form, one was my wife's daughter, who had died decades before I'd even met my wife. The other was the mother of my best friend, someone I'd never met though I knew about, who had been an activist in the Civil Rights Movement, in America in the Sixties, and had messages for me and my friend. And the third was a holy man who died a hundred years ago. Interestingly, the holy man was not someone I in particular revered and for the most part I knew of him second-handedly. So you can scratch that explanation, which is that I somehow drew him to me or conjured him out of some desire of mine.

There were, altogether, ten No-Form Personalities who relayed information to me, including and especially the holy man. There were another five, who I had known when they were alive, who were either mentioned by these beings or simply showed up to my friend, with no apparent message to me, exactly. To me their appearance to my friend — who had never heard of let alone known them previously — and my friend's descriptions of them and some of the things they thought or felt was just more confirmation of the validity of my friend's experiences. She even got the sound just right of the way one friend of mine laughed. She was so right about so many things that she could not possibly have known that it constantly had my mind blown.

A total of fifteen No-Forms came to her, that I know of. There may have been more who my friend interacted with, and I did not receive all the information that the ones I knew about wanted me to have or tried to give me. For these interactions, for my friend, were difficult, ongoing, and rather overwhelming. She had a great deal of time with these beings. They interacted with her as friends, actually the word she used was "family," for them. Yet she complained about the fact that she could not "close the door" on them, and they wanted more interaction than she was physically able to give. She had long conversations ... both verbal and non-verbal ... with these No-Form personalities, these friends and family, who had passed on, of myself and my wife. Altogether, because it was too overwhelming and there was too great an amount of it, I only received a fraction of the information that came to her. Oh, and there was one planetmate who had passed on and was known to my wife who was involved.

Six of the ten who conveyed actual information to me I had ongoing interaction with, over the course of those months, through my friend.

By the way, my friend knew none of these people and only knew me for a few months before this began happening. These all began after she, my friend, "died" and returned. During her death, her *DDE* — her *Death-Death Experience*, to distinguish it from a *Near-Death Experience* — she met my wife's daughter who had passed on tragically, forty years previously. It might be relevant that if the daughter had lived, she would have been about the same age as my friend. Mary Lynn's daughter helped my friend when she was in that afterlife state as well as conveyed information to my wife and I through my friend, both right after the initial experience, the DDE, and for a while afterward. For my friend continued having ongoing contact with the daughter. My friend said things about the daughter and another No-Form, who had been a close relative of mine, that indicated a buddy-type of relationship with each; like they "hung out" together.

My friend described the daughter as being like an "angel," in her kindness, assistance, and her beauty, upon her first meeting with her, right after my friend's death. Considering her use of the word, "angel," I should mention, for this will be important to some, that my friend was anything but a religious person. She was quite educated and cultured, had a life characterized by service and compassion as a midwife, and knew quite a bit about religion in general, as sophisticated people do. She knew John Lilly when he was alive, and for some that might give an indication of the kinds of intellectual thought and circles in which she traveled. Hardly was she overtly religious, let alone fundamentalist, is the point. Indeed, neither she, nor I, are. Our views are spiritual and universalist, as you can see in this work. Both she and I are saddened by the way religions have hurt and used people, often tragically, and for ends that are not spiritual. Another indication of her and my views relates to her contact with a relative of mine who *was* very fundamentalist — indeed he was doctrinaire and quite proselytizing — in his views when he was alive. And her comment about him was that "he knows better, now." That should tell you something.

Subsequently, my friend was visited by more No-Form personalities who were important in my life and were seeking to get information to me.

I can be as bold as saying all this and standing upon the validity of these communications, for the character of the information that was relayed to me, the content of it, involved some things that *only I knew,* and that I had never told *anyone.* My friend knew, through these personalities, of deep feelings about myself and my life that I carried within me but never expressed, ever. Much else of the communications from these No-Form "intimates" were things that only they could have known about our relationships in Form; and the content was detailed, very private, very personal. In some cases the communications resolved left-over issues between us, with their being able to communicate from a much greater understanding about themselves, as well as with an astonishingly heartfelt honesty they didn't have as much of while in life.

Indeed, my No-Form friends, or "family," and I actually progressed forward in our relationships from the place we had left off in life. We developed greater affinity and stronger bonds, based upon newer understandings of each other — for example, with amends being made to me by a few of them. The main reason for contacting me, for some others, although this was true of all, was support for and confirmation of my work in this life. I dare say, it was impressed on me repeatedly that I was being helped and would not fail, among other things too startling for me to offer. Well, just yet.

One of those others was a colleague with whom I shared a rare perspective — something that pretty much he and I were the only two in the world to have arrived at. It was the basis of our connection in life. And the last time I saw him, with him not knowing he was going to pass on not too long after that, he enjoined me to bring that information to the world, in the "Twenty-First Century." His actual words, from over two decades ago, included, "Bring primal therapy into the Twenty-First Century."

During our interactions later, with his No-Form personality, we continued that collaboration, and he conveyed some things to me that he had not in life, about his work. He added some things he had learned since he had "died."

And by the way, my friend who had the DDE, who relayed all this, was completely unaware, prior to these events, of the field of pre- and perinatal psychology, within which my colleague friend and I interacted, and about which we collaborated in Form, and now also in No-Form. Even subsequent to her conveying ideas of this nature between us, she did not have the detailed perspectives of it that my colleague and I did, though she tried to understand. Often, she conveyed information not knowing what it meant and told me, "He said you would understand this." Lol. And I did, by the way.

Oh, and one more thing. None, absolutely none, of this was sought by either my friend or me. It came about *totally* through the initiative of these No-Form personalities. And neither of us dabbled in this kind of thing previous to it happening or even knew, or believed, that it was possible. It was only through the fact that she "died," that she was able to do this. And it was only through the fact that she came to me, troubled and confused by it all in the beginning, and began revealing what was happening to her that I found out about it. I didn't seek her out, at all. And quite frankly, at the outset, I was highly skeptical.

Indeed, I didn't believe its veracity till I received proof of it beyond any shadow of a doubt for me. Hell, I am not even comfortable revealing this in this book, and I haven't in the two books previous to this one that I have written and published since our interaction. I am only revealing it now for it is relevant to what I am saying in this chapter about the increasing interaction between Form and No-Form personalities. And I must be honest here, regardless how it might make me look and/or any effect it might have on my credibility with my readers.

Incidentally, my friend's description of the way the DDE changed her is reminiscent of the "scrim" analogy offered by Mack. The analogy we came to, together, that to her helped to explain what had happened to her was that she had died and something that was always there in some way was suddenly clearly apparent. And once she was able to see it, she could no longer not see it ... even after returning to Form. It was like discovering that your whole life you had imagined yourself like a fish out of water, seeing yourself and the water as separate. Then, you realize you have been in water the entire time, and you cannot unknow that afterward.

Five of those ten No-form Personalities who had actual messages for me, including the holy man, had ongoing contact with me through my friend, going on for months. A few actually helped me in writing the book I was working on at that time (*Funny God*, 2015). With three of these five I developed an especially warm and close relationship. For the two of the three that I knew in life, that relation carried forward and exceeded what I had with them while they were in Form.

Teehee, and I was "adopted" by two of them. They took over, in a sense, from my biological parents; meaning only that they have taken me on as a responsibility to support and assist me from the No-Form state in rather maternal and paternal ways. Beyond even that, the holy man expressed kind of an identity with me — that I "was him" or "was his" or both. Soul, oversoul, perhaps? Some sort of overlapping identities?

Regardless, per the "adoption," this time the "fit" was perfect. Or it became the way it was always supposed to be. For this "mother" and I, in our From lives together, both felt we had that relationship and that being mother and son was the way it was supposed to be, or simply was, on a different level, all along. To be honest, as a child I had several times tried to "run away," so as to live with her, instead of my own parents. Indeed, she had served as my "godmother" in life. For the "father" part, well, that is part of that too-startling-to-share-just-yet stuff. Sorry.

The actual content of all those interactions, beyond what I have said, will have to wait till another time, though obviously what I learned from and through my process of interacting with them has gone into everything I have written since then. Although, truth be told, ninety-five to ninety-nine percent of what I am writing I had in mind previous to those interactions. What I mainly received from them about my work was confirmation on it through those communications and an incredible amount of encouragement and support for my continuing.

## Going "Ec-static"

Getting back to the book I was writing at that time, in it, in *Funny God* (2015), I described, in story form, details of an increasing contact between humans and the after-death state and the personalities therein through the increasing incidence of NDE and what my friend and I termed Death-Death Experiences (DDEs). For it seems these last can occur after a person has actually been dead for a while — from fifteen minutes up to forty-five minutes and even longer, I am told. And it appears these DDEs, unlike the NDEs, do not have that tunnel phenomenon. I attribute that to a difference in the degree of "Formness" one is retaining when having the experience. … with more Formness meaning more of our bioculturally constituted overlay — the constructs from our birth and conception experiences — configuring and slanting the experience in the case of NDEs, thus the appearance of "tunnels." It appears the longer you are "dead," the more Form-ly constructs (constituted realities) you lose.

And, of course, in this book I am framing that coming together of heaven and earth in a way to emphasize a change in our human understanding to allow us a vision of that No-Form reality which underlies our existence and gives us truer maps and better guidance for our lives. I have stressed that it amounts to going outside our Form-ly biases and prejudices — all our constituted realities, especially the biologically and bioculturally constituted ones. And I have described it as going ec-static, *ex-stasis*, ecstatic, in getting a peek into a cosmic overstanding — beyond the severely limited human one — as I have been describing it in this book. Using the analogy of a fish and water again, this time in a completely different way, only a fish who leaves water can know it lives in it. In this case, the water is the constituted realities and leaving it amounts to that peek into the No-Form, that going ecstatic. That peek allows for changes in virtually everything. For when one knows one can be free, can "leave water," one is open to radically more expansive options for one's life

## A "Family" Reunion?

So, if you were to ask me, "Do you really believe we are on the verge of some kind of world shattering contact with other consciousnesses — No-Form, alien, planetmate, whatever — that will bring us for the first time into the "family" of Universal Consciousness that we have split from in becoming human?" My answer would be an unqualified, "Yes."

For I see it is already happening. And it has most definitely begun happening in my own life. Look for it happening in a big way, an unmistakable way ... and soon ... for we have very little time left. However, right now, at this point and with increasing prominence over the last fifty years, folks like myself are having experiences outside of normal Form boundaries in all kinds of ways, both informally and spontaneously as well as formally as in a multitude of shamanic-type psychotechnologies such as holotropic breathwork, rebirthing, vivation, and expanded forms of primal therapy.

Folks, as well, are having NDE and DDE experiences and are contacting No-Form personalities and bringing back information from them. No-Forms are contacting loved ones still in Form and telling them about their after-transition reality. Beings and entities are contacting us in all kinds of forms — from simple inspiration and vision to more thingly ways as UFOs, aliens, spaceships, and involving alien abductions. Often they bring a message of wake-up to our environmental crisis and for the purpose of consecrating us into roles to pass on the information and take on the tasks involved in doing something about it.

Lastly but not leastly, the Earth speaks. Or the Universe is speaking to us on the "tablet" of the Earth in the form of crop circles telling us all of the above: We need to correct our ways and "get back to where we once belonged"; we are at the doorway to a transition of immense importance — a shift as epochal as for an individual it is in being born from the womb, in dying and going from Form into No-Form, or coming into Form out of No-Form around the time of conception.

And why? Of course the Universe is reaching out a hand to help us, for the Universe is friendly. As I have stressed throughout, the Universe is us, so why would we not expect It to be on our side? In a sense you can say that we are coming to ourselves to help ourselves. You can put it that we are the ones we have been waiting for, too.

# 33

# Birthing Into the Universe:

And The Humanity Show. Stay Tuned! The Universe Is a Bible … Read It. The Universe Is Ever Teaching Us … Matter Is a Language … We Are Stars/ Stars Are Us … World Tree … Primal Philosophy

*"Ten thousand years of insanity and now they're about to blow themselves up! What will happen? Mark your calendars. Don't miss it. Aaaannyy-thing can happen!!"*

*"...we just might be the hottest ticket in No-Formity at the moment."*

# Physical Reality As an Epiphenomenon of Consciousness

Regardless of one's interpretation of crop circles and UFOs, the point is that an opening to the possible understanding of phenomena such as crop circles arises with the acceptance of the new-paradigm primacy-of-the-psychic-world postulate — that is, if one simply considers psychic reality as the true reality and physical reality as only an "epiphenomenon" of it … instead of the other way around.

The conclusion is that the physical world cannot be anything but a manifestation of the psychic in its basic rootedness and concurrence with the psychic. It follows that the messages that one discovers in contemplating the phenomena, as "given," of the physical world are endless. They are as endless as the infinite "things" that exist in the Universe and the infinite experiences, information, awarenesses they essentially are.

It follows that these messages are both universal and personal, corresponding … exactly, one might guess … to the fact of there being shared physical realities as well as individual physical realities — that is, spaces which one sees in one's unique way, or in which one has sole or near-sole dominion. There are shared physical realities which are shared Truths, such as the wisdom embodied in stream, ocean, and tree. There are less shared or not-shared physical realities for each of us, related to the environment we create for ourselves and the particular features or items of the physical world we encounter. If we look around us, our physical world is telling us eternal and all-encompassing Truths, applicable to all existence as well as individual and personal things related only to us and our current life, through the things, and of course the people, we encounter around us.

## Primal Philosophy

Now, as shown by Robert Lawlor (1991) especially, this sort of perception of Reality is the common view of those peoples who we indicate with pejoratives such as "primitive," "savage," and "uncivilized." Displaying our fear of our own primal roots in this way, we cut ourselves off from a perception which has been our birthright for possibly ninety-nine percent of our existence as a species. Furthermore, as mentioned earlier, it is a viewpoint our science is beginning to give back to us.

As similarly pointed out, this is the common perspective of mystics — who we also commonly denigrate and even persecute, thereby displaying those same things about ourselves in relation to them.

## Anthropocentrism

We do these things on the basis of an extremely recent ... in the grand scheme of things ... Western hubris and anthropocentrism which rose up its head at the time of the Renaissance in Europe in the late Middle Ages. Placing ourselves on pedestals comprised of our ethnocentric beliefs in an overweening ego and of an all-powerful — a supreme and superior but unfortunately anthropocentric — "rationalism," we presumed ourselves like unto gods.

The symbol of this Renaissance "humanism" — from Leonardo da Vinci's sketch originally — is that of man, arms and legs wide, in the center of a circle and touching it at the ends of each of his limbs, which is called the *Vitruvian Man*. You've all seen it. It is ostensibly supposed to demonstrate some symmetry in the human body involving the length ... the "perfect" length, you see ... of our four limbs. Even that, on the surface of it, is saying we are perfect within Nature. Chimps should hide in shame. As for lobster, are you kidding me? You'll never see a crawdad depicted within a circle, a symbol of the Universal Crustacean. (omg)

However, the Vitruvian Man says far more than that. And while it is widely acknowledged that this symbol depicts humanism, it is totally unacknowledged that this is a perfect representation of anthropocentrism as well. Dare I venture, and hubris, too? For, in da Vinci's symbol, "man" is placed in the center of the circle, thus, in the center of the Universe ... the world revolves around "him."

Indeed, it is the veritable opposite of the peace symbol I described previously. That image represents going inward, retreat, reconsideration before going forward. The opposite of that would be a cross in a circle with arms up, not down. Which is pretty much the da Vinci symbol. So the Vitruvian Man symbol is saying to humans everywhere, reach for the stars, you can touch all the Universe if you but extend yourself freely.

Indeed, in Western culture it is hard to find a person who does not beam with pride, become breathless in awestruck wonder at him or herself, contemplating da Vinci's drawing. It is no wonder that it is an icon of such importance in science — worshipped, revered by nerds everywhere — as it inspires ever more expanding hubris in regard to Nature and the Universe. It is practically an imagic form of a cosmic permission for us to do so. It is a kind of Ayn Rand philosophy in simple lines on paper, granting us Promethean permission to steal fire where we may, despoil, like Gilgamesh, all in Nature and the Divine that we might wish, and rape and take whatever within our vision we choose, to the veritable ends of the

Universe (the circle, you see). We'd never say out loud that we are "Lords of the Universe," but we'll think it; and we'll let those words Freudian slip in the images we revere in our scientific communities.

This depiction is so much a part of our experience, so much a part of our pedagogy and culture, that it is only by looking to other cultures, with other perspectives, that we might by contrast see its significance.

# World Tree

In many parts of the world, and from time immemorial, the center of the cosmos, as depicted in a rendering of the center of a circle, would no doubt be a figure or symbol of Nature, or of the Divine. It is often a tree in the center of a circle — for example, the "tree of life" — in a great many other, less-dissociated cultures; for example, the vast majority of the indigenous ones. For those cultures see Nature and the interconnectedness of Nature as the center of the Universe and themselves as a part of that larger whole.

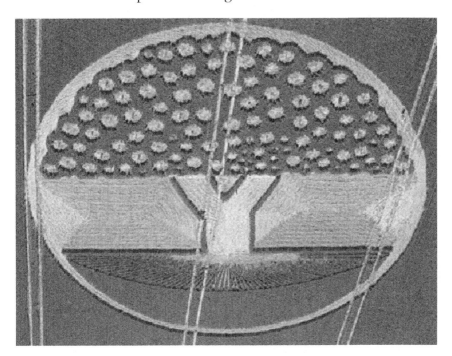

Lawlor (1992) says of the Australian Aborigine:

*The subjugation and domestication of plants and animals and all other manipulation and exploitation of the natural world — the basis of Western civilization and "progress" — were antithetical to the sense of a common consciousness and origin shared by every creature and equally with the creators. To exploit this integrated world was to do the same to oneself.*[1]

By contrast, our Western symbol of humanism — and we see now, anthropocentrism — coincided with vast advances in technology and science. But also — we are only now finally acknowledging — it coincided with extermination of indigenous peoples ... by these *same*, so-called, "renaissance" peoples ... and with the beginnings of the rape of Nature, which we are now seeing the fruits of in the global environmental crisis.

Nevertheless — no doubt because of the impending ecological crises — this is changing; and more and more this anthropocentrism/ egoistic "humanism" is on the wane. The *deep ecology* movement is the perfect example of this, but the renewal of interest in primal, indigenous cultures and in their perspectives is also evidence of this change.

With this change, "man" is no longer the center of the circle, the center of the Universe. Instead, the Cosmos, or Nature, is returning to the center. God is once again becoming the focus of consciousness and "man's" ego is taking a powder, so to speak, or, at the least, is stepping aside a bit.

Theodore Roszak (1992) speaks powerfully about this development and its being required as part of any chance we might have of avoiding eco-apocalypse. Using the term *ecopsychology*, he says we need a new way of understanding our human psyche that puts it firmly within Nature. He records the history of our understanding of ourselves and shows how and why those perspectives lack that rootedness in Nature. His reasoning is terribly consistent with my own in this book, and especially that in *Planetmates* (2014b) and *Prodigal Human* (2016a).

## "The Dewdrop Slips Into the Shining Sea"

So the symbol of the World Tree is manifesting, fortunately, in our thinking on this edge of a new paradigm. In it, we are part of Nature, not estranged from it. Our ego seeks to no longer be a dominator of it all but to integrate with it all, to harmonize with Nature and with the Divinity extending beyond that.

This is the stage described in Buddhism as the waterdrop becoming one with the ocean: "The dewdrop slips into the shining sea." It is expressed by Sathya Sai Baba as a stage when the individual disappears into God, or becomes one with God. And it is exemplified everywhere in Zen Buddhism, especially in Zen art, which likewise depicts naked Nature — that is to say, a consciousness truly reflecting, in an undistorted way, that which is, or, one might say, the still lake that perfectly reflects the sky and moon. It is also wonderfully depicted in the ninth frame of the ten ox-herding symbols, where neither ox nor herder is visible, and all that is, is Nature Unsullied.

So it is in this sense, at this stage, that we see ourselves not as the center of the Universe, and not even as babes (our "inner child"-ren) in the Universe. But we have physically disappeared from the center of the circle, the center of consciousness. We are then simple awareness, simple foci of consciousness in the vast expanse of the Universe.

# Birthing Into the Universe

Furthermore, it is interesting that the evolution of this symbol — specifically, from man in the center of the circle to the Universe in the center of the circle ... or life force or consciousness in the center of the circle — appears to have gone through the stage of "birthing into the Universe." This is exemplified, for example, by the symbol at the conclusion of *2001: A Space Odyssey* wherein the fetus is seen as suspended in the Cosmos, like a star.

Remember what I said about mandalas being representative of birth, as I continue. As well as that when spherical, like a star, they are portals, transition places. Now, consider that Arthur C. Clarke indeed had that prenate, in the movie, *2001,* become a star as metaphorical of that next step in consciousness we need to take.

Thus, at this stage — before we actually become one with the Universe ... and become just foci of light in the vast Universe of Consciousness, that is, become akin to stars against the blackness of space — we go through a process of focusing on our perinatal origins. In other words, we go through our personal, pain-driven reality constructions — a product of our earliest experiences in the womb and at birth. We place them in the center of the Universe, the center of consciousness, and we clear them out.

We do this so we might truly see the Universe as it is, not distorted by our personal psychic overlay. We do this to get beyond the biologically constituted realities — those arising from our common experiences at conception, in the womb, at birth, and as infants. To all of which experiences, our cultures add further specificity and thus adulteration to Unsullied Experience through the way it handles, the way it configures those events culturally, creating our bioculturally constituted realities.

So, we need to get beyond these constructs to return to our unity with the Universe, first. Clearing out our biocultural distortions — our pain-riddled pre- and perinatal screen — is equally as important as, and often is necessary prior to, taking the step outside of our biologically constituted realities, which are those arising from the fact we are of the species, human, with its unique biology and characteristics of perception.

However, the end point of this process is hinted by Clarke, as well. For, later, in the stages of evolution of our consciousness, we no longer are even "babes" (or fetuses) in the Universe but instead have transcended even that. In this stage the personal disappears ... *we* disappear (in the symbol) ... and then the Universe alone exists.

## We Are Stars/ Stars Are Us

We are much like the stars in the vastness of the sky ... points of light, or Experience, with the awareness from each of us in this gigantic hologram of What Is traveling everywhere else in the Universe, to everyone else of us and interconnecting us all and participating us all in the reality of the whole. Just as the light from the stars travels everywhere in the Universe, to all the other stars in the Universe, interconnecting, through ever-traveling and infinite light, each and every one of them.

## And Pleiadians Are Stars, Too!

A fascinating extrapolation of this we-are-stars idea is the fact that much of the channeling/UFO stuff that is emerging concerns aliens coming from the Pleiades, who are said to be contacting us in order to help us right now. The Pleiades is a star cluster that is one of the nearest to Earth. However, it is still an impossible 444 light years away. These alien beings are reputedly able to come to us by mechanical means *or* psychically. They are being said to contact us physically, via some sort of spaceship, as well as via channeling, evidently related to our ability to accept and give validity to the inner world.

Applying the perspective I am advancing in this book, then, they might be considered other foci of consciousness within the "inner" psychic universe that are reflected in the outside universe as the star system, Pleiades. In other words, rather than they being humanoids like us who happen to have flown in spaceships from other planets in that part of outer space ... a very anthropocentric view ... they might actually be the star cluster itself. More correctly, they might be the psychic foci in the That Which Truly Is of Consciousness-Experience that is seen by us as a "star system," which we label *the Pleiades*, in the same manner that we create all the rest of the physical world out of the pure "mind-stuff" of the Universe.

Hence, the Pleiadians might far more easily be seen, or connected with, within us. Such helpful star cluster might be much easier traveled to within ourselves than via any kind of space vehicle we might imagine. Astonishingly, they just might, and more significantly, be the psychic reality of the star cluster itself, not merely physical beings looking somewhat like us. Which is a crude, unsophisticated view, woefully lacking and woven with species-centrism. However, comprehended as a psychic reality and as the stars themselves, they would be much like the planets in our solar systems. These also, from our perspective in nonordinary states of consciousness, are psychic realities, or entities, who influence us. As we monitor in our astrologies.

# The Universe Is Ever Teaching Us

So it is, once again, in this example of the stars and our individual points of awareness, that the physical universe again reflects the spiritual-metaphysical reality of us: We are interconnected points of awareness in a vast expanse, ever reaching out to and ever meeting with each and every other one of us. The world of matter is, we see, forever teaching, as it were, ever showing, and demonstrating to us. Ever hoping, so to speak, it is that we will just look up and see ... and in so doing come to realize our true nature, our true place in the universe of awareness — free, once again, from the limitations and suffering of attachment to form ... of attachment to reflection, of attachment to separation and delusion.

# We Do Not Anthropomorphize the World, It Has Deified Us

It is not that in looking at the world we project human characteristics onto it. It is that the world has looked at us and reflected its universal characteristics. We don't anthropomorphize the world, it has deified us.

## The Universe Is a Bible

Or, as Lawlor (1992) phrased it, in describing the worldview of the indigenous Australian Aborigines:

> While the Aborigines refer to the forces and powers that created the world as their Creative Ancestors, they believe all creatures — from stars to humans to insects — share in the consciousness of the primary creative force, and each, in its own way, mirrors a form of that consciousness. In this sense the Dreamtime stories perpetuate a unified world view. This unity compelled the Aborigines to respect and adore the earth as if it were a book imprinted with the mystery of the original creation.[2]

You might say that to the Aborigines, the Earth is like our Bible. For upon it is printed the knowledge of the ages, the story of our beginnings and our nature, and the guidance for how to live and how to find our way back to our source. We can read the Earth, Nature, the Universe ... the world of matter. Everyone can. It is a book of God and philosophy that cannot be hidden and hoarded by any elite and is available, always, to each and every one.

## Matter Is a Language

Further, according to Lawlor:

> The Dreamtime stories extended a universal and psychic consciousness not only to every living creature, but also to the earth and the primary elements, forces and principles. Each component of creation acts out of dreams, desires, attractions and repulsions, just as we humans do. Therefore, the entrance into the larger world of space, time and universal energies and fields was the same as the

*entrance into the inner world of consciousness and dreaming. Exploration of the vast universe and a knowledge of the meaning of creation was experienced through an internal and external knowledge of self.* [3]

*The Dreamtime creation myths of the Aborigines guided them to see the physical world as a language, as a metamorphosis of invisible spirit, psychological and ethical realms. In this way, the Aboriginal involvement with the physical world includes and resonates with all other aspects of human experience.*[4]

Let me just add to that, for any more is not necessary: Well said!

Of course the root of the word, *matter*, is *mater*, which is the Latin term for mother. For like a mother, matter teaches us the important things of life.

# Last Night I Had the Strangest Dream

Last night I had a dream in which I was shown how this complementarity between Form and No Form works. Think of it as like two sides of something with each facing each other and each is the outward manifestation of the other. The dividing line between the two is death. We face the afterlife world; the afterlife world faces us. So that life and death is about the switching back and forth between the two. Flickering, we turn on and off like Christmas lights on the Universal Tree.

## The Tao

As I continued looking, I saw the one side in light and the other side in dark. Then I realized it was looking like, it was morphing into, a Tao symbol. And each of us beings was either the dot of light in the darkness, as humans. Or one was the dot of dark in the lightness, the No-Forms. It dawned on me that existence was simply a swirling of perspectives, alternating. The swirling quality of the Tao symbol expressed that, and I could see, at times, the image moving, swirling around, showing the dynamic quality of existence as well.

I began understanding how we, here on Earth and in the dark, are small specks of light amidst a Universe of darkness, which is our ignorance of our true nature as Divinity. And which more specifically, as we look around, is our perception of the world of matter around us, the physical universe. For we, like someone on the dark side of the moon, in the dim lighting cannot make out the beingness, the aliveness of that which surrounds us. Thus we — like the blind wise men thinking the elephant to be various things, all of which are non-alive — think what we are immersed in and interacting with is non-alive as well.

## Why We Look to the Light

Then when we seek to face the light, to discover our true nature, it is like we have hunkered back in our semicircle of dark and are peering over to the other side, the light side, the No-Form side. So we — being in dark and when we wish to awaken — are like the spot of light in the dark peering over to the light side of the Tao symbol. And why? Well, because we are light and we are drawn to light. It is the beginning of our understanding that we are not the dark, like what surrounds us, and that our essence is the same as the light we look to. Atman is Brahman.

So, you could say they — the No-Form Beingness and Beings — are the backdrop or the context of all that we do; we play in It. No-Form Personalities, individually, are the dark spots within their light. That is, they are the denser part of the light. They are relatively more configured, slightly contained or bounded. Being dark relative to light explains, by the way, why they, though god-like, might be mistaken as dark or demonic to us at first, as will be explained in the next chapter.

Anyway, they show up in our reality as the relative "darkness," too. No-Form Reality is light seen correctly, on its side, from its perspective. It is dark seen on our side, on the other side of the life-death line. By that I mean they show up as the matter we do not see for what it is. We do not see the secret life of stones; hence their beingness is darkness, is unseen, relative to our perception of World.

We operate in It All, appearing to us as matter and as a mere context or backdrop of our human ad-venture. Yet it — matter as the physical world — channels and creates, supports and directs, every act we make. It is God's Divine hand, the physical universe is. The world of matter is like the configuration of the streambed which determines exactly the path and the speed of flow of its stream. It is like the boulders and rocks that bring obstacles and tribulation to the flow of life. It is like the heights and drops bringing falls of euphoria; and the wide and deep parts offering deep pools of peace.

It is All Reality. It is seen as darkness around us, but it is seen as Reality on the light side. It is seen, by No-Forms, clearly to be the Divinity, the All That Is, that it is. That it is light on that side indicates it is being seen correctly there, or like "in the light of day."

Similarly, on the light side, the No-Form side, there is the obviousness about Divinity being All. For light is all around. However for the purposes of fun, out of the light, a sort of parameters and a loose boundedness is created, a conscribing of Experience into discrete individual experiential units. These are the configured No-Forms or the No-Thing configurations. They are denser, thus dark spots, in relation to the light of the All and Undifferentiated they are immersed in. Yet they never forget their existence is in Divinity — in the light, the love, the bliss, the infinity of possibilities.

So we know who they are in relation to us. They are from the light and so they can get us to face correctly, toward the light, not into the darkness surrounding us — which darkness is the ignorance that leaves out the aliveness of the Universe in what amounts to the Basic and Grand Mistake of Being Human. They are on the light side and can align us with our inherent Divinity. Yet we are surrounded by darkness, by matter seen in its reduced or incorrect way as non-alive.

Got that? Yeah, I know. This bends my mind, too.

## Why The Light Looks to Us

But now, another thing, the other side of that. Along this line of reasoning, what are *we* then, to them? I mean, they are in light. Why would they want to even look over into the darkness.

Well, for one thing, they usually do not. That is why there is and has been so little contact between No-Forms and Form Personalities in the past. If you are surrounded by Divinity, metaphorically you are in heaven, you can do anything you like, you are unbounded and can participate in anything in space and time. So why even bother with us who are in darkness?

Well, remember, they are surrounded by light and we are a speck of light. So there's a hint. There is affinity between us. We are alike or kin to each other.

Second, think of how folks in modern times consider the unfortunates stuck in war zones, regions of brutal oppression, and places where unspeakable tragedy or natural catastrophe has occurred. Be honest. If it is not happening to us, we almost always turn away. So also, probably, do No-Forms look elsewhere. Why would they want to see *our* futile struggles and pathetic suffering?

However, think back now to that dream I had where I was in a between-life state, with a companion. I was in a No-Form state. We were observing the unfortunates in Form going through all their trivial machinations above those tables. I said my companion and I metaphorically shook our heads.

Well, there is a hint on why they would look at us. For we are specks of light, which they know to be their essence as well, yet we are stuck in darkness, such a darkness.

As a former Catholic — marinated in it, actually — I am thinking of what we were told about the saints in heaven reaching out to give a hand to those in purgatory to lift them up. I am also thinking of bodhisattvas, who, when you think about it, would be like those No-Form configurations, those personalities choosing to retain or take on a little dark (they are the dark spots) and not "go completely into enlightenment." Consider a spot of darkness within light as meaning having a little bit of form, a little configuration or separating out from the infinite sea of Experience. And why? Out of compassion. Bodhisattvas like Guanyin, Avalokiteshvera, and Ksiti-garbha show us the nobility in that.

Remember also that my response to the superficiality I saw in humans was, eventually, to "boldly" go back into the room (womb). Which I think is what those of us here continue to do, either for our personal growth — that is, we *must*, for some reason for ourselves, go back into Form. For an example of that reason, consider the other dream where I was on the celestial plain and I chose to come back to learn more about being able to connect with ordinary folks about complex things, not just the scholastic types.

The other reason, though, exemplified in the dream about transactions over tables, is because we are drawn here, like bodhisattvas, out of compassion for the suffering we see here. If so, we come into life with a powerful compellant to help, which we know from the beginnings of our lives. I think there are many of us like that, and no doubt many of you reading this know, deep inside, what I am talking about. But if you fail to see it, think of clear examples of that like Jesus and Sathya Sai Baba, both of whom showed the qualities of Divinity even as children and both of whom began their missions at very early ages.

So, why would No-Forms bother to look over to us? Why would they be concerned with our doings? Well, partly out of compassion. And there might even be specific sympathy and concern for particular individuals who they knew in life, perhaps loved.

But not just that. Consider the No-Forms who wanted to contact me, as I described last chapter. Certainly, they helped. They gave me a shot of confidence that I could use at that time of my career when I was beginning the process of releasing the most important and radical of my writings. But they didn't give me what I lacked, for I had always had some of that confidence, even as a child. (Well, that's another story. Some other time, perhaps.) However, beyond what I came into life with, I had many more lessons throughout my life pounding away at and fashioning me so as to get me to the place of finally believing in myself totally.

So the No-Forms came to me when I already had acquired what they offered. Probably that is the way it works. For otherwise, one would be deprived the experiences involved in the lessons. So when they came to me, it was not needed, it was merely "nice." Hell, what was happening and what they blessed me with didn't even have to be true … still doesn't though I cannot find a way invalidate it. Consequently, what I got was unnecessary but nice; like a cherry on top that makes for a nice appearance but that I can without problem do without.

So they helped some. Perhaps they gave me a shot of belief in myself that will become more necessary as time goes by. I'm "staying tuned." It's a pretty good show from *my* seat, I'll tell ya.

But the main thing, as I said in the previous chapter, is they wanted to participate. They wanted to help it along. Not just by supporting and encouraging, like cheerleaders on the sidelines. But they gave additional information that catalyzed what I was already doing, understanding, and writing … and that was in concert with it … just as it had been coming to me nearly my whole life and certainly from the age of nineteen.

And I believe there are more and more No-Forms who are wanting to participate in our "show" right now. Why? Well, consider the enormous interest in a show when it is the season finale. Consider even more if that was a soap opera that was going on for decades and was having its final show, forever.

Well, as for *our* show, The Humanity Show? "Ten thousand years of insanity and now they're about to blow themselves up! What will happen? Mark your calendars. Don't miss it. Aaaannyy-thing can happen!!"

Yes, we just might be the hottest ticket in No-Formity at the moment. Not that it has to be the last episode of the Humanity Fall and Return Show. Or Return and Fall Show. For how much is the attendance increased at the climax of the season, too? Or consider in a movie you are watching how much greater is your interest at its denouement.

## They Are the Stage, We Are the Actors

Backing up, so then the Alive Universe, which we mistake as being dead, which includes the No-Forms, is the stage upon which we as actors, we as participants, perform our roles and experience the drama, the fun of Existence.

But correspondingly, we are their entertainments. They as audience view us the actors. That is, when they want to. When we are interesting enough. So don't worry about them being voyeurs, lol. We're simply boring, lame, perhaps tedious to them, most of the time. And, like we say of doctors, they've "seen all that." Indeed they've "been" all that. So no big deal.

However, they apprehend us, when they choose, like the gods of Olympus were depicted to be viewing humans. We are their reality show, their game show. We are their Survivor, their Amazing Race. They are our Big Brother, and we are locked in a house called the Earth in which we interact with each other, working out our drama and feelings, being watched 24/7 by them. For those who "tune in," anyway.

They view us as their documentaries and comedies as well. They face us, from their places on the light side of the Tao. And we are those spots of white in the midst of black; we are the bits of light on the dark screen of unconsciousness. We see them as world, as our context, our theater. They see us as actors in plays, in scripts and dramas. And life and death is simply about shifting awareness back and forth between the two perspectives. We alternate between being in the audience and on stage.

The No-Form state is where we go to watch Universal TV, to kick back from direct engagement for a while. Here in Form is where we engage in the drama of realizing that we are on a Truman Show. There are all these clues and hints, if we but watch … and listen closely.

# 34

# One at First Sees a God as a Demon:

Why We Crucify Our Angels and The Perinatal Veil on the Paranormal … If You Don't Hear the Heavenly Song, You Need More Spiritual Experience

*"One at first sees a god as a demon until one is 'wholly' enough to recognize him." — Carl Jung*

*We See Our "Angels" Through the "Fog" of Our Individual Vapors of Pain. Are They Aliens or the "Hounds of Heaven"?*

*"…entities might be seen … as frightening assailants, they are later seen as guides…."*

# Abducted by Angels?

An important sidelight on all this needs to be pointed out. It spins off from what I was saying about the Pleiadians and how that gives us insight into the UFO abduction phenomenon, and much more that is revelatory to us beyond that.

As I said, these entities can be thought to come to us physically or inwardly, and that has to do with us, with our frames of perception, our levels of understanding. If we are too bogged down in the Form-ly, they can only connect through the medium which seems to be Form. If we are more inner seeing, we are contacted by them on the inner plane.

Compare also how levels of interpretation affect alien abductees' understanding of their experiences. Initially, these encounters are frightful, terrifying. But as Mack has shown, through integrating these experiences abductees come to realizations about the encounter which has them seeing these experiences as transformative, even blessed. It has to do with the extent to which one has removed the psychic overlay of the all too human fear with which we view the unexpected and the unfamiliar.

If these alien abductors or these Pleiadians are, indeed, psychic forces that are attempting to aid us and will come to us in any way that makes sense to us, then it is understandable that they can come as spaceship jockeys for the technologically and materialistically minded Westerner, as forces of inspiration about crucial current environmental events to someone less fearful, or as psychic helping allies to the spirituality minded. For that matter they can appear as the Mother Mary to the devout Catholic … these sightings are *also* on the upsurge. Conceivably, they can appear as any of a number of gods or sages to the Hindu; or they can appear as a grandfather figure, in the form of a planetmate, or as some sort of supernatural being in an indigenous culture. And so on.

Herein we have a parallel to what Carlos Castaneda (1977) once expressed in his descriptions of the allies who in reality are just forces or "lights" but can be seen as everything from monsters to "leering men." We also see parallels to John Lilly's (1972) descriptions of the allies that came to him in his experiences.

Let us take a moment to review what Castaneda wrote. Regardless of the actual source of his writings, he revealed great spiritual insight. And that is what he can give us right now.

## "Allies"? Or, "Monsters"?

Carlos Castaneda's works contain much of encounters with forces or psychological or spiritual energies that, let us say, appear to emanate from "the dark side of the Force." At one point he indicates why this is so in a manner that is parallel to the point being made here. In his book, *The Second Ring of Power* (1977), Castaneda had just had an encounter with the "allies," which he had seen as grotesque monsters. In describing this to his companion, la Gorda, he begins to realize that she, who had been there also, had not seen the same things as he:

> "The allies have no form," she said when I had finished. "They are like a presence, like a wind, like a glow. The first one we found tonight was a blackness that wanted to get inside my body.... The others were just colors. Their glow was so strong, though, that it made the trail look as if it were daytime."[1]

## "You Haven't Lost Your Human Form Yet."

And further on:

> "Why do I see them as monsters?" I asked.

> "That's no mystery," she said. "You haven't lost your human form yet. The same thing happened to me. I used to see the allies as people; all of them were Indian men with horrible faces and mean looks. They used to wait for me in deserted places. I thought they were after me as a woman. The Nagual used to laugh his head off at my fears. But still I was half dead with fright. One of them used to come and sit on my bed and shake it until I would wake up. The fright that ally used to give me was something that I don't want repeated, even now that I'm changed. Tonight I think that I was as afraid of the allies as I used to be."

> "You mean that you don't see them as human beings anymore?"

*"No. Not anymore. The Nagual told you that an ally is formless. He is right. An ally is only a presence, a helper that is nothing and yet is as real as you and me."*[2]

Okay, Form, No-Form, the path of ec-stasis or going out of Form. Need I say more?

An important aspect of this, again using the example from Castaneda, is how we manage to distort these encounters. It follows from our fallenness from grace into physical form that whatever we experience will be framed within the parameters of limitations imposed by our separation from the All That Is in this particular set of delusions which we call the biological body of the species human. But we know that our encounter with these foci of consciousness will be further distorted by our cultural apparatus — representing the second separation … the second fall from spiritual grace … see "Part One: Being Shiva — Destroying and Creating Worlds." Thus, not only will they appear in some way physical or humanoid or form-like to us, representing that first instance of the fall as depicted in the creation of a physical species constitution, but they will also come colored with our cultural paintbrush. Therefore they might appear as Mother Mary, space pilots, or Trickster, depending.

Finally, and extremely importantly, they will be further distorted and cloaked, and clothed as well, by our personal experience in this separated state and, thus, very profoundly by our traumatic experiences here, especially our earliest ones. What I am saying is that these spiritual foci of consciousness will be further colored by our individual pain. It is in this sense that Castaneda talks about the allies appearing like monsters to one person … in this case, himself … and to another person — la Gorda — as lecherous men who want her as a woman. In other words, one's personal fears, borne of one's experiences of pain and trauma, pervade our perceptions of these helping "psychic spots." We see them through the "fog" of our individual vapors of pain.

## Why We Crucify Our Angels

This should not be too hard to understand, for we do it all the time toward things that are strange and unfamiliar to us. We project upon the best and the brightest of our culture the pains and darkness we have within, just as project the same upon the Divinity and angels who approach us.

In my own experience, this tendency was blatantly expressed in the way the people at large viewed our counterculture in the Sixties and Seventies. We were demonized, slandered. Remember back to the scene in the coffee shop in the movie, *Easy Rider,* where Peter Fonda and Dennis Hopper are stared at by the patrons of a restaurant ... you can hear a pin drop. That night, some of those folks kill Hopper's character in his sleep.

I had a near exact experience — obviously I avoided the murdering part, lol — at a breakfast joint in Florence, Oregon, in 1979, when I showed up at its door at five in the morning while hitchhiking through. There was complete silence, and I was watched as avidly as if I were on stage. Humorless audience. Tough crowd!

Just yesterday, I was at the Oregon Country Fair, near Eugene, Oregon, where I live. It is a hippie-alternative phenomenon that is a mainstay of Eugene and counterculture life since 1969. For three days, it is pure bliss, happiness, silliness, oneness, surrealness. You cannot help but smile. People are free; they dress up madly. Some women walk around without tops. One guy showed up totally nude. I watched a parade of about one hundred folks go by, playing instruments, dressed in costumes, smiling. The group at the end wore clothes of bright green. One of them looked at me and explained they were "lime-backers." Others of them made similar puns about limes, silly as can be, as they went. A guy at the end held a sign proclaiming, "The end of the lime."

People reach out to each other, everyone around. Total strangers become instant friends. People speak of oneness, how we are all the same; how we are one being. That is near exactly what was said by the guy sitting across from us as we ate our stir-fried rice and chicken. His name happened to be "Magic," and he was a musician who got money occasionally as a busker — a street musician. Of course I relayed to him, before parting, how "It's all fucking magic!" And of course he heartily agreed.

And we all dance madly. At any of the six or seven stages scattered over many acres and at any one of the ongoing perfor-mances or musical events going on continuously at each of them throughout each of the three days. There are tens of thousands of people showing up daily, and it is an important feature of Eugene cultural life for all of Eugene, even the middle class.

It is the closest thing I've experienced to heaven on earth, simply because of the people there. Indeed, any negativity coming out anywhere around, were it to occur, would be such an oddity that it would be a phenomenon, a curiosity all its own, warranting quizzical attention. Indeed, I literally smiled the entire day. I had no problem putting my hand out to the shoulder of a total stranger, for loving emphasis, as I talked. I saw hugging of strangers that someone might have been dancing near. On my way out, dancing, not walking, a woman joined in with me and we free styled together for a bit along the path; a man gave me a side-sliding five for what he saw as I passed. I cannot say enough about it, and it appears it is a spot where Divinity overlaps with our Form reality, for a spell.

Yet the day before I was telling someone at the place where I live, a senior apartment building, that I was going. She is about ten years older than I, I would guess. She said, "Well, just be careful." "Meaning what?" I asked. "Just keep your things close." "Why's that? You saying someone might take it?" "Well there are certain elements that work that event. They prey on the folks there."

This was astounding to hear, especially coming from a Eugenian who should know better. But then *sigh* consider her age. For in actuality, regarding folks "preying" on others there, that was a total fabrication from that obviously fearful elder. People there are more likely to blow bubbles your way, bop a balloon to you, than rob you.

The next day, at the Fair, which was yesterday, then, I was talking to someone who attends annually. We were discussing the use of pot there. We were talking about how even though marijuana was now legal in Oregon, in the one smoking spot in the place — it was ostensibly for tobacco smokers — pot smokers were still necessarily secretive about their use. Why? Well, because, at this hippie haven, open pot smoking was not allowed; its use was even discouraged and had been for all thirty-two years of the Fair's existence.

I wondered why. My "new" friend, Will, said, "Well, you know the people 'out there' are looking for any excuse they can find to shut this down." I nodded knowingly. For I knew that no matter the goodness — actually because of the pureness, the heavenliness — of a phenomenon or event, the more it is likely to be demonized and attacked by folks ... folks who have those demons within them. People are more likely to drown a kitten, smash a butterfly, than they are to confront annoying people. They are more likely to hate the best of us than the worst. Why? Because the best of us make folks feel they are missing out, and they cannot stand that. It makes them feel inferior.

And, hell, secretly folks are happy about the worst of us, for it makes people feel better about themselves to be able to point to others who are worse. Not to mention, you ever notice how a truly bad person, or the group's necessary asshole, tends to unite people? Folks have a common concern, then — one which they can use and abuse to let other people know just how "good" and "above that" they themselves are. Ahem. And it becomes the group's pathetic way of bonding, too. Substituting for genuine one-on-one connections, a sense of belongingness ... and, importantly, safety from being oneself judged that way ... can be had by affirming one's solidarity in the group's Good Citizens Club. However unconsciously, the KKK have used that to great effect over the years. So also, on a grander scale, did the Nazis.

Indeed, this is why Christ was crucified. He made the people of the time feel bad about themselves by comparison. And it is why good women and men, sadly — not the evil ones, of all time, you see — are assassinated. Hitlers and Mussolinis and Stalins, Nixons and George W. Bushs don't get assassinated. But folks like the Kennedys, John Lennon, Martin Luther King, and Gabrielle Giffords get targeted ... predictably, almost routinely.

So in the way we commonly cast our negativity judgmentally upon the ones who least deserve it, I cannot help seeing a parallel to Castaneda's perception as "monsters" of those who were actually allies — lights who were helpers, but were nothing (no-thing) really, and most definitely were nothing threatening.

## Transformative Abductions

This understanding is important because it explains how these encounters — in the form they are taking in our culture currently, that is, as UFO "abductions" — contain so many reflections of pain and trauma. In particular, experiences are colored by our deepest, most powerful trauma, that from the time surrounding our births.[3] You see, just like that elder woman thinking the angelic humans at the Fair were thieves and la Gorda thinking the allies were leering men, upon the bright screen of goodness is the place we project our pain.

It is not entirely without meaning to project our worst onto our best. For where else, except in relation to what it is exactly NOT can a negativity, a pain, an evil be seen to be merely a projection ... and not true ... so as to better allow our growth in awareness when that is learned. This has been the function of many a guru; Sathya Sai Baba was used that way. People rarely saw him; he was the projection screen upon which his devotees saw their hidden issues, and he knew and acknowledged that as a necessary "evil," if you will. He accepted it as part of his function, knowing he would rarely be seen for who he really was or be truly understood. He knew his message would only sink home in bits and parts, randomly and "accidentally," because of this failing of humans. When it occurs in a psychotherapeutic setting it is called *transference*. In any of these situations it can be growthful, if used correctly

We rarely do learn, of course. Most of the time we just hate and are judgmental. We love having those feelings of righteousness and superiority. Pathetic and petty substitutes for authentic self-regard, though they be. But still our soulular psychology puts it out there for us to see. For the time when we are ready to be better and can do so.

Yes, it happens, this growth in self-understanding, especially so if there is a some kind of therapy or personal growth in the works for someone. So it was that, as John Mack (1995) made clear, in his therapeutic work with abductees, there was a tendency for a kind of evolution in the understandings of some of them concerning what was happening to them as they went about therapeutically processing their feelings about the experiences. What was initially traumatic became transformative. What was frightening turned into an intensely meaningful experience of powerful bonding.

Therefore, while these entities might be seen at first as frightening assailants, they are later seen as guides toward a greater role and an expanded identity, often centered around an ecological mission.

## Vision Questy Encounters

In this respect, then, abductions and encounters similar to them can be very much like the vision quests and walkabouts I referred to in an earlier chapter. I am not alone in seeing that parallel. Keith Thompson (1989) makes exactly this comparison between encounters with aliens/ abduction experiences and the hero's journey as described by Joseph Campbell (1972).

Keep in mind that the hero's journey in its purest form is something like a vision quest, where one leaves one's social "container" and goes off to a place where one has experiences which unveil for one a larger reality. There, a kind of consecration into a new role occurs for a person, along with the receiving of or "insertion" of new information that is missing or needed by the culture of one's origins. The conclusion of the cycle occurs when the "hero," meaning everywoman/ everyman, returns to his or her society and brings forth, shares with it, what was learned. Often this hero's cycle involves the fashioning of a role, perhaps a new one for that society. This role is one through which — perhaps for a good chunk, if not the rest, of one's life — one brings forth or actualizes what was learned in the "liminal" state, the state on the outskirts of one's society. This is how societies stay vibrant; it is how cultures grow.

However, keep in mind, there is hardly much allowance for such quests in our modern culture, and there is very little respect for it or for those who might take it up. For conformity is what is wanted, is *demanded*, in a complex technological-industrial culture that relies on ever new cogs — of the same shape and exact size as before, naturally — to keep its motors of industry churning and pumping out the stuff of an omnipresent consumption-obsessed, profit-driven culture.

Still those needs for meaningful roles and authentic beingness remain, however unmet. And they just might not be able to be so completely snuffed out as the titans of commerce would wish of us.

So it is, that Keith Thompson explains how the result of that need for authenticity, unmet and repressed, might have something to do with UFOs and alien abductions. He professes that these phenomena have interesting correlations with Campbell's well-known portrayal of the "refusal of the call" during the "hero's journey."

Thompson (1989) saw this connection to the abductees, expressing it this way,

> *"Refusing the call," writes Campbell, "represents the hero's hope that his or her present system of ideals, virtues, goals, and advantages might be fixed and made secure through the act of denial." But no such luck is to be had: "One is harassed, both night and day, by the divine being that is the image of the living self within the locked labyrinth of one's own disordered psyche. The ways to the gates have all been locked: there is no exit."[4]*

You see, he is saying that these phenomena have psychological overtures. He compares it to the necessary journey, in life, to discover self and mission. His point is that these experiences can be seriously and disturbingly negative and distressing because they might be opening up to something that a person is trying hard not to have happen. They might embody messages that one is fervently attempting not to hear.

This correlates with Mack's finding that given time and compassion, these frightening encounters actually can, and do, begin righting themselves into the kind of rites of passage or initiation rites into important new roles that we need right now and that are apparently being demanded of these people regardless how hard they resist.

And speaking purely psychologically, as Jung would view it, these entities and beings who would initiate one into one's dharma, mission, and authentic role are representations of one's higher Self. They are representatives of our whole self, our authentic Self. And in one sense that makes them reflective of our future selves, as well.

# One at First Sees a God as a Demon

This idea that aliens — whether "channeled" or encountered — are somehow connected with our higher or our "future selves" is common thinking in UFO-believing encampments I've wandered through. The important point, however, is that we do not see them that way at first. Initially, these forces are imbued with all the pain and "garbage" from our polluted inner worlds, especially with that emanating from our particularly severe birth trauma. Or, as Jung phrased it, one at first sees a god as a demon until one is "wholly" enough to recognize him.

One current example of this mistake is the way David Icke sees transpersonal realities through the filter of his pain, and sees reptiles in government and alien reptiles watching us from the far side of the moon. These reptilian elements, which are "alien," you see, have obvious corollaries to the reptilian brain, from which emanate many of the constructs of our biologically constituted realities. This also we have made "alien," for we have separated from it and we strive to suppress it whenever it pops up its head.

I have referred endlessly in this book, as well, to the meaning of our lives as being like we live in the dark, like on the far side of a planet or moon. Those "aliens" watching us from the "dark side of the moon" might just be us, symbolically distorted by Icke's psyche. Even more provocatively, he might be picking up on those No-Forms watching us right now, as I explained in the last chapter. But you see how we automatically make negative what is unfamiliar to us? How anything outside the lit and sanctioned circle of information created of our cultural daylight is seen as a foreboding darkness in contrast to the bright familiarity of normal reality?

Keep in mind, along these lines, that Icke's perception of reptiles came out of an experience on an entheogen (a psychedelic); and it is well known — Grof for one makes it absolutely clear — how nearly always those experiences raise up perinatal elements which must be dealt with prior to a more encompassing vision. Grof shows clearly how we go through a "birthing into the universe," prior to our reunion. I believe part of that relates to our reptilian experiences in the womb, where we constructed our biologically constituted realities, our species constructs.

So, yes, as Icke thinks, we *do* live in a kind of matrix that has been constituted for us from our very beginnings in life. But they are hardly any government's arrangement. They are the biologically and bioculturally constituted realities which, from our beginnings as single cells on, create our reality as separate and distinct from all other species in the process of making us human. I suppose, as wrong as

Icke is, and as dangerous and fear-mongering his fantasies are as disseminated, there is a positive aspect to his work. That is, that it is an indication that people are beginning to wake up to the realization that a) their reality is construed and concocted, and b) that there is a greater and truer reality outside the boxes of perception, the matrix, which is our normal everyday reality. Now, if some of those folks who are open to hearing him would catch wind of some of what I am saying, we might have some actual awakening. We would also have people less fearful and more easily ecstatic, even euphoric, in viewing the truth as I am presenting it here.

Getting back to how these prenatal and perinatal distortions affect the experiencers, abductees might color their experiences with elements of being poked and prodded, of having things inserted into them, of being surrounded by alien medical-type beings in a laboratory setting, of having "samples" removed from them for testing, and of being swooped from one place to another without any control or say on their part. Compare this with what might be an infant's interpretation of their experience upon coming out of the ordeal of birth into a brightly lit room of masked medical personnel and weighed on cold scales, having thermometers stuck up them, having suctions and fingers inserted into their mouths with their jaws stretched wide, having medical samples taken from them for testing for various indicators of health and possible disease, being roughly scrubbed, and then moved to strange places where they are left for periods before being moved around again. And then there are all the other aspects of the perinatal which color the experience as described by Alvin Lawson (1985, 1987).

If you want a clear and blatant example of the way our alien encounters are imbued with, are virtually painted over with, the elements of our prenatal and perinatal experiences, check out the movie, *Fire in the Sky*. It is based on a book that purports to reveal the details of one person's actual alien abduction. The sequence of detailed scenes at the end, revealing the elements of that person's experience, could not be more obviously related to womb and birth experiences. I'll leave you to judge for yourself how and why.

# I Called It "Grace." Not "Abduction."

The foregoing is *not*, however, to say, as Lawson does, that these experiences are not in some sense real, or that they are entirely derivative of birth trauma. I can say this emphatically for I myself have had at least the one experience described in my works which contained many of the elements of a UFO abduction. See Chapter 18 of *Experience Is Divinity* (2013c), titled "'Don't Despair. There Are Others Doing It With You, and We're Here, Too': Always Are We Helping You"; and Chapter 28 of *Wounded Deer and Centaurs* (2016b), titled "For Earth's Sake, Get Real! 'Sure It's Hard but Always Are We Here Helping You.'"

As well, and even more so, it was like a vision quest experience, I should add. It was almost a pure example of how it is done in a vision quest, actually, including that it was an experience in which I was given information that was *severely* lacking in my culture and society at the time. And now, too, sadly. As well, I was enjoined upon to enter a role to bring forth that information or at least to help in some way. My enrollment, not coincidentally, was exactly into the kind of role described by Mack as what abductees are consecrated into — one involving doing something about our imminent environmental collapse. And this was way long, over a decade, before Mack had begun his work, let alone I had ever heard of him.

Yes, there are rites of passage, in all times, and in all cultures … and then there are *rites of passage!* There are initiations that are unique for our times — times which are so unbelievably different from any other faced by any human, nor for that matter, any planetmate, ever … ever, on this planet.

And why wouldn't they be different? For unlike any other time or culture, we are not bringing back information or blessings to some simple or singular culture of use to it alone. We are now a worldwide culture. We are a global uniculture. And we, all seven billions of us, are confronting the same crisis and must find solutions to the dilemma in which we all find ourselves. So, of course what is needed now by our global culture and society is different from ever before.

Not only is it different in being applicable to so many, indeed, all; but it involves bringing what is needed to a culture that is an amalgamation of all cultures currently. And that uniculture is comprised of virtually all cultures that have ever been, or at least the significant number that we are aware of through the diligent research of our social scientists, going back over a hundred years.

So, think, what could it possibly be that is needed to know now, for it fits any of the blind spots such an encompassing culture has? What is needed now would then be the information denied virtually all humans of all times. Not only does that make the vision quests and hero's cycles of today different in being relevant to so many more people, but it involves bringing forth that which is still needed by our world and societies and cultures.

Thus these openings to the infinite involve, sometimes, bringing forth the information that *no* human society, throughout time, has ever contained. They are about bringing forth the perspective that no human or culture has ever offered or held. Another way of saying this is that we, at this particular time, are having revealed to us the *Unapproved and Hidden*, as I call it, of all times. See *Planetmates*, by the way, on this in particular. The Unapproved and Hidden is the knowledge that, because of our species-centric blinders, no human or culture could fathom before now. See, specifically, in that book, *Planetmates*, the First and Second Prasads, titled "1st Prasad — Hidden: The 'Unapproved and Hidden' ... Our Wisest Humans Shared the Same Blind Spot" and "2nd Prasad — Invisible: What It Means to Be Human Became Increasingly Invisible" to get an exact idea of what I mean by this.

For now, just realize how these encounters, these initiations and the information being revealed through them — needed at this time and no time previously — will be different ... vastly different ... from ever before.

Consider also that, for example, only within the last fifty years has it come about, this environmental crisis, which is often the focus of these visionary revelations or encounters with Other. Now that I think about it, is that not the exact time period in which we have been seeing these extraordinary openings to the No-Form realities and this upsurge of experiences and information coming out of nonordinary states of consciousness? I said earlier how it was fifty years now that this upsurge in paranormal encounters has been going on. If we map the two trajectories — awareness of environmental crisis … coincident with actual apocalyptic environmental events, I need add … and this outpouring of psychic and nonordinary experience — I believe they match up exactly. Is that coincidence? I believe it is not.

In any case, my "initiation" left me with a profound understanding of our current environmental emergency as well as it motivated me to a calling, which has stayed with me to this day, thirty-six years later, as evidenced by this and the other books I have published in the last three years.

However, what I wish to point out right here is how my vision quest, "alien abduction," initiation, had none of the usually reported painful, perinatal-reminiscent elements described by abductees … at all! It was the most unusual experience of my life, and it was incredibly profound. But I called it "vision," and "grace," not an abduction.

# Are Aliens Actually Angels?

I am not claiming to be special; my experience was not completely without apprehension and fearfulness. Furthermore, from Mother Mary in *The Bible* to John Lilly (1972) and Terence McKenna (1991) in modern times, people have frequently reported encounters with higher beings — whether termed visitations from angels or experiences of "the Other," "guides," "Logos," "guardians" and "entities," or "allies."

It is also possible that the fact that I had been processing my birth, in a deep experiential way, for several years before my "abduction" may have had something to do with the relative lack of fear or perinatal overlay in my experience. For one clears out these birth-related distortions and dissolves the terror of that time, through facing and experiencing the pain involved in them. On the other hand, if these traumas remain unacknowledged, unfelt, and unconscious, they becomes manifest in the way one sees things. It shows up as the screen through which we perceive our surroundings and becomes the frame within which we interpret our experiences. Witness David Icke, for one, regarding this. Consider how it happened for Castaneda and la Gorda, as well.

All these things in mind, the question that arises is, are these beings we vilify, calling them *aliens,* actually entities more like what in the past would be called angels? In which case, as they seem to have done with Mack's abductees as well as in my experience, are they attempting to midwife us into the next higher stage of our ascension to hOMe?

## Biblical Prophets Do Not Report Being Probed.

Then again, if they are beings more like angels, why are they appearing so much more nefarious than in other times and places when they might have been called something more positive, like angels?

Naturally, our answer is given partly in the title to this chapter, and indeed entities have been perceived as menacing in the past and called demons ... or as Castaneda misperceived them, "monsters." However, if it is simply that our perinatal pain is blocking clear perception of them, why does it seem those folks in the past did not perceive them the way we do? After all, it is said of Jesus's disciples that they "fell on their face, and were sore afraid" at the time of the Transfiguration and the appearance of Moses and Elijah. But nowhere do we see anything like being medically examined and probed in these earlier visitations.

## Angels in Medical Gowns?

In answer to that, something stands out immediately. Notice in the reports of frightful encounters with seemingly ill-willed aliens how much they appear like something we know doing something we recognize. They are reported to have features pretty much like our anatomy and they do things that we would recognize to be medical.

Now, keep in mind what I have been saying about the biologically constituted realities and what that says about the unlikelihood that any actual aliens would be anything at all like us. Let alone would they be engaging in procedures that are familiar to us. For each of those notions assumes that the unique, precise set of factors creating us on Earth — or for that matter any of the other planetmates, from which we are only slightly different — occurred pretty much the same, only slightly modified, on other planets we know to be vastly different from ours. Even the theories about alien origins of humans does not explain the fact that so many beings here have bodies like ours — four-armed, mammalian, air-breathing, and so much more. For if we were seeded, what of the other life here like us?

Nor does alien origins address the nearly exact match between our DNA and that of our close primate relatives — chimpanzees, bonobos, and guerillas. As I said earlier in the book, ninety-eight to ninety-nine percent of the DNA we have is exactly like that of our sister planetmates. So, if Earth was seeded by aliens and that is why they would be like us, did they also seed the chimps and bonobos? So why aren't they portrayed like chimps … ever? How about the species only slightly removed from them in DNA … say, the wolves? Seeded also? Okay, then how about the ones whose DNA is slightly different from wolves … let's say, a ferret. More seeding? Man, those aliens had quite the sex life! That's more work than I would *ever* want!

I know our species-centrism makes it nearly impossible to understand how absurd it is to presume that aliens would be anything like humans. For we have this notion that our consciousness, again, is some singular achievement created in one and only one way — the way we evolved.

But if consciousness pervades the Universe, and we with our limited perceptions are already able to perceive nine million of kinds of consciousness (the number of species, sans bacteria and some forms of microorganisms), nine million *vastly* different ones, on Earth alone, as well as to be able to imagine an infinite number of kinds as possible out from that … just considering the beings, like dinosaurs, who once lived here allows that. And including bacteria and the other microorganisms there are as many as one trillion species of life on Earth alone. Hence, what are the chances extraterrestrials or extradimensionals would be anything like us? Not to mention, what are the chances they would be like *any* of Earth's planetmates? My calculations, based on what I have said, is that possibility has a likelihood of an infinitesimally tiny percent.

One might say, and it is common to advance this notion, that higher beings would come to us in ways we can understand. That is no different from us learning the language of a newly discovered indigenous tribe and wearing their clothes, adopting some of their ways, in order to speak to them. In fact, this is the most natural thing in the world — to adjust the way we communicate to the audience we have or the kinds of people we are talking to. But we do any of that so as to communicate and connect. Armies do not have such concerns when they invade. The folks of the epic Western expansion during the renaissance did not bother to learn the ways of the natives in any of the regions they entered. No, if you're going to exterminate a people you hardly care about their "sensitivities."

Yet we hear of abductions by greys or other two-armed, two-legged humanoid types, arriving in mechanical spaceships much like we might build, and engaging in medical procedures — procedures that we of all the 8.7 million species here are the only ones to perform. The mind boggles that somehow they would, beyond even that, evolve medical instruments similar to ours. Considering what I have been saying in this book, let me say that is preposterous! And arrogant and species-centric to boot! What hubris to think that! What vanity! Oh, what a real piece of work is this "man."

## High Tech Births ~ High Tech Aliens

Yet there is an obvious answer to my question about why we would perceive them more "medically" and intrusive than other times. We have already seen how birth trauma affects perception of the supernatural. So, the question arises, does the *way* we are born in modern times have an influence? Specifically, does our high tech perversion of birth in modern times have something to do with our perceptions of aliens?

By that I mean that the fact that Western culture is the only known culture to have so perverted the natural birthing process — with high-tech and sterile gadgetry, drugs, and machine-like efficiency — might just account for the cuttingly stark medical-like robes in which we outfit our modern angels. It might have something to do with the fact that they are often perceived with eyes prominent, the rest of the face inconsequential, so much like a baby might perceive a doctor or nurse wearing a surgical mask. Hence, this might help us understand why the encounter with Other in modern times would initially seem extra-threatening and painful — and in that particular perinatal-reflecting way.

## The Perinatal Veil on the Paranormal

Let us shine this light over to another supernatural phenomenon. Consider what this says about the past-life experiences that people report. In one sense, this explanation of a perinatal overlay to perception of the paranormal supports Arthur Janov in his pointing out the personal trauma elements of so-called past-life memories. He claims they are not real. Indeed, Janov proclaims any and all seemingly supernatural or paranormal experiences to emanate from primal pain, that is, from unfelt repressed traumas from our early lives. This would be the ultimate in the "biological materialism" I mentioned earlier. And I take this issue on, disputing it, in the first major article (1985) of mine published. Consistent with what I have said in this book, my contention is that such supranormal realities exist but we taint them with our unconscious; we see them through our Shadow, as Jung would put it.

Correspondingly, in the same way that one's pain, and especially perinatal pain, colors and "constitutes" one's encounter with these other foci of consciousness — these allies, aliens, No-Forms, or the Other — might it not also color and imbue one's past-life memories?

That is to say, is it possible that, contrary to Janov, there actually *are* memories from other times trying to come through to us? But that unintegrated pain elements from this life are mixed with them? Thus it is not that the past-life parts are not there, are not true, or are not coming through. Rather, that one's remembering of them and one's interpretation of them is not going to be correct until one clears away the competing and interfering this-life elements. Much of that would be those deep and early imprints from our especially traumatic births.

Roger Woolger's (1987) work taking people into past lives confirms my speculations that there is unconscious primal pain imbuing these experiences, yet they are nevertheless real. His work also demonstrates that to the extent one feels, emotes, and clears out that repressed pain and trauma, one is able to accept and be informed and benefited by these experiences. Again, one at first sees a god as a demon.

## Is Good News

And how many and what other kinds of nonordinary experiences are so tainted, so imbued with primal and perinatal pain elements, yet occurring nonetheless? Seems we have a lot of sifting through to do when we consider the extraordinary. It would also seem that since we would invariably see anything unfamiliar as negative ... "one at first sees a god as a demon" ... then what truly exists is more likely to be far more positive, auspicious, and helpful than we are capable of seeing or knowing. But it would not be seen that way at first. That should at least be wonderful news for any of you who are truly groking this. And I contend that the perspective I am presenting in this work is the kind of vision more aligned with such an auspicious reality, truly existing.

# If You Don't Hear the Heavenly Rhythm, You Need More Spiritual Experience

Look at it this way: It is like when you are picking up a channel on your radio but there is too much static obscuring it. Or, perhaps a better analogy would be when that particular spot on the radio is near and picking up from two channels ... a little nudge of the dial here and there and you pick up from one or the other, predominately. In this case you — and I am sure we have all had this experience at one time or other — are hearing parts of both broadcasts alternating and mingled, neither one too clearly. Thus, you hear, say, Lindsey Stirling's heavenly violin from the one channel, resonating in you the beginnings of solace, poignant and bittersweet loves, self-forgiveness-acceptance and homey divine belongingness.

Okay, yes, this would have to be a world where they actually play inspiring and feelingful music on a radio. And not merely the corporately pleasing twaddle keeping the masses unfeeling soululary, yet stimulated and desiring bodily so as to be fertile for their suggestions to buy. Or the trivel they broadcast to keep the masses mesmerized into states of idiocy and numbness so that folks will not realize their chains and will not rise up … or to keep them soothed into unconscious states ripe for subliminal directives. So, yes, I suppose I am asking you to conjure a fantasy world. But for the purpose of illustration, imagine, or remember back to the days when, heartfelt stirring feelingful music could be heard there on a radio. Okay?

In any case, near that radio band, is a religious channel. Little tweak of the dial and you hear overtones from there of how bad you are, how everyone's going to hell in a water bucket, how you had best turn your thinking to syrup and have it ooze out your ears and be like them … or else. Or else you are in danger of being cast to the other side of that syrupy sweetness and their smiles become devilishly demonic as you are categorized as one of them unelect and expendable. It's okay if you die, sinner, when the Rapture comes, for your life is of no worth, daughter of Satan son of Lucifer….

Okay, okay. I'll stop. When my laughter subsides, I'll continue.

But you get it. Heavenly rhythms and Divine hands of consolation and ease get mixed with the fearful and hateful stuff lying dormant on our insides. At times you hear the heart-tugging music clearly, with only some faint bombastic rhythms in the background. At other times, you hear the heavy pounding of fundamentalist verbiage, with only a sweet and yearning harmonious tinge to it, coming from Stirling's soulful stradivarius.

In this example, if you do not know otherwise, how do you interpret your experience? If you are hearing the pounding rhetoric foremost, let us say, do you not interpret this experience in the cataclysmic, assaultive, and brimstone tones of the punishing preacher talk? Of course you do. Yet does this mean that the heart-opening Stirling song does not exist? Of course it does not.

Similarly, and this is the way we have observed this process to work, as you clear out and recognize the personal-pain aspects of the bombastic preacher overlay, you are more able to tune-in to and clearly take in the Universe's deeper, truer symphony and get its message of blissful embracing belongingness and love.

Too bad David Icke didn't do that.

You see, at first all you did was get access to something beyond yourself — that is to say, you "turned on the radio." Your interpretation of your radio experience is obviously going to be colored by all aspects of what you pick up at that time. It may be a while before — in looking within, or in gaining access, or in having transpersonal encounters — you are able to discriminate the personal pain from the transpersonal beauty and to hear the underlying heavenly harmony.

## Demons Can Later Be Seen as Angelic Midwives Helping Us Get Back hOMe

In sum, it is not that the encounters with alien entities or certain paranormal phenomena such as the emergence of past-life memories are either exactly false and derivative of underlying pain — as Lawson and Janov would have it — or that they are entirely accurate in all their details, as Mack and past-life therapists might sometimes view them. It is possible instead that the truth lies in a "both-and" — a paradox ... as is so often the case on these borderlines of the ordinary. It might just be that these realities and memories are *real*, that these experiences *do really happen* ... but that our interpretations and perceptions of them are highly distorted by our individual pain.

In the same way Jacob, in the movie *Jacob's Ladder*, could only see demons hounding him until he had relinquished attachment to his former self and finally saw what they truly were — angels attempting to midwife him into the next higher stage of his ascension to hOMe.

# 35

# Sing the Body Ecstatic:

## The Path of Ecstasy … We Are Embraced and Loved by a Universe We Finally Know to Be Our hOMe

*"We can be proud and noble in our rightful and truly honored place in the Universe…. We can feel … the joy of cosmic belongingness, which is the right of all beings."*

*"…we peer through a portal wherein we are once again one with the Universe. We find ourselves on the edge of a coming together as grand as that which we experienced at conception."*

*"…we find our minds opening to a grand overstanding, bringing comfort, humor, solace, and light-heartedness into our lives. Knowing … we have huge tasks, huge responsibilities, but that we are immensely helped, infinitely blessed, and unable to truly fail, regardless how it goes."*

This has been a long long journey, in this book, through the secret life of stones. I'm tempted to quip, "The end is near!" After that last chapter, however, I wonder how many would take it that I'm talking about the book.

Regardless, I am. We have flowed all over and under and even been immersed in the world of matter, not to mention Divinity. I have tried to show you how the world, the Universe, is alive; and that that is the most important thing for any one of us to know; that it changes everything; and that it is the necessary component, indeed it is the missing component, of virtually all mainstream as well as new-age ideas of us — what we are and what we need to do.

Yet it *has* been missing, sadly. It has been nearly impossible for folks, even the spiritually minded, to not refer to aspects of the material world — light, energy, atoms, vibrations, and so on — as ways of validating their inner experience — their feelings, intuitions, visions. When it should be the other way around. As I have stressed in this book, we don't go toward actual "light"; we proceed to actual bliss, actual love. We don't "raise our vibration"; we become *kinder,* more compassionate. Just as a few examples. And it is important to know this so that one will stop futilely looking for a light within or without, trying to experience energy "tingles." So that one will leave off trying to mechanically or through meditation raise the vibration of one's atoms. So that one will leave off trying to rid oneself of feeling and emotion to make an empty space for "realer," more "scientific," more tech-sounding, energy-like things to manifest; and so on. And thus miss out on the love, the kindness, the compassion, the searing poignancy, the despair and then ecstasy, and the laughter that are the actual components of our path, our authenticity, and our deeper Divinity.

And it does change everything, knowing this. It is the crucial part, the catalyst, the tipping point that reveals a new world — one in which you are immersed, like a fish in water, in aliveness, consciousness, experiential units … and all of it friendly, compassionate, reaching out to you and helping you … even in spite of you.

This awareness is the crucial element, the catalyst, and the tipping point for a world on the edge of disaster, too. I have been compelled to write this book, along with the others of mine, like many of my compadres right now, out of a sincere and heartful concern and compassion for the life around us now, as we can see a little ahead to what is coming.

Be that as it may, in this book I have shown how it makes sense that the world is alive and that a simple switch in an assumption or two, revealed to be completely baseless and vain to boot, allows a vision of a new world. One that you belong in.

Thinking back to what we have seen, we have had revealed to us that the world is constructed of many things that have to do with the experiences we have gone through in the past as well as having to do with our physical, biological constitutions. From that we learn there is nothing ultimate to be had by insisting on our limitations, which are imposed on ourselves that way.

We have learned that throughout history and in all cultures there have been "magical" people with ways of accessing nonordinary states of consciousness that have allowed them glimpses ecstatic; which is to say, outside their bounds of Form, body, and culture. We have seen that society resists, like mad, these kind of visions out of two motives:

In traditional cultures, first of all, the worst that could happen was that the society and its elders had a vested interest in shunting its members along avenues of perception suiting themselves and their status. Truly authentic visionary experience would be counterproductive. The example of a particularly grotesque form of that was given in the tribesfolk of Papua New Guinea who since time immemorial held elaborate initiation rites which were in modern times admitted by them to have only the motive of ensuring the elders' power ... and pleasure.

In modern culture, second, something similar but different is going on. Our entire culture is built upon the assumption of these realities and visions not existing or being real. We have institutions of commerce, religion, and vested moneyed interests, people, and corporations who are so inextricably embedded in something — the status quo, the establishment — which would be threatened if these things of which I speak were true.

So we are not talking about a few men's and women's power and prestige at this time. We are looking at what would seem to be the downfall of "civilization" were we to take this vision seriously.

Hence, contemporary cultures, orchestrated by their puppet-masters, abjure such authentic roles and experiences for the modern masses. Indeed, that is why LSD was made illegal, as just one example I make out of many I could. Instead, especially since 1971, these orchestrators of culture and mainstream thinking have been impressing upon us a Frankensteinian identity, wherein the usual renewal of culture is not being allowed through these new roles and identities. (See my *Culture War, Class War*, 2013b.)

However, it is merely our fear that this new paradigm of cosmic overstanding will bring down civilization; it is not the reality. Remember, we almost always see a god as a demon until we are wholly enough to receive her. And that is indeed our situation now. We would not only benefit from the inclusion of these new and grander overstandings. We would not only experience a new renaissance — with these ideas, which resonate with those of indigenous and primal cultures, marrying together with the findings of science and modern times so as to create a primal renaissance.[1] Not only that. But our survival itself, as a species, and indeed the life of all on this planet depends on such a reversed, and expanded, overstanding. So any threat we fear of disintegration of modern culture and commerce is far less, or nothing, compared to our *actual* eco-apocalyptic threat right now.

Such new identities, roles, and perspectives are not only pushing themselves out of us, or coming to us despite us, they are necessary … and profoundly helpful. So how do we do it? How do we incorporate that which is so alien, but needed, now?

To do that we can take our clue from primal cultures. There were many other cultures — of primal and indigenous societies and unlike the one of Papua New Guinea — that instead aided individual opening to these visions. Particularly we saw this in the Native American vision quests, the Australian aboriginal walkabouts, and the ecstatic dance ceremonies of the San of the Kalahari. We should include in that any of the cultures — and there are many — who have used in sacred ceremonies entheogens such as ayahuasca, iboga, peyote, magic mushrooms, psilocybin, Tabernanthe, Salvia divinorum, mescaline, kava, and more.

We have also reviewed that there are nondrug technologies of consciousness, for the first time in Western history, that are allowing folks worldwide to get a peak outside of those conscriptions of understanding. I have mentioned, from my own experience, holotropic breathwork, primal therapy, and rebirthing, in that regard. All kinds of other shamanistic type or deep-feeling experiential approaches abound currently, as well.

In addition, Westerners have been reintroduced to the traditional visionary entheogens as well as newly discovered ones like LSD, MDMA (ecstasy), ketamine, and more. We are opening the doors of perception; we are singing the body ec-static....

There are developments as well, in modern times, contributing to a profound leap outside of our Form-ly understandings to a more cosmic overstanding. In the chapters previous, I discussed the influence of worldwide information — mass media and the Internet most significantly — and the multiculturalism that comes of that. I talked about the advances of medical technology making possible access to No-Form realities in the form of NDEs and DDEs. Not to be underestimated are the discoveries from quantum physics of the previous century, which are only gradually being integrated into scientific understandings, let alone the common lay culture of the world. Yet they are. And they put everything we thought we knew on its head.

Then, of course, we are prodded, indeed compelled, into a cosmic overstanding that embraces the consciousness of the Universe and of all matter and life on this planet ... or what I call, metaphorically, "the secret life of stones." This comes from our pendulum swing to the extreme opposite of that. Our denial of life and consciousness has led to the grievous harm we continue to inflict on the Earth, the planetmates living on it, and even our fellow humans. This has reached such an extreme that in horror we recoil. Hopefully we learn and adjust.

It comes down, simply, to this: You want to clean the doors of perception? Scrub away the vanity, then. What do I mean by that, you ask? How can we do that? Well if you think of an idea and it is obvious its truth is dependent upon us, as a species, being the pick of the litter, the crown of creation, pretty good chance it is not true. If you see a theory woven through with an assumption of human's more evolved consciousness, let alone superior intelligence, cast it to the side and look to see what is there instead. What truth is that hubristic defense hiding? Do that, for starters. That by itself reveals a world of wonder beyond the purview of merely normal, purely self-and-species-congratulating humans.

In truth, vanity, egotism, self-aggrandizement are the hugest blocks to awareness of any kind. And they are as much the psychological defenses of our species blocking our higher awareness, as individual humans have psychological defenses covering up what they need to know to grow. In either case — individually or as a species — the mental defenses we use to block our pain and prop up our fragile esteem conceal what is real, what if embraced would expand our horizons.

We see this on an individual level, where we in the course of personal growth or therapy learn that it is the petty glories we insist upon that keep us from the grand awakenings possible for us ... in realizing our actual Divinity, for one. But for that — for personal growth — we at least are aided. For we have plenty of people around us busting our chops and letting us know whenever we stray too far over that line. Though many do not hear and careen over anyway.

But who keeps the society in line when it is doing this vanity, this species-congratulation, as a major assumption of its culture? As a primary building block of the modern ego being demanded of our industrial societies? Find me a speech by any leader or political figure that isn't riddled with hidden and not-so-hidden praise and glorification of the character and values of those addressed, out of their motive of gratuitous pandering. You'll never hear from the psychotherapists or politicians, or the new-age prophets of prosperity, what the culture and its society are missing. They're too busy trying to get paid or popular.

So, who "busts the chops" of Western culture? Or Eastern culture for that matter. Sure, there are national and cultural differences that come into play to sometimes keep nations in line.

But what if what is blinding us is a culture, a scientific culture — truthful in so many ways that it is hard to see perhaps some major misconception it is making. Also, this scientific paradigm is one that transcends all cultures currently; it is omnipresent as any god. For good reason it has attained dominance. And much of that is beneficial. Wonderful advances. I'd rather go to a doctor than a medieval priest with my ailments. I'd much rather seek the information of the ages on the Internet than have to rely on accessing the Akashic records all the time. Wouldn't you? As Sathya Sai Baba once put it, "Sure I can move through walls. But most of the time it is easier just to open the door."

But what if that entire world view — of all that modern convenience and technological magic — depends on adhering to a dogma that is unseen as dogma, as a believed assumption, and beyond that is destined in the near future to kill us?

My point is, now and in this book, that vanity and societal and species aggrandizement has led to not only the evils of all time and the current impending apocalypse but is also the cause, that actual base root, of our estrangement from Nature. My hope is that merely my shining the light on these egoic limitations has awakened in you an ability to see beyond them — to what is there ... and which is comforting as well as noble and uplifting.

And this is good news! For it means that estrangement from Nature, taken forever as a horrible given, and unchangeable, is actually changeable, reversible.

Our separation, like our limitations, are self-imposed. Indeed, we can become one with the Divine. Indeed we can reunite with Nature. Indeed we can rejoin the Universe. We can be proud and noble in our rightful and truly honored place in the Universe. Not just fearfully bucked up in our esteem in such a fraudulent and dangerous place. We can feel instead the joy of cosmic belongingness, which is the right of all beings.

With everything at stake — and with all these blessings coming to us from all these quarters, including, as I have been laying out in the last few chapters, even from entities beyond ourselves, No-Form realities and personalities — we peer through a portal wherein we are once again one with the Universe. We find ourselves on the edge of a coming together as grand as that which we experienced at conception. And we find our minds opening to a grand overstanding, bringing comfort, humor, solace, and light-heartedness into our lives. Knowing both that we have huge tasks, huge responsibilities, but that we are immensely helped, infinitely blessed, and unable to truly fail, regardless how it goes. And where we are embraced and loved by a Universe we finally know to be our hOMe.

# EPILOGUE — The World Is Out to Love You:

## Expect Less … and More … from Your Wasps. The Rest of the World, Given the Chance, Is Out to Love You

*The Teachings of Some Insect Planetmates: Knowing the Truth Doesn't Make You Paranoiac, It Makes You Pronoiac.*

Akin to Hesse's insights in his book, *Siddhartha,* which I described throughout a number of the previous chapters in the final Part, "Matter Is Message," I have an example of teaching coming from the physical world occurring in my own life a few years ago.

In November of 2012, my wife, Mary Lynn, and I picked up our trailer on our annual sojourn south for the winter, from Oregon to California. It had been stored on a friend's rural property, deep in the California farm country, three hundred miles north of our eventual destination and six hundred miles from our origin.

We discovered soon enough that not quite a family of wasps, an actual *nation* of wasps had taken up abode in our trailer.

Now, my wife and I are both spiritual and pacifists, totally uninclined to kill anything, even insects. The death of other things is inevitable in living … we are not fools about it. But we try to learn a different attitude from what we were taught and try to see if peaceful coexistence, if not outright harmony and love, is possible with all that exists.

So our first inclination was to see how the wasps would react if they were simply left alone. We were not deluded in our efforts. Where they were clustered in spots we needed to use, I had to kill off entire families. As near as I could make out … and I am still not sure … their nest was in a vent above the stove, accessible from the outside and allowing entrance to the inside. But it was not a place I could get at to dislodge it. Still, the little buggers left us alone and were mysteriously absent except when we were in direct sunlight, when they would become agitated and would come out.

So after our minimal mopping up campaign, we continued down the road the hundreds of miles to our destination. You would think our invaders would be swept away by the sixty-mile-per-hour winds blowing through their home. But they were not.

Day after day when the sun would be the greatest they would come out. On the second day of this, they were out in forces that reminded me of Hitchcock or Stephen King movies. Scores if not a hundred of them flew above and around us. I had flashbacks to scenes from *The Birds*. One particular image from *The Hunger Games* came to mind, where the tracker jackers attacked and covered one unlucky contestant, stinging her into a puffy ghastly death.

Nevertheless, I tried to remain calm, lying on my bed, wondering what the proper response should be. I mean, this was extraordinary. My cat, Muff, who had been curiously focusing on these creatures at times, at this point looked up at me from the floor with wide terrified eyes and bared his teeth in a meow of terror and confusion. Also, being the guy I felt it my obligation to protect wife and cat at any and all costs, even if it meant throwing my body between interlopers and family.

Still, I was keen to find a different way than all-out war. I know that is what we need to do if we are to survive on this planet (writing this even now as a wasp friend of mine just came in and circled around my right hand as it was typing before flying on over to the window again). So at this time of full infestation, I stopped and watched and remained calm, having faith that Hichcockian horrors only exist in fantasy, not God's real world.

Meanwhile, my wife went into action. To my amazement, she got out a Mason jar and its lid and began enticing one after another of these beasty things into it, then releasing them outside. She encouraged them to leave by keeping the door open as well. I knew this was futile because they could and would come back inside, most of them. Or they would retreat to that inaccessible nest that we could not get rid of despite the hours of freeway driving. Still, I was awestruck by her complete lack of fear in her task. She was as aware as I that we could not live calmly in a tiny twelve-by-seven trailer with hundreds of wasps buzzing about our heads and filling the air all around. Yet she methodically and without a trace of skittishness, let alone fear, went about collecting and removing our unwanted visitors.

Knowing we could not live like this and realizing that my wife's choice, while admirable, was ultimately futile, I watched and pondered my course of action. What came to mind was Sathya Sai Baba's words on this, which were that though you should never kill another living thing, you must of course kill insects inside your house.

So, being also aware that there is no death anyway just transformation of consciousness from one form to another, I must confess I went about helping those tiny beings along in their "transformations." I was inspired by my wife's example of fearlessness, too, and with respect for each and every one of them, and with love and appreciation for their existence, I went about ending said existences for them, one after the other.

They were amazingly stupid and inept. They apparently were literally born yesterday, as I began to consider what might be the short and brutal life span of wasps. I could easily kill or disable them with the sole of my sandal. They were much less able to withstand blows than comparable insects such as flies or mosquitoes. They were unbelievably less nimble. And they, unlike flies or mosquitoes, did not return or retaliate either. I swear, I am not sure they could sting you except by accidentally backing into you! They seemed to have enough trouble just dealing with their confusion of being in an enclosed space with patches of light they could follow but which did not lead to any open space and was blocked to the outside ... with glass, you see, or similar obstruction. I watched them going nuts on every sunlit window. They moved, much like humans do, in endless ritual processions of futility.

Between both of our efforts we reduced the number of the trespassers to a livable amount — less than ten visible at any one time. And we relaxed again into our routine. It was at this point that again I could return to my pacifist approach of peaceful co-existence.

I lie there on my bed watching these insect planetmates, wondering what it was like to be them. I held no animosity toward them ... quite the opposite. They were rather cute. They careened about on newly formed wings, their many legs, arms, and stinger bottoms dangling below. Jerking left and right as they flew peripatetically about, I was reminded of cartoons of such insects — Disney-like and from commercials. Hardly offensive these depictions, they were enchanting and affable. All this overlaying my perception, these youngsters from a different kind of mother seemed like infants trying to walk. They were charming and delightful.

It filled me with warmth and love to feel this connection to another life form, which in my way of thinking could easily be me, have been me, or is me right now being a part of me I am not presently aware of. At any rate, I felt love for them, and because of them for all creation extending out from them. There was a palpable love filling up all space around me and I bordered the euphoric as I welled up in the poignancy of it all. Tears came, in apprehending such beauty and love.

And it occurred to me that this encounter with the wasps was like our relations with all things. Oh yes, we know the parable of the frog and the scorpion: The frog and the scorpion have an arrangement for the frog to carry the scorpion on his back across the stream (a wasp just said hello to the underside of my left wrist just then, as I was typing, and continued on). In exchange for this service the scorpion says he will not sting the frog. But in the middle of the stream the scorpion stings the frog and they both drown. The frog before dying cries out, "Why did you sting me? You know we will both drown!" The scorpion answered. "You should know I can't do otherwise. For it is my nature."

Well, watching the wasps I thought of that parable and had a different way of seeing it. Of course beings will do what is in their nature. I might even get stung by a wasp. But I might also get hurt by another human. I might get slighted or slandered in a way that is a great deal more painful than any insect bite.

And aren't they much the same? Do I refrain from relationships because they can hurt me at times? No. Do I seek to kill off all other humans on the chance that one of them might hurt my feelings at some point? Of course not! So why do we kill off insects who would even more infrequently harm us?

More importantly, I realized that just as we could accept a sting from an insect, knowing it was only doing what is in its nature and not taking it personally, we could also see the people in our relationships that way: They only do what is in their nature; we do not need to take it personally. And as long as there are not too many of them — these hurts or such people — we can live in peaceful co-existence with potentially hurtful humans, knowing that the stings of relationship are almost always unintentional.

Indeed, it occurred to me that all things can live in peaceful harmony and co-existence if we but notice the love and attraction all beings have for each other — which truly is our Divinity ... that tendency to want to be One again. If we can remember that all beings are more likely frantically focused on getting to a light that is mysteriously blocked off and hardly intent on hurting us .... if we can recall that like wasps the stings from others are unintentional byproducts of the ritualistic machinations of their struggles to be free ... then perhaps we can let go of those horror picture fears that the world, and its people, would swarm over and hurt us, if given the chance.

Of course we occasionally get stung, but, unlike the frog, we hardly drown from it. No. To know the truth does not make you paranoiac. It makes you pronoiac — that is, inclined to believe that the rest of the world, given the chance, is out to love you.

# AFTERWORD

## Continue with Book Two, *Womb with a View,* and about The Path of Ecstasy Series

At this time, I have plans for there to be another series of books, paralleling the one already in print — the Return to Grace Series of twelve volumes of which nine are in print at this time — which I am considering titling, The Path of Ecstasy Series. Here, I wish to share with my readers what they can look forward to.

### Book One, The Secret Life of Stones

This would be the first book in that series. Obviously, as a first book, it introduces and touches on many of the things that will be brought out in the subsequent works.

### Book Two, Womb with a View

The next will be titled, *Womb with a View,* and it will continue this exposition. Much of it is already written, so I can tell you a little about what it will contain. In *Womb with a View,* I will continue this look into the screens of distortion across human perception by focusing on the ways our womb experiences — our prenatal events and traumas — create our beliefs in life.

Several other theorists, beginning especially with Grof, have noted the cross-over of birth experiences and traumas with religious and mythological beliefs and symbols. Grof's view in particular is that they are distinct — pre- and perinatal events, and transpersonal events — and that birth events represent a kind of junction spot between the transpersonal and the personal. Seen this way, mythological events have an *a priori* standing; they are not reducible to life events such as the traumas of birth. The term *biological materialism* has been used by those in his camp to describe the idea that birth-like mythological and archetypal symbolism and experiences are derived from birth events. Saying they are derived is saying that they would not occur except for the birth traumas, and to that they do not agree.

I have a different take on it. I do not dispute that some of their view is true. I really do not know of their ontological status, these birth-like mythological and archetypal symbols. However, I view the actual events of one's life as having strong determination on the way one views and interprets everything that comes after them.

My difference lies in two things: One, that these events *form* or they configure our religious and spiritual understandings, especially our religious ones. I do not know the extent to which they *create* them. Further, that those events that configure our species world view go all the way back to conception, way before birth. In *Womb with a View* I will be bringing out the mythological, psychological, and archetypal elements and relating them to underlying womb, and to some extent birth, events.

My view, if you remember back to Chapter 34 on how one sees a god as a demon, is that they overlay and configure the way we will view what might be considered truly non-Formular events or entities. What I will say is consistent with what I have laid out here in *The Secret Life of Stones*, relating to biologically-constituted realities, in particular the bioculturally-constituted realities. Consistent with what I have said here, my aim will be to show how by wiping away the distortive effects of biocultural experiences at birth, womb, and conception, we might come closer to purer perception. This is how, indeed, we cleanse the doors of perception; that is, by clearing away the personal pain and pre- and perinatal trauma imbuing and slanting them, if not out and out creating them.

In doing this clearing away of fear- and pain-laden prompts to our perception and interpretations of them, we might approach that view ec-static, that cosmic overstanding that is normally denied us out of the fact that we have such powerful determinants on our perception at the beginnings of our lives as the traumas prenatally and perinatally.

# Book Three, Cells with a View

The book following *Womb with a View* in The Path of Ecstasy Series of books is to be *Cells with a View*. In it I will show how the events around *conception*, this time — the *periconceptional* experiences — configure even more of our biocultural matrix even prior to our "beliefs" about things outside the natural. It is my view that our very perception of Form reality is created there. You might say that is where we not just read the rules of the game we will be playing in life, we imprint them on all of what we will perceive ever after in life.

So, prior to religious and spiritual beliefs we have seemingly indisputable assumptions impressed on us related to the existence of duality in the world and the existence of space as well as time. If we accept a mystical position that both of those are illusions, then it is my contention that we can look to our pre- and periconceptional experiences and events as to why we have such deep-rooted assumptions about reality, such "illusions" as to the existence of space and time.

This is where — at the periconceptional experiences — we are looking more at the biologically constituted as opposed to the bioculturally constituted realities. For while our experiences in the womb and at birth are much influenced by the mother's experience in her culture and thus the way those events are construed in her culture, there is not a lot of influence from culture on the way the conception experiences unfold.

Not a lot, but some. Certainly the health of the father and the mother go into it, somewhat, and that is affected by culture. Certainly the emotional and psychological characteristics of the parents, which are influenced by culture, influence their very cells, including their sperm and ova. And astonishingly, with test tube babies and other high-tech, modern interventions into the processes of fertilization and conception going on, suddenly there are huge influences on its processes emanating from culture. We can only wonder, at this point, what kinds of beliefs and notions about the Universe will be had by those who come from those origins.

However, that to the side, there is a great deal of uniformity in our experiences at and around conception. Whereas there is far more variability and cultural input with each advance of time in gestation. Thus it is that we live in pretty similar physical worlds because we have rather the same experiences, periconceptionally. These events are part of our species makeup, our biologically constituted realities, as opposed to the bioculturally constituted realities, which are more variable and that come in with the influences of culture in later womb life and at birth.

The result and aim of looking at our perceptual prejudices, from birth, womb, and conception, as will be done in the two books — *Womb with a View* and *Cells with a View* — is to arrive at something astounding. As I said in this book, *The Secret Life of Stones*, the way to get a peek outside our biologically-constituted realities, the way to go ec-static, is to drop our vanity and self-congratulation at all levels.

Now, in these two books I will show how we can view even beyond that into what is the Nature of Reality. How? By peeling back not just the veils of ego and vanity, but those of even more fundamental pain and early experience. Our earliest experiences form, they create, our prejudices about Reality. So what would we see, what Reality would reveal itself, with those constraints pulled to the side?

Whatever it is, it would necessarily be Truth, or truths, far beyond what we come up with enslaved as we are within the boundaries of concepts formed from our early, our profoundly influential, experiences. An example? What is the reality we experience before we have the one of duality when we come into Form as cells, as sperm and ovum? When we experience not just separation, from father and mother, but then duality in the coming together of the two at conception? At that point we have laid — through the experiences we have had there of duality — a foundation of seeing all the rest of the Reality we will experience in life in terms of male and female, separation and union, struggle and peace, pleasure and pain, satisfaction and discontent, inner and outer, and all the rest.

But what was Reality before we stamped that particular cookie cutter on Reality? What was the bigger "game" or the larger reality outside the game before those rules of consensual reality, involving dualism, were initiated? At this point we are metaphorically looking for what the "room" looks like that we are sitting in when we are playing the board or virtual reality game of life. What is the room like? What are we like? Who else is there and what are they like? What does it feel like? What is it all about at that "level"? And more — anything else we will find out when we have removed more than just vanity from our prejudices, but the formative early experiences, many of them painful, which give rise to all the other prejudices on our perception.

You could say that outside our perceptual biases and all our biologically and bioculturally constituted realities, it is nothing. That there is a fundamental nothingness, like some mystical types and their literature profess. But I contend that is a cop-out. It is easy to say something does not exist — there is "nothing" there — in "places" where we are not able to see at our level of spiritual growth. As I have said throughout this book, all the evidence points to a rich and infinite variety of experience, a colorfully profound and interesting mix, as a more fundamental reality. Something that is no-thing, but hardly nothing! Indeed, quite the opposite!

So this is where we will go in those books. We will, like Salome, do a Dance of the Seven Veils and find out what naked Reality is more likely to be like.

# Book Four, The Prenatal Matrix of Human Events

Following *Cells with a View*, I have plans to write a more elaborate exposition of the "prenatal matrix of human events," as I introduced it in my recent work, *Wounded Deer and Centaurs: The Necessary Hero and the Prenatal Matrix of Human Events*. There is much more to be said on this topic, and it is vitally important. As I explained in that work, this prenatal matrix is virtually the root of the evil that humans distinctively manifest, out of all of Nature. More than that, it is essential we see it and remove those weeds from the meadow of human nature if life is to continue on Earth. This book, Book Four, like *Wounded Deer and Centaurs*, will elaborate on why and how that can be done.

# Book Five, The Centered Path Through Hell

Beyond these first four — this one, *The Secret Life of Stones*, *Womb with a View*, *Cells with a View*, and the one elaborating on the prenatal matrix — six more works are in this queue, at this time. These include one that would be about the centered path through hell. This one follows logically the one elaborating the prenatal matrix and explaining the source of human evil. For this one begins discussing the path that is necessary in order to go beyond those hellacious influences. It is one that involves facing and going through them in order, like Dante proceeding through Inferno and Purgatorio, to release oneself from their influences.

This work will include important corrections to common spiritual thinking, including stressing the knowledge that the path to liberation involves facing the darkness. Or, as Jung put it, "One does not become enlightened by imaging figures of light, but by making the darkness conscious." This book, as well, will highlight a fundamental acknowledgment that the path to authenticity, to rootedness in Divinity, is not a ladder-style one, as Wilber and transpersonal ego psychologists think of it. Rather, an authentic spiritual path embraces, as Hesse phrased it, "seeking the depths." As Jung also wrote, "There is no coming to consciousness without pain." My book on the centered path through hell, correspondingly, acknowledges that "the way forward is down."

This work reveals the equally disastrous matriarchal and patriarchal mistakes that are made in the spiritual quest. And in noticing the mistakes to the left and to the right of true-footedness it carves a road, a centered path, avoiding them. It shows how to keep oneself centered and unharmed while also proceeding in the direction down, into one's feelings, into life experience, hence metaphorically, into "hell." This book would be Beatrice to Dante in his *Divine Comedy*.

So this work focuses, for one thing, on the matriarchal mistakes we make on the path, which delays or blocks our progress. These matriarchal mistakes have to do with opening to overwhelm through various reckless means, at the times when actualization, not more access to potentiality, is what is warranted, as I explained in Chapter 27 on "Identity and the Sea of Potentiality." At this time, I expect to include, additionally, in this particular book some of the ideas I was laying out in that chapter on identity and potentiality about the dangers of mysticism for "modern" youth. So "the centered path through hell" book will also deal with identity, potentiality, rites of passage, youth and mid-life and other liminal crises, drugs and their effect on the process, multiculturalism, the occult, and generations — mine of the Sixties and the ones subsequent.

However even more importantly this work on the centered path through hell deals with the much more widespread patriarchal mistakes we make. Especially in that we live in a patriarchal world, almost totally, and going back ten thousand years and more in some places, the patriarchal mistakes virtually riddle our religious and spiritual beliefs and even our ideas of personal and psychological growth. These patriarchal mistakes predominantly involve the use of control, versus surrender, and mastery, versus vulnerability, on the path. These are ego mistakes, they are ones that are ladder-like and intellectual and are rooted in a false reliance on rationality as a tool of spiritual growth, which is an aspect of ego, as opposed to intuition, faith, guidance from within and without, and grace.

## Book Six, The Journey of Re-Membering ... Four Phases of Self-Awareness

After this in line is a book on the "the journey of re-membering," with a title something like that. Following the corrections to the misunderstandings of spiritual evolution unveiled in the previous book, I have laid out a volume detailing the path to ecstasy and Self, or Divinity, as it proceeds in four stages, or phases. These are four phases of self-awareness that those who become liberated embody and go through in this life and over the course of lives. It is the path involved in moving out from the prejudices and the evil that accrue to us all as described in the first four books. The last book, the centered path, focuses on the mistakes. Whereas this one on stages takes a look at what that path involves. And it is the one that is the true and authentic route avoiding the pitfalls of matriarchality and patriarchality which in one way or another keeps one stuck in hellish misery.

Once one realizes the way of the centered path through hell, there are four phases of expanding self-understanding that are related, roughly, to four stages of life, correctly lived. More importantly these four phases are related to levels of the unconscious — each deeper and more expansive than the previous — and thus they lead to the superconscious, once those levels are embraced, incorporated, and gone beyond.

These phases of self-awareness were inspired by Masters and Houston (1966, 2000) in their seminal work, *The Varieties of Psychedelic Experience.* They are the sensory, the recollective-analytic, the symbolic-existential, and the integral. Don't worry I'll come up with "sexier" labels for them by print time. lol. At any rate, these stages are found in virtually all valid spiritual, psychological, transpersonal paths of evolution or growth to liberation. Therefore, they provide a yardstick against which one can evaluate one's progress. They can provide direction, when needed; and confirmation, when that is what would help.

## Book Seven, Primal Spirituality and the Primal Process ... The Second Half of "The Cure"

The book following that, a seventh book in the series, is the one I am anxious to bring to print. It is on "primal spirituality." I have several parts of it currently online, including "Unconditional Acceptance and the Primal Process" (1993) and "The Other Half of 'the Cure'" (1995b, 1995d). These are ideas that have already melded into the culture of the field of primal therapy, by now, as I brought these ideas out initially in the early Nineties. But I have much much more to say on them. And it is very important.

For one thing, the fact that it is radical unconditional acceptance that truly allows growth, that truly heals, is hardly known. Outside of the primal modality and unfortunately sometimes even under its aegis it is missed. If it is known, it is rarely understood sufficiently for it to bring about the powerful transformation it can. It goes way beyond Carl Rogers's admirable therapeutic advances termed "client-centered."

However, it is truly difficult for facilitators to apply it without having done considerable deep experiential work themselves. For, predictably in a patriarchal culture and a capitalist system of economy, everything pushes in the direction of a medical-type model of growth and healing where facilitators can get paid to give direction, provide advice, and so on … to be authorities and to be esteemed and paid that way. Fine for them, but basically that usurps the growing person's primary mechanism for growth — which is the self-realization coming from within. Beyond that, the authority-citizen, the teacher-student, the doctor-patient mode is the only one that a person, whether counselor or client, has encountered in life, usually. The client expects it; the counselor often does not know there is anything wrong with it. Hell, what else would they be getting paid for? Why else should folks give them money except for they telling them what they need to know and fixing them wherever one thinks one can?

Nonetheless, there is a mode of radical unconditional acceptance, as we learned it in primal therapy. It is close to what Tav Sparks — the current director of Grof Transpersonal Training — is getting at in his manual *Doing Not Doing: A Facilitators Guide to Holotropic Breathwork*. Hard to explain, it is, but I will in my forthcoming book. For now I offer this as analogy: I am reminded that as a one-time community activist I was taught that organizers do not succeed by doing what is needed to be done, but rather by encouraging others in the group, and then stepping to the side when an event arises, so that those in the community can be motivated to step up and can learn to be leaders and initiators of change. That in no case should one step in, even if failure results, for that precludes people finding their own power, their own ability to lead and initiate progressive action.

Well, the vast majority of healers and psychotherapists are way behind the curve in learning this, unfortunately. The temptation of wanting to be seen as an authority, to be able to label oneself a "professional" … the ego, and the remuneration, involved in that … is virtually impossible for most would-be healers to forego. So, that point is important to bring out in this upcoming work.

The other aspect of this book, which I see now is also very very important … I think even more so as time goes by … has to do with the final movements in the spiritual symphony. This is where so many get stuck. My experience is that even primal people, not to mention folks in virtually all spiritual and psychological paths, get this wrong. Think back to what I said about the spherical path versus the circular ones, in Chapter 31. Virtually all spiritual and psychological modalities see everything in terms of "balancing" opposites or "integrating" dualities within the person. And there is a huge flaw in that. I want to make a joke and say it implies that being an asshole is fine as long as one does it only half the time. And while that hits on part of it, the problem far surpasses that.

503

Even in my "centered path" book, I stress that it is not about "balancing" or "integrating" matriarchal and patriarchal ways but foregoing them, for what good is it to make two mistakes, however equally? One is not benefited by opening to overwhelm, a matriarchal mistake, and then alternately enlisting will power, a patriarchal error. What is best is to avoid both blunders and learn to surrender to an inner flow that has one naturally unfolding and effortlessly actualizing, not in a "balanced" way but in a seamless way.

Hence, as one would expect in models that are circular, indeed yes, they go round and round and go nowhere. For they are ever trying to fix the person prior to or outside the person's engagement in the world. This is another aspect of the medical model. For the medical model doesn't only have the problem coming about because of its paid authorities, but it also has a category of "sickness"; hence, withdrawal from the world is included as an aspect of that. So also do virtually all spiritual paths. This is the "monastery" stage — the contemplative or meditative or therapy arc of the process of growth.

Now, certainly it is important to have liminal times for growth. I stressed that several times in this book, especially when I referred to experiences mimicking vision quests or hero's cycles. But there is a problem in this as well. For what usually happens is those liminal times get clung to by sick people. Then to add to that, these folks are encouraged in their dependency by professionals who can hardly keep from operating out of motives of financial gain, since they live in and are constantly pressured by the demands of a capitalist system. Dependent clients make for steady streams of income, you see.

So a huge realization is missed: It is what I call the second half of the cure. And it is embodied in this statement, that:

**_It is only when one aligns oneself with a cause beyond oneself that one is truly healed._**

For in doing so, one is lifted out of oneself into a larger, and higher, reality in which one's pain is not focused on, is inconsequential, hence becomes forgotten.

Another reason this is not seen is that professionals who might lead — whether in psychotherapeutic or spiritual milieus — are often ones who are themselves stuck. Indeed, they then are pied pipers. They are stuck themselves, are often unhappy and unliberated, yet they feel the need to pass on what has not worked for them … for regardless its barrenness of results, hell, they worked and paid _hard_ for it! They tell themselves that it is okay for them to do that for — with faith as blind as any fundamentalist — surely they will at some point, somewhere in the future, sometime, succeed in what they have been trying to achieve.

What is funny is how they sometimes will try to convince others — they will brandish it as some kind of badge of courage — that there are no real answers, as a way of rationalizing to themselves their failure and avoiding the necessary correction in their path that their failure is trying to reveal to them. Saying silly things, meant to come across as bravado, like "the only answer is there are no answers," and such, they affirm their stuckness as a value. And they hate like hell any insinuation that there are actual answers and that they have simply been failures in finding them in this life. This cul de sac is often the street signed, Existential Circle. Folks living there do not know of the freeways beyond where they live and try to convince you to live there with them. They would have you believe the "no-exit" and "dead end" signs you notice are just more proof of their hardiness in living there anyway. Though perhaps being tough-minded in a losing cause is not very smart? However macho it might seem to be in some kind of existential no-nonsense "real-world"–worshiping way?

The other reason the second half of the cure — the one involving higher causes, fate, actualization, destiny, and atmidharma — is missed is related to that monkish mistake in that once retreat is taken as a value, one finds all kinds of ways to deprecate more active paths, paths of activism and service in this world. You will hear such folks decry politics, as in some egoic way of trying to put out that they are above that stuff, would not get their hands dirty. They call it "negativity," perhaps, or "drama." And they proclaim how they are superior in "not getting caught up in that" — those "petty concerns of *this* world." However, in truth, it is simply that they are fearful of venturing outside their cocoon of the monastic, the fearful, the narcissistic, the self-obsessed — that hypochondriacal cul de sac they have made a home and rationalized as a value.

Regardless the reasons, all these folks miss the culmination of the healing process, which is expressed in the final stage of the hero's cycle, when one brings back to the world what one has learned in the liminal state. It is related to what Maslow called self-actualization. It is parallel to what Sathya Sai Baba called the path of service, which according to him was far far superior to the meditative route. Indeed, Baba explained how the meditative route was not a properly fruitful spiritual route at all. That it was just a kind of way of doing mental spring-cleaning, so to speak. That it was only the paths involving service in the world and to society or to something beyond oneself that are any kind of spiritual paths. Castaneda in enjoining one to choose "a path with a heart" was saying something similar. In any case, this is what I agree with, what I think it is vitally important for folks to know, and what I bring out in the ideas on "the second half of the cure."

So in terms of being healed, it is true in practice that one will not be really complete or authentic until one finds a way to bring what one has learned out into the world in some kind of helpful way, often by applying it to some cause of importance, often involving the relief or prevention of suffering to some beings other than oneself, for a change.

And, yes, this activism is the missing component in virtually all spiritual and psychological paths. I touched on it in this book, as well. When I talked about the bodhisattva path, for example. But again there is far far more to be said about it. What I want folks to get out of this upcoming book on primal spirituality and the primal process is the release into knowing that one gains oneself when one gives oneself. That sickness and neurosis and pain cause one to look inward — that is fine. But staying constrained and fearful keeps one stuck in misery and neurosis, in directionlessness and meaninglessness. What I want folks to know is that there is a grand and beautiful and fulfilling world out there to engage in. And that at a certain point, far earlier than most folks know, the way to grow is to stretch out to it, to stretch past one's pain. And to align with something that measures up with what one discovered within.

It is because spiritual paths tend to draw to them introverts that this is not seen. Introverts hate like crazy having to do anything that would seem to require something like extroversion. Understandable, of course. However, they then rationalize it is not needed and is inferior to them and their path. But this is out of a mistaken notion of what activism or a higher cause is. So this is their fear or prejudice that they need to put behind them in order to feel free.

By the way, though I am not planning a book on it, extroverts, who naturally embrace activism as a matter of course, have the complementary problem in the way they pooh pooh inwardness. Yet, as I have been saying in my books, especially *Funny God,* that is their tragic mistake, as well. And it is the one needing correction in order for actual success on the pressing problems of the world to be had.

Now, this notion regarding a necessary engagement in the world and alignment with a cause greater than oneself is something I did actually say a bit about in this book in the chapter on gods being seen as demons, Chapter 34. I pointed out the hero's cycle aspects of the alien abduction phenomena. And quoting Campbell and Thompson, I was making the point that a liminal time — a time of social "alienation" and living on the borders of one's group, of retreat and reevaluation, of moratorium — is an absolutely essential stage in the cycle. But that if one does not come back to the world ... one is "harassed night and day by the demon within."

The point is that one needs to take what one learns and bring it back to the world. It is only then, with the cycle complete, that one gets relief. Indeed, one gets liberation. And more important than those, one feels fulfillment in the surety that one has been helpful; and one is rewarded being at home in a place among the noble ones who have lifted the suffering of the world a tad. Knowing that is the wholiest blessing of all.

So, in summary, the book on primal process will explain how to traverse the path of Re-Membering described in the previous book on the four phases of self-discovery. It will explain the process, its permutations, and show how to go in — that unconditional acceptance and the primal process. But also it will unveil how to come back out — the second half of the cure.

# Book Eight, Authenticity Rising

The book planned for after that is one about current times and its cultural changes which involve a shift to the importance and valuing of authenticity. It is a book on "authenticity rising." And it will show how the current state of the world in so many aspects — multiculturalism, mass media, social networking and the internet, and the environmental and political and civil crises of the day — are pushing for more and allowing for more in terms of personhood. I will show how this powerful and promising trend is raising itself up, as well I will show the powerful forces seeking to push it back down … to snuff it out. There is authenticity vying with conformity and the status quo. There is original and dharmic roles and living going head to head with the incessant, relentless demands of a material industrial corporate culture and its governments, geared to keep the masses compliant, unmoving, uncomplaining … but also ungrowing.

# Book Nine, Return to Grace … The Crisis and Opportunity of End Times

What follows naturally from a book on current times and its craving for authenticity is the outer — or the social, historical, current events aspect of that. For not only is there an increasing hunger for realness and truth, the times themselves are demanding genuineness and integrity of us. No less than the survival of all life on this planet is at stake. This is the greatest crisis.

However, it is also the grandest opportunity for folks to find themselves and to participate in a cause beyond themselves. There has never been a time so ripe for personal fulfillment alongside and within a time so dire and having such momentous consequences. There has never been a better time for heroes to come forth and rainbow warriors to awaken. This is the grandest adventure of all time, the greatest story ever being told on Earth and it is happening in our lifetimes. We are lucky to be here, despite the dark cloud of gloom and doom approaching. For we can never be better than we are able to be now. The brightest angels of our beings are being summoned now, like never before.

Sot this book, book nine, will explore the unique and apocalyptic character of our times … in all its wondrous implications.

# Book Ten, The Cosmic Overstanding … You, God, and Identity

The final book in this series, at least the way it is all being envisioned at this time, not only caps off the entire series in a kind of culmination, but brings it back around again to some of the themes of this book. For this book dealt with the nature of Reality in all its components. And it pointed to some implications of that for one's life.

Well, in this final book, I will put forth the greatest overstanding — *The Cosmic Overstanding* — of us in relation to the Universe as revealed in the current book. If this book was about the nature of Matter and Divinity, the final book will be about the Nature of the Game, our script, and how we can be liberated within it. It will expand the ideas of "The Mind's True Liberation" as put forth in Part Three of *Funny God* (2015), as well as in Part Three, "Experience Is Divinity" of the book by the same name (2013c).

It will do far more than explain the path of liberation, or give you steps to achieve it — that is something I would *never* do — it will *embody* it ... embody liberation. It might also open your eyes to the realization that you already are.

# The Path of Ecstasy Series, Summary

In summary these books are:

Book 1, this one: *The Secret Life of Stones: Matter, Divinity, and the Path of Ecstasy*.

Book 2. *Womb with a View*. It will be about how our womb experiences create our religions and supernatural beliefs and how those pre- and perinatal experiences show up in our mythologies, our spiritualities, and our theologies.

It will go into biology as both metaphor and mythology to elaborate upon what our bodies and our early biological experiences tell us about life, Reality, and our purpose and meaning of life ... and how that is reflected back again upon us in our mythologies and religious beliefs.

Book 3. *Cells with a View*. It will tell how our earliest experiences of life at the cellular level create our physical world and our deepest assumptions about Reality. And how these early imprints show up in the makeup of the world of matter and Nature, which we share, and of the time, cosmos, and supernatural that we assume.

Book 4. On the prenatal matrix of human events. It will lay out for review and insight how our late-stage gestation experiences configure our actions ... how they give rise to evil ... how they are the origins of the brutality and atrocities of all time and how they are hence not our true human nature. So they can be finally gone beyond when that is recognized and addressed.

Book 5. On the centered path through hell and the way forward is down. This work will take up and strip away the matriarchal and patriarchal mistakes which mar a true apprehension of our journey. Hence it will also unveil a centered and safe navigation of our way through our pain and dis-ease on the way to our liberation.

Book 6. On the journey of re-membering and the four phases of self-discovery. This one delineates the path of ecstasy to Self, or Divinity, as it is found in the transpersonal paths of all times and places. It shows how each of us travel from pain and darkness to ecstasy and reunion, from the prenatal matrix to the cosmic overstanding.

Book 7. On primal spirituality and the primal process. It will reveal how radical unconditional acceptance heals and how anything less hurts or diverts. More importantly, it will unveil the necessary stage, the second half of the cure, which involves aligning with something greater than oneself — a cause, a principle, a duty, or a blessing — as the way to finally achieve release from the tortuous prison of ego, of primal pain.

Book 8. On authenticity rising, this book will go into some auspicious trends in our postmodern society involving the goals that the masses are fashioning and the feelings and personalities that are being valued. This craving for genuineness, this adherence to only the real, this no-nonsense insistence on truth … "Just give me some truth!" – John Lennon … could not have happened at a better time. And it is none too soon.

Book 9. On return to grace and the crisis and opportunity of end times. It will bring out the unparalleled fortune of our times even as we stand on the brink of disasters as great as eco-apocalypse.

Book 10. Finally, *The Cosmic Overstanding: You, God, and Identity* will present the good news involved in a new paradigm as it rises up from all these understandings, and more. Consistent with consciousness studies and quantum physics, yet revealing a friendly and loving reality, it says what we can rely on, why we should have hope, and how there is no reason not to be happy and free, at this time, even as we apply ourselves. For we are always and everywhere assisted and saved, uplifted and loved, even "in spite of ourselves."

# Other Books and Series

## The Stages of Re-Membering Series

Just an fyi, I have intentions for other series — some of which I have done already considerable work on.

For a very long time, in the works has been the elaboration, in four volumes, of the phases of re-membering or the four stages of self-understanding that I plan to release in one work, first, as Book 6, above. This Stages of Re-Membering Series would include, again with sexier titles by print time:

**Book 1. The Sensory.** This describes the place we all start from. It is a way of apprehending world and life where sensory experiences are all that matter and the sensory and the material are all that has value. Regardless what "religious" beliefs people have, we start with a "fundamentalist" view of the world of it being comprised of *things*. We might be the average person seeking, in the "venerable" words of George W. Bush, to "throw food on their families," (lol). We might be the careerist. We might be the religious-minded, thinking that God created us five thousand years ago in a Garden of Eden, who can't wait to get lifted up in the skies physically when the Rapture comes. It could be the Catholic thinking that at the end of time, God is going to raise all the bodies from the graves, refurbish them somehow, and then the lucky of us are going to get to hang out in "heaven" in those bodies. I just hope they have grilled cheese sandwiches, in that case.

And regardless, what is valued as a goal is the accumulation of sensory experience in life, as much as possible. So it comes together with the struggle for wealth, as well, in that it is seen that it is money that allows more sensory experience — whether that is the finest vacations, the most elegant residences, the most sophisticated dining, or the most daredevil of stunts … or having the most accomplished of sexual partners, the most variety and amount of sexual experiences.

If there are any goals beyond surviving and increasing the pleasure quotient of life to the max, they center around stuffing as much as possible of different experiences into one's life, having the longest "bucket list" and accomplishing them. The more parties, the more sexual partners, the more cars, the more planes jumped out of, the more motorcycles raced, horses rode, medals won, the more lavish repasts and exotic locales visited, the winner … or as they boast, those who are at this level, "the one with the most toys at the end wins."

This is the sensory level of evolution back to grace. This is where we start after having been diminished by the four falls from grace as we came into this world. It is the one everyone knows; it is the one you are the most familiar with, even if you have grown past it. For we each contain it even if we supersede it. For these levels are not about different stops on a bus route, they are about expanding outward in all directions at once. So the innermost circle, this sensory one, is encompassed in all beyond it. It is integrated within one's personality, even if one has reached beyond it to place the focus, the interest, of one's life elsewhere and beyond it, in the domain of one of the outer rings from it.

As a stage of life, the sensory level is childhood. Regardless how we evolve afterward, virtually every one of us in childhood apprehends the world this way and has these kinds of values. As a spiritual experience, it is the one most are aware of, where there is enhanced sensory experience; sensory experience that is open and wonderful as a child's, but which doesn't go beyond that.

**Book 2. The Recollective-Analytic.** Some folks, however, enter upon a search for identity in youth that involves more than simply finding out what route one might best take to acquire the materials of life and to draw to oneself the sensory experiences desired — the pleasures of the world including all the above from stage one as well as sex, spouse, family, and friends. Such individuals, instead, seek a grander identity and wish to know a more ultimate truth. And it might arise at any time of life, actually, not just youth. Especially so it might arise after the occurrence of a life-shattering tragedy. Often it emerges in mid-life, as Jung chronicled, when life's material and sensory attainments are revealed as the shallowness they are. Nevertheless, it is an identity stage that contains all the components of the one at youth, and some folks in youth do embark on it.

People often do not choose it — this opening into self-reflection. For it is frequently fallen into as a result of a tragedy — one experiences a serious illness or the death of someone close to one or has an accident, a career disaster, a heart-breaking love disappointment, or some other major misfortune — and this unexpected stumbling block on one's well-planned route to material, sensory, and social success, this enforced "moratorium" from life, causes the initial inward turning. One wants to know "Why?" As in "Why me (Lord)?" "What's it all about?" "What's *wrong* with me?" "What did I do to deserve this?" In response one becomes reflective. One turns self-analytical. One begins the process of self-inquiry that is the initial and necessary stage of any and all spiritual or personal evolution.

This stage of spirituality has its corollary in the life stages as the student phase of life. Indeed, often this quest begins in college. But the recollective-analytic as a spiritually evolutionary phase involves more of a vision quest, or an existential search for meaning than occurs for the average youth or student. And all things considered this search for identity, for who to be in life and what to do, takes on the character mostly of a more profound and wider search — that for self-understanding.

**Book 3. The Symbolic-Existential.** This phase of spiritual evolution comes about after one has discovered some aspects of self (and Self) on the inner plane, through the previous stage, that one wishes, rather needs, to express and bring to the world. I talked above how this is a necessary stage in the primal process. Indeed it is, but in all other processes of growth it is vital as well. In terms of the primal process, the therapy stage would be the recollective-analytic above, from Book 2; and this would be the actualization phased required, or, as explained above, "the second half of 'the cure.'"

This stage is existential for it involves immersing oneself fully in existence, in the game here and now that one came to human form on Earth to play. It is symbolic as well, for it has mythological overtones. This is the phase often depicted in mythologies, which portray the path, the journey, of everyman-woman through life. It is the life as lived by the "hero of a thousand faces," as Campbell laid it out, and as exists in all cultures and is available for all peoples.

It is the facing of challenges, the overcoming of obstacles, the expression of what was discovered within and now in the context of society and the rest of life and the world. From stage one to stage two it was a leaving of the fold, the community, society. From stage two to stage three it is a returning to the fold, the community, the society, although perhaps not the same one. For as Tom Wolfe said, "one can never go home again." In that case it is about finding one's tribe and then participating in it.

It is dramatic; it is the grandest theater, for the stakes are high. It is the life that is worthy of a soundtrack, so to speak. For it is urgent and necessary to bring to the world what one uniquely can. No one else can do it. And if you fail in it, the world will simply lack forever whatever it is you came here to contribute.

This stage of spiritual evolution is full and fulfilling but stressful, intense, and all-encompassing. Failure in one's task is the thing most feared. Not loss of material things or lack of avenues for sensory gratification. Not either is the problem that of confusion and wondering about "it all." One does not feel here that one lacks meaning in life or considers life to be empty. There are always periods of self-reflection and re-evaluation at every stage. But in this one, one is not obsessed by that, is not paralyzed by that. One does not retreat from the world; one throws oneself into it. Eager to do and belong in it. For here, at this stage, one knows enough about "it all" to know that the world lacks and needs what one can uniquely bring it. So responsibility is laid upon one's actions as well.

It is the heroic quest, thus mythologically important, and is in that sense "symbolic." It is immersion in life experience; it is the experiential path of evolution, it is one where one is lined up with a cause higher than oneself ... thus it is existential.

It corresponds to the adult stage of life, though few adults in any society bring adulthood to fruition in the way it needs to happen in order for it to be a stage in liberation. But some do. Creative and spiritual people in particular know what I am talking about here. And when one fulfills one's life and purpose in this grandest of fashions, the next ring of the circle of growth becomes accessible.

Notice, these are rings outward, with each one encompassing all the ones that preceded it. They are not rungs of a ladder in which each step takes one further away from what was below and the earliest efforts are left behind and forgotten, no longer feeding or fulfilling the ones following, no longer being a headspring for ever greater wisdom.

So one edges outward along the circumference of one's self, bordering on the Divine. Here is where the magic is palpable. One has grown in purpose to the point where it brings about the next stage, the Integral.

**Book 4. The Integral.** This is the one the spiritual literature talks about. It corresponds to the sannyasi stage of life in the Indian culture. It corresponds to Jung's Wise Old Man and Crone archetypes, framed as stages of life and spiritual evolution. At this point one has fulfilled oneself in relation to the society; one has done one's atmic duty. One approaches the cosmic. It is not about getting anywhere at this point, it is about being here.

As I said in a previous chapter, first there is a mountain, that is the Sensory. Then there is no mountain, that is the Recollective-Analytic. Then there is, this is the Symbolic-Existential. And at this stage of the Integral one has gone beyond even that, and one has merged into Self. And if still alive, one expresses and operates out of that Source. This is the stage of the individuated person, using Jung's terminology. In the spiritual literature, much more is said about this stage of spiritual evolution than any other, for it is the one wherein one is on the doorstep of the "goal."

However, that reveals a mistake as well. For although in Hindu culture these stages are reflected as the four stages of a human life, if one looks in the spiritual literature it is as if this is the only stage and one can attain liberation from any of the other stages of life. Whereas that is not the case.

We now know that one cannot jump from sensory experience to enlighten-ment. If one takes an entheogen at that first stage, the Sensory one, all one can expect is enhanced sensory experiences. At the most there is possible an opening to the Recollective-Analytic. The experience might lead to deeper self-reflection and/or the undertaking of a spiritual quest for understanding and liberation. It might even lead to a break-*down* that hopefully, sooner or later, will be seen to be the break-*through* it in actuality is. In such case it is termed a *spiritual emergency,* and it is not at all pleasant or comfortable ... one's self-esteem gets wrecked, for one thing ... regardless how growthful and necessary it turns out to be. In any case, that is just the beginning.

Similarly, one cannot expect to jump from the Recollective-Analytic, the monastic, the student phase directly to liberation. That is what I was stressing in what I said regarding the book that will be about the second half of the cure. One needs to bring one's re-freshed, re-newed, re-born self into the world and add what one can to it, in engagement with the community of souls and the life on this planet. One can do that in parts, for one should always keep one foot in the world of self-evaluation, but one needs to embark on self-actualization where and when one can. It is the dialectic between the two that catalyzes growth. One goes from realization to worldly actualization and inevitably confronts obstacles. Leading to more self-inquiry, then back to expression and participation, which sooner or later finds stumbling blocks. Leading one inward again for another stint at the drawing board, followed by another ad-venture, and round and round again.

Nevertheless, this fruitful and often ebullient process is not the Integral stage. The Integral stage is the dawning of wisdom, or at least the beginning of that. It is open-hearted beingness in the world; palpable reunion with all life, all Experience; it is both cosmic and community belongingness at once. And that can only come about through participation and immersion, fully, in the pulsing phases of expansion, previous.

## The Quadrilogy, *Remembering*

The other series I have planned at this time has to do with the quadrilogy, the novel in four books that I have worked on over the years. The name of the quadrilogy is *Remembering*. It comprises four books. Book One: *Leaving*. Book Two: *Looking*. Book Three: *Arriving*. And Book Four: *Being Here*.

Perhaps these titles make sense after what I was just relating about the four stages of re-membering above? In any case, it is true these novels are fictional expressions of the ideas of the four stages of self-understanding of the Journey of Re-Membering Series described above.

Finally, I have plans to fill out the ideas of *Falls from Grace* (2014a) in a series of four books covering each of the phases: The First Fall, Conception. The Second Fall, Birth. The Third Fall, the Primal Scene. And The Fourth Fall, Identity. And more immediately in the future, with no apparent series for them to find a home, are the books in process, *The Psychology of Apocalypse* and *The Psychology of Generations*.

I am not going to say any more, and I have already said too much. For these plans are likely to change, indeed they undoubtedly will. What usually happens is these plans expand as put into practice, so that more books will be added. But you see here the grandest overview possible of what you can look forward to in the upcoming years. This is a look at what is enroute and will appear, barring unforeseen circumstances. That is, as they say, this is what will arrive, "the Lord willing and the creek don't rise." Lol

We will see what the Universe wants and what it will support. Stay tuned.

# ACKNOWLEDGMENTS

Who to thank for this one? This is a difficult Acknowledgments to write for this has been a mostly No-Form production throughout. Seriously. Even this acknowledgment came to me upon awakening today, just as some of the ideas of this book were there at dawn or came to me in actual dreams, as I have explained in the text.

The one inspiration that first came to mind upon awakening today was Carl Jung. And he is not in Form, anymore. I thought of how his book *Memories, Dreams, Reflections* (1961) was inspirational to me in my youth, but also how it contributed to the style in which I would allow parts of this book to come out.

Others of note are also in No-Form now. Sathya Sai Baba was a chief inspiration, through his works, especially. And I acknowledge him in most of my works for he is an inspiration and has been a source of reflection since the Eighties.

And this leads me back to the dedication I made for this work. Therein contains the ones who should get most of the credit for assisting in this work. Carl Jung, Hermann Hesse, Arthur Janov, Stanislav Grof, and Sathya Sai Baba. All of these are people who inspired me primarily through their works.

In a practical sense, I want to thank my friend, a talented artist, Mark Lawrence for his generosity in providing the graphics for Chapter 15. Tolerating my painstaking attention to detail, he graciously provided the three graphics mapping the inner realms, as seen in that chapter under "The Map of All Reality" and "Sri Yantra."

Beyond that, and these are the ones who deserve the most of my gratitude of all, is my No-Form family, especially Graham Farrant, Martha D. Ello, and Shirdi Sai Baba. Graham Farrant, a colleague, catalyst, and friend, his encouragement and input sustains me. Shirdi Sai Baba, I am buoyed up in the inspiration of your example and humbled in receipt of your love.

As for who else, well, the fact is that there are few who are in Form who have thought along these lines.

And of course, as in everything I do, the greatest help I receive is from Mary Lynn Adzema, my wife. She is my partner in crime in everything I write. She listened to these ideas as they came through in the text. She supported them. She, like I, learned from them.

Peter Radford and Ceila Levine I want to thank as well, as they listened to these ideas and discussed them with me.

Others I want to thank for their support are Peter Lavender. Thanks for showing up, Peter.

Thanks for your support as well, Jeanine Parvati Baker.

Much love to you, Terry Larimore. What a true ally you have been.

Thanks for your modality, Stan Grof. And for creating the circumstances within which I would learn so much

My mother, my father — thanks for coming through and for the message, Dad.

Jeanne Levine and Lynn Radford, I am humbled by your assistance.

To Martha D. Ello — eternal love and gratitude for your love and your help and all else. Who but you, in Form, saw me? Few others, that's damn sure. And you never left and you aid me always. How can I ever thank you except to continue to acknowledge and dedicate my works to you.

For reasons I must leave out, I need to thank Mary Elisabeth Dupont for having played a huge role in this work. I am forever grateful to you, Mary Elisabeth, wherever you are.

# NOTES

## Chapter Two

1. Gary Zukav, *The Dancing Wu Li Masters*, 1979, p. 30.

2. Ibid., pp. 30-31.

3. Roy D'Andrade, "Cultural Meaning Systems," 1984, p. 92.

4. See "Allegory of the Cave" in *The Republic of Plato*, by Plato, with Allan Bloom (trans.), 1991.

5. I need to explain my use of the terms *perceptor* and *percepter*, which I use quite a bit in this part. I use perceptor to mean a being who perceives, also could be called an experiencer. In the dictionary a *perceptor* is defined as "that which perceives," a receiver, an imbiber, and, in Spanish, a recipient. I need to acknowledge this term, for it is not even included in many of the most popular dictionaries. But it is in some, and I needed to use this term, even if I would have had to coin it, in that I needed a word for *being, entity, person, animal, experiencer,* and so on. I needed a term that would encompass all those possible receivers or beings who experience, without any of the differing connotations each of them bring. All have connotations I want to exclude. For in making my case, as you will see, I need to define *something* ... not necessarily anything that we can imagine to be a being ... something that is a receiver of perceptions. An experiencer comes closest, but that, too, has all kinds of connotations I do not want. So *perceptor* it is; plural is *perceptors*.

Now, in terms of *percepter* (with an *e* instead of an *o*), I *did* have to coin a word for the sense organs that such a perceptor might employ, and I needed to avoid the connotation that, as in *sense organ*, they would necessarily relate to a body or an organ, or anything connoting human, bodily, or even physicality, for that matter.

For what I am talking about is not necessarily even "embodied" in any sense I am using. What I am indicating with my term, *percepters*, is the unimaginable "sense organs" of a perceptor ... which are not necessarily physical and so are not really organs.

Now, if we consider an alien, a planet, or some being we are unable to perceive, except in its effects in our world and which is therefore invisible to us, something ghost-like that way, but living and experiencing, who therefore perceives and uses whatever they do to perceive with, and some of my examples of possibilities of perceptors are that far out there, then it would be ridiculous to say the "sense organs" of an invisible or planet-like being... lol. You see, *sense organs* or *senses* assume a physical world as well as one that is distinctly divided between living and non-living things.

So, I coined the term *percepter* to mean whatever is used by a perceptor to perceive. And the plural of that is, of course, percepters. None of the possible terms for this — receptors, senses — say what I am trying to. For they either indicate a specific cellular area that receives stimuli, which implies a body, again, or they refer to the character of the stimuli that are received. Senses are hearing, touch, and so on. But a percepter would be the sensory organ that picks up the sound. But it would also be applicable to whatever a not embodied or not imaginable being would have that would sense an aspect of Reality.

Thus, *perceptors* are beings who perceive, and they use *percepters* to do that.

6. While this is not important to point out for the purposes of this book; in this analysis, in order to be consistent, I need to say that the idea that cultures are separate and that they cannot be understood outside of them, as is the traditional anthropological understanding, coming down from Boas, is full of logical lapses as well. For, is there anyone even *within* a culture who does not see that culture as different from any other one in that culture?

I mean, at base, is not culture reducible to personality and to individual psychology? In which case, there is as much relativity to individual culture, to "personality" culture, if you will, as there is to collective culture, what we call *culture*. And it follows from this, conversely, that there is potentially as much *reality* or truth — as well, then — to someone from another culture's interpretation as is from someone within the culture under discussion.

To see this, compare someone outside that culture who is imbued with the cultural understandings of that culture relative to someone within that culture who for some reason is lacking in understanding of their cultural elements or is misunderstanding, or alternately understanding, that culture from the way the majority of that culture is understanding it. So this idea of cultural relativity is itself relative as truth. For it is based on a reified construction of culture as being something absolute with distinct boundaries. Which is not and is nowhere true in Reality. The boundaries of culture are permeable and overlapping, like so many other realities, entities, and items we mistakenly think of as distinct for the sole purpose of being able to talk about them.

7. I define and describe the *Unapproved and Hidden* in several of my works, but especially, and initially, in *Planetmates, The Great Reveal* (2014b). For here, note that the *Unapproved and Hidden* is the species unconscious for our species, humans, which exists in *all* cultures, for all times. It is pretty much *the same* in all cultures, based as it is, on both a common human biology as well as a common human psychology — specifically having to do with our unique psychological invention of Ego. Indeed, the Unapproved and Hidden can be considered one of those brute facts, those species-specific facts, I have been referring to.

# Chapter 3

1. Stanislav Grof, *The Cosmic Game*, 1998, p. 17.

2. Ibid. p. 86.

3. Roy D'Andrade, "Anthropological Theory: Where Did It Go? (How Can We Get It Back?), 1987, p. 5.

4. Ibid, p. 6, *emphases mine*.

# Chapter 4

1. The works in which I have detailed how our conception, gestation, and birth condition and shape all later experience are *Womb with a View: Spiritual Aspects of Intrauterine Experience* (1981); *Cells with a View: Spiritual and Philosophical Aspects of Sperm and Egg Experience* (1984); "A Primal Perspective on Spirituality" (1985); *Falls from Grace: Spiritual and Philosophical Perspectives of Prenatal and Primal Experience* (1994); *Falls from Grace: The Devolution and Revolution of Consciousness* (2014a); and *Wounded Deer and Centaurs: The Necessary Hero and the Prenatal Matrix of Human Events* (2016b). Look also to updated and readily available versions of *Womb with a View* and *Cells with a View* which I will be bringing to print quite soon, probably in 2017-2018.

2. A good place to start in looking into what we now know about the influences from the womb on later personality and the ability to remember extending that far back is Thomas Verny's *The Secret Life of the Unborn Child* (1981). That, along with the publications from the Association for Prenatal and Perinatal Psychology and Health (APPPAH) and its many members and the works of mine detailed in the note above, which give an overview of the field, are pretty good correctives to our common mistaken notions about unconsciousness and lack of memory in the prenate and about how far back we can go in looking at the earliest influences on our lives.

# Chapter 5

1. See Adzema, *Falls from Grace*, 2014a.

# Chapter 7

1. Aldous Huxley, *The Doors of Perception*, 1956, p. 22.

2. Ibid., pp. 22-23.

3. Ibid., p. 23.

4. "Mind-meld," for those not familiar with the term, is a term popularized by the *Star Trek* series. The character, Spock, would be able to do a complete merging of his mind with another's and be able to experience their actual thoughts and images in the way they did.

# Chapter 8

1. This perspective has much in common with Wilber's (1977) *spectrum of consciousness* view of reality. Though, for reasons which will become clear as we proceed, I must stress that this position does not synchronize with Wilber's later formulations (e.g., 1980, 1981), where he has conformed his view to the more traditional and presumptuous Western biases. And these biases are distinctly at odds with an essential point I have emphasized in this section of making diligent our attempts at wiping away any ethnocentric as well as anthropocentric residue from our lenses if we are to have any chance at all for even minimal success in our venturing into Reality. (Cf. Winkelman 1990; Adzema 1995a)

2. Some of Stanislav Grof's work and findings can be found in Grof, 1970, 1975, 1980, 1984, 1985, 1988a, 1988b; Grof and Grof 1980, 1989, 1990; and Grof and Halifax 1977. He has more recent works as well, extending over a period up to the present.

3. For the video, "Holographic Universe," check online at

   https://www.youtube.com/watch?v=lMBt_yfGKpU

4. For a discussion of this subject of the difference between the new transpersonal paradigm and the old religious one, and how they are, against all the facts, confused, see my article "Christ's 'Religion' — The Spiritual Practice of Jesus," 2009. Online at

   *https://sites.google.com/site/primalspirituality/*

5. See Thomas Kuhn, *The Structure of Scientific Revolutions*, 1970.

6. Thomas Kuhn was an American science historian and science philosopher who held that science was not a steady, cumulative acquisition of knowledge but is "a series of peaceful interludes punctuated by intellectually violent revolutions." Here are some especially prescient and relevant quotes from and about Thomas Kuhn:

> *Under normal conditions the research scientist is not an innovator but a solver of puzzles, and the puzzles upon which he concentrates are just those which he believes can be both stated and solved within the existing scientific tradition.*

> *Normal science does not aim at novelties of fact or theory and, when successful, finds none.*

> *In a sense that I am unable to explicate further, the proponents of competing paradigms practice their trades in different worlds.*

> *Later scientific theories are better than earlier ones for solving puzzles in the often quite different environments to which they are applied. That is not a relativist's position, and it displays the sense in which I am a convinced believer in scientific progress.*

> *Scientific development depends in part on a process of non-incremental or revolutionary change. Some revolutions are large, like those associated with the names of Copernicus, Newton, or Darwin, but most are much smaller, like the discovery of oxygen or the planet Uranus. The usual prelude to changes of this sort is, I believed, the awareness of anomaly, of an occurrence or set of occurrences that does not fit existing ways of ordering phenomena. The changes that result therefore require 'putting on a different kind of thinking-cap', one that renders the anomalous lawlike but that, in the process, also transforms the order exhibited by some other phenomena, previously unproblematic.*

> *The success of the paradigm ... is at the start largely a promise of success ... Normal science consists in the actualization of that promise ... Mopping up operations are what engage most scientists throughout their careers. They constitute what I am here calling normal science ... That enterprise seems an attempt to force nature into the preformed and relatively inflexible box that the paradigm supplies. No part of the aim of normal science is to call forth new sorts of phenomena; indeed those that will not fit the box are often not seen at all. Nor do scientists normally aim to invent new theories, and they are often intolerant of those invented by others.* — Thomas Kuhn

And more recently, from Carl Sagan,

> *At the heart of science is an essential balance between two seemingly contradictory attitudes — an openness to new ideas, no matter how bizarre or counterintuitive they may be, and the most ruthless skeptical scrutiny of all ideas, old and new. This is how deep truths are winnowed from deep nonsense. — Carl Sagan*

# Chapter 9

1. Aldous Huxley, *The Doors of Perception*, 1956, p. 26.

2. See my works, *Planetmates: The Great Reveal* (2014b) and *Prodigal Human: The Descents of Man* (2016a), especially on this topic of how morality gets construed along lines beneficial to elites with the beginnings of hierarchical societies.

# Chapter 10

1. For Rupert Sheldrake's ideas see, among others, Sheldrake, 1981, 1991a, 1991b, and 1995.

2. For my ideas on secondary altriciality and culture, see my works, *Planetmates: The Great Reveal* (2014b) and *Prodigal Human: The Descents of Man* (2016a).

3. For an idea of "the different planetmate views," see my work, *Planetmates: The Great Reveal* (2014b).

4. Thomas Kuhn, *The Structure of Scientific Revolutions*, 1970.

# Chapter 11

1. For Ken Wilber's works, see, among others, Wilber, 1980, 1981, 1982, and 1983.

2. Roger Jones, *Physics as Metaphor*, 1982, pp. 6-7.

3. Ibid., p. 7.

4. Ibid., p. 3.

5. Ibid., p. 5.

6. Ibid.

7. See, as one variation on this, "Masculinization or Dehumanization? The Sambia Tribe of Papua New Guinea," available online.

8. For an explanation and description of cargo cults, one can check out Wikipedia, online, at

*https://en.wikipedia.org/wiki/Cargo_cult*

# Chapter 12

1.  Rupert Sheldrake, "Is Nature Alive?" *Human Potential*, 1991a, p. 17.

2.  Ibid.

3.  Robert Lawlor, *Voices of the First Day: Awakening in the Aboriginal Dreamtime*, 1991, p. 33.

4.  Ibid., p. 34.

5.  Sheldrake, op. cit., p. 17.

6.  Ibid.

7.  Ibid., p. 18.

8.  Experiments testing the theory of morphogenetic fields have been reported in a number of places, including *New Sense Bulletin* (1991), *Noetic Sciences Bulletin* (1991), and of course Sheldrake's own works and presentations.

9.  Sheldrake, op. cit. p. 33.

10.  Ibid., p. 35.

11.  Ibid.

12.  Lawlor, op. cit., p. 24.

# Chapter 13

1.  On Emanationism, see also my works, which view suffuses them. See especially, *Falls from Grace: Spiritual and Philosophical Perspectives of Prenatal and Primal Experience* (1994); *Primal Renaissance: The Emerging Millennial Return* (1995c); *Falls from Grace: The Devolution and Revolution of Consciousness* (2014a); *Planetmates: The Great Reveal* (2014b); *Funny God: The Tao of Funny God and the Mind's True Liberation* (2015); and *Prodigal Human: The Descents of Man* (2016a).

2.  Philip Merlan, Emanationism, *Encyclopedia of Philosophy*, p 473.

3.  To be completely accurate, Ken Wilber did follow his spectrum of consciousness theory forward into his next book, titled *No Boundary* (1979). However, in his book following that, *The Atman Project* (1980), he reversed himself. Notice how *The Atman Project* even in its title implies such an effortful view of growth and progress whereas *No Boundary* implies the opposite, a freely giving and growing and emanational view. So, Ken Wilber, in the subsequent work and thereafter retreats from the implications of his original position. He does a reconceptualization of his theory in all of his later work.

Interestingly, I followed the exact opposite path in that my first work was one espousing the stance Wilber eventually came to, but I reversed my position upon my coming into my understandings of the primal and holotropic sort, arising from my years of experience doing primal therapy and holotropic breathwork.

# Chapter 14

1. Sheldrake, op. cit., p. 17.

2. Ibid.

3. Ibid.

4. Ibid.

5. Ibid., p. 18.

6. Ibid., p. 19.

7. I prefer to use the term *psyche* with which to distinguish universal subjectivity from all of matter, rather than *Mind*, or "the mental," as is traditionally done in philosophy. For I find that *Mind* means much less than what is intended here and leads in general to many misinterpretations in philosophy. Let me explain.

Despite its long tradition of use, *Mind*, meaning subjectivity in the abstract, is still confused with *mind*, in the common sense of the term, meaning a person's intellect, thoughts, ideas, concepts, and so on. Hence *Mind* ends up being equated with language or thoughts, as in in "I think, therefore I am." Such a way of looking at subjectivity, which excludes the feeling or "bodily" component of the psychic or subjective (cf., Gendlin, 1992) or the experiential part of existence (cf., all existentialists) bespeaks a reality compatible to Rationalists, and most intellectuals, who appear to know of no experience outside of their thoughts.

But there are others of us whose subjectivity, I insist, comprises much more than what is thought of, commonly, as "mind," which is that it is merely thoughts, cogitation, cognition. Hence, in the tradition of Carl Jung, it seems *psyche* is the appropriate term, at least for starters. For it is a term that points to the possible inclusion, in subjective reality, of "feelings," "passions," archetypal and transpersonal noncognitive-nonverbal experience, and the psychic.

The best term of all for what is meant here by the Absolute Idealistic Reality — as I contend in this book and an earlier formulation of it, *Experience Is Divinity* (2013c) — is, in my considered opinion, *Experience*. That is a term that is also, on its surface, heavily loaded with connotations and the baggage of a traditional philosophical heritage. Still, it is the most accurate term and enjoys the most usage of all in contemporary personal-growth, experiential-psychotherapy, and consciousness-research conclaves. For that reason, I affirmed it in my work, *Experience Is Divinity*, and I seek to apply it consistently in this book. I contend *Experience* is the best term, with *psyche* a suitable second, to explain the difference between the theory I advance in this work and traditional Idealistic conceptualizations in philosophy.

However, it is a position I lead up to gradually and attempt to demonstrate in the analysis throughout this work. For beginning purposes, Jung's use of *psyche* — as more inclusive than mind — suffices to point us in the right direction.

8. This is a description, according to Toms (1992, p. 89), that has been originally attributed to C. E. M. Joad.

9. Wittgenstein, 1953, 2009, *Philosophical Investigations,* Sec. 390, p. 119e.

10. Peter Tompkins and Christopher Bird, *The Secret Life of Plants,* 1979; and Thomas Verny and John Kelly, *The Secret Life of the Unborn Child,* 1981.

11. Patrick, 1952, p. 185.

12. Arthur S. Eddington, *Space, Time, and Gravitation,* 1920, 2009, pp. 200-201, from Patrick, 1952, p. 116, *emphases mine.*

# Chapter 15

1. W. T. Stace, *The Theory of Knowledge and Existence,* 1932, pp. 65-66.

2. From Patrick Gardiner's article, "Arthur Schopenhauer (1788-1860)," in *Encyclopedia of Philosophy,* 1967.

3. Erwin Schrödinger, *Mind and Matter,* 1958.

# Chapter 16

1. On *devolution* occurring in the course of human history, as opposed to what we normally call *evolution,* especially see my works, *Prodigal Human: The Descents of Man* (2016a), which is being published concurrently with this book; and *Planetmates: The Great Reveal* (2014b).

# Chapter 17

1. I have several works-in-progress in which I do focus on these levels of experiential reality, this Map of the Universal Mind. See, in the Afterword of this book, my descriptions of "Book Six, The Journey of Re-Membering ... Four Phases of Self-Awareness" and "The Stages of Re-Membering Series" to get an idea of what is coming.

2. This would be David Icke. Since his works are paranoia and propaganda built around some actual elements of truth, I will not further him by referring to his works. You can do that on your own, if you wish.

3. For explications of how distortions arise in and influence spiritual perceptions and realities, see especially *Apocalypse NO: Apocalypse or Earth Rebirth and the Emerging Perinatal Unconscious* (2013a); *Falls from Grace: The Devolution and Revolution of Consciousness* (2014a); *Wounded Deer and Centaurs: The Necessary Hero and the*

*Prenatal Matrix of Human Events* (2016b; and "A Primal Perspective on Spirituality" (1985), among my other readily available and published works.

# Chapter 18

1.  I explore the prenatal and perinatal influences that cause us to look away from direct Experience especially in my works, *Apocalypse NO: Apocalypse or Earth Rebirth and the Emerging Perinatal Unconscious* (2013b); *Falls from Grace: The Devolution and Revolution of Consciousness* (2014a); *Funny God: The Tao of Funny God and the Mind's True Liberation* (2015); and *Wounded Deer and Centaurs: The Necessary Hero and the Prenatal Matrix of Human Events* (2016b), of my works that are currently in print and readily available at this time.

2.  In several of the books following from this one in The Path of Ecstasy Series, I will go even further than Part Five, "Matter Is Message," into the deepest and closest conceptions to be laid upon raw Experience. These works especially would be *Womb with a View*, which is the book following this one in the series and scheduled for 2017; *Cells with a View*, the one following that in the series and scheduled 2017, as well; and *The Cosmic Overstanding: You, God, and Identity*, planned to be the last one in the series and scheduled 2018.

3.  Clark Moustakas, *Heuristic Research*, 1990, p. 9.

4.  Ibid., p. 11.

5.  One such monograph, demonstrating the espousal of strict boundaries be-tween academic fields, is Max Gluckman's (ed.) *Closed Systems and Open Minds* (2006).

6.  For a description of The Path of Ecstasy Series and the Return to Grace Series, see the Afterword of this book.

# Chapter 19

1.  Sathya Sai Baba, "Joy of Surrender," 1991, p. 16.

2.  Robert Lawlor, "Sexuality and the Universe Evolving," 1989, *emphases mine*, p. 43.

3.  Robert Lawlor, "Voices of the First Day," 1992, p. 22.

4.  Ronald D. Laing, [Interview with R. D. Laing], 1988, p. 62.

5.  Gabriele Uhlein, "Hildegard of Bingen," 1991, p. 54.

6.  Ibid.

7.  Ibid.

8.  This idea that the world, perceived, gives us lessons in ultimate truths was ex-pressed wonderfully in this poem by Antler, 1991, p. 61, titled "Proving What?"

How in autumn, even before the leaves fall,
When they're all at their height of color,
Next year's leaves are already there, tiny,
on either side of the stem of each leaf
where it meets the branch,
Already there, waiting,
Before the leaf that is still there
is dead and falls,
Tiny folded leafbudsheath
Resembling two hands in prayer
Palm to palm with fingers extended.

Proving what?
Life after death exists
even before you're dead.

Or how when a redwood tree is cut down or blown over
It doesn't die because the roots
Curl up out of the earth and become
new trees,
Each of which can grow to be
Just as tall just as old
as the tree which was there before.
It'd be as if you were cut off at the ankles
And your top taken away to make *The Milwaukee Journal*
And your toes curled into the ground and came up
as ten new "you's — looking exactly like you
and being exactly like you.
And so a redwood you see now that's 2000 years old
may've come from the root of a redwood that was
2000 years old
that may've come from the root of a redwood that was
2000 years old
so far back that it's literally one million years old!
And *that's* why they're called *Sequoia sempervirens*,
ever-living.

Proving ... what?
Even before you're dead
life after death exists.

9. I am referring here to the Jungian notion that the process of individuation is one that is necessarily taken up later in life. I am saying here that any time is a good time to begin, with an important qualification. This is an issue close to me as it relates to my first book (1970), written at the age of 20, in which I asserted

exactly the Jungian position. I discuss this at length in a later chapter, Chapter 27, "Identity and the Sea of Potentiality."

For here, I want simply to say that the important qualification for taking up the path of mysticism and individuation earlier in life than mid-life is that it should come with some kind of experiential way of handling the unconscious materials that arise ... and in a way that is integrative and expressive, as for example as is done in primal therapy, holotropic breathwork, or the experiential psychotherapies ... and not in a way that is repressive, as in meditation, which is the way these materials are usually attempted to be dealt with, often with tragic results. Also, it should be combined with actualization of experience. This part about actualization I especially cover in Chapter 27.

An important aspect of this is that since we have these new psychotechnologies of experiential integration we might, for the first time in Western history, be able to approach these realities and truths; not only earlier in life, though that is huge and significant in itself; but that these paths of individuation might be for the first time in any culture or time be undertaken by the masses, by average folks not just specially fortunate ones.

10. Francine Schiff, "The Mystical Experience, 1991, p. 9.

11. My experience with alcoholism is a book-length story on its own. For here, just let me say that, in addition to all my paths of spiritual and psychological endeavor and all those practices, I went also through periods of addiction and recovery.

This is hardly something I am ashamed of, for they were perhaps the most transformative experiences of purification through fire I experienced in life. I am reluctant to say this, but it fits with the experiences of others in recovery from addiction and alcoholism and has been noted by Jung; Bill Wilson, the co-founder of Alcoholics Anonymous; and Stanislav Grof that the addictive processes and the spiritual processes have much in common. In fact, such experiences can be manifestations of what Grof has termed *spiritual emergencies* which are actually times of *spiritual emergence.*

Let's put it this way: I mean, I don't actually *recommend* alcoholism as a technique of higher consciousness. But, hey, it worked for me.

12. Michael Adzema, *Falls from Grace,* 2014a, p. 91. Also it appears in "A Primal Perspective on Spirituality," *Journal of Humanistic Psychology,* 1985.

13. The places where I go into the issue of how tortuous and counterproductive it is to act-out one's Pain, rather than feeling it, are especially my works, *Apocalypse NO* (2013a), *Falls from Grace* (2014a), and *Wounded Deer and Centaurs* (2016b).

# Chapter 20

1. Shakespeare, Macbeth Act 5, scene 5, 19–28.

2. The full quote from Shakespeare goes

*What a piece of work is man! How noble in reason! how infinite in faculties! in form and moving, how express and admirable! in action how like an angel! in apprehension, how like a god! the beauty of the world! the paragon of animals! And yet, to me, what is this quintessence of dust?*

Hamlet speaks to Rosencrantz and Guildenstern in Act II, scene ii (287–298).

# Chapter 21

1. Stanislav Grof, *The Cosmic Game*, 1998, pp. 62-64, 179-180.

# Chapter 23

1. For my writing on human prematurity, secondary altriciality, and fetal malnutrition, see especially, in the books cited, *Planetmates* (2014b), *Falls from Grace* (2014a), *Wounded Deer and Centaurs* (2016b), and *Prodigal Human* (2016a).

2. I have elaborated on the seed of light that lies within darkness in Chapter 37 of *Funny God* (2015), titled, "The Truth One Dare Not Speak: How Evil Is Reality? How Much Fear Is Real? … Even in the Seemingly 'Darkest' of Places, There Is Light"; and Chapter 55 of *Experience Is Divinity* (2013c), titled, "What I Can Tell You About the Seed of Light in the Deepest Darkness: The Witness Self, The Beneficence of Experience, and the Secret About Oneself One Dares Never Reveal."

# Chapter 24

1. To clarify, *Planetmates: The Great Reveal* (2014b) is a book I wrote, as inspired by our non-human friends. Animals did not write it. I do not claim it to have been "channeled," though I do not know what "channeling" feels like. If that was channeling, then all my books are "channeled." I prefer to call it inspiration, like any other writer.

However, in *Planetmates,* I use a literary device, which amounts to framing it as if it is an event and the planetmates are speaking to us and I am only elaborating, as inspired by them. Still, whether it was channeled or I was "inspired," it is still the only book, as far as I know, that professes to speak for them, for all the beings with whom we share this planet, for *planetmates.* And I speak for them saying things I am sure they would applaud, perhaps even be proud of. Their interests, along with our illumination, are paramount in the book.

# Chapter 25

1. Hermann Hesse, *Siddhartha*, 1951, p. 104.

2. Ibid.

3. Ibid., pp. 107-108.

4. Ibid., pp. 109-110.

5. Ibid., p. 111.

# Chapter 26

1. Ibid., pp. 136ff.

2. Ibid.

3. Ibid.

4. Ibid.

5. Yoko Ono, from the song, "We're All Water," on the album, *Some Time in New York City*, 1972.

6. Hesse, op. cit., pp. 136ff.

7. Ibid.

# Chapter 27

1. On The Trilateral Commission, the quote in the text is from Michael Kasenbacher, 24 December 2012, "Work, Learning and Freedom," in New *Left Project*. A humorous, albeit telling, additional quote from that work:

> *Conservative pundit Charles Krauthammer sardonically alluded to the conspiracy theories when he was asked in 2012 who makes up the "Republican establishment," saying, "Karl Rove is the president. We meet every month on the full moon... [at] the Masonic Temple. We have the ritual: Karl brings the incense, I bring the live lamb and the long knife, and we began... with a pledge of allegiance to the Trilateral Commission.*

From "Trilateral Commission," on Wikipedia, online at

https://en.wikipedia.org/wiki/Trilateral_Commission

2. From "Oklahoma City Bombing," on Wikipedia, online at

https://en.wikipedia.org/wiki/Oklahoma_City_bombing

3. From "Jared Lee Loughner," on Wikipedia, online at

https://en.wikipedia.org/wiki/Jared_Lee_Loughner

4. Ibid.

# Chapter 30

1. The idea has become pervasive that crop circles have been shown to be hoaxes. I have just reviewed an article on the website Skeptical Inquirer that stated that "Most crop circle researchers admit that the vast majority of crop circles are created by hoaxers." First of all, how can researchers "admit" anything unless they themselves are the hoaxers? Indeed, what "crop circle researchers" amounts to is people who like the author have thought about crop circles and assumed they are hoaxes. That is what they consider "research," when you look at their sources.

Secondly, saying most "crop circle researchers admit" anything is like saying most folks in primitive times admit the world is flat. That is, these debunkers are claiming the assumptions of other debunkers as some kind of evidence.

This kind of irrationality masquerading as reason abounds in times of changing paradigms. Whether it is political or scientific paradigms changing — and both are moving right now — it is common to hear skeptics and debunkers to have a "well, everybody knows" kind of rationale for why the new ideas cannot be true. Again, like the scientists building theory upon theory that have no basis in reality, many really solidly established castles have been created in the air. The fact that illusions are persistent says nothing about their truth.

What is not known by these "skeptics" is that the "hoaxers" have themselves been debunked. Here is one good article out of several I have seen that addresses this. It should be looked at before one goes assuming that something extraordinary cannot be real simply because it is too fantastic or too outside one's beliefs about the way things work. This also gives the history on the hoax about the hoaxes. Check out, "Crop Circles," on the Walking the Labyrinth website, online at

http://walkingthelabyrinth-cameron.blogspot.com/2010/11/crop-circles.html

# Chapter 32

1. John Mack, 1992a, "Other Realities," In *Noetic Sciences Review*, p. 10.

2. Sara Terry, 1992, "Alien Territory," in *The Boston Sunday Globe, The Boston Globe Magazine*, p. 27. Also available online at

http://johnemackinstitute.org/1992/10/alien-territory/

3. Ibid.

4. Ibid.

5. Ibid.

6. Ibid.

# Chapter 33

1. Robert Lawlor, 1992, "Voices of the First Day: Awakening in the Aboriginal Dreamtime," in *New Frontier*, p. 22.

2. Ibid., p. 20.

3. Ibid.

4. Ibid., p. 22.

# Chapter 34

1. Carlos Castaneda, 1977, *The Second Ring of Power*, pp. 151-152.

2. Ibid.

3. Alvin Lawson (1985, 1987) details the way abduction experiences are dense with elements of our repressed birth traumas.

4. Keith Thompson, 1989, "The UFO Encounter Experience as a Crisis of Transformation," in Grof and Grof, *Spiritual Emergency*, p. 127.

# Chapter 35

1. For the idea of a *primal renaissance* — one in which modern technology and scientific advances marries with the ideas of primal peoples and cultures to create a cross-fertilization and flowering unlike anything ever known — see my works, *Primal Renaissance: The Emerging Millennial Return* (1995c) and *Primal Return: Renaissance and Grace* (scheduled, 2017). This idea is also strewn throughout issues of the journal I produced and edited for the International Primal Association, *Primal Renaissance: The Journal of Primal Psychology* (1995, 1996).

# REFERENCES

Adzema, Michael. 1970. *The Dangers of Mysticism for Modern Youth*. Unpublished manuscript. sillymickel@gmail.com.

Adzema, Michael. 1972. *Remembering: The Four Stages of Self-Understanding*. Unpublished manuscript. sillymickel@gmail.com.

Adzema, Michael. 1981. *Womb with a View: Spiritual Aspects of Intrauterine Experience*. Unpublished manuscript. sillymickel@gmail.com.

Adzema, Michael. 1984. *Cells with a View: Spiritual and Philosophical Aspects of Sperm and Egg Experience*. Unpublished manuscript. sillymickel@gmail.com.

Adzema, Michael. 1985. A primal perspective on spirituality. *Journal of Humanistic Psychology*, *25*(3), 83-116.

Adzema, Michael. 1993. Only half a cure: Unconditional acceptance and the primal process. *IPA Newsletter: International Primal Association*, Summer, 4. Available online at

  *http://primals.org/archives/newsletters/1993%20Summer.pdf*

Adzema, Michael. 1994. *Falls from Grace: Spiritual and Philosophical Perspectives of Prenatal and Primal Experience*. Published Master's Thesis. Rohnert Park, CA: Sonoma State University.

Adzema, Michael. 1995a. Biologically constituted realities: An anti-anthropocentric (species-relative) and new paradigm perspective. *Primal Renaissance: The Journal of Primal Psychology*, *1*(1). Available through sillymickel@gmail.com.

Adzema, Michael. 1995b. Creating positive scenarios: The other half of the cure. *Primal Feelings Newsletter*, Spring, 1995. Available online at

  http://www.primal-page.com/madzema.htm

Adzema, Michael. 1995c. *Primal Renaissance: The Emerging Millennial Return.* Gonzo Sage Media: Eugene, OR. Available through sillymickel@gmail.com.

Adzema, Michael. 1995d. Reunion with the positive (self), part 1: The other half of "the cure." *Primal Renaissance: The Journal of Primal Psychology, 1*(2), 72-85. Available through sillymickel@gmail.com and online at

http://www.primals.org/articles/adzema01.html

Adzema, Michael. (ed.) 1995, 1996. *Primal Renaissance: The Journal of Primal Psychology.* Published by the International Primal Association. Available through sillymickel@gmail.com.

Adzema, Michael. 2009. Christ's "religion" — The spiritual practice of Jesus. Available online at

https://sites.google.com/site/primalspirituality/

Adzema, Michael. 2013a. *Apocalypse NO: Apocalypse or Earth Rebirth and the Emerging Perinatal Unconscious.* Return to Grace, Volume 4. Eugene, OR: Gonzo Sage Media. Available on Amazon, Kindle, and at book stores.

Adzema, Michael. 2013b. *Culture War, Class War: Occupy Generations and the Rise and Fall of "Obvious Truths."* Return to Grace, Volume 1. Eugene, OR: Gonzo Sage Media. Available on Amazon, Kindle, and at book stores

Adzema, Michael. 2013c. *Experience Is Divinity: Matter As Metaphor.* Return to Grace, Volume 8. Eugene, OR: Gonzo Sage Media. Available on Amazon, Kindle, and at book stores.

Adzema, Michael. 2014a. *Falls from Grace: The Devolution and Revolution of Consciousness.* Return to Grace, Volume 9. Eugene, OR: Gonzo Sage Media. Available on Amazon, Kindle, and at book stores.

Adzema, Michael. 2014b. *Planetmates: The Great Reveal.* Return to Grace, Volume 6. Eugene, OR: Gonzo Sage Media. Available on Amazon, Kindle, and at book stores.

Adzema, Michael. 2015. *Funny God: The Tao of Funny God and the Mind's True Liberation.* Return to Grace, Volume 7. Eugene, OR: Gonzo Sage Media. Available on Amazon, Kindle, and at book stores.

Adzema, Michael. 2016a. *Prodigal Human: The Descents of Man.* Return to Grace, Volume 10. Eugene, OR: Gonzo Sage Media. Available on Amazon, Kindle, and at book stores.

Adzema, Michael. 2016b. *Wounded Deer and Centaurs: The Necessary Hero and the Prenatal Matrix of Human Events.* Return to Grace, Volume 5. Eugene, OR: Gonzo Sage Media. Available on Amazon, Kindle, and at book stores.

Adzema, Michael. work-in-progress. *The Cosmic Overstanding: You, God, and Identity.* The Path of Ecstasy Series, Volume 10. Scheduled for release in 2017.

Adzema, Michael. work-in-progress. *Primal Return: Renaissance and Grace.* Return to Grace, Volume 11. Scheduled for release in 2017. Some of it was originally published in *Primal Renaissance: The Emerging Millennial Return,* 1995. sillymickel@gmail.com.

Anscombe, G. E. M. (Elizabeth). 1958. On brute facts. *Analysis 18*(2).

Antler. 1991. Proving what? [poem]. *The Quest, 4*(3) [Autumn 1991], 61.

Baba, Sathya Sai. 1991. Joy of surrender. *Sathya Said Newsletter, 15*(4) [Summer 1991], 15-18. [Adapted from *Sathya Sai Speaks, Vol. VII,* pp. 78-86, Second American Printing, 1985.]

Bohm, David. 1980. *Wholeness and the Implicate Order.* London: Routledge and Kegan Paul.

Campbell, Joseph. 1972. *The Hero with a Thousand Faces.* Princeton, NJ: Princeton University Press.

Castaneda, Carlos. 1977. *The Second Ring of Power.* New York: Simon & Schuster.

D'Andrade, Roy G. 1984. Cultural meaning systems. In *Culture Theory: Essays on Mind, Self, and Emotion,* R. Shweder and R. LeVine (eds.), Cambridge, UK: Cambridge University Press (88-119).

D'Andrade, Roy G. 1987. Anthropological theory: Where did it go? (How can we get it back?). University of California, San Diego. (Unpublished paper)

deMause, Lloyd. 1982. *The Foundations of Psychohistory.* New York: Creative Roots.

deMause, Lloyd. 2002. *The Emotional Life of Nations.* New York & London: Karnac.

Eddington, Arthur S. 1920, 2009. *Space, Time, and Gravitation.* Rockville, MD: Wildside Press.

Gardiner, Patrick. 1967. Arthur Schopenhauer (1788-1860). In *Encyclopedia of Philosophy.*

Gendlin, E. T. 1992. The primacy of the body, not the primacy of perception. *Man and World 25*(3-4), 341-353.

Gluckman, Max. 2006. (ed.) *Closed Systems and Open Minds.* Piscataway, NJ: Aldine Transaction.

Grof, Stanislav. 1970. Beyond psychoanalysis I. Implications of LSD research for understanding dimensions of human personality. *Darshana International 10*(55).

Grof, Stanislav. 1975. *Realms of the Human Unconscious: Observations from LSD Research.* New York: Viking Press.

Grof, Stanislav. 1980. *LSD Psychotherapy.* Pomona, CA: Hunter House.

Grof, Stanislav. (ed.) 1984. *Ancient Wisdom and Modern Science.* Albany, NY: State University of New York Press.

Grof, Stanislav. 1985. *Beyond the Brain: Birth, Death, and Transcendence in Psychotherapy.* Albany, NY: State University of New York Press.

Grof, Stanislav. 1988a. *The Adventure of Self-Discovery: Dimensions of Consciousness and New Perspectives in Psychotherapy and Inner Exploration.* Albany, NY: State University of New York Press.

Grof, Stanislav. (ed.) 1988b. *Human Survival and Consciousness Evolution.* Albany, NY: State University of New York Press.

Grof, Stanislav. 1998. *The Cosmic Game.* Albany, NY: SUNY Press.

Grof, Stanislav, and Grof, Christina. 1980. *Beyond Death: The Gates of Consciousness.* London: Thames & Hudson.

Grof, Stanislav, and Grof, Christina. (eds.) 1989. *Spiritual Emergency: When Personal Transformation Becomes a Crisis.* Los Angeles: Jeremy P. Tarcher.

Grof, Stanislav, and Grof, Christina. 1990. *The Stormy Search for the Self: A Guide to Personal Growth Through Transformational Crisis.* Los Angeles: Jeremy P. Tarcher.

Grof, Stanislav, and Halifax, Joan. 1977. *The Human Encounter with Death.* New York: E.P. Dutton.

Hesse, Hermann. 1951. *Siddhartha.* New York: New Directions.

Huxley, Aldous. 1956. *The Doors of Perception and Heaven and Hell.* New York: Harper & Row.

Institute for Noetic Sciences. 1991. *Noetic Sciences Bulletin.*

Jones, Roger S. 1982. *Physics as Metaphor.* Minneapolis, MN: The University of Minnesota.

Kagan, Annie. 2013. *The Afterlife of Billy Fingers: How My Bad-Boy Brother Proved to Me There's Life After Death.* Charlottesville, VA: Hampton Roads Publishing.

Kasenbacher, Michael. 24 December 2012. Work, learning, and freedom. *New Left Project*. On The Trilateral Commission.

Jung, Carl G. 1978. *Flying Saucers: A Modern Myth of Things Seen in the Sky*. Princeton, NJ: Princeton University Press.

Jung, Carl G., and Jaffe, Aniela. 1961. *Memories, Dreams, Reflections*. New York: Random House.

Kuhn, Thomas S. 1970. *The Structure of Scientific Revolutions*. Chicago: University of Chicago Press.

Labbe, Armand. 1991. Consciousness versus awareness in the light of classical Eastern perspectives on the nature of transcendence. Paper delivered at the 1991 Annual Conference of the Society for the Anthropology of Consciousness, 21 March 1991.

Laing, Ronald D. 1988. [Interview with R. D. Laing]. *Omni*, [April 1988].

Lawlor, Robert. 1989. Sexuality and the universe evolving. *New Frontier*, November, 1989, 9-10, 43.

Lawlor, Robert. 1991. *Voices of the First Day: Awakening in the Aboriginal Dreamtime*. Rochester, VT: Inner Traditions International.

Lawlor, Robert. 1992. Voices of the first day: Awakening in the aboriginal dreamtime. *New Frontier*, April-May, 1992, 19-20, 22, 48.

Lawson, Alvin H. 1985. UFO abductions or birth memories? *Fate*, *38*(3) March 1985, 68-80.

Lawson, Alvin H. 1987. Perinatal imagery in UFO abduction reports. In *Pre- and Perinatal Psychology: An Introduction*, T. Verny (ed.), New York: Human Sciences Press.

Lilly, John C. 1972. The Center of the Cyclone. Oakland, CA: Ronin Publishing.

Mack, John E. 1992a. Other realities: The "alien abduction" phenomenon. *Noetic Sciences Review*, No. 23, Autumn 1992, 5-11.

Mack, John. 1992b. The UFO abduction phenomenon: What does it mean? Presentation at the Twelfth International Transpersonal Conference, Prague, Czechoslovakia, 25 June 1992.

Mack, John. 1995. The UFO Abduction Phenomenon's Challenge to Consensus Reality. *Primal Renaissance: The Journal of Primal Psychology*, *1*(1), 96-110. Available through sillymickel@gmail.com

Masters, Robert E.L., and Houston, Jean. 1966, 2000. *The Varieties of Psychedelic Experience*. Rochester, VT: Inner Traditions.

McKenna, Terence. 1991. *The Archaic Revival: Speculations on Psychedelic Mushrooms, the Amazon, Virtual Reality, UFOs, Evolution, Shamanism, the Rebirth of the Goddess, and the End of History*. San Francisco: Harper-Collins.

Merlan, Philip. 1967. Emanationism. In *Encyclopedia of Philosophy*, 473-474.

Moustakas, Clark. 1990. *Heuristic Research: Design, Methodology, and Applications*. Newbury Park, CA: Sage Publications.

*New Sense Bulletin*. 1991. Contest-winning studies support Sheldrake theory. *New Sense Bulletin, 17*(1) [October 1991], 8.

Patrick, G. T. W. 1952. *Introduction To Philosophy*, Revised Edition. New York: Houghton Mifflin.

Plato, with Bloom, Allan (trans.). 1991. "Allegory of the Cave" in *The Republic of Plato*. New York: Basic Books.

Pribram, Karl. 1971. *Languages of the Brain*. Englewood Cliffs, NJ: Prentice-Hall.

Pribram, Karl. 1976. Problems concerning the structure of consciousness. In *Consciousness and the Brain*, G. Globus (ed.), New York: Plenum.

Rajneesh, Bhagwan S. 1976. *Meditation: The Art of Ecstasy*. New York: Harper & Row.

Roberts, Jane. 1972. *Seth Speaks*. San Rafael, CA: Amber-Allen Publishing.

Roberts, Jane. 1974. *The Nature of Personal Reality*. San Rafael, CA: Amber-Allen Publishing.

Roszak, Theodore. 1992. *The Voice of the Earth*. New York: Simon & Schuster.

Sahlins, Marshall. 1976. *Culture and Practical Reason*. Chicago: University of Chicago Press.

Schiff, Francine. 1991. The mystical experience: An interview with David Spangler. *The Quest, 4*(3) [Autumn 1991], 8-14.

Schrödinger, Erwin. 1958. *Mind and Matter.* Cambridge, UK: Cambridge University Press.

Searle, John R. 1969. *Speech Acts: An Essay in the Philosophy of Language.* Cambridge, UK: Cambridge University Press.

Sheldrake, Rupert. 1981. *A New Science of Life: The Hypothesis of Formative Causation.* Los Angeles: J.P. Tarcher.

Sheldrake, Rupert. 1991a. Is nature alive? *Human Potential,* 16-21, 33-39.

Sheldrake, Rupert. 1991b. *The Rebirth of Nature: The Greening of Science and God.* New York: Bantam.

Sheldrake, Rupert. 1995. Nature as alive: Morphic resonance and collective memory. *Primal Renaissance: The Journal of Primal Psychology, 1*(1), 65-78. Available through sillymickel@gmail.com

Stace, W. T. 1932. *The Theory of Knowledge and Existence.* Oxford, UK: The Clarendon Press.

Terry, Sara. 1992. Alien territory. *The Boston Sunday Globe, The Boston Globe Magazine,* 11 October 1992, 20-27.

Thompson, Keith. 1989. The UFO encounter experience as a crisis of transformation. In *Spiritual Emergency: When Personal Transformation Becomes a Crisis,* S. Grof and C. Grof (eds.), Los Angeles: Jeremy P. Tarcher.

Tompkins, Peter, and Bird, Christopher. 1979. *The Secret Life of Plants.* New York: Harper & Row

Uhlein, Gabriele. 1991. Hildegard of Bingen. *The Quest, 4*(3) [Autumn 1991], 48-85.

Verny, Thomas, and Kelly, John. 1981. *The Secret Life of the Unborn Child.* New York: Dell.

Washburn, Michael. 1988. *The Ego and the Dynamic Ground: A Transpersonal Theory of Human Development.* Albany, NY: SUNY Press.

Washburn, Michael. 1990. Two patterns of transcendence. *Journal of Humanistic Psychology, 30*(3), 84-112.

Wilber, Ken. 1977. *The Spectrum of Consciousness.* Wheaton, Il: Quest.

Wilber, Ken. 1979. *No Boundary.* Boston, MA: Shambhala Publications.

Wilber, Ken. 1980. *The Atman Project*. Wheaton, IL: Theosophical Publishing House.

Wilber, Ken. 1981. *Up from Eden*. New York: Anchor Books.

Wilber, Ken. 1982. The pre/trans fallacy. *Journal of Humanistic Psychology, 22*(2), 5-43.

Wilber, Ken. 1983. *A Sociable God*. Boulder, CO: Shambhala Publishing.

Winkelman, Michael. 1990. The evolution of consciousness: An essay review of *Up from Eden* (Wilber 1981). *Anthropology of Consciousness 1*(3-4), 24-31.

Wittgenstein, Ludwig. 1953, 2009. *Philosophical Investigations, 4th Edition*. Wiley-Blackwell: Hoboken, NJ.

Woolger, Roger J. 1987. *Other Lives, Other Selves: A Jungian Psychotherapist Discovers Past Lives*. New York: Bantam.

Zukav, Gary. 1979. *The Dancing Wu Li Masters*. New York: W. Morrow.

# ABOUT THE AUTHOR

Michael Adzema is an author, activist, former university instructor, and psychotherapist, now retired, who specialized in primal therapy, breathwork, and rebirthing. He was the editor of *Primal Renaissance* — a professional journal of primal psychology — and was the first person in the United States to teach prenatal and perinatal psychology at the university level, which he did at Sonoma State University in the early Nineties. In the early Eighties, working as an anti-nuke activist with Oregon Fair Share, he was one of a small group of people whose actions led to the lawsuit that put a stop to nuclear plant construction in the United States.

He is a regular contributor to Extinction Radio, broadcast by Activate Media, formerly Occupy Boston Radio. His voice can be heard on other broadcasts, as well, speaking on topics of activism, spirituality, ecopsychology, the environment, prenatal and perinatal psychology, metaphysics, and philosophy.

Over the last twenty years, Michael Adzema has managed and authored a number of popular websites and blogs, including *Primal Spirit; Becoming Authentic; Culture War, Class War;* and *Michael Adzema, Author.* Currently he publishes prolifically and often on his primary blog, *Michael Adzema, Author,* at sillymickel.blogspot.com. One can find a number of his videos on youtube, as well, under the name, sillymickel. He teaches and publishes frequently on Facebook under Michael Adzema and on Twitter under Mickel Adzema, @sillymickel.

In addition to *The Secret Life of Stones,* he has authored the books, *Wounded Deer and Centaurs; Funny God; Falls from Grace; Planetmates, The Great Reveal; Experience Is Divinity; Apocalypse NO; Culture War, Class War; Apocalypse Emergency, Love's Wake-Up Call;* and *Primal Renaissance.* The book, *Prodigal Human: The Descents of Man,* is scheduled for release concurrently with this book, in Fall of 2016.

His books can be found at Amazon, are available on Kindle as well, and can be ordered through any major book outlet.

Printed in Great Britain
by Amazon

81668154R00325